THE LIENZO OF TLAPILTEPEC

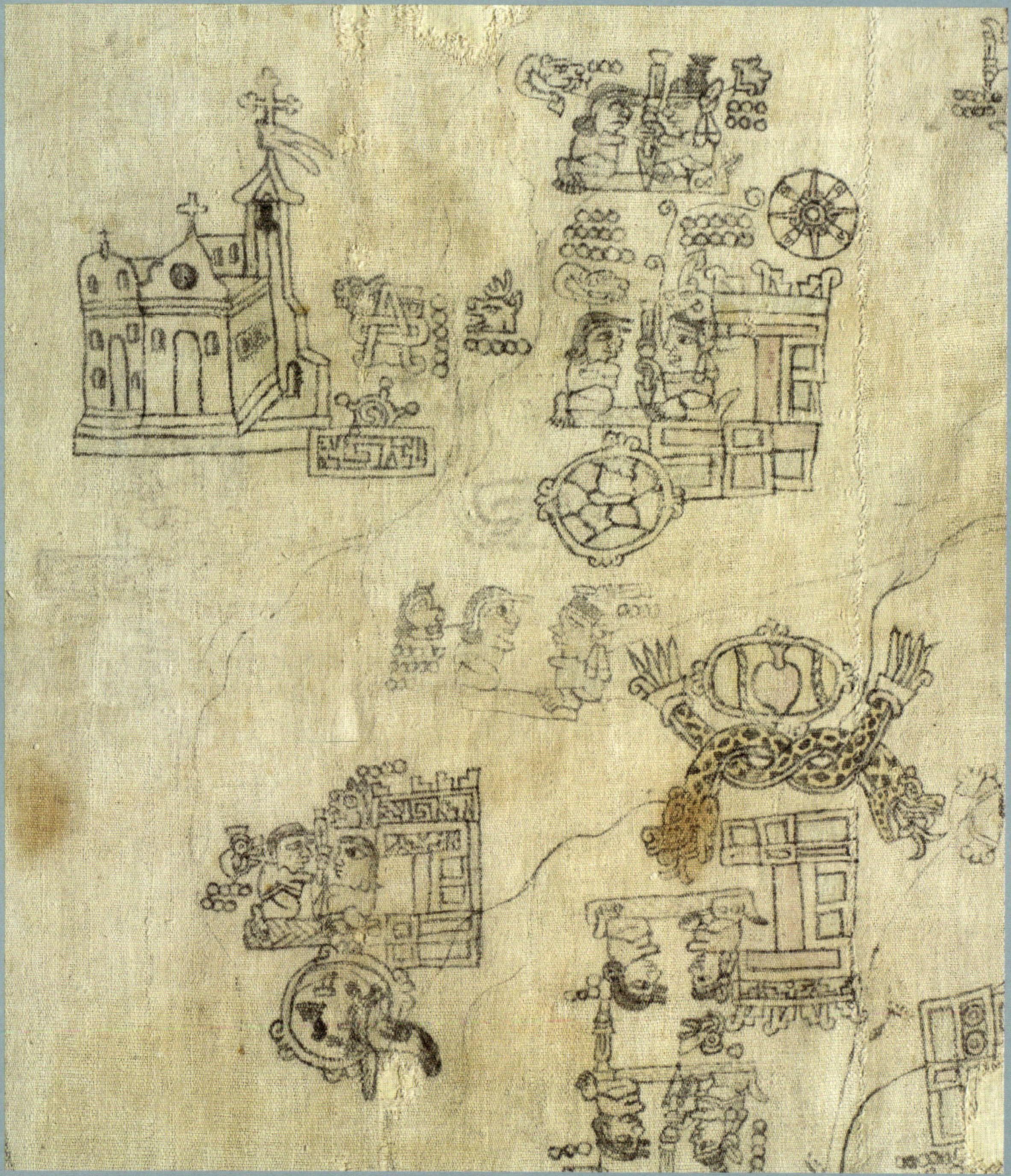

THE LIENZO *of* TLAPILTEPEC

A Painted History from the Northern Mixteca

EDITED BY Arni Brownstone

WITH CONTRIBUTIONS BY Nicholas Johnson & Bas van Doesburg

FOREWORD BY Elizabeth Hill Boone

ROYAL ONTARIO MUSEUM

UNIVERSITY OF OKLAHOMA PRESS : NORMAN

ALSO BY ARNI BROWNSTONE

War Paintings of the Tsuu T'ina Nation (Lincoln, Neb., and Edmonton, Alberta, 2015)

The Royal Ontario Museum gratefully acknowledges the
Louise Hawley Stone Charitable Trust
for its generous support of this publication.

Library of Congress Cataloging-in-Publication Data
The Lienzo of Tlapiltepec : a painted history from the northern Mixteca / edited by Arni Brownstone ; with contributions by Nicholas Johnson and Sebastian van Doesburg ; foreword by Elizabeth Hill Boone.
pages cm
Includes bibliographical references and index.
ISBN 978-0-8061-4629-4 (hardcover : alk. paper)—ISBN 978-0-8061-4630-0 (pbk. : alk. paper)—
1. Lienzo de Tlapiltepec. 2. Manuscripts, Mixtec—Mexico. 3. Mixtec Indians—History.
4. Mixtec Indians—Antiquities. 5. Coixtlahuaca (Mexico)—History. 6. Coixtlahuaca (Mexico)—Antiquities. I. Brownstone, Arni, 1947–
F1219.8.M59L54 2014
972'.7401—dc23 2014016216

The paper in this book meets the guidelines for permanence and durability of the Committee on Production Guidelines for Book Longevity of the Council on Library Resources, Inc. ∞

1 2 3 4 5 6 7 8 9 10

CONTENTS

ILLUSTRATIONS

FIGURES

MAPS

TABLES

FOREWORD

The Painted Histories of Mexico and the Lienzo of Tlapiltepec

ELIZABETH HILL BOONE

In the centuries before Europeans set foot on Mexican soil, indigenous rulers recognized the need to situate themselves conceptually in time and space. Regardless of whether they governed a vast empire, a bustling city-state, or a small polity, the rulers desired to tie themselves to the past and secure themselves in the present, in essence to explain how they achieved their current station and relations with other polities and peoples around them. Like political leaders elsewhere in the world, the indigenous rulers looked to histories to support their authority. Histories functioned to define the rulers and their polities, place them securely within the stream of time, and connect them with both their predecessors and contemporaries. The historical past, as interpreted and recorded, was a potent resource for the rulers and their communities.

In Pre-Columbian Mexico much history was conveyed in long narrative discourses that arose out of the discipline of advanced rhetoric. But oral discourses are always subject to contestation, as specialists on orality and literacy have shown, so indigenous rulers had records painted to keep the fundamental features of the histories pure. They looked to painter-scribes to document the past correctly, as they conceived it.

Indigenous record-keeping in central and southern Mexico had not developed along the same trajectory that writing followed in the Old World. Unlike Old World scripts, the principal goal of Mexican pictographic writing was not to record speech but to record meaning; it thus developed not as a glottographic system that concretized linguistic streams of utterance, but as a semasiographic system in which images and glyphs usually signified meaning directly to the reader without a detour through speech.[1] Only in the names of places, and perhaps in the names of persons, did the indigenous system record the sounds of language. This pictographic system achieved meaning by manipulating form, color, relative placement, and context, instead of the morpheme, word, and sentence of glottographic systems. Founded on a broadly understood corpus of visual conventions, Mexican pictography could communicate across ethnic and linguistic boundaries. It was well adapted to the multilingual and multiethnic world of Mexico in the century before the Spanish conquest.

The Spaniards arriving in Mexico remarked on the excellence and profusion of indigenous painted books, which they saw stored in large palace repositories or kept individually by persons in power, such as rulers, priests, and officials. Those books that were painted on long folded stripes of native paper or hide we now call "codices," and those that take the form of large sheets of cotton cloth we now call "lienzos," after the Spanish word for canvas, linen, or a panel of cloth. Almost all the preconquest painted histories perished during the destructive and chaotic years during and following the Spanish conquest, but histories endured as an important genre in the early colonial period. Histories continued to be painted for the indigenous leaders even under Spanish rule. The Spaniards recognized the truth value and utility of indigenous histories. Indigenous rulers, for their part, continued to need painted histories in order to support their respective positions, to maintain their lands, and to advance their claims to rights and privilege under the Spanish administrative system. The Lienzo of Tlapiltepec is one such history. It was painted in the Coixtlahuaca Valley of Oaxaca several decades after the Spanish conquest, but it records events that go back deep in time.

As a history, the lienzo calls up and organizes memories of the past. Because no history can include everything that happened over the years, it selects, among all the innumerable people who once lived and events that once happened, only those individuals and actions that support its particular story. It then organizes these into a singular, fixed, and unalterable past, a past that can be inspected in the present. It is also a past that serves the interests of the present. As Bas van Doesburg says in chapter 2 of this volume, the Lienzo of Tlapiltepec records events and constructs a past that support the aspirations and probably also the struggles of the colonial present. Don Domingo, the young heir to the rulership of the kingdom of Coixtlahuaca in the years after his father's death, probably had the lienzo created to reaffirm his rule and Coixtlahuaca's position as a major power in southern Mexico before the conquest. The last male ruler depicted in the lienzo may well have been Don Domingo's father. This ruler, known locally as Lord 11 Vulture (his calendrical name) and called Cozcacuauhtli (Vulture) by the Spaniards, was the culmination of two royal lineages that once jointly ruled the kingdom of Coixtlahuaca. The lienzo affirms that he was the descendant of the original ancient founders, that he was the last in an unbroken succession of rule, and that the original founders emerged supernaturally from a specific place of origin. Every person, place, and action in the lienzo helps to support Lord 11 Vulture's position as the noble and legitimate ruler of an important and widely influential kingdom, in this case Coixtlahuaca.

Like other Mexican histories, the Lienzo of Tlapiltepec is a story about elites for elites; there are no commoners or ordinary people in the story. Instead, the protagonists are supernaturals, male and female rulers, their noble offspring who marry rulers or become rulers themselves, and occasionally warriors and other actors who were sufficiently important to be individually named. These were the individuals who created and shaped the community kingdom of Coixtlahuaca and expanded its domain and influence.

THEMES OF THE LIENZO

Although the Lienzo of Tlapiltepec is a unique document created within the local context of Coixtlahuaca in the middle of the sixteenth century, it participates in the larger world of the Mexican painted history, sharing many features with other painted histories. Coixtlahuaca was a multiethnic kingdom in a region where Nahua-speakers from Central Mexico interfaced with Mixtec-speakers from Oaxaca. The lienzo therefore blends features from both Nahua and Mixtec traditions. Its individual story is a local story, but in outline, its story is paralleled in general terms by other communities' stories, and its narrative is structured in the same way that many others are.

Like other pictorial histories from central and southern Mexico, the story in the Lienzo of Tlapiltepec attends to three major themes.[2] These themes concern the people's origin, the founding of the community kingdom, and the continuity of this polity and rule. Although different pictorial manuscripts may emphasize one theme over the others, the histories that cover the full extent of a polity's past attend to all three.

Most painted histories begin with an account of origins. This genesis take can various forms, but it often involves the first people or their supernatural ancestors originating from some special place. They do not simply appear on the surface of the document but are recorded having emerged or migrated from somewhere. In the histories painted for the Aztecs and their Nahua-speaking neighbors northwest of the Coixtlahuaca Valley, the leaders of the first people came out of a cave with seven openings, called Chicomoztoc (Place of Seven Caves), the metaphoric place of emergence for all central Mexican peoples. From here, these central Mexican histories record, the people dispersed and migrated to the locations where they would establish the capitals of their kingdoms. Even though the Aztecs from Tenochtitlan specify that they originated in Aztlan—and they begin their own migration stories with their departure from this ancestral homeland—they usually either blend Aztlan with Chicomoztoc or include Chicomoztoc as one of the stages along the migration. Chicomoztoc also figures in some Mixtec histories and in histories from the Coixtlahuaca Valley, including the Lienzo of Tlapiltepec.

The opening passage in the Lienzo of Tlapiltepec, on the lower left corner of the sheet, features this seven-chambered cave of Chicomoztoc, with lines connecting it to the home of the ancestors pictured above it. Another painted history from the Coixtlahuaca Valley, the Selden Roll, fleshes out this story: it describes in some detail how a group of priests went to obtain the cult bundle of the Mixtec creator god Lord 9 Wind (whom the Aztecs called Quetzalcoatl), emerged with it from a seven-chambered cave, and brought it to the place where the ruling dynasty was to be founded. This is one of the origin stories summarized in the Lienzo of Tlapiltepec. The lienzo does not actually picture 9 Wind's bundle, but it signifies the bundle and the deity by placing the calendrical name 9 Wind within the cave. The second date in the cave is 1 Reed, which is the calendar name of the Aztec version of 9 Wind, Quetzalcoatl. By employing both the Mixtec and Aztec names, the history painter ensures that readers from both Nahua and Mixtec traditions will understand what is meant. In chapter 3 of this volume, Nicholas Johnson describes the imagery and this episode of origin in more detail.

Most Mixtec histories, however, begin not with the Chicomoztoc of central Mexican tradition but with more local points of origin. The ancestors of the Mixtec ruling families, we are told, emerged from trees, clefts in the earth, or openings in the heavens, places all located in the Mixteca. They did not migrate but were locally born. This Mixtec tradition also appears in the Lienzo of Tlapiltepec, where a second origin story is presented just above Chicomoztoc. In this local Mixtec genesis, the first man and woman to appear in the lienzo emerge from the precious waters of twin rivers, one of quetzal feathers and one of jade, as discussed more fully in chapter 3. Three generations later, their great-grandson will found the principal lineage being tracked in the lienzo, which will finally join the secondary lineage to produce the last depicted ruler, Lord 11 Vulture, and thereafter his presumed son Don Domingo.

In its account of origins, the Lienzo of Tlapiltepec merges two traditions by recording two complementary stories. One is that a cult bundle (of the creator god 9 Wind) is brought out of a seven-chambered cave and carried to the home of the ancestors; this story establishes the religious underpinnings of the polity. The other account is of the first ancestors who are supernaturally born from the waters of precious rivers. These two stories complement each other in establishing the basis of royal authority: divine ancestors who emerged from an extraordinary feature of the landscape, joined with the cult of a principal supernatural. The two stories merge in the lienzo at the point where the descending ancestors and the sacred cult bundle come together at the home of the ancestors.

The second major theme treated in almost all the indigenous painted histories is the founding of the community kingdom (Boone 2000a). Although different pictorial traditions and individual manuscripts record different kinds of events after the first origins episode, these scenarios all lead up to and prepare the protagonists for the founding of the polity. Aztec and Mixtec histories agree on the significance and basic components of this founding event, which is often the most prominent presentation or scene in the pictorial histories. Its major features are the marking of the place (which can include defining its territory), establishing a cult (sometimes also the construction of an altar or temple), lighting a new fire (to inaugurate the ritual space), and defeating any hostile neighbors. The Aztec histories tend to focus on naming the place and identifying the human leaders who shepherded their people to that location, whereas the Mixtec and Coixtlahuaca Valley histories emphasize divine participation and the actual ritual of foundation.

The founding event in the Lienzo of Tlapiltepec is the manuscript's most prominent scene, located about halfway up the left side of the sheet. As Johnson explains in chapter 3, it involves the largest place sign on the lienzo, a complex and elaborate sign composed of both geographical and metaphoric elements. There, on top of the place sign, emphasis is placed on the ritual that actualized the foundation, in particular the placing of a staff of authority and the drilling of a new fire, both actions executed by priests who, according to other sources, were responsible for bringing the cult bundle of 9 Wind to this place. Specific locales that surround this place of foundation are identified by their smaller place signs. The place signs of the four cardinal directions are spaced around the edges of the scene and are here affixed with glyphs of chevron roads that signify the enemy. By centrally positioning the place of foundation between the cardinal directions, the historian affirms that the place being founded is in effect the center of its world. But, because the cardinal points are characterized as enemy points, the historian also suggests that the founders carved out this kingdom within a hostile land. This event is closely paralleled in other histories from the Coixtlahuaca Valley and in some from the Mixteca in Oaxaca.

The third theme treated in all the Mexican pictorial histories is the duration of the family, line of rule, or polity. Different traditions emphasize different aspects, but all assert a direct connection between the original founders of the kingdom and the rulers at the time the history was painted. If there has been a rupture in this connection, such as the death of a ruler or conquest by another polity, the histories either ignore the mishap or take pains to explain how the situation was repaired. The histories thus emphasize the continuity and duration of the dynasty or unbroken sequence of rulers, or the endurance of the polity as a corporate body since its founding. Aztec histories do not pay much attention to the bloodlines of their rulers, because rule was not strictly governed by primogeniture descent; instead they focus on the succession of individual male rulers and track the achievements of the polity as a corporate whole. In contrast, Mixtec histories focus on the royal family. They take great care to record genealogical descent along both male and females lines, because rights to polity and territory flowed along both lines. It was understood that Mixtec rulers (male and female) held authority because they were directly descended from known supernatural ancestors and were the legitimate offspring and heirs of royal kings and queens. In the process of demonstrating duration and continuity, whether of the polity or the ruling family, both Aztec and Mixtec histories record successful efforts to preserve or enlarge the kingdom.

The Lienzo of Tlapiltepec devotes most of its surface space to this post-foundation history. The upper half of the left side of the lienzo records the succession of ruling couples. Two columns of couples—the female and male seated facing each other on the royal mat—rise from conventionalized palace structures painted beside the place signs of their respective homes. The two lineages jointly ruled until their offspring married and united the lineages one generation before the Spanish conquest. The heir of this union was Lord 11 Vulture, who inherited along both lines. This upper left side of the lienzo, then, proclaims the unbroken and conjoined succession from the founding couples to Lord 11 Vulture.

The whole right side of the lienzo is dedicated to explaining how Coixtlahuaca's power and influence developed. This great expanse of cotton cloth is given over to a conceptual map of the Coixtlahuaca Valley and the places and polities outside the valley that were important to its history. It is not simply a map but a cartographic display of individual places that forms the substrate on which Coixtlahuaca's history is arranged. Attached to the places are the many events that increased Coixtlahuaca's power and influence. These events are manifested by people and their actions and by the red and black lines that connect the actors and places with others. Chapter 2 relates many of these events to Coixtlahuaca's sixteenth-century situation; chapter 3 describes and explains them in more detail.

This juxtaposition of ruler lists with a map distinguishes the Lienzo of Tlapiltepec and other lienzos from the Mixtec screenfolds. All these histories are concerned with showing dynastic continuity, but the lienzos reduce the dynasty to one or more lists of couples in sequence, whereas the screenfolds track all the individual births, marriages, and offspring. The lienzos identify and describe the kingdom geographically and politically in an abstracted cartographic display; the Mixtec screenfolds, in contrast, only identify individual kingdoms by adding their place signs to the images of events and actions. Although the subject of the screenfolds is the royal family, the subject of the lienzos is both the kingdom as a territorial construct and the dynasty that ruled it.

STRUCTURES OF HISTORY

As chapter 1 explains, the historical facts of the Lienzo of Tlapiltepec are recorded by means of figural images and glyphs that either picture or symbolize by convention what they mean. We can think of this collection of graphic marks as the semantic content, or vocabulary, of the pictorial system. How these figures and glyphs come together to form a historical narrative belongs to the realm of syntax or grammar.

In pictorial histories these grammars are spatial. By arranging the images in certain ways on the two-dimensional surface, the native historian can fashion the data into a concrete narrative of the past. The data of these histories, like all histories, include the four elements of person, event, time, and place: the who, what, when, and where of historical imagination. Usually one of these elements dominates the account and provides the structural basis for the story; time might dominate, or event, or place, for example, with the other data arranged to fit around it. Mexican manuscript painters usually organized their histories in one of three ways: by time, event, or place.[3] Occasionally, such as in lienzos, they used two arrangements in combination.

The Aztec annals histories were time-based, tying people and events to the years. In such annals histories, a ribbon of time, composed of consecutive year-dates placed side by side, forms a spine that runs along the length of the manuscript (unless it is broken in places). To this ribbon are attached the events important for the history, each event appearing adjacent to its year and sometimes linked to the year by a line. A cluster of events can clearly indicate just how eventful a particular year might have been. The events themselves are often represented only by glyphs, but in other cases, human figures record the action by their poses, gestures, and interaction with other figures. The place where these activities occur is assumed to be the kingdom of those who commissioned the history. The place of the kingdom is not usually given except at the moment of its founding, when it is named by its place sign and often characterized geographically. Otherwise, the subject place does not usually reappear in the history. When events happen in other locales, such as when foreign lands are conquered, these exterior locales are identified by their place signs. Time-based histories excel at recording the events that punctuated a single kingdom's history over time. They largely ignore genealogy and territory, however, and they cannot easily convey spatial relationships between polities or present many contemporaneous events.

Other histories privilege the events themselves, organizing their narratives as a series of events. Elsewhere I have characterized these event-oriented histories as *res gestae*, or "deeds done," accounts (Boone 1994a:53–60; 2000b:70–71). They are close to what we usually consider to be a history, for they tell the story by means of a sequence of related events, in much the way that a written chronicle does. The individual events are often expressed by means of human or supernatural figures shown in the act of being or doing something, but shorthand versions can take the place of these figures. For example, humans or supernaturals can be signified merely by the presence of their calendrical names, or events can be recalled merely by glyphic symbols. The historical elements of time and location are subsidiary to the event itself; they take the form of date glyphs and place signs that are attached to the event. It is the sequence of events, however, that drives the story. The Mixtec screenfold histories follow the event-oriented structure; they measure and organize history in terms of related events rather than in terms of years elapsed. In them, events are compressed along registers in a tight linear sequence.

A third structure for recording history is the diagram or map, in which the broad spatial arrangement of events by location takes precedence over their linear sequencing. Such histories are spread on a single cartographic display in which events are shown in the locations where they occurred. Although the events may be temporally fixed by date glyphs attached to them, usually they remain undated, for time is not a central concern. Cartographic histories measure the past not according to chronology, but according to territory. They excel at recording migrations, where the story is the movement of people across the land, and at recalling actions that secure land or tie people to their geographic neighbors. They are ideal for recording a polity's territory and for recognizing that territory is secured and made meaningful by the events that occurred there.

These three organizational structures bring with them different narrative strengths and weaknesses that shape the stories they tell. Accounts of a kingdom through time are best told in the annals format. Stories about ruling families are best told as sequences of events. Stories about land and territory are best told from a cartographic perspective. The Aztecs preferred the annals for many of their histories, but they also used the cartographic and mixed formats, especially for stories of their migration. The Mixtecs relied on both event-oriented and cartographic structures to preserve their dynastic histories and record the events that secured their kingdoms.

The Lienzo of Tlapiltepec brings together both the event-oriented and cartographic structures to tell about the ruling family and its land. Like many other lienzos, it organizes the stories of ancient origins and the succession of rulers as a series of events, and it attaches this to a conceptual map of the territory in question. The lienzo uses the map to hold and structure the events that compose the military and diplomatic aspects of its history.

As a lienzo, it is compositionally looser than the screenfold histories because it does not employ registers. The events of its story are therefore not confined to a tight linear sequence but are freer to flow across the surface of the sheet. This allows the history painter to highlight visually the most important events by enlarging them and setting them apart with surrounding blank space. We see this on the left side of the Lienzo of Tlapiltepec, where the large place signs pertaining to the episodes of origin and the ritual of foundation dramatically dominate the lower half. Blank spaces around them help them cohere as individual thematic units. These blank spaces also provide pathways for the several red and black lines that connect them to other parts of the history, but the blank spaces are otherwise neutral. They convey neither geographic nor temporal information.

This spatial neutrality changes in the upper half of the left side, where the two parallel lists of ruling couples rise majestically from the two place signs of their seats. The lists represent the two lineages who jointly ruled, the one on the left based in Monte Verde, the more prominent lineage according to this lienzo, and the one on the right based in Miltepec, whose place sign is unfortunately largely lost to a hole in the fabric. Chapter 3 details the story of these dual lineages. These lists of ruling couples are insistently sequential, for each couple immediately follows and supplants the one just below it. This charges the space they occupy with a strong but somewhat ambiguous temporality. Time runs from the first couples at the bottom of the lists, who date to the eleventh or twelfth centuries (according to Johnson in chapter 3), up to the topmost ones in the years before the Spanish conquest. We are not told at what rate time is passing, and certainly it is variable, for some couples may have ruled only a few years and others for many years; all we are given is their sequence. This upper left half of the lienzo continues the narrative begun with the origin and foundation scenes in the lower left corner, for it carries the story of Coixtlahuaca's dynasty from its ancient origins up to what is close to the presumed present. A black line that runs vertically along most of the length of the lienzo separates this event-oriented section from the map to its right.

The map, as chapter 3 explains, describes the territory relevant to Coixtlahuaca as a geographic entity, with the Coixtlahuaca Valley in the upper half and Coixtlahuaca's more northern neighbors in the lower half. It is a conceptual map rather than a strictly geographic one, in that it presents what is known about the territory rather than what might actually be seen or encountered there. It emphasizes certain features to the exclusion of others and thereby signals what was important to the history, omitting what was not. A few rivers flow through it, but other landscape features are absent. Major places within and outside the Coixtlahuaca Valley are located in a roughly geographic arrangement, centered on the place sign of Coixtlahuaca itself in the upper middle right. As Johnson points out in chapter 3, their place signs are all oriented in a centrifugal relation to the Coixtlahuaca place sign, with their bases toward it. As chapter 3 also reveals, some of the place signs have been moved from their actual geographic location in order to provide space for the presentation of events and persons and to allow for the important red lines that tie places and events together. It is in this map that many of the events that empowered Coixtlahuaca to greatness are pictured, adjacent to the places where they occurred.

The map is the substrate for these historical events, preserving, above all, the spatial relationships between events. Its diagrammatic structure carries a force of contemporaneity that unites all the events in the map as a set and obscures their distinctive placements in time. It tells the viewer that while one event occurred at one location, another occurred elsewhere, and another elsewhere still. Although dates attached to some events may establish them more precisely in time, the cartographic presentation, as a tableau, overrides individual temporalities in order to privilege the collective whole as a set of events relevant to Coixtlahuaca's history.

As in other pictorial histories from Mexico, the Lienzo of Tlapiltepec employs the organizational structures that best suit the stories it has to tell. The narrow left side of the great cotton cloth tracks the dynasty as a series of events that lead from the supernatural origins, to the founding of the polity, through the sequent ruling couples, and finally to the last inheriting ruler and his wife. The right two-thirds of the lienzo displays the lands controlled and influenced by Coixtlahuaca as a great cartograph on which the story of the polity's growth is detailed. The lienzo is both a history and a charter for the kingdom.

The Lienzo of Tlapiltepec today exemplifies three truths about the value of Mexican painted histories. The first is that history painting was a deep-seated tradition before the Spanish conquest. Every independent polity had its history, likely in multiple versions and variations, which supported the political and social order. Historians could choose to organize their stories from a range of presentational structures, depending on which aspects of their history they wished to privilege. Each structure helped them record a particular kind of story. The second truth is that histories continued to be painted after the conquest. Indigenous leaders and Spanish administrators recognized pictorial histories as authentic records of the past, ones that were closer to Pre-Columbian sensibilities than accounts written alphabetically and were thus considered more authentic and likely more accurate. These histories stemmed from the traditional forms but often came to include post-conquest features. A third truth is that the ancient sixteenth-century pictorial histories, such as the Lienzo of Tlapiltepec, have continued to remain valuable as containers of historical memory over the centuries. As Arni Brownstone tells us in the preface, this lienzo was held in the town of Tlapiltepec until the early years of the twentieth century, when it was brought to Coixtlahuaca to help settle a land dispute (and never returned).[4] Even though those who brought it forth could not read its story in its entirety, they did not question its value as a historical record. Today, the value of the Lienzo of Tlapiltepec as a repository of historical knowledge about polity, dynasty, and territory remains as strong as when it was first painted.

Thanks to the in-depth research and sure insights of Nicholas Johnson and Bas van Doesburg, it is possible again to read with some precision the lienzo's story and its episodes and to understand something of the specific colonial situation that gave rise to it. The lienzo's majestic color reconstruction, achieved by the collaborative labors of Brownstone, Eckehard Dolinski, and Georgia Guenther, allows us to see it in its former colorful state. These combined efforts to interpret, analyze, and recreate the sixteenth-century pictorial history have brought the Lienzo of Tlapiltepec back to life.

NOTES

1. For a discussion of glottographic and semasiographic writing systems, see Sampson 1985; Jansen 1988; Boone 1994b.
2. This summary is based on the more detailed discussion of Mexican pictorial histories in Boone 2000b.
3. These Mexican manuscript structures were first articulated in Boone 1994a and are elaborated in Boone 2000b:64–86.
4. For other accounts of painted manuscripts being employed in legal cases, see Smith 1973a:89; Parmenter 1982:46–48; Doesburg, chapter 2 of this volume.

PREFACE

One by one, the authors of this volume were drawn to Toronto's Royal Ontario Museum by their deep interest in the Lienzo of Tlapiltepec, a pictographic document painted on a large sheet of cotton in sixteenth-century Mexico. Their converging interests only partly explain how this book came to be, for a number of events unfolded that gave the lienzo an almost talismanic quality and destined this book to be written.

The lienzo's journey from Tlapiltepec to the Royal Ontario Museum is a complex tale, and its circuitous travels are best illustrated by the many names given to the document over time. Its first title, "Códice *Wave*," is inscribed in pencil on the earliest known photograph of the lienzo, taken around 1908. The term *Wave* is one of a number of spellings for Huave, an indigenous group living on the Isthmus of Tehuantepec.[1] Several years later, the lienzo was mentioned in the newspaper *El Imparcial* in 1909, where it was named "Códice Chochonteca" (Doesburg 1998:61). Next, at the Seventeenth International Congress of Americanists in Mexico City in 1910, Abraham Castellanos, a Oaxacan educator and scholar of ancient Oaxaca, christened the document "Lienzo Antonio de León" in honor of an important nineteenth-century Oaxacan general. Several weeks later, the great German archaeologist and president of the congress, Eduard Seler, made a tracing of the lienzo. In his own hand, Seler inscribed in two places on the resulting illustration his title for the manuscript, "Lienzo de Tlacotepec, Mixteca Alta." Seler's student and colleague Walter Lehmann labeled a series of early photographs of the lienzo with the same name (Lehmann papers, Ibero-American Institute, cat. no. Y 1812). Constantine Rickards, a British vice-consul in Oaxaca who was born in that state to Scottish parents, was a onetime owner of the lienzo. He presented a paper on the document in London at the 1912 Congress of Americanists, where he referred to it as "Codex Rickards" (Rickards 1913). Meanwhile, Castellanos added several more titles, "Lienzo Antonio de León de Papalutla y Miltepec" and "Lienzo Antonio de León de Atenango," so-named after the villages in the region where he thought the document originated (Castellanos 1912a, 1912b, 1917). Several years later, in a caption, Castellanos quietly renamed the document "Lienzo de Tlapiltepec" after a village in another region (Castellanos 1917). Herbert Spinden (1940), the eminent curator of Amerindian collections at the Brooklyn Museum, later coined the title "Lienzo de Chicomostoc," based on a prominent scene on the lower left corner of the document. A dozen years later, Alfonso Caso (1954:18), the father of Mexican archaeology, compounded most of the previous terms and referred to the document as "Lienzo Antonio de León, Códice Rickards, o Lienzo de Tlapiltepec, de Papalutla y Miltepec."

In 1961 the Mixtec manuscript scholar Ross Parmenter (1912–1999) carefully examined the histories of these names in his quest to discover the origin of the lienzo. Based on Caso's (1958:389) research, Parmenter understood the lienzo to be from the Coixtlahuaca Valley, and he calculated that Castellanos must have had good cause to drop his former village names in favor of one within the valley. Parmenter tested his theory in October 1961, when he brought a three-foot photograph of the lienzo to Tlapiltepec, hoping that a village old-timer might recall having seen the manuscript while it still resided there (Parmenter 1961:11–12). One elder, Don Severo Hernández, had never seen the lienzo but recalled that it had been stolen in 1904. Several years later, Parmenter came across a Oaxacan newspaper article on the life of Fidel López Sandoval, who was a teacher in Tlapiltepec from 1888 to 1892. The article noted that at the request of the historian Manuel Martínez Gracida, López Sandoval had made several drawings of the lienzo in that village. A few years after that, Parmenter met López Sandoval's son, Fidel López Carrasco, who confirmed that in 1904 the elders of Tlapiltepec had brought the lienzo to the town of Coixtlahuaca and put it in the hands of their lawyers in an effort to settle a land dispute with two neighboring communities. The case was settled, but the lienzo disappeared and never came back to Tlapiltepec, despite the town council members' repeated appeals to their lawyers to secure its return (Parmenter 1972:3). López Carrasco also recalled that his father had persuaded Castellanos to use the term "Lienzo de Tlapiltepec" in his 1917 article. However, to be certain that the Royal Ontario Museum lienzo was the one from Tlapiltepec, Parmenter needed to find the drawings López Sandoval made for Martínez Gracida. Martínez Gracida's massive, unpublished manuscript on the ethnology and archaeology of Oaxaca came to light in 1972 when it was accessioned into the Sala de Asuntos Oaxaqueños of the Biblioteca Pública Central Margarita Maza de Juárez in Oaxaca. There, Parmenter found a sketch and an accompanying note stating: "This hieroglyph is from the lienzo or codex of Tlapiltepec, where it was copied by Fidel López." He immediately recognized that the sketch was indeed of a hieroglyph on the Royal Ontario Museum's lienzo, and in doing so he had finally established without question the location of the lienzo when it was last in indigenous hands (Parmenter 1982).

Parmenter also learned that Antonio Chávez, the legal assistant who had worked directly with the Tlapiltepec town council, had stolen the lienzo. On May 23, 1907, Chávez had sold the lienzo to Constantine Rickards for 400 pesos in a transaction formalized by a sales contract signed by a Oaxacan notary and two witnesses (Doesburg 1998:59). In November 1908, Rickards commissioned Castellanos to sell the lienzo to the Ministry of Education for 4,000 pesos. The three experts hired by the government to assess the lienzo recognized its great importance but advised the ministry to counter with an offer of 2,000 pesos for its acquisition. Castellanos proposed a compromise of 3,000 pesos, and despite his strong arguments on the importance of the lienzo, the ministry declined to buy it.

Meanwhile, Chávez learned of these negotiations and was so incensed by how little he had received for the lienzo that he took legal action. He accused Rickards and Castellanos of robbing him of the manuscript, alleging that the sales contract referred to another, less valuable, lienzo. The judge in the case ruled against Chávez. The fact that Chávez stole the lienzo in the first place was apparently never mentioned in the legal proceedings (Doesburg 1998).

Toward the end of 1911, Rickards offered the lienzo and his archaeological collection of some 1,500 pieces, largely Oaxacan ceramics, to the National Museum of Mexico for 25,000 pesos. Acting on the advice of Fernando Sologuren, a prominent collector of Oaxacan antiquities, the museum director, Cecilio Robelo, turned down the offer (Doesburg 1998). One hundred twenty Zapotec funerary urns make up the most visually interesting subsection of archaeological material in the Rickards collection. However, two-thirds of these were later proven inauthentic (Sellen 2004). Perhaps Sologuren recognized the urns were fakes and advised against their acquisition.

However, Rickards was also looking elsewhere for a buyer. In a letter dated July 13, 1911, to Charles Currelly, director of the Royal Ontario Museum, he offered his collection for US$15,000 or 30,000 pesos. Currelly's archival papers, held in the Royal Ontario Museum's registration department, contain no further correspondence on Rickards's offer until September 18, 1918, when Francisco Diez Barroso, of the law firm Cancino and Riba, wrote to Sir Edmund Walker, the museum's chairman of the board, that after a yearlong search he had finally located the Rickards collection. Soon after, Cancino and Riba hired two antiquities experts who assessed and recommended the purchase. The museum accepted Rickards's offer, and around March 16, 1919, Currelly left by rail for Mexico City. On April 14 the Mexican Ministry of Agriculture and Public Works issued a letter permitting the export of the majority of the objects in the collection, and by April 21, Currelly was on his way back to Toronto. Shipping agents Berea, O'Kelly and Co. were hired to transport the twenty-three packages of "pottery," which sailed by steamer from Veracruz bound for New York on May 2.

Currelly's correspondence after November 14, 1927, traces the shipment of an additional five crates said to contain Zapotec funerary urns. Sir Edmund Walker had apparently acquired this material shortly before the first shipment was approved for export and had stored it in the basement of the British embassy in Mexico City. The Mexican government officials inspected and approved export of almost all the 136 small and 72 large pieces contained in the crates, and the Royal Ontario Museum received the material in November 1934. In later years, both shipments were combined into the Rickards Collection.

Any knowledge concerning the questionable ownership of the lienzo appears to have been absent from these transactions. However, in correspondence dating from 1937 between Herbert Spinden and T. F. McIlwraith, curator of ethnology at the museum, there are suggestions that something was amiss. Spinden mentioned to McIlwraith that he would like to show photographs of the lienzo to people in Oaxaca. McIlwraith, however, noted that some "relatively ancient [museum] history" had recently come to his attention and wrote Spinden the following cautionary note: "I do not know the full ramifications but I understand that there were certain personal matters involved in the acquisition of the lienzo of which I recently sent you photographs. I have just been speaking with Dr. Currelly on the subject; apparently some of the people involved live in Oaxaca,[1] and he thinks that it would be wise to ask you not to show the photographs there." Spinden replied, "I suspected that there might be some sensitivity as regards your codex. I think I know the man who originally owned it but in any case you may depend on my being very discreet."

It would not be until 2004, in the context of planning an anthropology gallery for its new addition, that the Royal Ontario Museum corresponded directly with the community of Tlapiltepec. The Tlapiltepec municipal council reacted favorably to the museum's plans to install a life-size illustration of the lienzo while allowing the light-sensitive original to remain in its darkened and climate-controlled storage environment. The council members expressed pride that the lienzo would find a place of prominence in the cultural landscape of the museum galleries and said that the study of the lienzo "gives us the hope of retrieving our cultural roots, to be passed down to our children and grandchildren, while, at the same time, making them known to Canada and the world."

Bas van Doesburg, Nick Johnson, and Eckehard Dolinski kindly assisted in the development of the display, a project that helped knit us together as a working group of authors who, along with Elizabeth Boone, would be responsible for this book. We were particularly excited about the lienzo illustration, which employed new electronic techniques to revitalize color passages that for centuries had been extremely faded.

The authors of this book were drawn together from many directions and over many years by our interest in the Lienzo of Tlapiltepec. The work of Ross Parmenter played a strong role in our coalescence. Around 1960 Parmenter learned that the lienzo was preserved in the Royal Ontario Museum, only a few blocks from his old high school in Toronto. By that time he had been away from Toronto for some twenty-six years, working for the *New York Times*, where he ended his career as its music news editor in 1964. Nick Johnson also found out about the lienzo only after leaving his adopted city of Toronto. In 1986 he became a student of the Mixtec manuscript specialist Mary Elizabeth Smith at the University of New Mexico. In his first class he learned of the Lienzo of Tlapiltepec and that the person who knew the most about it was Smith's good friend Ross Parmenter. In the following year, Christmas brought Parmenter and Johnson to Toronto, where they met for the first time and discussed the lienzo. A week later, in my capacity of curatorial assistant in the ethnology department, I (Brownstone) met Johnson and facilitated his firsthand study of the lienzo.

I also had the pleasure of meeting the three other contributors to this volume through their interest in the lienzo. During the 1990s, Bas van Doesburg was one of a group of six scholars headed by Maarten Jansen in the department of archaeology of the University of Leiden. The Leiden group was at the leading edge of research on Mexican pictographic documents. Its members became interested in producing digital, multimedia programs about lienzos from the Coixtlahuaca Valley, and in this context, Van Doesburg traveled to Toronto to study the Lienzo of Tlapiltepec in August 1997. The following year, Boone came up from Tulane University, New Orleans, especially to study passages that illustrate the mythological origins and historical foundations of the rulers whose history the lienzo records. Later that year, Eckehard Dolinski also arrived to study the lienzo. He had been employed by the Ibero-American Institute in Berlin, where his interest in the document stemmed from his research on the colorful tracing of the Lienzo of Tlapiltepec made in 1910 by Eduard Seler.

The distinctive backgrounds of these authors are reflected in the variety of viewpoints that they bring to this volume. There are three major essays in the book. Nick Johnson, who completed his doctorate in Latin American Studies at Tulane University and is today a visual artist and scholar living in Port Bruce, Ontario, wrote two chapters, "What Is a Lienzo?" and "The Language of Lines on the Lienzo of Tlapiltepec." They focus largely on the lienzo as an entity unto itself. He discusses the large cloth format of the manuscript, analyzes its painted contents in relation to the format, and shows how cloth and paint combine to communicate ideas and tell a story. The chapter "The Lienzo of Tlapiltepec: The Royal Historiography of the Coixtlahuaca City-State," by Bas van Doesburg, emphasizes the lienzo as a product of local political circumstances. On the basis of colonial documents in archives, Van Doesburg reconstructs this early colonial political context. Van Doesburg lives in Oaxaca, where he is a full-time researcher for Mexico's National University (UNAM) and a senior advisor to the Alfredo Harp Helú Oaxaca Foundation. Eckehard Dolinski and I have contributed a brief chapter on illustrations of the Lienzo of Tlapiltepec, particularly the illustration used throughout this volume. Dolinski trained as a visual artist and anthropologist. His contribution draws on his extensive knowledge of primary documents on Mesoamerican archaeology and ethnology held in German archives. As assistant curator at the Royal Ontario Museum, I have devoted much of my career to the study of Plains Indian pictographic painting, and in this context developed the techniques for illustrating pictographic documents applied to our current rendering of the lienzo. The glosses on the lienzo are discussed by Michael Swanton, an investigator at the Coordinación de Humanidades, UNAM, whose research focuses on the linguistics and philology of the languages of Oaxaca, Mexico, especially the Popolocan and Mixtecan languages. Elizabeth Boone is the Martha and Donald Robertson Chair in Latin American Art, Tulane University, and former Andrew W. Mellon Professor, Center for Advanced Study in the Visual Arts, U.S. National Gallery of Art. Her foreword to the book provides a theoretical overview of the essays and a general orientation to the Lienzo of Tlapiltepec within the larger Mesoamerican tradition of pictorial narrative manuscripts. We have endeavored to write a book of the highest scholarly level while ensuring that its contents are accessible and of interest to non-specialist readers. We also bore in mind that the book should be generously illustrated. Since the lienzo employs sixteenth-century concepts of combining pictures and writing, we have worked particularly hard on the successful integration of pictures and words in our twenty-first-century manuscript.

There are many individuals and institutions whose contributions have made this book possible, including a number of colleagues at the Royal Ontario Museum. A special note of thanks is due Georgia Guenther, ROM artist, who dedicated her high standards of precision and clarity to the digital rendering of the illustration of the lienzo that is used in whole and in part throughout this book. Along with Tara Winterhalt, ROM graphic designer, Georgia also kindly converted maps and diagrams into vector-based illustrations. Brian Boyle, ROM photographer, with great patience and skill took the photographs of the Lienzo of Tlapiltepec found inside these covers. Annette Boenke-Jarek, budget officer of ROM's World Cultures Division, expertly handled the allocation of finances. Administrative assistant Gwen Adams generously gave of her time to help prepare hard copies of the manuscript. Sheeza Sarfraz, project coordinator, ROM Publications, kindly sorted out details regarding the contract with the University of Oklahoma Press.

It has been very pleasant to work with the staff of the University of Oklahoma Press. Alessandra Tamulevich, acquisitions editor, and her assistant Thomas Krause were extremely helpful in shepherding the manuscript and illustrations into the editing and production phase. Emily Jerman and Katrin Flechsig exercised great patience, care, and intelligence in editing the text. I would like to thank the following individuals who worked on the production side, all of whom clearly understood the important role of design in this book: Anna María Rodríguez, production assistant;

Emmy Ezzell, production director; Julie Rushing, designer; Julie Allred, compositor and designer; and Tom Jonas, who redrew the maps. Thanks also to Amy Hernandez, marketing assistant, and Sandy See, publicity director, whose efforts ensure that this book reaches a wide reading audience. The two anonymous peer readers made several key recommendations, and I am very grateful for their well-considered thoughts on the manuscript.

Allan Kosmajac and Sam Slotnick kindly took the photographs of the lienzo that were very useful in the DStretch photo-enhancing software analysis. Jon Harman, developer of DStretch, generously gave us a copy of his software. I am indebted to staff of the Canadian Conservation Institute, guided by Kate Helwig, for lending their expertise in the scientific examination and analysis of the paint mediums employed on the lienzo.

Too many to name individually, many colleagues on both sides of the Atlantic have enriched this volume with information and images held in the following institutions: Benemérita Universidad Autónoma de Puebla, Mexico; Universidad Francisco Marroquín, Guatemala; Museo Regional Casa de Alfeñique, Puebla; Biblioteca Nacional de Antropología e Historia, Mexico City; Archivo General de la Nación, Mexico City; the Brooklyn Museum; the Bodleian Library, University of Oxford; the British Museum, London; Museum der Kulturen, Basel; Österreichische Nationalbibliothek Bildarchiv und Grafiksammlung, Vienna; and Ethnologisches Museum Berlin.

Special thanks to María de los Ángeles Romero Frizzi, researcher at the Instituto Nacional de Antropología e Historia, for freely sharing copies of her prints of the Tequixtepec lienzos I and II. Gregor Wolff, director of the Ibero-American Institute, kindly permitted us to make a photographic record of Eduard Seler's traced illustration of the Lienzo of Tlapiltepec. Harry Persaud of the British Museum Library greatly assisted with information concerning the negative blueprint of the presumed Paul Henning illustration of the Lienzo of Tlapiltepec. I am grateful to the American Museum of Natural History and the Latin American Library, Tulane University, for kindly undertaking the first professional photographs of two very large and complex documents, the illustrations of the Wilhelm von den Steinen copy of the Lienzo of Coixtlahuaca (Lienzo Seler II) and Lienzo A (Lienzo Meixueiro), respectively.

Finally, I am humbled by the deep knowledge possessed by the authors of this book and am extremely privileged to have had the opportunity of channeling their intense interest in Mexican pictorial documents into this volume.

NOTES

1. The photograph is preserved in the Archivo General de la Nación, Fondo de Instrucción Pública y Bellas Artes, caja 154, exp. 22. It bears the following inscription: "Códice *Wave*. Mixteco—Castellanos—5000$." It is signed, "M.[anuel] Ramos. FOT."
2. Note in Freed (2012:756). Herbert Spinden attended the Congress of Americanists in Mexico City in 1910. Possibly he learned there that there was a cloud over the lienzo.

THE LIENZO OF TLAPILTEPEC

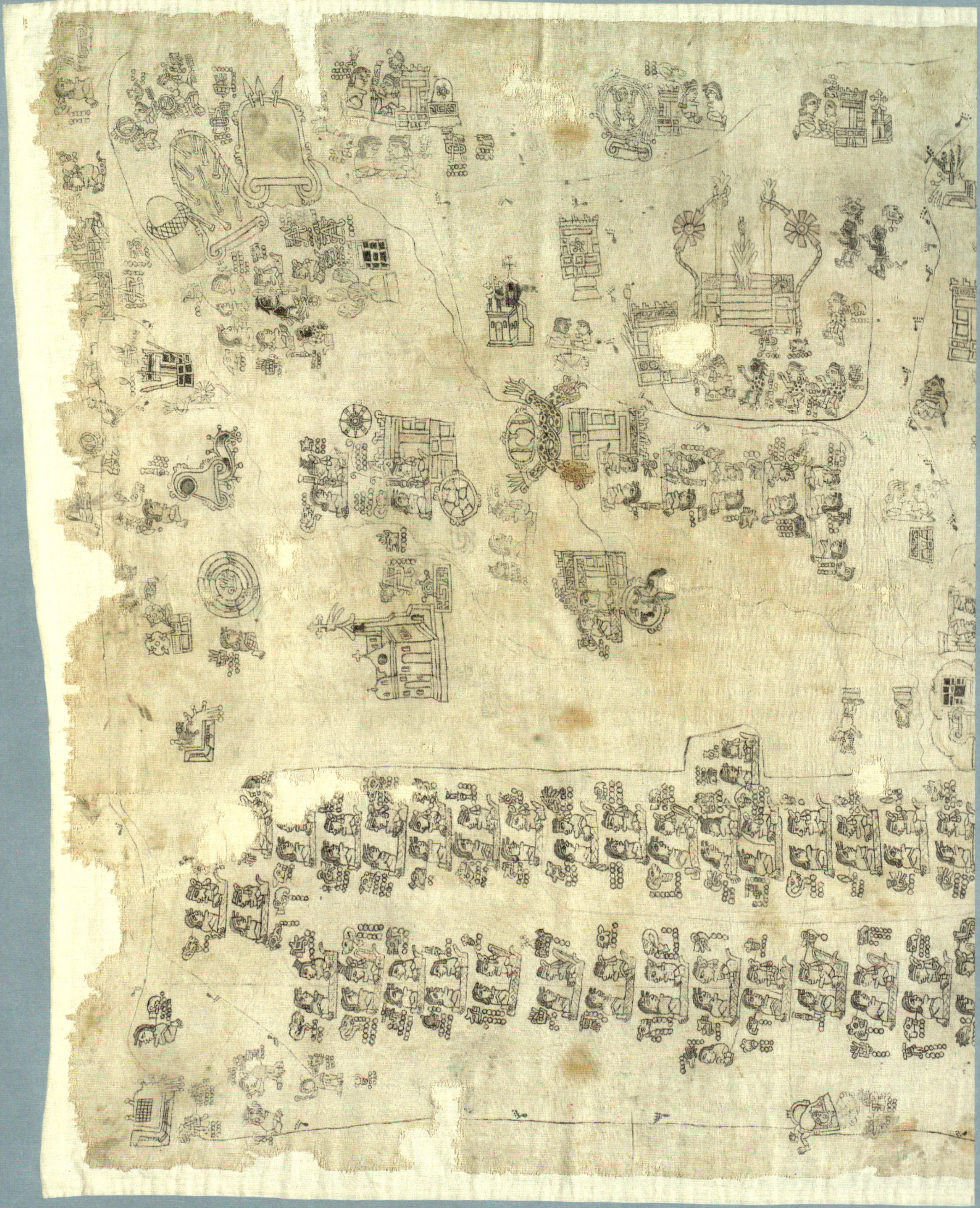

FIG. 1.1.

Lienzo of Tlapiltepec.

On the next three pages, the complete image is shown in three panels. Note that the images have been rotated ninety degrees counterclockwise; the lienzo's proper orientation is vertical rather than horizontal. Woven cotton, 3.97 × 1.67 meters. Courtesy of Royal Ontario Museum, acc. no. 917.3, photo by Brian Boyle.

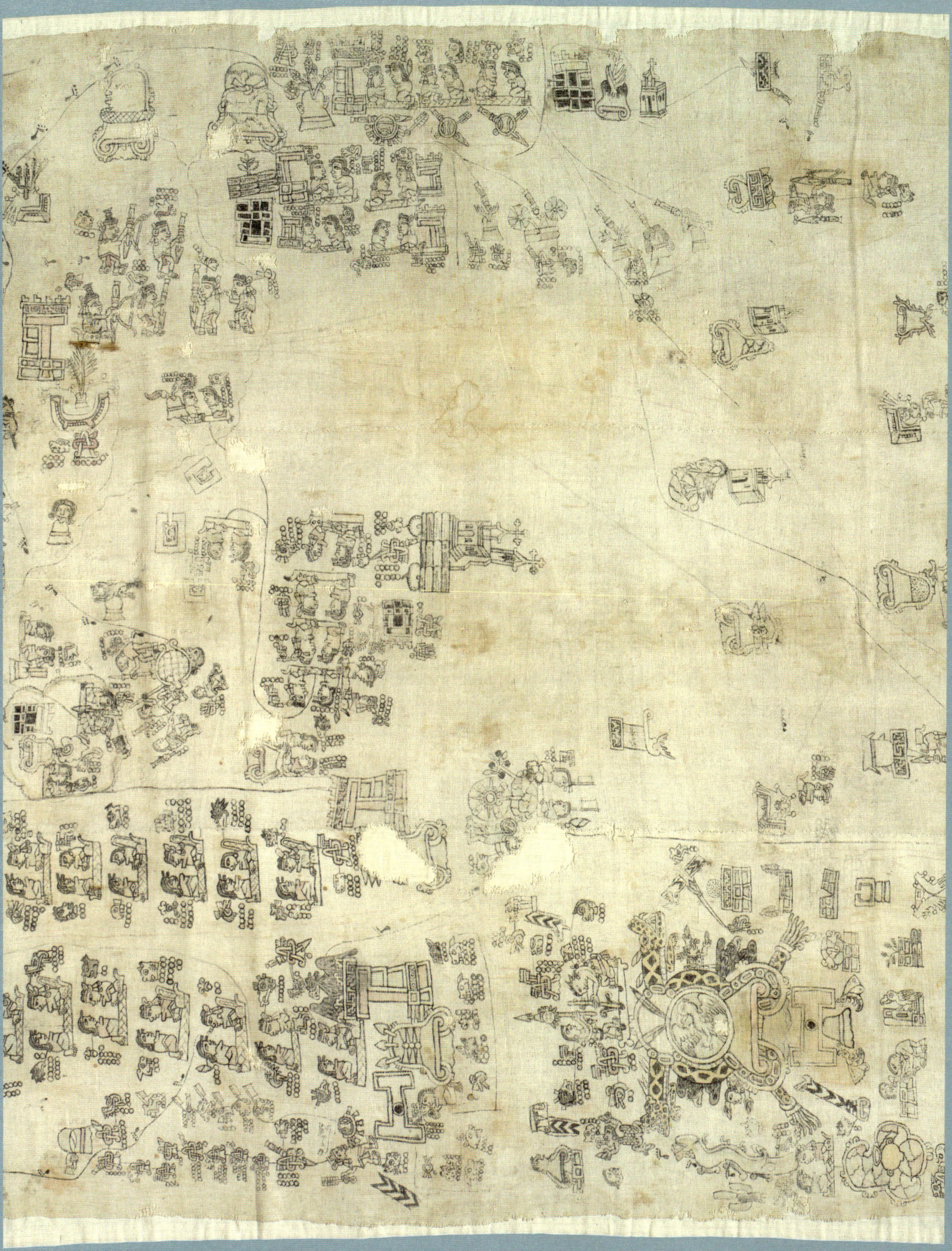

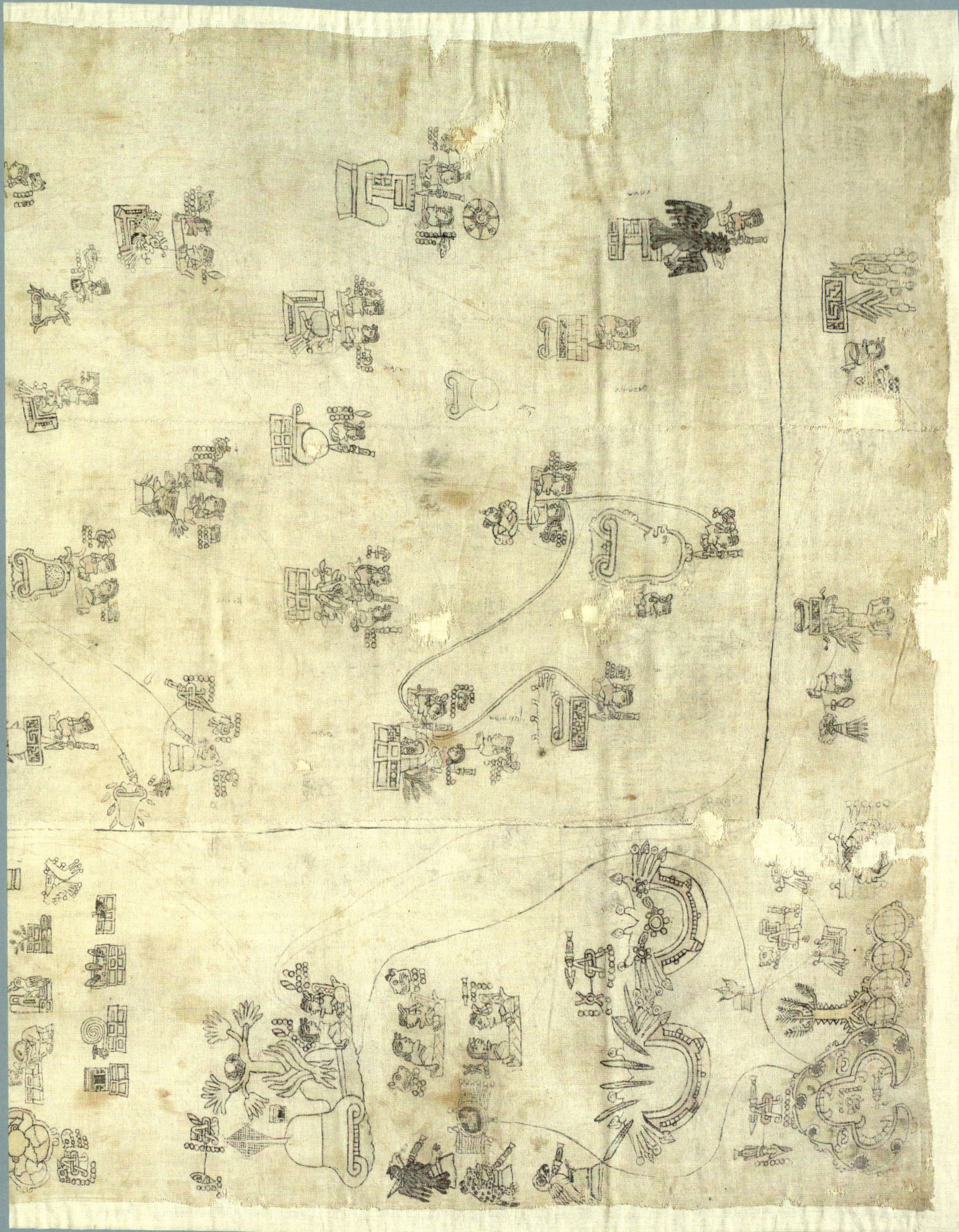

CHAPTER 1

What Is a Lienzo?

NICHOLAS JOHNSON

The Lienzo of Tlapiltepec is a major sixteenth-century native picture-writing manuscript of large size and elaborate composition (fig. 1.1). Originally from the region known as the Mixteca in southern Mexico, the manuscript is now housed in the Royal Ontario Museum in Toronto, Canada. *Lienzo* is the Spanish word for a native manuscript inscribed on a large sheet of woven cloth, and Tlapiltepec is the village in which this particular lienzo at one time resided. Like many other lienzos, the Lienzo of Tlapiltepec's painting is a combination of map and visual history.

In my contribution to this study of the Lienzo of Tlapiltepec, I place emphasis on the object itself. I begin with the geographical and cultural origins of this lienzo, and for readers less familiar with Mesoamerican writing and manuscripts, I provide a brief guide to the pictorial conventions it employs. The remainder of the chapter is devoted to aspects of the lienzo format. I explore lienzos as maps, their large size, the cloth they are made of, their scale and orientation, and how they might have been viewed and read. This includes comparison with other Mesoamerican manuscript formats, especially the screenfold. The Lienzo of Tlapiltepec is one in a small family of pictorial manuscripts known as the Coixtlahuaca Group, after the valley in which they originate. One of the features that defines the group is that most of its manuscripts are of the lienzo type—maps and histories painted on large sheets of cloth such as the Lienzo of Tlapiltepec. The question, "What is a lienzo?" is thus, in this context, particularly relevant.

THE COIXTLAHUACA VALLEY LIENZOS

A relative handful of manuscripts retained in museums, libraries, and state archives, and in some village archives and private collections, is what remains of the great number and variety of pictorial manuscripts that helped to preserve and communicate knowledge in Mexico before and several decades after the Spanish conquest of 1519–21.[1] There were histories and genealogies, books of religious knowledge, maps, and accounts of goods and services. Rulers of small communities and larger political entities kept detailed records of their origins, lineages, and affiliations. Priests and healers depended on almanacs for daily guidance. Old manuscripts were copied and revised and new ones compiled generation after generation. Spanish conquerors mention coming across rooms full of manuscripts—the original archives and libraries (Boone 2000b:22).

There were numerous variants in the writing systems of ancient Mexico, which spanned more than two thousand years. These writing systems were partly pictographic, employing the direct pictorial representation of things and ideas. To a greater or lesser degree, they were also partly phonetic, employing the representation of sounds in the native languages.[2] The oldest known Mesoamerican inscriptions, carved in stone, date to around the fifth century BC. The oldest painted manuscripts still in existence may not be older than the fifteenth century AD, though scenes on seventh-century ceramic vessels appear to show Maya scribes painting in manuscripts similar to those in use when the Spaniards arrived nearly a thousand years later (Coe and Kerr 1997; Tedlock 2010:146–64).

To the Spaniards and other Europeans of the sixteenth century, the native writing systems and manuscripts of Mexico were of great intellectual interest. They were also a source of practical information on the history, religion, politics, and resources of the lands and people the Spaniards would now be governing and converting to Christianity, the lands and people they would be tending to and exploiting. Many manuscripts were burned during the early years of the conquest in zealous attempts to destroy the native religion. Many more were lost to the ravages of time.

Pre-Hispanic writing systems continued in use for about three-quarters of a century after the Spanish conquest, to around the end of the sixteenth century, by which time they were well on their way to being replaced by European alphabetic writing. Most examples of native manuscript painting extant today, including the Lienzo of Tlapiltepec, derive from this early colonial period. Of the less than a thousand major and minor manuscripts that survive, probably no more than fifteen predate the arrival of the Spaniards in Mexico and so are free of Spanish and European influence.[3]

Early colonial manuscripts combine pre-Hispanic writing and manuscript painting traditions, still retained in various degrees, with changes in style and content as well as materials and formats used. In both subtle and more obvious ways, the early colonial manuscripts inevitably reflect the disruption of the conquest and the changes brought about by the importation of Spanish culture and the imposition of Spanish government, social order, and religious beliefs on the people and lands of Mexico.

The surviving pictorial manuscripts are diverse in their origins, and their distribution is uneven. Many of the preserved manuscripts were made by the Aztecs and their neighbors in and around the densely populated and politically important Valley of Mexico, location of the Aztec city of Tenochtitlan, now Mexico City (map 1.1). Many others originate from the large, culturally and geographically distinct area of southern Mexico that corresponds approximately to the modern Mexican state of Oaxaca. Others are from states surrounding the Valley of Mexico, plus a small number from outlying areas in the northwest. Few examples are left of the unique manuscripts of the Mayas of far eastern Mexico and Guatemala.

In the ruggedly mountainous state of Oaxaca of southern Mexico, the largest native populations were and are the Zapotecs of eastern Oaxaca and the Mixtecs of western Oaxaca and smaller, adjacent parts of the states of Puebla and Guerrero. The Mixteca, as this western tri-state region as a whole is known, comprises three subregions: the Mixteca Alta, centrally situated and of high elevation, the lower but still

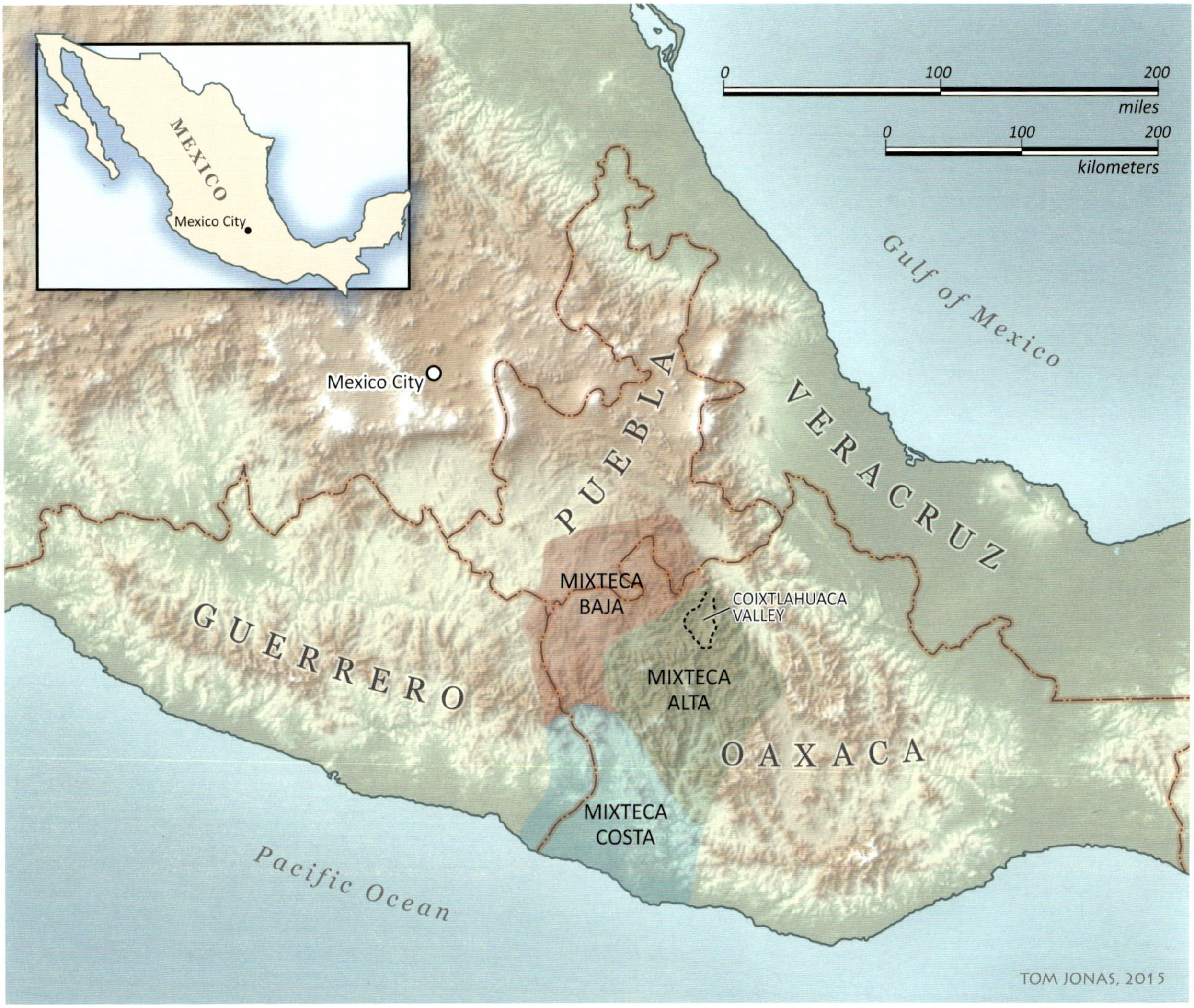

MAP 1.1. Central and southern Mexico, showing the Mixteca and its subregions and the location of Coixtlahuaca Valley.

mountainous Mixteca Baja west and northwest of the Alta, and the Mixteca de la Costa along the hilly Pacific coastal plain (see map 1.1).

The Coixtlahuaca Valley, source of the Lienzo of Tlapiltepec, lies on the northern edge of the Mixteca Alta. Tlapiltepec is one of several dozen small towns and villages, surrounded by farmlands, that occupy the valley, many since long before the Spaniards arrived in Mexico. In late pre-Hispanic times, united around the principal town of Coixtlahuaca, these valley settlements formed one of many small, autonomous kingdoms that made up the political map of Oaxaca and other areas of Mexico during this period.

The Coixtlahuaca Valley is of medium size, some thirty kilometers wide east to west and forty kilometers long north to south, surrounded by large mountains with rounded and conical tops (Rincón Mautner 1999:93–100). The broad, rolling valley floor lies at an elevation of approximately two thousand meters. At dry times of the year, the valley is an austerely bare landscape of pale colors—tan, greenish, salmon, as well as white where erosion has exposed a calciferous substratum known as *tepetate*—with dark vegetation on the upper slopes under blue skies. In the summer, after it rains, the landscape softens and turns green (fig. 1.2).

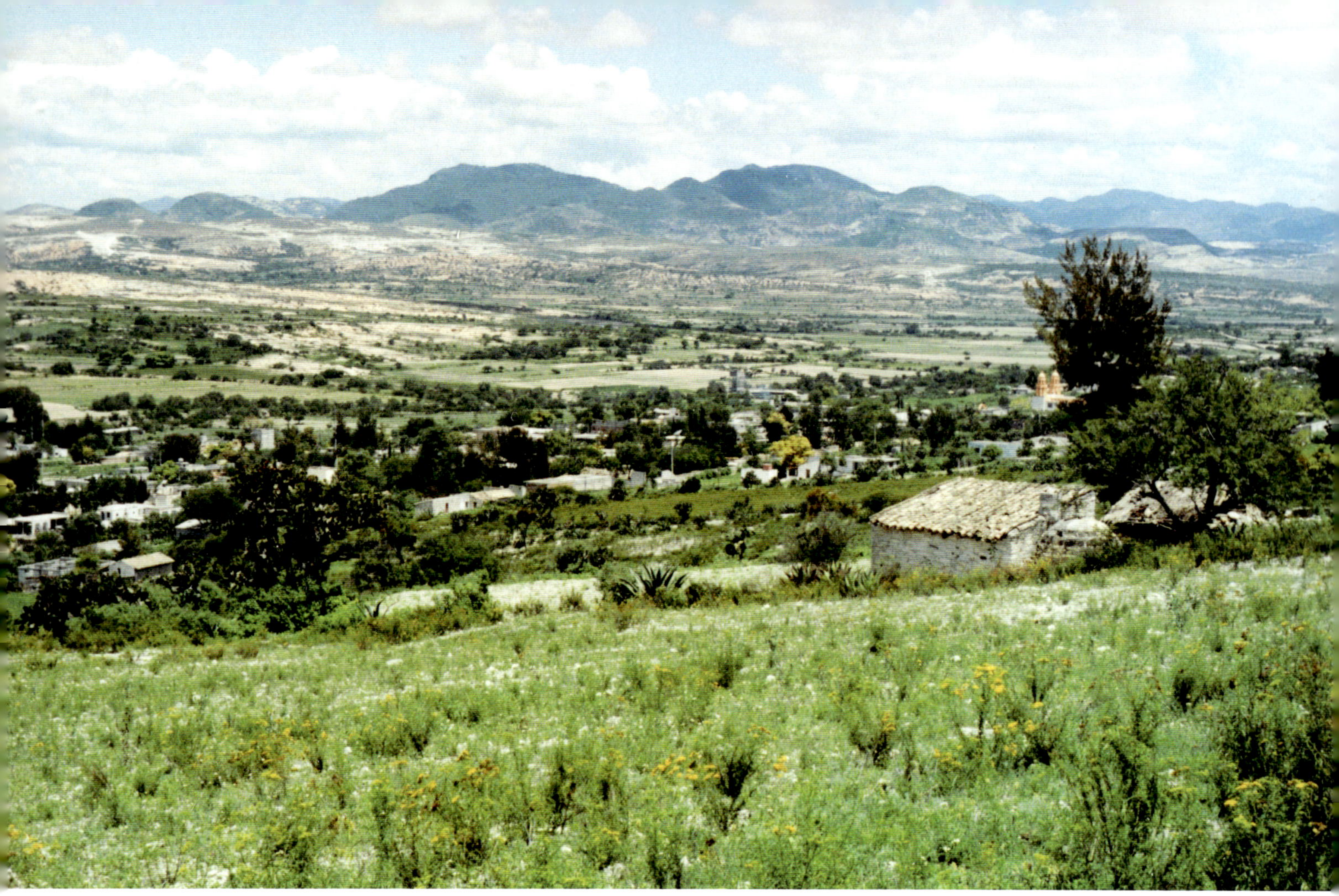

FIG. 1.2. Coixtlahuaca Valley, looking west from hillside above Coixtlahuaca, June 1992. Photo by Nicholas Johnson.

The Lienzo of Tlapiltepec, in addition to its individual importance as a historical document and major manuscript of its type, derives significance from the rare circumstance that a large number of early colonial pictorial manuscripts have survived to the present day from this one, relatively small, geographical area. The Lienzo of Tlapiltepec is thus not an isolated artifact but a member of a concentration of closely related painted documents known as the Coixtlahuaca Group.[4]

Eleven lienzos—manuscripts painted on large sheets of cloth—plus several manuscripts of other formats compose the Coixtlahuaca Group (table 1.1). Most or all are from the sixteenth century and originate either in the town of Coixtlahuaca itself or in other Coixtlahuaca Valley dependent towns. The maps and histories contained in these documents record overlapping accounts of the pre-Hispanic past and reflect interlocking adjustment to the early colonial present. They describe a common geography, history, and mythology, while at the same time they set in relief the individual perspectives of the parties who produced them in the mid-to-late sixteenth century. All together, they preserve something of the entire Coixtlahuaca Valley microcosm.

The Mixtecs of southern Mexico tend to be less well-known than their Aztec contemporaries in the Valley of Mexico; their archaeology less prominent and their communities more isolated in remote mountain locations. Still, they flourished and were influential in the late pre-Hispanic, or Postclassic, period (circa 950–1521 AD). In particular, the Mixtec pictographic writing system and artistic style were of importance to the wider Mesoamerican culture.

The majority of the manuscripts known from the Mixteca today are histories or combinations of maps and histories. Detailed genealogies of community rulers distinctively structure the painted histories from this region. Many are paintings on large sheets of cloth—lienzos—and many others take the form of book-like screenfold manuscripts, painted on long accordion-fold strips of animal hide.[5] Mixtec screenfold manuscripts, to which the Lienzo of Tlapiltepec is in some ways related, are among the landmarks of Mesoamerican pictorial narrative art.

TABLE 1.1. Pictorial manuscripts of the Coixtlahuaca Group

Lienzos	*Size (height × width in meters)*
Coixtlahuaca II (Seler II)	3.75 × 4.25 (15.94 m^2)
Lienzo A[a]	3.80 × 3.60 (13.68 m^2)
Coixtlahuaca I	4.25 × 3.00 (12.75 m^2)
Tequixtepec I	3.05 × 2.48 (7.56 m^2)
Tlapiltepec	3.97 × 1.67 (6.63 m^2)
Ihuitlán	2.48 × 1.57 (3.89 m^2)
Nativitas	1.73 × 1.75 (3.03 m^2)
Tequixtepec II	2.97 × 0.70 (2.08 m^2)
Tulancingo I	1.45 × 1.15 (1.67 m^2)
Otla	1.40 × 1.12 (1.57 m^2)
Aztatla[b]	0.50 × 2.64 (1.32 m^2)
Other manuscripts	
Selden Roll	native paper, 0.38 × 3.50
Gómez de Orozco Fragment	animal hide, 0.21 × 0.69
Codex Baranda	animal hide, 0.37 × 2.28

Sources: See chapter notes 4 and 11; also Glass and Robertson (1975). Table 1.1 lists only the major manuscripts of the Coixtlahuaca Group. A more comprehensive list would include such documents as the Land Grant Map of 1590 (Archivo General de la Nación, Tierras 2729-5; Smith 1973a:182, 184) and the Map of the Lands of Santo Domingo Tepenene of 1617 (AGN, Tierras 2812-11; Sacchi 1986), among others. Also not included in Table 1.1 is the late colonial Lienzo of Tulancingo II, of 1753 (Rincón Mautner 1994). Although as a map of the lands of one of the valley settlements, the Lienzo of Tulancingo II is related to other, earlier lienzos from the Coixtlahuaca Valley, it is largely disconnected from the pictographic writing system that produced them. It is a European-style oil painting on canvas of the village landscape.

Present locations: Coixtlahuaca II (Seler II), Ethnological Museum Berlin. Lienzo A, Latin American Library, Tulane University, New Orleans. Coixtlahahuaca I, Museo Nacional de Antropología, Mexico City. Tequixtepec I and II, San Miguel Tequixtepec, Oaxaca. Tlapiltepec (formerly Lienzo Antonio de León), Royal Ontario Museum, Toronto. Ihuitlán, Brooklyn Museum, New York. Nativitas, Santa María Nativitas, Oaxaca. Tulancingo I and II, San Miguel Tulancingo, Oaxaca. Otla, San Jerónimo Otla, Oaxaca. Aztatla, San Miguel Aztatla, Oaxaca. Selden Roll, Bodleian Library, Oxford University. Gómez de Orozco Fragment, present location uncertain. Codex Baranda, Museo Nacional de Antropología, Mexico City.

[a] Lienzo A is a late 19th- to early 20th-century copy of a lost 16th-century original (Parmenter 1970; Doesburg 2010b; also Doesburg 2001:30–31 n. 7). Sometimes known as Lienzo Meixueiro.

[b] The painting on the Lienzo of Aztatla is badly damaged and said to be mostly illegible (Doesburg and van Buren 1997:105 n. 1). The cloth has ribbed borders on some of its edges.

Manuscripts from the Mixteca are notable for a continuity of style that remained strongly indigenous even into the late sixteenth century. The corpus of surviving examples spans many years, for in addition to a substantial number of early colonial origin, one-third of the Mesoamerican total of about fifteen manuscripts made before the Spanish conquest are Mixtec. Furthermore, the pre-Hispanic Mixtec manuscripts are the only preconquest manuscripts still in existence from the whole of Mesoamerica that are devoted to the recording of history. The other pre-Hispanic manuscripts are dedicated to matters of religion.

The Coixtlahuaca Valley, as noted, is located on the northern edge of the Mixteca Alta, and the Coixtlahuaca manuscripts are in some ways a sub-group of Mixtec manuscripts. Like the Mixtec manuscripts, history and geography are their principal subject matter. The genealogies that are their central theme are constructed like those in the Mixtec manuscripts. The Coixtlahuaca manuscripts employ the same type of calendrical notation and same system of personal names as do manuscripts from other parts of the Mixteca.

In other respects, however, the Coixtlahuaca manuscripts are a separate entity. For example, genealogies in the Coixtlahuaca lienzos as a rule do not overlap with the network of genealogical ties and political affiliations emphasized in pre-Hispanic and colonial manuscripts from more central areas of the Mixteca south and west of the Coixtlahuaca Valley. The same people do not usually appear in the two groups of manuscripts. One of the underlying reasons for this separation is that the population of the Coixtlahuaca Valley was only partly, and perhaps, secondarily, Mixtec. The valley was also home to a people known as the Chochos, closely related to the Popolocas of southern Puebla.[6]

Much that is distinctive about the Coixtlahaca Group of manuscripts is in fact associated with an orientation northward toward this southern Puebla region, into the sphere of influence of the Toltecs and Aztecs of the Valley of Mexico, rather than southward into the Mixteca. Intermarriage and political interaction linking rulers of Coixtlahuaca and those of Puebla towns are featured on several of the Coixtlahuaca lienzos and are especially salient on the Lienzo of Tlapiltepec. The Coixtlahuaca manuscripts reflect central Mexican historical traditions and show the influence of central Mexican painting styles.

Style remains a largely unexplored aspect of the Coixtlahuaca Group. The painting styles of the lienzos and other manuscripts from the Coixtlahuaca Valley show varying degrees of external influence—Central Mexican indigenous on the one hand and European on the other. While there is a great variety of individual painting styles, there is evidence of interaction among the artists. For example, a number of human figures on the Lienzo of Coixtlahuaca II, also known as Lienzo Seler II, of the Coixtlahuaca Group, are so similar to figures on the Lienzo of Tlapiltepec as to suggest the possibility that these figures on Coixtlahuaca II were drawn by an artist who also worked on the Lienzo of Tlapiltepec (fig. 1.3).[7]

To sum up, the manuscripts of the Coixtlahuaca Group are related to manuscripts from the central and western Mixteca but separate from them. They are a concentrated entity corresponding to Coixtlahuaca Valley geography, history, and political organization. They are further defined by the combined Mixtec and Chocho population of the valley and by a historical orientation northward that is documented especially well on the Lienzo of Tlapiltepec. They show influence of central Mexican

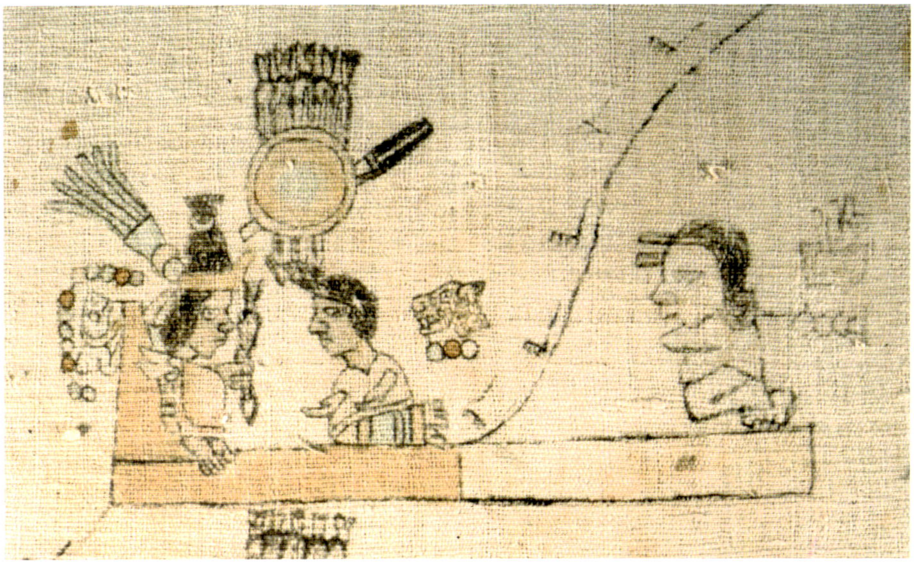

FIG. 1.3. Lienzo of Coixtlahuaca II (Seler II), detail showing woman, *right*, drawn in style of figures on Lienzo of Tlapiltepec. Courtesy of Ethnologisches Museum Berlin.

manuscript painting and historical traditions. They are sixteenth-century or early colonial in date. Last but not least, the majority of them are large lienzos.

The Lienzo of Tlapiltepec is today a faded painting on a sheet of discolored cloth approximately 4 m long × 1.7 m wide. The woven cotton was presumably once white. Now the visual impression it makes is of a soft, sandy beige color, gently mottled with brown and rust-colored stains. There are about sixteen small holes in the interior of the sheet, the largest approximately 8 × 15 cm, and eight fragments are missing along three of the edges. The entire upper edge is badly frayed.[8] The black outlines of the figures painted on the cloth are mostly intact and still clear, but the red, blue, green, yellow, yellow ochre, and brown colors that filled in these outlines are now pale and in places barely visible or not visible at all.[9]

One of the most serious color losses suffered by the lienzo has been the near disappearance of long, red connecting lines. One is aware of many black lines leading from one place to another over the length and breadth of the lienzo, but only gradually do the red lines emerge from the faded, fragmented traces of them still detectable and add themselves to the network. Gradually, the full extent of the web of red and black lines, and the original prominence of color and position of the red lines, becomes apparent (fig. 1.4).

The style of drawing is consistent throughout the lienzo, implying it was the work of one artist, or several artists trained in one style. The one notable addition to the otherwise pictographic manuscript consists of ten single words in European letters inscribed here and there on the lower right quarter of the lienzo. These words, some of them now badly eroded and difficult to decipher, appear to be place names in the Chocho language and to be related to place glyphs found nearby. They seem to be written in the same black paint used for drawing elsewhere on the lienzo.[10] These glosses are discussed by Swanton and Doesburg in chapter 2, appendix B, of this book.

Exactly when the Lienzo of Tlapiltepec was made is unknown. Events recorded on the lienzo took place before the Spanish conquest of Mexico of 1519–21, but several Christian churches and chapels included in the painting are an indication that it was produced at least several decades afterward. The drawing and painting style

FIG. 1.4. Illustration of Lienzo of Tlapiltepec with colors enhanced. Courtesy of Royal Ontario Museum, drawing by Georgia Guenther.

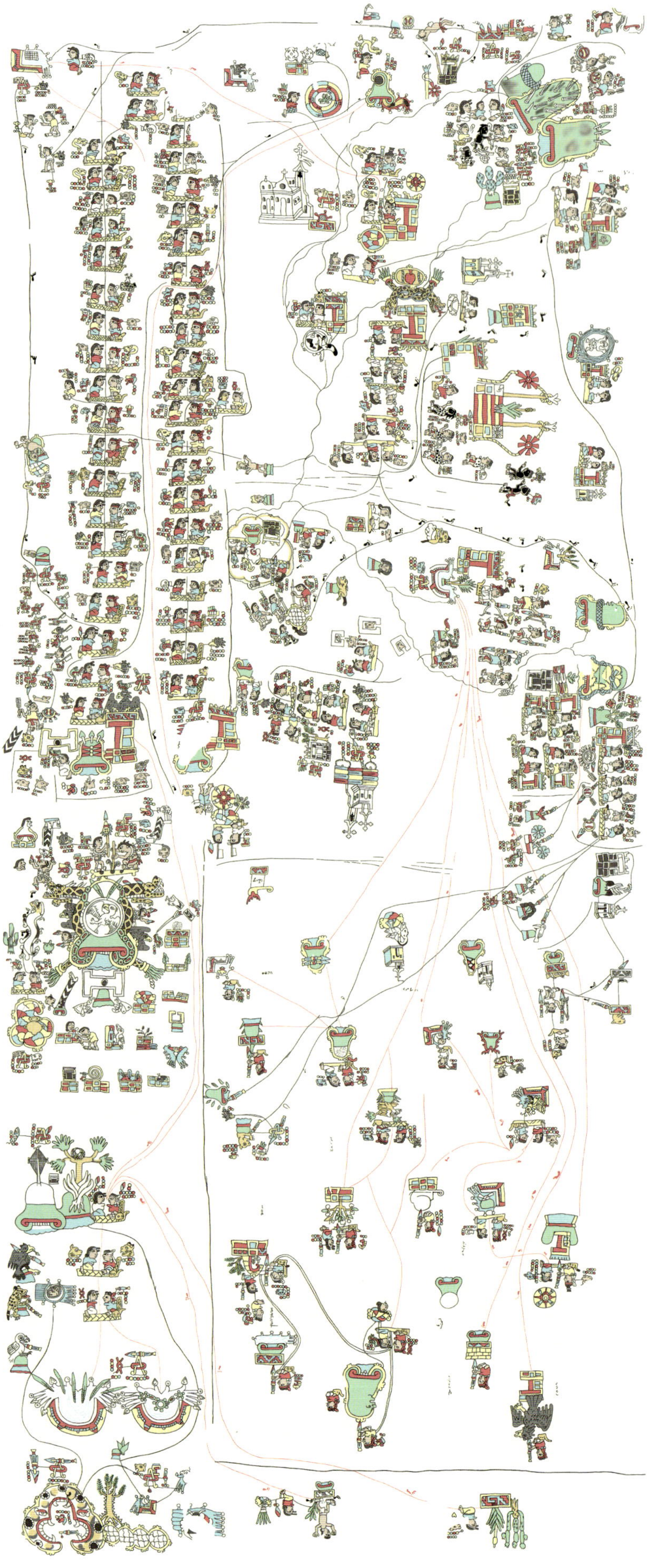

of the lienzo is close to that of known pre-Hispanic manuscripts. Shapes are two-dimensional, colors mostly flat, and human figures drawn in profile. People's names, place names, and calendrical dates are, by and large, represented in the conventional pre-Hispanic manner.

Exactly where the lienzo was made is also uncertain. The principal town of Coixtlahuaca is a strong candidate for its place of origin, as is proposed by Bas van Doesburg in chapter 2 of this book. The namesake village of Tlapiltepec, where, thanks to Ross Parmenter (1982:15–44), the lienzo is known to have resided at one time, is a less likely possibility.[11]

PEOPLE, PLACES, AND DATES ON THE LIENZO

Before continuing, especially for the sake of readers new to Mesoamerican manuscripts and writing systems, it may be helpful to provide a brief guide to the details of the painting. Just what is it that the viewer of the lienzo is seeing in the hundreds of small motifs dotted, clustered, aligned, and tied together over its surface?

On an introductory level, the lienzo is not difficult to follow. It records the history of actual people, places, and events with dates. Using conventional depictions, people are represented by male and female figures, places by glyphs or "place signs," events by simplified scenes or shorthand references to the activities, and dates by date signs.[12] The people are exclusively members of the local nobility. The lienzo is a history of the political affairs of the rulers, and by extension, the community they ruled, but not otherwise of ordinary people.

The human figures are distinguished by gender through their costumes and postures (fig. 1.5). Men on the Lienzo of Tlapiltepec usually wear headbands, short tunics, breechcloths, and sandals, while women wear longer, curling hair, long blouses or *huipiles*, and wraparound skirts, and are barefoot. Women's hair was braided on top of the head, and on the lienzo the ends of the two braids project forward, forming what look like horns on the women's foreheads. Women kneel, men sit on thrones, with their knees bent and feet in front of them.[13] Alternations in the colors of their garments and a certain rubbery variation in their outlines give them a lively sense of individuality, but essentially the figures are formulaic.

The name attached to each figure is its most important identifying feature. The name is placed close behind or above the figure, often attached by means of a short connecting line. The person's name is the calendar day on which he or she was born.

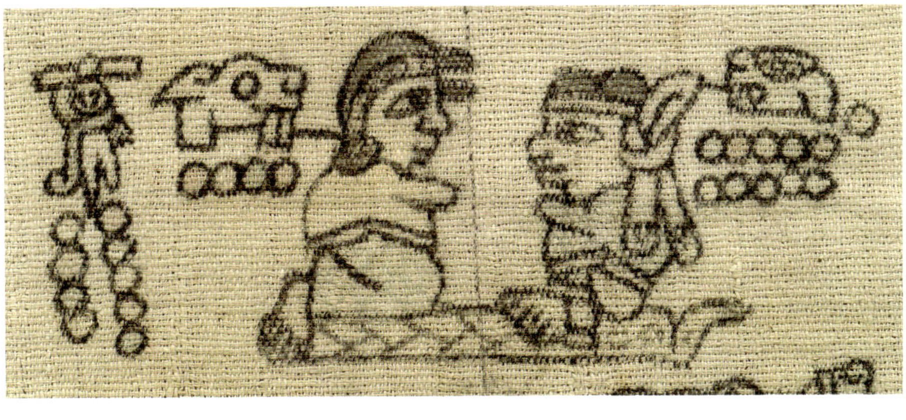

FIG. 1.5. Eleven Lizard, *right*, and wife 4 Rabbit on Lienzo of Tlapiltepec. A second wife, 9 Rain, is only mentioned by name. Courtesy of Royal Ontario Museum, acc. no. 917.3, photo by Brian Boyle.

FIG. 1.6. The twenty day signs as they appear on the Lienzo of Tlapiltepec.

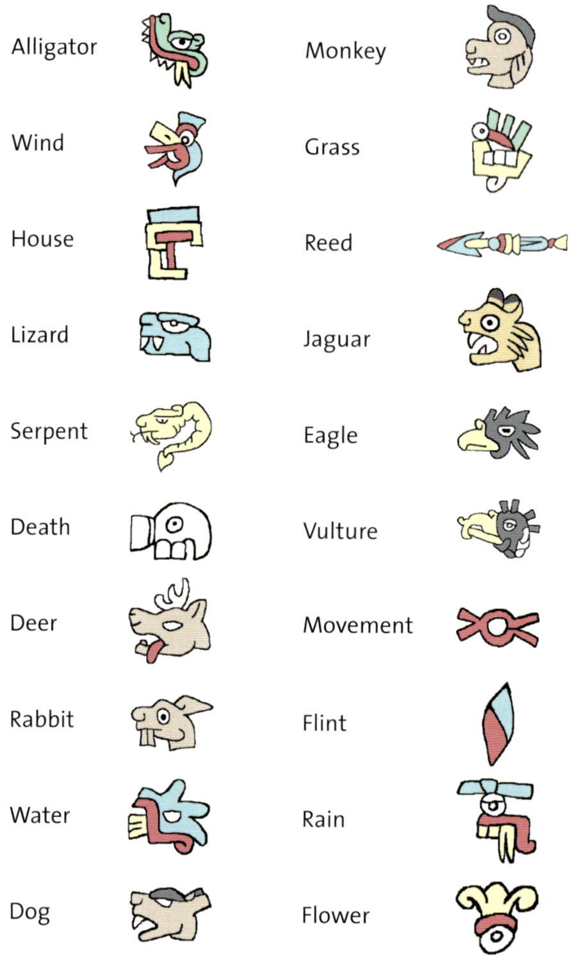

These are the animal heads and other motifs and accompanying rows of small circles seen everywhere on the lienzo. Days in the ancient Mexican calendar were identified by means of a combination of a day name proper and a number, or numerical coefficient. For example, the man seated with his wife on a palm or reed mat in figure 1.5 was born on the day 11 Lizard, his calendrical name, indicated by the head of a lizard and eleven circles positioned behind him. His wife was born on the day 4 Rabbit, which became her name.

There are twenty different day names in the native calendar, beginning with Alligator and ending with Flower, and thirteen numbers, 1 through 13 (fig. 1.6). Running concurrently and repeating endlessly, Flower is always followed by Alligator and the number 13 by the number 1. The combination of the series of twenty names and shorter series of thirteen numbers yields a total cycle or "calendar round" of 260 differently named days, which itself repeats ad infinitum.

In addition to calendrical names derived from the days of their birth, Mixtec and

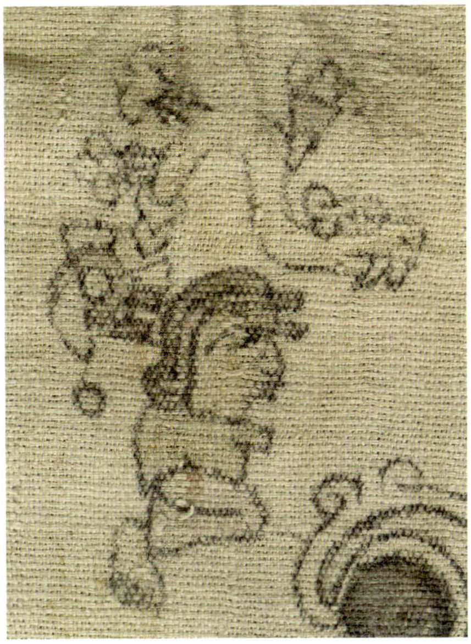

FIG. 1.7. One Wind "Flower Serpent" on Lienzo of Tlapiltepec. Courtesy of Royal Ontario Museum, acc. no. 917.3, photo by Brian Boyle.

FIG. 1.8. Tlapiltepec, "Hill of the Knot," on Lienzo of Tlapiltepec. Courtesy of Royal Ontario Museum, acc. no. 917.3, photo by Brian Boyle.

Chocho men and women also had given or "personal" names, though on the Lienzo of Tlapiltepec, in most cases, these additional names have been omitted. One of the five or six exceptions, human figures on the lienzo who *are* identified by their complete combination of calendrical and personal names, is a woman whose calendrical name is 1 Wind (the wind sign consists of the mask of the wind god). Her personal name on the lienzo is a serpent decorated with flowers (fig. 1.7). Thus her personal name would have been something like "Flower Serpent." She was 1 Wind "Flower Serpent." Or, with the honorific prefix that, as a member of the hereditary nobility, would have been attached to her name, Lady 1 Wind "Flower Serpent."

Places are represented on the lienzo by conventionalized place signs, sometimes called place glyphs. These are the many bell-shaped hills, bowl-shaped river cross-sections, houses and temple platforms, and other geographical and architectural motifs seen on the lienzo. They name the towns the rulers inherited or conquered; towns, ceremonial sites, or features of the landscape from which the men and women came or to which they traveled; and locations where important events took place.

The village of Tlapiltepec, for example, is represented on the lienzo by a place sign that consists of a hill, faintly perceivable as having once been colored green (or green mottled with yellow), that has a knotted rope tied around it (fig. 1.8). The knotted rope is the important qualifying element, because Tlapiltepec means "Hill of the Knot." Rounded contours drawn within the Tlapiltepec hill, fringed as if with vegetation, do not appear to be part of the place name per se, though they might refer descriptively to certain physical characteristics of the actual mountain that rises steeply above the village of Tlapiltepec. Place signs on the Lienzo of Tlapiltepec vary considerably in size and elaborateness but only a few are descriptively embellished like the Tlapiltepec sign. Most contain only the name-signifying elements.

Within the lienzo's multitude of forms and its expanse, place signs are visual

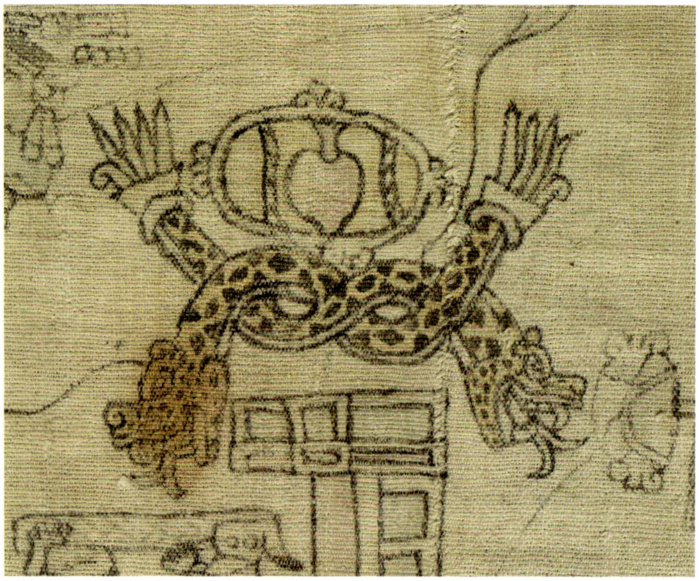

FIG. 1.9. Coixtlahuaca, "Serpent Plain," on Lienzo of Tlapiltepec. Courtesy of Royal Ontario Museum, acc. no. 917.3, photo by Brian Boyle.

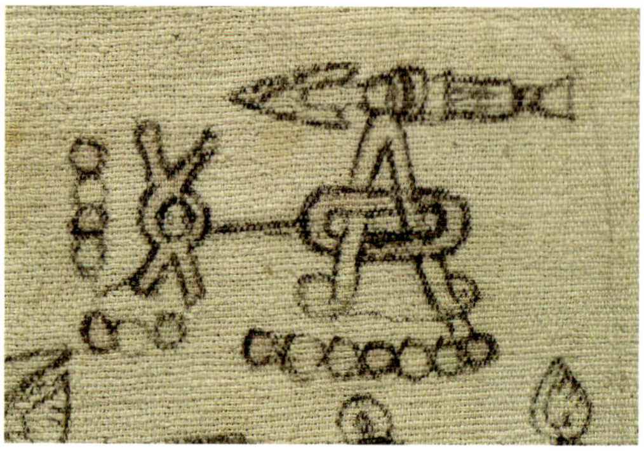

FIG. 1.10. A date on Lienzo of Tlapiltepec: day 7 Movement of year 7 Reed. Courtesy of Royal Ontario Museum, acc. no. 917.3, photo by Brian Boyle.

centers of gravity around which other elements revolve. The important town of Coixtlahuaca is shown on the Lienzo of Tlapiltepec as an entwined pair of ochre serpents with black markings and feathered tails (fig. 1.9). Coixtlahuaca means "Serpent Plain" (Smith 1973a:65–66). In some other lienzos from the Coixtlahuaca Valley, the serpent has a fully feathered body.

Dates on the lienzo usually include both the day and year, with the day appearing in exactly the same form as a person's calendrical name. In the system of notation employed in manuscripts from the Mixteca, the year portion of the date is distinguished from the day by the use of what is referred to as a year sign, resembling a large letter *A* interlaced with an *O*. An example from the Lienzo of Tlapiltepec is the day 7 Movement, year 7 Reed (fig. 1.10).[14]

Named human figures, place names, dates, connecting lines, dividing lines, as well as some faintly visible sketch lines, are the elements of drawing and painting on the Lienzo of Tlapiltepec.[15] The elements are economically assembled in standardized combinations to represent historical events and relationships of the types important to the Mixtecs in general and to the Mixtecs and Chochos of the Coixtlahuaca Valley: origins; the founding of towns and rulerships; conferences and large gatherings; the formation of alliances; journeys and migrations; conquests; religious rituals; marriage; and genealogical ties.

CHARACTERISTICS OF A LIENZO

The Spanish word *lienzo* is defined as: cloth, or a sheet of cloth, woven of linen, hemp, or cotton. The term may also refer to a painting done on cloth, comparable to similar usage of the word "canvas" in English. In Mexico and in the field of Mesoamerican manuscript studies, native pictorial manuscripts painted on sheets of cloth, usually of woven cotton and often large, are known as lienzos. The word comes from the Latin *linteum*, linen or linen cloth. The lienzo format is just one among the variety of different physical formats of native pictorial manuscripts that have survived from

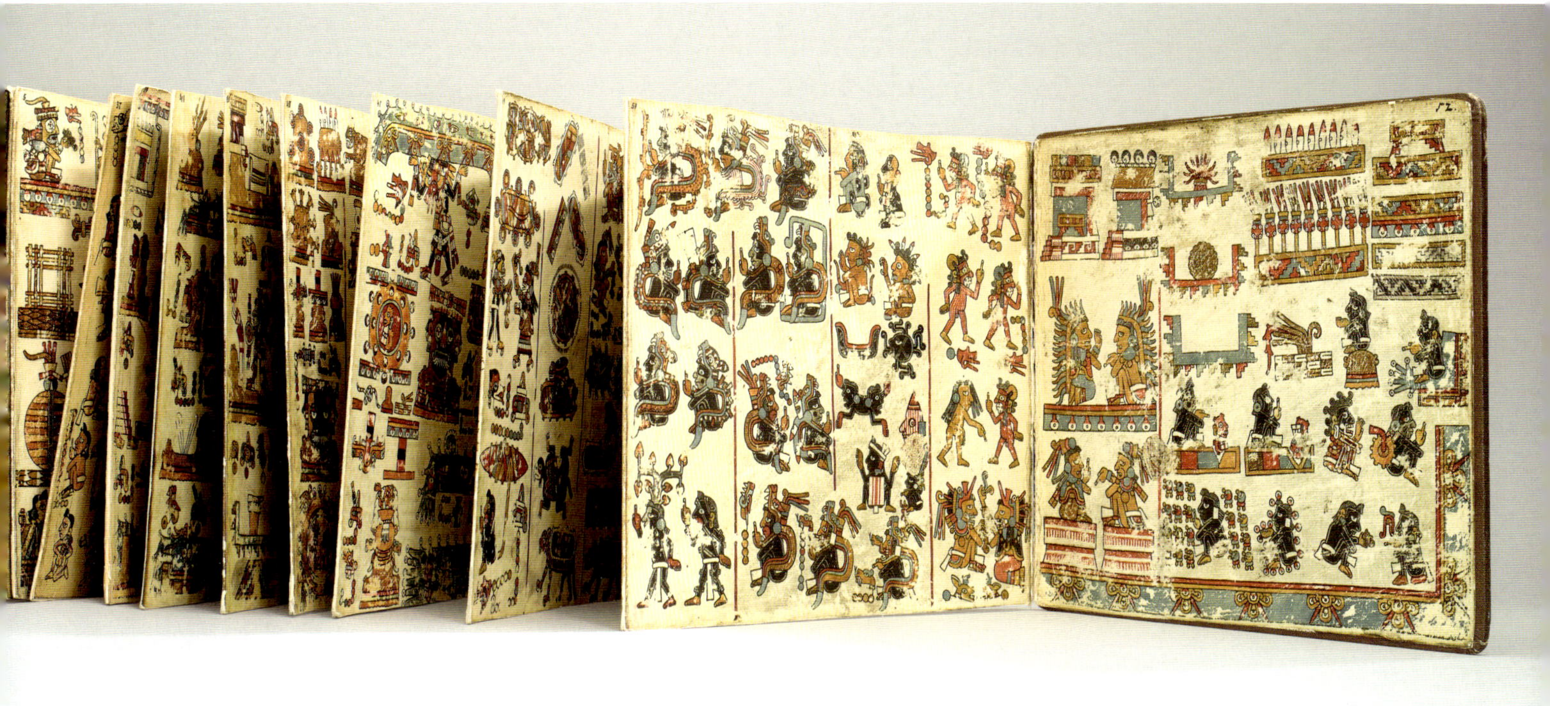

pre-Hispanic and early colonial Mexico.[16] Some indigenous formats are of preconquest origin and others are influenced by the design and uses of European books and manuscripts and modified by the adoption of European materials.

FIG. 1.11. Codex Vindobonensis, a pre-Hispanic Mixtec screenfold manuscript held in the Österreichische Nationalbibliothek (Codex Mexicanus I). Animal hide, 52 leaves, 22 × 26 cm, total length 13.52 meters. Pictured: first pages of the facsimile (Adelhofer 1963). Photo by Brian Boyle.

We are aware of two different types of preconquest format. There were strip-shaped manuscripts on the one hand, made of animal hide or native paper. Strip-shaped manuscripts include screenfolds and *tiras*. On the other hand there were single sheets or panels of cloth, hide, or paper.[17] As far as is known, the ancient Mexicans before contact with Europeans did not have manuscripts constructed like European books, consisting of multiple leaves bound together along one edge. Various native manuscripts made after the conquest take this form.

The most elaborate as well as most unambiguously indigenous of the manuscript formats is the screenfold, as it is known (fig. 1.11). The screenfold manuscript consists of a strip of animal hide or native paper scored at equal intervals and folded back and forth like an accordion or folding screen. The folds divide the strip of hide or paper into a regular series of page-like spaces. A type of gesso applied to the manuscript provided it with a smooth surface and bright white background for the painted inscriptions. In its collapsed or closed state, the screenfold forms a book-like block. Sometimes this block had covers consisting of thin slabs of wood or other material affixed to its two outer surfaces.

The screenfold manuscript is a defining artifact of Mesoamerican civilization. The screenfold was not a common manuscript format in Europe, nor to my knowledge did peoples of other regions of the Western Hemisphere make use of it. It is also almost the only preconquest Mesoamerican manuscript format for which there is abundant concrete evidence, since all but one of the fifteen or so extant preconquest manuscripts are of this type, and there exist at least another twelve screenfolds from the sixteenth century after the conquest. The sole known manuscript from the preconquest period that is *not* a screenfold is painted on a sheet of gesso-coated animal hide of medium size.[18] This, then, may be the only manuscript of the single-sheet or panel type in any material that has survived from preconquest times.

Also long and relatively narrow in shape is a type of manuscript referred to as a *tira*, from the Spanish word meaning "strip." Tiras, made of hide or native paper and sometimes European paper, lack the regular back-and-forth pattern of folds of the screenfold manuscripts, though they may be folded in other ways or may remain unfolded, and bear some resemblance to the European roll or scroll. No tiras survive from preconquest times. The tira, particularly the unfolded variety lacking built-in spatial subdivisions, is a less well-defined manuscript type than the screenfold. There is sometimes little physical difference between a short, wide tira and a long, narrow panel.

None of the existing lienzos, nor manuscripts painted on sheets of native paper, is thought to have been made before the Spanish arrival in Mexico. Because of the scarcity of preconquest examples, the exact nature, uses, and importance of lienzos and other single-sheet manuscripts in preconquest times is hard to determine. How closely the known exemplars from the early colonial period resemble similar manuscripts produced before the conquest is difficult to know with certainty. The same is true of the tira.

LIENZOS AS MAPS

While no lienzo still in existence is considered to date to before the conquest of Mexico, Spanish accounts of the early conquest years do include various mentions of lienzos seen by, or made specifically for, Hernán Cortés. Though brief, these early Spanish descriptions are evidence that cloth had indeed been an important material for pictographic inscriptions in pre-Hispanic Mexico.

The Spanish accounts also give an indication of the subject matter of pre-Hispanic cloth manuscripts. All of the paintings on sheets of cloth mentioned in the letters of Cortés to King Charles V of Spain, written between 1519 and 1526, were maps in one form or another (Cortés 1986:94, 192, 340, 365).[19] One such map, showing rivers and coves along the coast of the Gulf of Mexico, had been made for the conqueror at the behest of the Aztec ruler Moctezuma. Another was a lienzo sent to Cortés by the people of Chalco along with a request for military assistance in the face of approaching Aztec enemies: "On a large white cloth they showed the symbols for all the towns which were to attack them and the routes they were to follow." Two other lienzos were route maps drawn for Cortés by native scribes to guide his expedition to Honduras in 1525.

Another, apparently extremely large, pictographic map on cloth that Cortés sent to Spain in 1522 was described by Peter Martyr, a Spanish official who examined the painting, as being "thirty feet long and not quite so wide. All the plains and the provinces, whether vassal or hostile to Muteczuma, are there represented, as well as the lofty mountains which completely surround the plain" (Peter Martyr, *De Orbe Novo*, 1530, in MacNutt 1912, 2:198–99).Thus, the cartographic lienzos of early colonial Mexico, of which the Lienzo of Tlapiltepec is one, did not represent a new, post-conquest development, but were a continuation of a pre-Hispanic practice of painting maps on sheets of cloth.[20]

Not all existing lienzos are maps, but the majority are. Approximately sixty manuscripts of the lienzo type survive from the sixteenth through early seventeenth century. These manuscripts still display substantial use of preconquest writing systems. Another sixty to seventy lienzos are known from the seventeenth to eighteenth centuries and even later.[21] These usually show considerable or almost total loss of native writing systems and styles, replaced by European-influenced alternatives, but they reflect similar concerns and make similar use of the lienzo format as those of the earlier period. Sometimes these later manuscripts are versions or variants of earlier ones.[22]

Of this total of approximately 130 earlier and later colonial lienzos currently known to scholars, about 85 percent (approximately 107 lienzos) contain maps. Most of the cartographic lienzos are either maps of a community's territorial boundaries or of its constituent village settlements, or both. Many (approximately 89 lienzos) are map-history combinations, incorporating into the cartographic context such elements as scenes of events or dates associated with the founding of the community's towns and villages and genealogies of its pre-Hispanic rulers.

Among the lienzos that are not cartographic (approximately 20 lienzos) are 11 sixteenth-century manuscripts devoted to historical matters such as genealogy, and several lienzos whose subject matter is unreported or damaged beyond recognition.[23]

LARGE SIZE OF THE LIENZO

Cartographic subject matter alone does not distinguish cloth lienzos from single-sheet manuscripts made of other materials. Indeed, many maps are drawn or painted on single sheets or panels of native or European paper and some on animal hide, rather than cloth. A feature that does set the cloth manuscripts apart from others of the single-sheet or panel category, however, is their size. Lienzos are commonly large- or medium-size, while manuscripts of paper or hide tend to be smaller. [24]

Thus, of approximately ninety cloth manuscripts that in terms of surface area are 1 m square or larger, ten are close to 7 m square or larger. In contrast, of some fifteen non-cloth manuscripts 1 m square or larger, only one is above 7 m square. These dimensions are listed in table 1.2, from the largest in terms of surface area at the top of the table down to the smallest at the bottom; also indicated are the region and period of origin and the subject matter of the manuscripts.

The Lienzo of Tlapiltepec, at the bottom of the list in table 1.2, is in terms of surface area, the smallest of these eleven manuscripts. On the other hand, in terms of its height of nearly 4 m, the Lienzo of Tlapiltepec is comparable in size to cloth manuscripts at the top of the table. This may not be coincidental, as three of the cloth manuscripts in the upper half of the table, all of which approach or exceed 4 m in one dimension or the other, are, like the Lienzo of Tlapiltepec, from the Coixtlahuaca Valley, and at least three if not all four Coixtlahuaca Valley lienzos are known to have originated specifically from the town of Coixtlahuaca itself. Doesburg in chapter 2 of this book shows that the Lienzo of Tlapiltepec, like the lienzos of Coixtlahuaca I and II and Lienzo A, is also probably from the town.

A fifth manuscript in table 1.2, the Lienzo of Tequixtepec I, is also from the Coixtlahuaca Valley. Thus the reputation lienzos have for being of great size rests substantially on the evidence of the group of mainly sixteenth-century lienzos that has survived from this valley. All eleven very large manuscripts listed in table 1.2 were likely made before the end of the sixteenth century. If the thirty-foot dimensions of

TABLE 1.2. Largest Mesoamerican single-sheet pictorial manuscripts

	Material	*Area in m²*	*Height × width in m*	*Century*	*Region*	*Subject matter*
Lienzo of Coixtlahuaca II (Seler II)	native cloth	15.94	3.75 × 4.25	16th	Coixtlahuaca Valley	cartographic-historical
Lienzo A[a]	native cloth?	ca. 13.68	ca. 3.80 × 3.60	16th	Coixtlahuaca Valley	cartographic-historical
Codex of Huamantla[b]	native paper	13.30?	ca. 1.90 × 7.00?	16th	Tlaxcala	cartographic-historical
Lienzo of Coixtlahuaca I	native cloth	12.75	4.25 × 3.00	16th	Coixtlahuaca Valley	cartographic-historical
Lienzo of Quauhquechollan[c]	native cloth	10.04?	2.35 × 4.27?	16th	Puebla	cartographic-historical
Lienzo of Tlaxcala[d]	native cloth?	8.53?	4.20 × 2.03?	16th	Tlaxcala	historical
Lienzo of Tequixtepec I	native cloth	7.56	3.05 × 2.48	16th	Coixtlahuaca Valley	cartographic-historical
Lienzo of Zacatepec 2[e]	native cloth	7.35	3.00 × 2.45	16th	Western Oaxaca	cartographic-historical
Lienzo of Zacatepec 1	native cloth	7.31	3.25 × 2.25	16th	Western Oaxaca	cartographic-historical
Lienzo of Tzoquietlan	native cloth	7.26	2.42 × 3.00	16th	undetermined	cartographic-historical
Lienzo of Tlapiltepec	native cloth	6.63	3.97 × 1.67	16th	Coixtlahuaca Valley	cartographic-historical

Sources: Glass and Robertson (1975). For Coixtlahuaca II, Lienzo A, Coixtlahuaca I, Tequixtepec I, Tlapiltepec, see also chapter notes 4 and 11. Codex of Huamantla, Aguilera (1984); Lienzo of Quauhquechollan, Asselbergs (2004); Lienzo of Tlaxcala, Kranz (2007), Reyes García (1993:207–209); Lienzo of Zacatepec 1 and 2, Smith (1973a:89–121).

[a] Lienzo A is a late 19th- to early 20th-century tracing of a lost 16th-century original (Parmenter 1970; Doesburg 2010b; also Doesburg 2001:30–31 n. 7).

[b] Codex of Huamantla, now fragmented and partly missing, is estimated to have been originally 190 cm high by 700 cm wide (Aguilera 1984:35; Reyes García 1993:219).

[c] Lienzo of Quauhquechollan, now incomplete and measuring 235 cm high by 320 cm wide, is estimated to have been originally one-third wider (Asselbergs 2004:74, 192).

[d] Lienzo of Tlaxcala exists only in the form of numerous copies (Glass and Robertson 1975:214–18).

[e] Lienzo of Zacatepec 2 is known only through a tracing made in 1893 (Smith 1973a:93) and a description of the original by Peñafiel (1900:2–3).

the lienzo that Cortés sent to Spain in 1522 are to be believed, large size was not a new development but a continuation of the scale of such manuscript paintings as they were sometimes made in preconquest times.

The themes of the manuscripts in table 1.2 are conquest, control, or influence over territory and its inhabitants. Several of the manuscripts, such as the Lienzo of Tlaxcala and Lienzo of Quauhquechollan, are literally "war paintings."[25] The Lienzo of Tlaxcala depicts and catalogs the part played by Tlaxcala and its warriors, as enemies of the Aztecs and allies of Cortés, in the Spanish conquest of Mexico. Similarly, as Asselbergs (2004) has demonstrated, the Lienzo of Quauhquechollan tells the story of Quauhquechollan's role as an ally of the Spaniards in the conquest of Guatemala. On

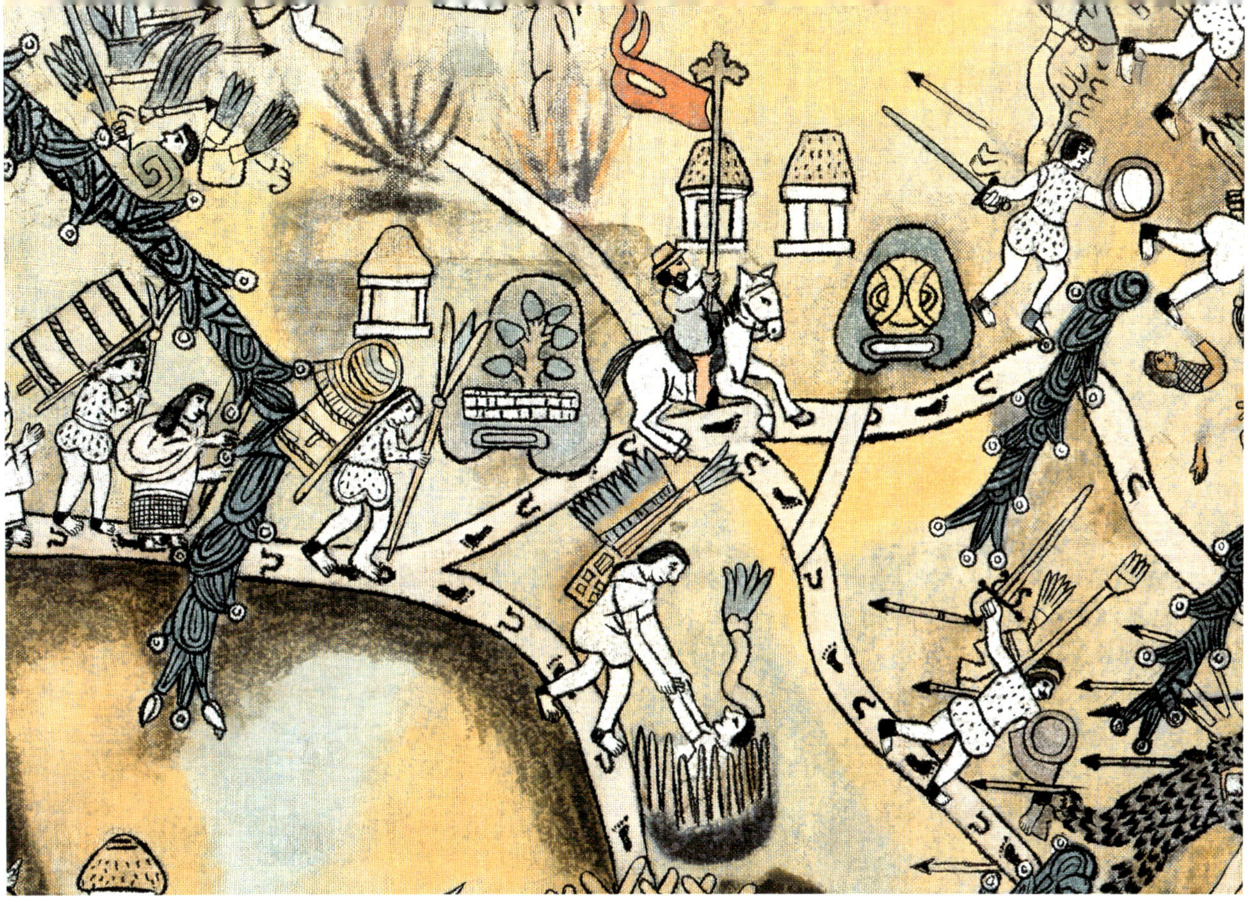

FIG. 1.12. Detail from the Lienzo of Quauhquechollan, ca. 1530. Digital restoration by Universidad Francisco Marroquín/Banco G & T Continental, © 2007 Universidad Francisco Marroquín, Guatemala, 🅭🅯🄏🄎, lienzo.ufm.edu. Original lienzo: Museo Regional Casa de Alfeñique, Puebla.

this lienzo, a small army of native and Spanish soldiers makes its way from Quauhquechollan, which lies east of the Popocatepetl volcano in central Mexico, to Guatemala. There, a tangle of switchback roads leads from place to place, and one scene of violent conflict and conquest leads to another (fig. 1.12).

In contrast to the crowded landscape and twists and turns of the Lienzo of Quauhquechollan, the cartography of the Coixtlahuaca manuscript known as Lienzo A, traced from a sixteenth-century original that is now lost, is spare and geometric (fig. 1.13; table 1.2). Like many other lienzos, Lienzo A is a map of the town and its boundaries. A large plumed serpent in the center of the lienzo represents the town of Coixtlahuaca, with satellite towns forming a circle around it. Smaller place signs arranged as a rectangle along the periphery of the lienzo give the names of Coixtlahuaca's boundary sites.

On Lienzo A, scenes of pre-Hispanic battles are associated with this important peripheral geography, as are later meetings with Spanish colonial officials mounted on horseback. A ribbon of wavy lines that accompanies the boundary signs on the edges of the lienzo frames the territory. On other Coixtlahuaca lienzos, this boundary ribbon is painted with black spots derived from the jaguar, a Mesoamerican symbol of authority from the most ancient times. A river crosses the left side of the lienzo, and roads extend outward from Coixtlahuaca in all directions.

Aspects of the lienzo tradition and of the compositional scheme exemplified by Lienzo A persist through the centuries into later colonial times. The Lienzo of Tamazulapan, from a neighboring valley west of that of Coixtlahuaca, painted in 1733, though not quite of the great size of the manuscripts in table 1.2, at 1.83 × 1.22 m is still a large sheet of cotton cloth of native manufacture (fig. 1.14).

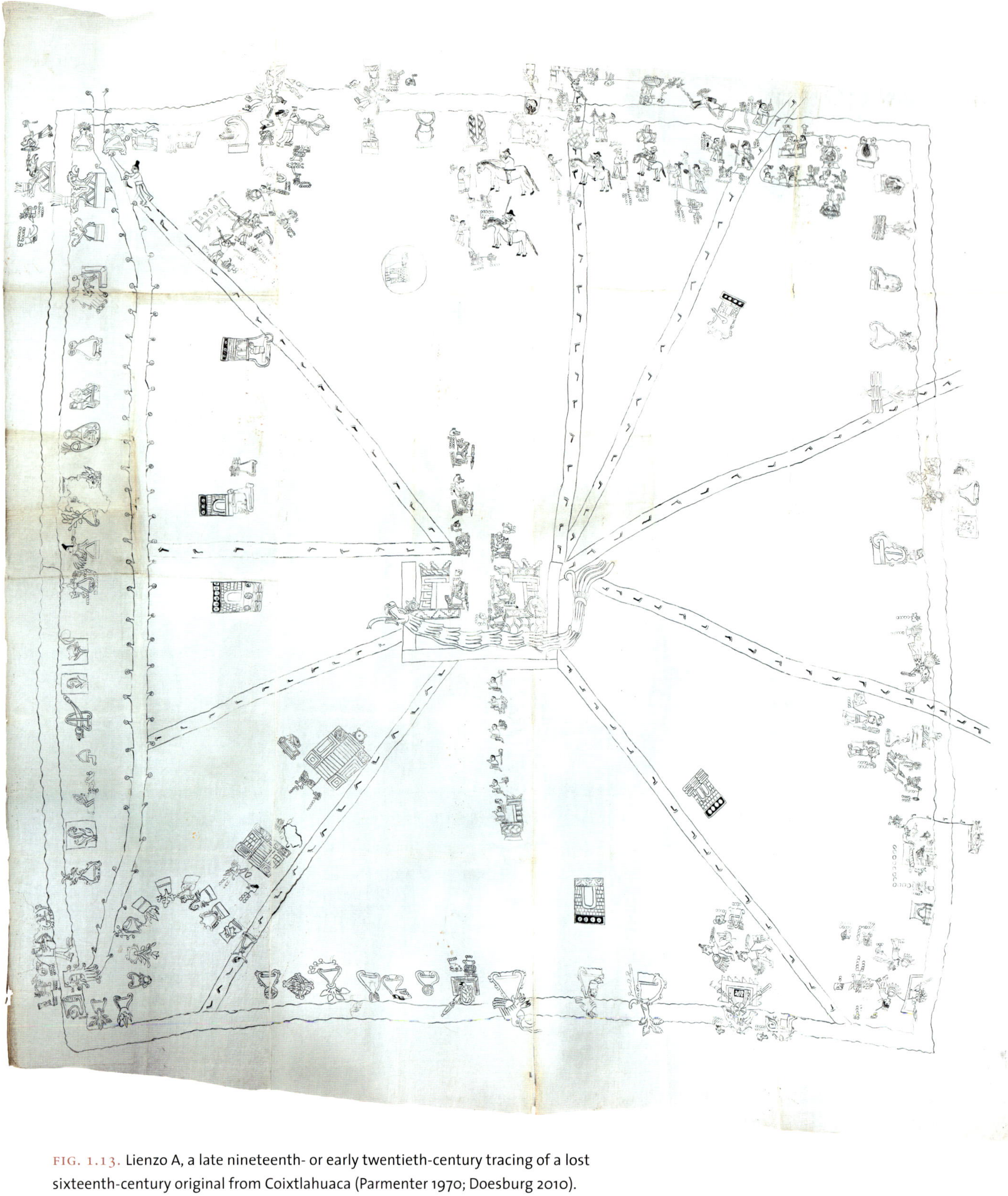

FIG. 1.13. Lienzo A, a late nineteenth- or early twentieth-century tracing of a lost sixteenth-century original from Coixtlahuaca (Parmenter 1970; Doesburg 2010). Tracing cloth, 380 × 360 cm. Sometimes known as Lienzo Meixueiro. Courtesy of the Latin American Library, Tulane University, photo by Jason Kruppa.

FIG. 1.14, FACING. Lienzo of Tamazulapan (Vischer III). Woven cotton, 1.83 × 1.22 meters. Courtesy of the Museum der Kulturen, Basel, photo by Peter Horner.

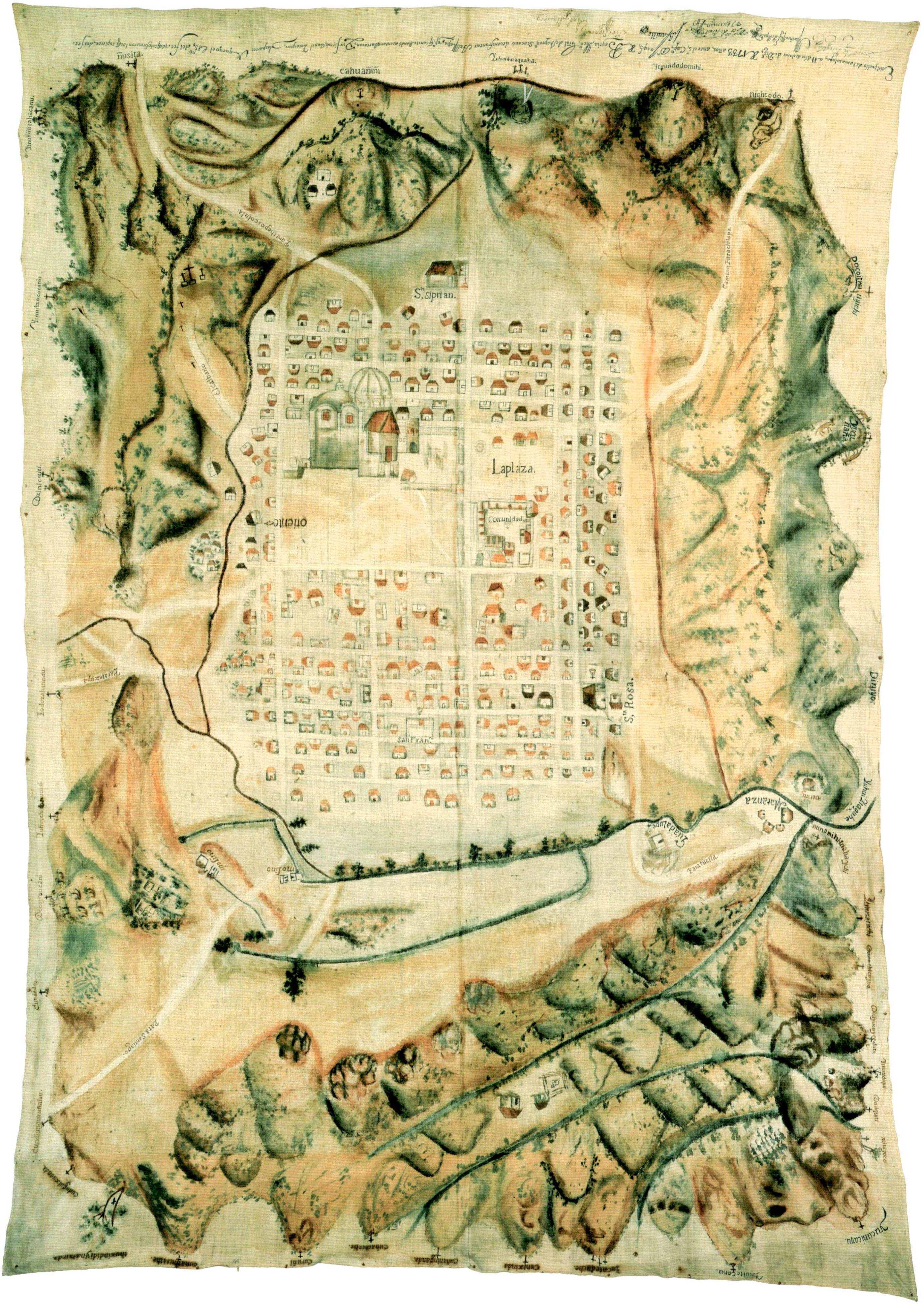

Laplaza
Comunidad
Sn. Siprian
Sta. Rosa
Matanza
cahuañini
ñusita

Here the pictographic representation of Coixtlahuaca as a plumed serpent in the center of the rectangle of boundary signs is replaced by a naturalistic bird's-eye view of the town of Tamazulapan, of gridded Spanish colonial design, situated within surrounding hills and mountains. Christian crosses on mountain peaks indicate Tamazulapan's boundary sites, and above the crosses, alphabetic inscriptions in the Mixtec and Chocho languages give the names of these sites.[26]

ANALYSIS OF THE TEXTILE

Another difference between the Lienzo of Tamazulapan and those of the Coixtlahuaca Valley is that except for a narrow band of exposed cloth along its outer edges, most of the surface of the Lienzo of Tamazulapan is painted. The white cotton cloth is not a significant part of the image in the way it was on Lienzo A.

White space visually separates and holds the individual signs and symbols in a certain order and distribution and gives them colorful prominence in the pictographic manuscripts of pre-Hispanic and early colonial Mexico. This white space is provided by the gessoed surface of animal hide or native paper, or by the textured white or light color of woven cloth.[27]

The Lienzo of Tlapiltepec and most other known lienzos of early colonial origin are made of white cotton native to Mexico that was spun into a yarn of medium weight, woven, and sewn by ancient indigenous methods. A native light-brown cotton and fibers from other local plants such as maguey and yucca were also probably sometimes used in the production of lienzo textiles.[28] Lienzos of later colonial centuries sometimes contain fibers not native to the Western Hemisphere, such as linen, and many of the later lienzos appear to be painted on commercially produced, more densely woven cotton cloth or canvas.

Cloth differed from the animal hide and native paper that were the other indigenous materials used for manuscript painting in pre-Hispanic and early colonial Mexico. Cloth was strong and durable, yet lightweight. It was flexible; it did not crack when folded. It was fluid, taking the shape of the body or surface it covered and moving with it or in the air that flowed around it. It was easily stored or transported; hung on a wall or as a curtain or banner; or spread out on a table, floor, or the earth. Furthermore, by stitching together smaller sheets of woven cloth, it was possible to produce an extremely large sheet that had all of these properties. The thirty-foot dimensions of the lienzo map sent by Cortés to Spain in 1522 and examined there by Peter Martyr were not impractical.

While lienzos of smaller sizes might consist of single pieces of cloth, most lienzo textiles produced by native methods consist of multiple strips of cloth sewn together to make a larger square or rectangle. In this respect, lienzos were a typical product—one might almost say, inevitable outcome—of the pre-Hispanic method of weaving on the backstrap, or waist-tension, loom, and the modular system of textile construction.

In this modular system, larger cloth items of every type were the result of a process of planning and weaving the individual component pieces, arranging them, and sewing them together to create the desired final product. No hemming was required. The cloth comes off the backstrap loom with four already finished edges, and there was normally no cutting or tailoring.[29] Depictions of articles of clothing and other textiles in native manuscripts sometimes show the seams, and even the stitches, joining the separately woven pieces. For example, sheets of cloth purchased for use in silk cultivation and pictured in a native book of expenses known as Codex Sierra (León 1982:38) show two seams uniting three pieces of cloth (fig. 1.15); the purchase was for fifteen sheets of cloth of this design with the eggs of silk moths adhered to them.[30]

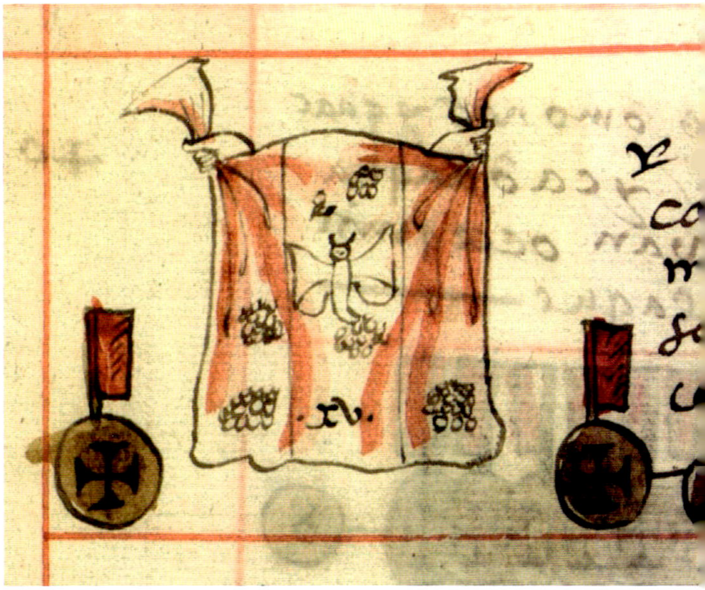

FIG. 1.15. Cloth for silk cultivation, detail of Codex Sierra-Texupan, p. 38. Biblioteca Histórica José María Lafragua (Fondo Restringido 48281-41010404). Courtesy of the Benemérita Universidad Autónoma de Puebla, Mexico.

The sheet of cotton cloth upon which the Lienzo of Tlapiltepec is painted was constructed much like the textile pictured in Codex Sierra. The lienzo consists of three individually woven strips of cloth sewn together side-by-side. Each strip is approximately 55 cm wide by 4 m long.[31]

Consistency in the cotton, spinning, and weaving of the Lienzo of Tlapiltepec and the economy of its construction suggest it could have been the outcome of a relatively simple design and production sequence.[32] The artist or the person who commissioned the manuscript asked a weaver to weave and construct the sheet of cloth to meet certain specifications. However, this is only one of various possibilities, and complications in the physical makeup of a number of lienzos indicate that lienzo textiles were not always so straightforwardly achieved.

Unlike the Lienzo of Tlapiltepec, the Lienzo of Coixtlahuaca II (Seler II) is sewn together of strips of cloth of several different lengths. Furthermore, the shorter strips are of several different widths. The Lienzo of Coixtlahuaca II, another sixteenth-century member of the Coixtlahuaca Group of manuscripts, is the largest of the cloth manuscripts listed in table 1.2. It would seem that at least some of the individually woven pieces of cloth comprising the Lienzo of Coixtlahuaca II were not woven specifically for it.[33]

Other evidence for the incorporation into lienzo textiles of cloth originally made—and possibly previously used—for other purposes is found in a number of lienzos containing a decorative feature known as a ribbed or corded border. The border consists of a series of small parallel ridges made by incorporating extra-thick threads into the cloth near its edges as it is being woven.[34] The ribbing in these lienzos is unrelated to the painting that covers their surfaces. It does not purposefully frame the images or have some other compositional or decorative function in relation to them. In some of the manuscripts thus far known to have this textural addition, it forms a complete border around all four outer edges of the sheet of cloth. In others, the ribbing is located along some sections of the outer edges of the sheet but not others, and it is also found lining some of the composite textiles' interior seams.

Cloth woven expressly to serve as a surface for the detailed drawing and painting of fine lines and small areas of color characteristic of the pictographic inscriptions would surely have been plain cloth, or cloth in which the ribbing was at least kept to the outer edges of the lienzo. It is evident that the strips of cloth that contain ribbed borders in these lienzos were originally woven as parts of textiles in which such embellishment would be more appropriate, such as clothing. The Lienzo of Ihuitlán, also of the Coixtlahuaca Group, is an example (fig. 1.16).

The Lienzo of Ihuitlán consists of nine separately woven strips of cloth and appears to have been put together entirely of cloth originally destined for other uses.

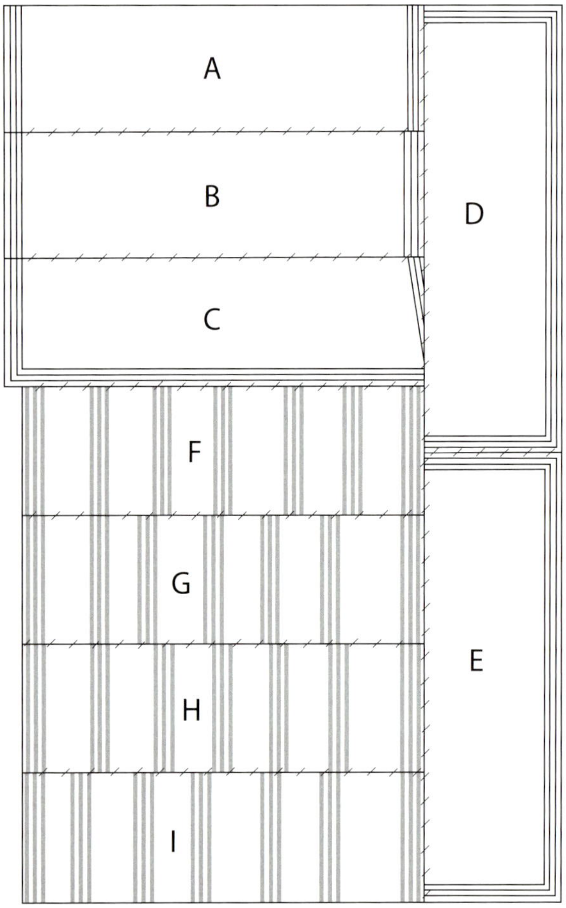

FIG. 1.16. Lienzo of Ihuitlán, textile diagram (Johnson 2000). Original lienzo illustrated in fig. 2.2.

Five of the nine strips contain a border of three single ridges on either two or three of their four edges (fig. 1.16, A–E). Four others contain textural bands of a different type (fig. 1.16, F–I). Furthermore, the strips are of two different lengths, with the result that the lienzo is not a simple rectangle but is wider at the top than at the bottom. The Lienzo of Ihuitlán is a puzzle literally and figuratively. It is a large manuscript (248 × 157 cm) containing an extensive genealogical and cartographic record, carefully drawn and painted on what appears to be an improvised textile.

Do such lienzos reflect stresses of the early colonial period, such as a shortage of raw materials or of weavers, or an increased demand for the production of manuscripts of this form? Cotton cloth made by native weavers was an important commercial item in the economy of early colonial Mexico; according to Borah and Cook (1958:27), cotton was second only to corn as a tribute commodity supplied by the natives to the Spaniards in the early and middle sixteenth century. Or had textiles for manuscripts of the lienzo type always been put together with ingenuity in this economical fashion?

Much might be learned from lienzos as textiles. While clothing and other utilitarian textile items were used until there was nothing left of them, a substantial body of native textiles of early colonial times has survived in the form of lienzos. As cloth, they contain evidence of the society, economy, and craftsmanship of the period. Lienzos in this regard appear to be an overlooked resource. Lienzo cloth, like painting style, is an aspect of the Coixtlahuaca Group that has yet to be systematically studied.

SCALE AND ORIENTATION

The screenfold manuscripts and tiras of pre-Hispanic and early colonial Mexico have features in common with books and manuscripts from many other parts of the world: long and narrow, compactly folded or rolled, with their inscriptions organized sequentially, often in rows or columns. The screenfolds in particular are familiarly book-like.

The cartographic lienzos, on the other hand, are not book-like, either in the way the inscriptions are organized or in their dimensions. The Lienzo of Tlapiltepec and several other manuscripts listed in table 1.2 are as tall as the roof peak of a one-story house. The Lienzo of Coixtlahuaca II (Seler II) is as big as the floor of a medium-size room. How were these large, inscription-filled sheets of cloth meant to be viewed and read?

It is not likely that the lienzos were handled and read in the same way as the screenfold manuscripts were. The large sheets of cloth were probably not somehow unfolded and read segment-by-segment. For one thing, the cartographic and cartographic-historical lienzos are not organized sequentially. Nor would any segment-by-segment reading of such a manuscript result in comprehension of the kinds of geographical spatial relationships it was intended to convey. For example, some towns and features of the landscape were located along the edges of the territory and others closer to the center. Some were in the north and some were in the south. For these relationships to be perceivable, there would be no option but to view the lienzo as a whole.

The viewer of Lienzo A (fig. 1.13) in its entirety sees, literally at a glance, the prominent size and position of Coixtlahuaca at the center of the lienzo, and the boundary sites and historical events concentrated on its four edges.

A screenfold manuscript may also be opened to its full length and viewed as a whole, but the relatively small scale of the drawing and the long, narrow proportions of the manuscript would make it legible only from a short distance away and a few pages at a time. Seen from a vantage point that would allow a comprehensive view of the extended screenfold, features of the painting might still be visually identifiable, and visual relationships active across multiple pages might even come to the fore, but it would not be possible to read the manuscript in detail.

Mixtec screenfold manuscripts are nearly miniature in scale and are related to other intricately patterned, small-scale works that the pre-Hispanic Mixtecs are particularly noted for. Such miniature items, along with the manuscripts, constitute much of their surviving artistic legacy: gold jewelry; incised carvings in shell, bone, and precious stone; and colorful ceramics (Covarrubias 1957:300–11). These objects were worn on the body or otherwise intimately handled, and like the screenfold manuscripts, appreciated at physically close range.

In contrast, to gain an overview of a large rectangular manuscript such as Lienzo A or the Lienzo of Tlapiltepec requires that the viewer be positioned a certain distance away, yet not so far away that details would become illegible. The figures on the Lienzo of Tlapiltepec are drawn 40 percent to 100 percent larger than those on the pre-Hispanic Mixtec screenfold manuscripts. Thus, even small elements of the drawing on the Lienzo of Tlapiltepec, such as persons' names, including those inscribed near the top of the four-meter-tall sheet of cloth, are legible when a full-size copy of the manuscript is hung vertically on the side of a building and viewed from about four meters away.

Colonial accounts of the actual circumstances of viewing and reading the manuscripts, whether screenfolds or lienzos, are scarce. The principal source for the Mixtec region is the writings of the Dominican friar Francisco de Burgoa (circa 1600–81). According to Burgoa (1934:210), it had been the custom in earlier times for the manuscripts to be displayed "in the rooms of the lords," that is, in the houses of the rulers who owned the manuscripts and whose family history and geography were documented and celebrated therein.

Burgoa does not state exactly how the manuscripts were arranged in these rooms, though the implication is that they were arrayed around the walls. Nor is it certain what types of manuscripts were displayed in this way. It is conceivable that Burgoa was referring to screenfold manuscripts (Smith 1994:122, 132 n. 14). When the rulers and their relatives gathered to listen to an orator interpret the accounts of their ancestors contained in the screenfold manuscripts, it is possible these events took place in these interior, private spaces (Mundy 2005:363).

It is difficult to imagine lienzos of great size displayed and viewed in such interior locations. The ceiling of the room would have to be over four meters high for the

Lienzo of Tlapiltepec to be hung on one of its walls. Such manuscripts seem better suited for exterior settings such as the outside walls of important buildings or the floors of central plazas. Mundy (2005:369) observes that the content of the lienzos also implies that they were exhibited in such public spaces, where they could be seen by members of the community at large, not only the ruling elite.

The lienzos' simplified history presented in map form, Mundy contends, was intended to give the lienzos wide public appeal. The screenfold manuscripts would have been of interest primarily to members of the hereditary ruling class, for it is their genealogies and related political affairs, the details of which fill page after page of these manuscripts. In contrast, the cartographic-historical lienzos, with their themes of land and territory, were something with which the bulk of the population, who lived and worked on the land, could identify. Mundy (2005:365) sees the scale of the large lienzos of the early colonial period as a manifestation of Mesoamerica's age-old tradition of monumental public art.

Another matter regarding the circumstances in which manuscripts of the lienzo type were displayed is the question of orientation. Whether the lienzos of late pre-Hispanic and early colonial times were hung vertically on a wall or laid out horizontally on a floor or the ground—or sometimes one way and sometimes the other—is difficult to decide. The viewer's experience of a lienzo would differ depending on how it was oriented.

An advantage of horizontal display in the case of a manuscript such as the Lienzo of Tlapiltepec or Lienzo A (fig. 1.13), in which the figures are not all oriented in the same direction, is that the lienzo may be viewed from any angle simply by walking around its edges. A disadvantage is that the lienzo is always seen from its edges, and from a distance no greater than that of the viewer's eyes above the ground. The angle of sight across or along the large sheet of cloth is acute, resulting in a degree of distortion and decreased legibility.

An advantage of vertical display is that the viewer is able to step back from the lienzo, improving the angle of sight and achieving a more balanced and still legible view of the inscriptions and the composition as a whole. If Lienzo A is displayed vertically and seen from several meters away, as opposed to being displayed spread out on the ground and viewed from one of its edges, Coixtlahuaca's boundaries will be clearly perceived as square and as having the place sign of Coixtlahuaca at their center. The Lienzo of Tlapiltepec's configurations also stand out more clearly from one another and from its welter of detail when displayed vertically.

On the other hand, if laid flat on the ground like the landscape it stands for, the Lienzo of Tlapiltepec has a kind of reality it loses when displayed vertically. Vertically it becomes more abstract, an icon that confronts the viewer, rather than, as noted by Asselbergs (2004:24), a "microversion" of the landscape to be explored by moving around its edges. Spread on the ground and viewed from above, its connecting lines flow out over its surface like rivers, and there is resonance between the trails of human footprints that lead here and there on the lienzo and the footprints the viewer makes on the ground surrounding the lienzo.[35]

NOTES

I am grateful to Arni Brownstone, creator of this book, for facilitating my study of the original Lienzo of Tlapiltepec at the Royal Ontario Museum on various occasions beginning in 1988, and now for the opportunity to work on this project, as well as for producing the illustrations that accompany my text. I am also grateful to Georgia Guenther, Royal Ontario Museum artist, for her transformation of my diagrams and maps. To Eckehard Dolinski, from whose generosity with research related to the Lienzo of Tlapiltepec and other matters I have benefited over the years. To Bas van Doesburg, whose comments on my contribution to this book have improved it throughout. To Elizabeth Boone for a clarification. To Susan Jarmain for analysis of the lienzo textile, and to Ian Johnson and Sallie O'Sullivan for figure 3.1. To Enrique Hugo García Valencia for sharing with me his articles related to lienzo textiles. Finally, I very much appreciate copyeditor Katrin Flechsig's more than expert help with my writing.

1. See Glass (1975), "A Survey of Native Middle American Pictorial Manuscripts," and Glass and Robertson (1975), "A Census of Native Middle American Pictorial Manuscripts." Their census catalogs the majority of such manuscripts known to scholars up to 1968. For a list of lienzos learned of since then, see note 21, below.
2. On the nature of Mesoamerican writing systems and their relationship to spoken language and to the important oral aspect of preservation and transmission of knowledge in pre-Hispanic Mexico, see Boone, "Introduction: Writing and Recording Knowledge," in Boone and Mignolo (1994), *Writing without Words: Alternative Literacies in Mesoamerica and the Andes*, as well as other essays in that book. The relationship between Mixtec pictographic writing and spoken Mixtec is a frequent theme in Jansen and Pérez Jiménez (2011), *The Mixtec Pictorial Manuscripts: Time, Agency and Memory in Ancient Mexico*.
3. The small group of extant pre-Hispanic manuscripts (see Glass 1975:12 for suggested list) may include a recent addition. The Códice de Yautepec, a three-page fragment of a ritual-calendrical manuscript found several years ago, bound in with a book of medieval music, in the town of San Bartolo Yautepec in southern Oaxaca, was possibly made before the Spanish conquest of Mexico (Bas van Doesburg, personal communication, 2011; Jansen and Pérez Jiménez 2011:64).
4. The Coixtlahuaca Group was first defined as a distinct subgroup of Mesoamerican pictorial manuscripts by Ross Parmenter in 1961 on the basis of the six lienzos from the Coixtlahuaca Valley then known to scholars (Parmenter 1961:1–2; see also Parmenter 1970, 1982, 1993, 1994, 1997). The group was next discussed by Mary Elizabeth Smith in *Picture Writing from Ancient Southern Mexico: Mixtec Place Signs and Maps* (Smith 1973a:182–84). Smith's list included two more Coixtlahuaca Valley lienzos that had by then come to light, as well as three manuscripts of other types that Alfonso Caso had shown to be related to the Lienzo of Tlapiltepec, although it is not yet known exactly where these three are from (Caso 1954, 1958, 1961:251–59). A ninth Coixtlahuaca Valley lienzo was subsequently published by Parmenter (1993) and a tenth, of eighteenth-century date, was added to the group by Rincón Mautner (1994). The existence of an eleventh, the Lienzo of Aztatla, was noted by Rincón Mautner (1997:134) and mentioned by Doesburg and Buren, who indicate it is now largely illegible (1997:105 n. 3). A twelfth lienzo, first learned of by outsiders in 2006, is the subject of a book by Ruíz Ortíz and Jansen (2009) and articles by Rincón Mautner (2007) and Doesburg (2010a).

   Investigators who, following Parmenter, have focused on the Coixtlahuaca manuscripts include Doesburg (1998a, 1998b, 2000, 2001, 2002, 2004, 2010a, 2010b, 2012; Doesburg and Buren (1997); Castañeda de la Paz and Doesburg (2008); Johnson (1992, 1994a, 1994b, 1997); König (1984, 1999); Rincón Mautner (1994, 1997, 1999, 2000, 2007, 2012); and Topsey (1985).

   Summaries of Coixtlahuaca history as contained in the manuscripts of the Coixtlahuaca Group include Caso's "La región de Coixtlahuaca" in vol. 1 of his *Reyes y reinos de la Mixteca* (1977:118–36, 231–39); Doesburg and Buren, "The Prehispanic History of the Valley of Coixtlahuaca, Oaxaca" (1997); Rincón Mautner, "Reading the History of Place-Becoming in the Codices from the Coixtlahuaca Basin" (1997). See also Boone (2000b:136-61).
5. On Mixtec pictographic writing and manuscripts, including those of the Mixtec and Chocho inhabitants of the Coixtlahuaca Valley, see Smith, *Picture Writing from Ancient Southern Mexico* (1973a); Smith, "The Mixtec Writing System" (1983); Jansen, "Mixtec Pictography: Conventions and Contents" (1992); Boone, *Stories in Red and Black: Pictorial Histories of the Mixtecs and Aztecs* (2000b); and Jansen and Pérez Jiménez, *The Mixtec Pictorial Manuscripts: Time, Agency and Memory in Ancient Mexico* (2011).
6. The Chocho and Popoloca languages, so closely related as to be nearly dialects of one another, are estimated to have diverged from a common parent language around 1200 AD (Hopkins 1984:43), resulting in Chocho being spoken in and around the Coixtlahuaca Valley, Oaxaca; and Popoloca being spoken in a triangular territory extending from the Tehuacán Valley west to Acatlan and north to Tecamachalco in southern and central Puebla (Jäcklein 1978:17; 1979:199; Winter, Gaxiola, and Hernández 1984:87, 90, 95). On the prevalence and distribution of the Chocho, Mixtec, and Nahuatl languages in the Coixtlahuaca and neighboring Tamazulapan-Teotongo-Tejupan valleys, see Swanton (2008) and Doesburg and Swanton (2008), who indicate that the language most widely in use in this area was Chocho. Of these indigenous languages, only Chocho is still spoken in the Coixtlahuaca Valley, and only in a few villages. The word Chocho derives from the Nahuatl name for this group of people, whose own name for themselves is Ngiwa.
7. Seven of the approximately 245 human figures that appear on the Lienzo of Coixtlahuaca II (Seler II) closely resemble the 229 figures that appear on the Lienzo of Tlapiltepec. A geometrically patterned frieze on Coixtlahuaca II also is nearly identical in design to some of the friezes on the Lienzo of Tlapiltepec; friezes of this particular design, out of all of the manuscripts of the Coixtlahuaca Group, are, to my knowledge, found only on these two lienzos: once on Coixtlahuaca II and six times on the Lienzo of Tlapiltepec. Eckehard Dolinski (personal communication, 2007) notes that Chicomoztoc, "Place of Seven Caves," is substantially the same on Coixtlahuaca II as it is on the Lienzo of Tlapiltepec. See König (1999:167–69) for a discussion of other aspects of the stylistic complexity of the Lienzo of Coixtlahuaca II.
8. Because the cloth of the Lienzo of Tlapiltepec is damaged all along its upper end, its original length is uncertain. If the only painting missing along this edge is the destroyed portion of the motifs visible there now, the lienzo would likely have been only slightly longer than its current length. The damage along the upper edge of the lienzo consists of a regular, mesa-like pattern of frayed threads across the whole width of the lienzo. Unless the lienzo was cut off with a knife or scissors, as opposed to natural wear and tear, it is

probable that the flat tops of these "mesas" are remnants of the original end of the lienzo.

Doesburg (1998b:59, 64–65) has published a sales contract from 1907 in which the length of the lienzo is given as 434 cm, more than 34 cm longer than it is now. I believe that measurement was inaccurate, and that the lienzo then was more or less the same length it is now. The 1907 contract gives the width of the lienzo as 175 cm, about 6 to 9 cm more than it really is. The lengths given for the lienzo in Rickards (1913; noted in Parmenter 1961:6 as 14 ft. 2 in. or 431.8 cm), Caso (1961:251 as 425 cm), and Glass and Robertson (1975:87 as 432 cm) are not correct. Photographs from the early 1900s formerly owned by Walter Lehmann (Ibero-American Institute, Berlin), kindly shown to me by Eckehard Dolinski, show the lienzo in approximately the same condition then as now. An inscription on one of the Lehmann photos gives the measurements correctly as 395 × 166 cm.

In sum: the width of the lienzo varies from 166 to 168.9 cm. The widths of the three individual strips of cloth from which it is constructed vary from 54.6 to 56.5 cm, with a variation of not more than 1.3 cm in any one strip. The maximum lengths of the three strips in their present condition are 391.2 cm (left), 395 cm (middle), 396.9 cm (right). In 1985 the lienzo was cleaned and sewn onto a linen backing (Johnson 1992).

9. The black used on the Lienzo of Tlapiltepec is a genuine black, carbon black, rather than brownish black. After black, the color that has survived most strongly is a tawny yellow ochre, most notably in large entwined serpents (or jaguar serpents), which are ochre with black spots and diamonds. A second yellow, currently a pale straw color, is barely detectable; the woven reed or palm mats on which ruling couples are seated are this color. The red paint used on the Lienzo of Tlapiltepec appears to have been a slightly bluish or cool red. A pale green is visible in hills. Ripple lines in some bodies of water, a crisscross design on some women's skirts, and Lizard calendrical signs show the remains of what seems to have been bright blue. It is often no longer possible to distinguish with the naked eye if something was green or blue. The faces, hands, and feet of human figures are brown but, again, this color is extremely faded. There is occasional use of a distinct gray. Eagles, for example, are gray with black markings. In several instances a color is shaded or mottled with gray and sometimes with yellow or ochre. White is also used. Some bodies of water are painted white with blue ripple lines. The colors of the lienzo and their pigment sources are discussed in more detail by Brownstone and Dolinski in chapter 4 of this book.

10. In addition to the ten single words in black paint or ink, a patch of faint marks on the lower right edge of the lienzo resembles the faded traces of several lines of slanted handwriting in brown ink, with a single word in larger letters printed above them (brought to my attention by Helmuth Fuchs, curator of ethnology, Royal Ontario Museum, January 1988). These marks are slightly more visible under ultraviolet light. The writing seems too small, fine, and fluid to have been made on the rough cloth itself, and seems made by a pen rather than a brush. As Fuchs suggested, perhaps something was written on a piece of paper placed on top of the cloth, and the marks are the result of the ink bleeding through the paper. The patch of writing, if that is what it is, is approximately 19 cm long by 10 cm tall and runs parallel to the right edge of the lienzo about 2.5 cm from the edge, 94 cm from the bottom corner.

11. Proof that the lienzo had once resided in Tlapiltepec was found by Parmenter in 1973 and published in his *Four Lienzos of the Coixtlahuaca Valley* (1982:15–44). Of its history prior to the late nineteenth century, nothing is known. For the twentieth-century history of the manuscript, see Parmenter (1961), Doesburg (1998b), and Brownstone, preface, this volume.

Abraham Castellanos was the first to discuss the Lienzo of Tlapiltepec in print (Castellanos 1912a, b; Parmenter 1982:18). Caso wrote the first detailed study of the lienzo (1961; republished 1989:75–104). Parmenter's *Four Lienzos of the Coixtlahuaca Valley* included his discovery that the lienzo was a map of this area and areas north of it (1982:34–38; see also Parmenter in Jansen and Gaxiola 1978:13–15). Other articles, chapters or sections of books, and theses focused partly or wholly on the Lienzo of Tlapiltepec include Boone (2000b:145–61), Brownstone (1996), Caso (1954, 1958, 1977:118–36, 231–39), Castañeda de la Paz and Doesburg (2008), Doesburg and Buren (1997), Hermann Lejarazu (2010), Jansen (1983), Johnson (1992, 1994a, 1997), Parmenter (1982:63–78), Rincón Mautner (1997), and Topsey (1985). Significant discussions of or references to the lienzo are also found in the works of Jansen (for example, 1989, 1992), Jansen and Gaxiola (1978:13–15), Jansen and Pérez Jiménez (2000:153–58; 2007:85, 215, 268, 272, 316 n. 6), and Pohl (1994a:147–53), among others. See additional relevant sources mentioned in note 4, above.

12. On the conventions of Mixtec pictographic writing, see works mentioned in note 5, above.

13. Another possible distinction between men and women on the Lienzo of Tlapiltepec is the color of their faces and other exposed flesh. On the copy of the lienzo made by Eduard Seler now in the Ibero-American Institute, Berlin, skin is a darker brown in men and lighter brown in women (the Seler copy is illustrated and discussed in Brownstone and Dolinski, chapter 4, this book). It is clear that flesh is colored brown on the original lienzo. However, the color is extremely faded, and it is difficult to know if men differ from women in this respect. On the Royal Ontario Museum's colored tracing of the lienzo reproduced in this book, men and women are both the same light brown. Some examples of other manuscripts that do contain differences of flesh tone between men and women are the Tira de Tepechpan (Diel 2008:31) and Codex Magliabechiano from central Mexico, and Codex Egerton from the Mixteca.

14. A year in the ancient Mexican calendar, as in our own, was the solar cycle of 365 days, identified by the name-and-number combination of the day on which it either began or ended. Because of the way in which the calendar's 260- and 365-day cycles mesh, these "year bearer" days make use of only four of the twenty day names. In the Mixtec version of the calendar, year bearers are House, Rabbit, Reed, and Flint. For the Mixtec calendar, see Caso (1965), Jansen and Pérez Jiménez (2011:22–29). For an introduction to the Mesoamerican calendar and its notation see Boone (2000b:39–42; Boone 2007:13–18).

15. At the upper left on the lienzo, fine black lines running vertically through the centers of tall columns of husband-and-wife couples appear to have been sketched on the cloth in advance of the figures as a guide to their placement. Scratchy horizontal marks on the right side of the lienzo in two locations also appear to be preliminary. The purpose of these marks, it seems, was to block out the space on this side of the lienzo. They divide the right side of the lienzo into upper, middle, and lower zones. In the lower zone, the artist put the section of the lienzo map that corresponds to

areas north of the Coixtlahuaca Valley. The middle zone contains Tlapiltepec on the right and Ihuitlán on the left, separated by a broad column of white space left open between them. Red lines leading from the Coixtlahuaca Valley to the towns and rulers of the northern section of the map pass through this opening. Also in the middle zone are Tequixtepec and the unidentified site from which the red lines originate. The upper zone contains Coixtlahuaca and Tulancingo and places south and west of them.

Dividing lines on the lienzo include a heavy black line extending vertically nearly the full height of the lienzo and separating the left third of the composition from the right two-thirds. This was apparently added to the manuscript after the drawings that surround it were already in place. The line detours around protruding figures and cuts through the edge of a place sign and possibly through the middle of a standing figure. This line follows one of the two seams that join the three long strips of cloth from which the lienzo is constructed. In this instance the seam itself was the original blocking-out line and guide to the artist. A second major black dividing line crosses the right side of the lienzo horizontally near the lower end of the sheet, and minor dividing lines separate and bracket material in various other locations. These various dividing and bracketing lines suggest a concern for clarity in the grouping and sequence of the material and perhaps are evidence that the Lienzo of Tlapiltepec was not a copy of another, similar manuscript but an original composition.

In addition to sketch lines and dividing lines, other faint lines and fragments of drawings partially visible in photographs of the lienzo are not traces of an earlier, incompletely removed, painting as was suggested by Caso (1961:251, 272). Some are the faded remains of lines that are part of the composition: the red connecting lines. Many others, as Helmuth Fuchs, then curator of ethnology at the Royal Ontario Museum pointed out to me (1988), are imprints of the black outlines of the drawings from one area of the lienzo onto another, apparently resulting from dampness seeping through folded layers of cloth. Some of these imprints are clear enough that their sources are readily recognizable, and the sources of others can be discovered since the imprints fall in mirror-image positions on the lienzo. Some of the imprints are the result of lengthwise folding of the cloth. Others show that the cloth was sometimes first folded widthwise. Unfortunately, details of the painting now lost to holes in the cloth have not been preserved in imprints.

16. For another discussion of manuscripts of the lienzo type including their format, painted contents, and layout; how they were viewed and read; and lienzos as maps; see Asselbergs (2004:21–29). The following are some books (all that I have been able to discover) devoted to Mesoamerican lienzos: Peñafiel, *Códice mixteco: Lienzo de Zacatepec* (1900), is a large-format book illustrating this large lienzo by means of 25 full-page sections plus an overview. Lienzos are the focus of Smith's fundamental *Picture Writing from Ancient Southern Mexico* (1973a).

Melgarejo Vivanco, *Códices de tierras* (1970), with photographs by Manuel Álvarez Bravo, contains high-quality overview illustrations and sectional color illustrations of a series of six closely related lienzos from Veracruz. Glass, *Lienzo Totomixtlahuaca 1570 (Códice Condumex)* (1974), includes an overview and 16 sectional illustrations of a lienzo from Guerrero. On Zacatepec Lienzos 1 and 2 there is also Fernández Gatica et al., *Proposición de lectura del Lienzo de Zacatepec: Método galarziano* (2002). Galarza, *Lienzos de Chiepetlan: Manuscrits pictographiques et manuscrits en caractères latins de San Miguel Chiepetlan, Guerrero, Mexique* (1972), is a major investigation of this group of six lienzos. Parmenter, *Four Lienzos of the Coixtlahuaca Valley* (1982), is a landmark in the study of manuscripts of the Coixtlahuaca Group, and by Parmenter there is also *The Lienzo of Tulancingo, Oaxaca: An Introductory Study of a Ninth Painted Sheet from the Coixtlahuaca Valley* (1993). Ruíz Ortíz and Jansen, *El Lienzo de Otla: Memoria de un paisaje sagrado* (2009), deals with this Coixtlahuaca Valley lienzo, which first became known to scholars in 2006. Oudijk and Doesburg, *Los lienzos pictográficos de Santa Cruz Papalutla, Oaxaca* (2010), concerns two lienzos from this village in the Valley of Oaxaca, also only recently known to the outside world.

Roskamp, *La historiografía indígena de Michoacán: El lienzo de Jucutacato y los títulos de Carapan* (1998), and Asselbergs, *Conquered Conquistadors: The Lienzo de Quauhquechollan: A Nahua Vision of the Conquest of Guatemala* (2004), are detailed monographs devoted respectively to the lienzos of Jucutacato, Michoacán, and Quauhquechollan, Puebla, based on doctoral dissertations. The latter contains a large, folded color reproduction of the Lienzo of Quauhquechollan in a pocket at the back of the book.

Lienzos of the later colonial period are the subject of Oettinger and Horcasitas, *The Lienzo of Petlacala: A Pictorial Document from Guerrero, Mexico* (1982), and Oettinger, *Lienzos Coloniales: Guía de la Exposición de Pinturas de Terrenos Comunales de México, Siglos XVII–XIX* (1983); Guevara Hernández, *El lienzo de Tiltepec: Extinción de un señorío zapoteco* (1991); König, *Die Schlacht bei Sieben Blume: Konquistadoren, Kaziken und Konflikte auf alten Landkarten der Indianer Südmexikos* (1993); König, *La batalla de Siete Flor: Conquistadores, caciques y conflictos en mapas antiguos de los zapotecos, chinantecos y mixes* (2011; Spanish version of König 1993); Cordero Avedaño de Durand, *Lienzo del Pueblo del Señor San Pedro Nexicho* (2001); Cordero Avedaño de Durand, *Interpretación y estudio del lienzo de San Juan Chicomezúchitl* (2004); Huerta and Berthier, eds., *El lienzo de Cuetzpala, Puebla: Un estudio integral* (2002); Sepúlveda y Herrera, *Los lienzos de San Juan Cuauhtla, Puebla* (2005).

17. The hide used in manuscripts is usually considered to be deer or antelope (see, for example, Alvarez, in Caso and Smith 1966:101–102), though frequently without scientific confirmation. A recent study by Maldonado and Maldonado (2004), combining investigation of traditional tanning practices in present-day Oaxaca with detailed description of the material of the nine animal-hide codices contained in the Biblioteca Nacional de Antropología e Historia, Mexico City, sheds light on material and artisanal aspects of Mesoamerican pictographic manuscripts. While the authors were unable to identify with precision the species of animals used in most of the nine manuscripts, one, an eighteenth-century copy of the Mapa de Popotla, was painted on goatskin. (See also Maldonado and Maldonado 1995.) The native paper used in manuscripts was commonly made from the pounded inner bark of wild fig trees and is known in Spanish as *papel de amate*, from the Nahuatl word *amatl*, "paper," and possibly at times from other vegetal fibers (Lenz 1973:72–111; Hagen 1999:31–49).

18. Most authors consider this piece, Aubin Manuscript no. 20, 51 × 91 cm, to be preconquest (Glass and Robertson 1975:90; see also Boone 2007:18, 255 n. 20). Batalla Rosado (2008) contends that this manuscript was not made in pre-Hispanic times but in the mid-eighteenth century.

19. For a comprehensive overview of Mesoamerican maps, see Mundy (1998).
20. Lienzos containing other types of subject matter are also mentioned in accounts of the Spanish conquest, for example, in the chronicle of the conquistador Andrés de Tapía (Fuentes 1963:44): "At this time Moctezuma called the Marqués [Cortés] to show him a mantle on which were painted eighteen ships, five of them wrecked on the coast and turned over in the sand. This is the way the Indians have of conveying news accurately." See also Díaz del Castillo (1956:257, 360).
21. These quantities are extremely approximate. Glass (1975:9) states that the Glass and Robertson "Census of Native Middle American Pictorial Manuscripts" (1975) includes "about 50 lienzos" but it actually itemizes or refers to about 90 lienzos from the sixteenth through the eighteenth centuries, and even the nineteenth and twentieth centuries, still in existence or possibly so as of 1968. See the following "Census" entries:

    Western Oaxaca: 8, 70, 71, 77, 157, 174, 195, 232, 242, 251, 299, 409, 419, 422, 423, 433, 434.
    Eastern Oaxaca: 7, 47, 66, 73, 130, 143, 241, 250, 295, 296, 301, 333, 413, 414, 416, 417.
    Northern Oaxaca: 51, 53, 54, 74, 137, 162, 265, 335, 420.
    Guerrero: 23, 58, 238, 342, 362.
    Puebla: 50, 89, 134, 199, 245, 432.
    Tlaxcala: 41, 45, 76, 275, 319, 337, 350, 411.
    Veracruz: 63, 214, 233, 320, 373–78.
    State of Mexico, Federal District, and Valley of Mexico: 12, 110, 198, 429.
    Morelos: 327.
    Regionally unclassified: 134, 380.

    Lienzos that have come to the attention of scholars since the 1975 publication of the "Census" include the following, by region:

    Western Oaxaca (all from Coixtlahuaca Valley): Lienzo of Aztatla (Doesburg and Buren 1997:105 n. 3; Rincón Mautner 1997:134); Lienzo of Otla (Rincón Mautner 2007; Ruíz Ortíz and Jansen 2009; Doesburg 2010a); Lienzo of Tulancingo (Parmenter 1994; Rincón Mautner 1994; Doesburg 2000); Lienzo of Tulancingo II (Rincón Mautner 1994).
    Eastern Oaxaca: Lienzo of Santiago Atitlan (Oettinger 1983:44–45); Lienzo of Santo Domingo Barrio Alto (Oettinger 1983:52–53); Lienzo de San Juan Chicomezúchitl (Cordero Avedaño de Durand 2004); Lienzo of San Bartolo Coyotepec (personal communication, Bas van Doesburg, 2014; unpublished); Lienzo of San Gabriel Etla (Oettinger 1983:42–43); Lienzo of Guevea I (Oudijk 2000:51–63; this lienzo presumed lost); two lienzos of San Bernardo Mixtepec (Oudijk 2000:170); Lienzo de San Pedro Nexicho (Cordero Avedaño de Durand 2001); Mapa antigua de Tiltepec Mijes / Lienzo de San Miguel Metepec (König 1993:140–53); two lienzos of Santa Cruz Papalutla (Oudijk and Doesburg 2010).
    Guerrero: Six lienzos from Chiepetlan (Galarza 1972; Jiménez and Villela 1998:142–47); Lienzo of Coachimalco (Jiménez and Villela 1998:140–41); Lienzo of Malinaltepec (Oettinger 1983:41; Jiménez and Villela 1998:158); Lienzo of Petlacala (Oettinger and Horcasitas 1982; Jiménez and Villela 1998:138); Lienzo of Tlamacazapa (Jiménez and Villela 1998:159).
    Puebla: Two lienzos from San Juan Cuauhtla (Sepúlveda Herrera 2005; also Oettinger 1983:54–55); Lienzo of Cuetzpala (Huerta and Berthier 2002).
    Tlaxcala: Six lienzos from Huamantla (Meade and Hernández 1984; also Reyes García 1993:230); Mapa de Santiago Tetla (Reyes García 1993:229–30, 299); Pintura de doña María Antonia Maxixcatzin Caxtilanxochitl (Reyes García 1993:222, 228); Lienzo de Tepeticpac (Aguilera 1986; also Reyes García 1993:217).
    Western Mexico: Lienzo of Carapan (Roskamp 1998:75, 279; Lienzo of Atapan and Lienzo of Comachuen are also mentioned, p. 75).

22. Most of the later lienzos, like many of the earlier ones, are maps of community lands. Oettinger (1983:23) observes that "lienzos that deal with the ownership of communal lands are the only examples surviving from pre-Hispanic and colonial pictographic traditions that continue functioning in a social and legal sense in contemporary Mexico."
23. The non-cartographic lienzos include several later colonial paintings on cloth that combine elements of native pictographs and European heraldry, such as three lienzos from Chiepetlan, Guerrero, that may have been hung as banners commemorating important official events that took place in this village in the late seventeenth to early eighteenth century (Galarza 1972:113–23). One contains a large image of a *nopal* cactus, part of the place sign of Tenochtitlan / Mexico City; another a rampant jaguar and lion wearing crowns; and the third a double-headed bird with crown. The painting on a late colonial lienzo from San Bernardo Mixtepec, Oaxaca, mentioned and illustrated by Oudijk (2000:170 n. 195, fig. 26) consists of the image of Saint Bernard seated on a jaguar (as, for example, are rulers of Tequixtepec on the Lienzo of Tequixtepec I of the Coixtlahuaca Group).
24. The smallest dimensions that I have found reported for a manuscript painted on cloth are 51 × 38 cm, given for the seventeenth-century Lienzo of Coachimalco, Guerrero (Jiménez and Villela 1998:140–41).
25. Reyes García (1993:207) notes that in the Acts of the Cabildo (governing council) of Tlaxcala of June 17, 1552, in which it was decreed that a manuscript showing Tlaxcala's role in the Spanish conquest of Mexico be made to be sent to Spain, the manuscript is referred to in the Nahuatl language as *yaotlahcuiolli*, "war painting or writing." The original of the Lienzo of Tlaxcala is lost, the manuscript surviving today only in the form of numerous copies, the earliest from 1773 (Glass and Robertson (1975:214–18).
26. Glass and Robertson (1975:200) observe that some boundary sites on the Lienzo of Tamazulapan are also represented by "what may be vestigial place glyphs." Tamazulapan, west of Coixtlahuaca, appears on the right-hand edge of the Lienzo of Tlapiltepec.
27. On the early colonial Lienzo of Quauhquechollan, a detail of which is illustrated in fig. 1.12, less typically, and perhaps in emulation of European depictions of landscape, the white spaces were colored in. Smudges of gray outline the curves and the crisscrossed roads that link the lienzo's scenes of travel and conquest, and spaces between the roads are colored ochre and pale blue-green (Aguirre Beltrán 1997:382; Asselbergs 2004:76 and color reproduction).
28. On lienzo textiles, see Weitlaner Johnson (1966), Altamirano Rocha (1982), Altamirano Rocha and Rubí (1989), García Valencia (n.d.a, 2010), Johnson (2000), Huerta and Berthier (2002:21–57), Asselbergs (2004:74–75).

29. For descriptions of Mesoamerican weaving and textile construction techniques, see, for example, Anawalt (1981:9–14, 214, 215), Weitlaner Johnson (1971, 1985), and Mastache de Escobar (1971).
30. According to Borah, *Silk Raising in Colonial Mexico* (1943:59), the moths were placed on cloth sheets where the females laid their eggs in a single layer and covered them with a gummy protective substance. Perhaps this is what the illustration in Codex Sierra is intended to depict: the cloth with the moth's eggs stuck to it. Codex Sierra is a partly pictographic, partly Nahuatl, alphabetic record of community expenses for the town of Santa Catarina Tejupan, Oaxaca, for the years 1550–64. I am grateful to Kevin Terraciano for help with translation of the Nahuatl text of this entry from the codex. Terraciano is currently preparing a new English translation of this manuscript. Tejupan is located just west of the Coixtlahuaca Valley and is represented on the right-hand edge of the Lienzo of Tlapiltepec.
31. Measurements of the Lienzo of Tlapiltepec are discussed in note 8, above.
32. The three strips of cloth sewn together to form the Lienzo of Tlapiltepec are made of cotton fiber all of the same type, consistently spun and woven. Three, or at least two, was likely the minimum number of such backstrap-woven strips needed to construct a sheet the size and shape of this one. (The maximum width observed for a single strip of cloth woven on a backstrap loom in Mexico that I have come across is 120 cm: Chamula man's shirt, Museo Nacional de Artes e Industrias Populares; source: Irmgard Weitlaner Johnson, as noted in Altamirano Rocha 1982:86.)

    The weave of the Lienzo of Tlapiltepec is a type of "plain weave," in this case each warp thread being crossed by a pair of weft threads. The density of the weave varies from approximately 32 to 44 threads per inch in the warp and 36 to 40 (18 to 20 pairs of threads) in the weft. There is occasional variation, such as two warp threads instead of one, or three weft threads instead of two. The three strips are arranged with the "joinings" (the final few inches of the weaving) aligned at the bottom end of the lienzo. The yarn from which the cloth is made is the weight of fine string, moderately evenly spun, though noticeably thinner in some places than others, and not tightly twisted. It is single-ply, Z-spun. The same yarn, S-twisted into a three-ply strand, is used to stitch the strips of cloth together to form the larger sheet. Paint on top of some of the stitches (simple slanted stitches about 0.5–1 cm apart) shows that the lienzo was sewn together before it was painted (Johnson 1992, with the assistance of textile expert Susan Jarmain).
33. The sixteenth-century Lienzo of Totomixtlahuaca, Guerrero (Glass 1974), appears to consist of three strips of cloth of one weave plus a fourth narrow strip of a coarser weave. The impression this gives is that the coarser cloth was not woven expressly for the lienzo but was available and was of the right size and shape to add to the three other pieces to produce a sheet of the desired overall dimensions. Bands of a different weave in Lienzo IV from Chiepetlan, Guerrero, and of different colors in Lienzos V and VI (Galarza 1972:113, 117. 121, photos D–F), suggest that parts of these lienzos also were not made specifically for them, but were used because they were available and were of suitable size.
34. A complex technique known as "curved weave" allows the ribs to continue around the corners of the sheet. The ribbed border was first described by Weitlaner Johnson (1966) in her analysis of the textile of the Lienzo of Ocotepec, Oaxaca. Ribbed borders on two lienzos from Tuxpan, Veracruz, are discussed by Altamirano Rocha (1982), and on the Lienzo of Quauhquechollan, Puebla, by Asselbergs (2004:74–75). In a paper suggesting that pieces of cloth with ribbed borders found incorporated into lienzo textiles were originally woven for other uses, I listed nine lienzos in which some or all of the component pieces display ribbed borders (Johnson 2000). Since then I have learned of three more lienzos with ribbed borders, all from the Coixtlahuaca Valley: the Lienzo of Aztatla, the Lienzo of Tulancingo I, and the Lienzo of Otla. With the Lienzo of Ihuitlán (fig. 1.16) this makes four lienzos of the Coixtlahuaca Group with this feature. I thank Bas van Doesburg for photographs of the lienzos of Aztatla and Tulancingo and Carlos Rincón Mautner and Van Doesburg for photographs of the Lienzo of Otla. The Mesoamerican "curved weave" technique and its variants in the colonial lienzos, but also as employed in modern times in *quechquemitls* (women's poncho-like upper-body garments) in the Sierra de Puebla and *morrales* (men's bags) in the Huasteca, are discussed in recent, some as yet unpublished, papers by Enrique Hugo García Valencia (for example 2008, 2010, n.d.a, n.d.b). I thank García Valencia for sending me drafts of these papers.
35. These observations are based on viewing a photocopy of my tracing of the Lienzo of Tlapiltepec enlarged to the size of the original, as well as seeing full-size tracings of two Coixtlahuaca lienzos spread out on the floor of the Latin American Library at Tulane University (April 2000). The two Coixtlahuaca tracings are Lienzo A, as it is known, 360 × 380 cm, a copy of a lost original (see fig. 1.13); and Lienzo B, 425 × 325 cm, a copy of the Lienzo of Coixtlahuaca I (Parmenter 1970; Doesburg 2001:30–31 n. 7; Doesburg 2010b).

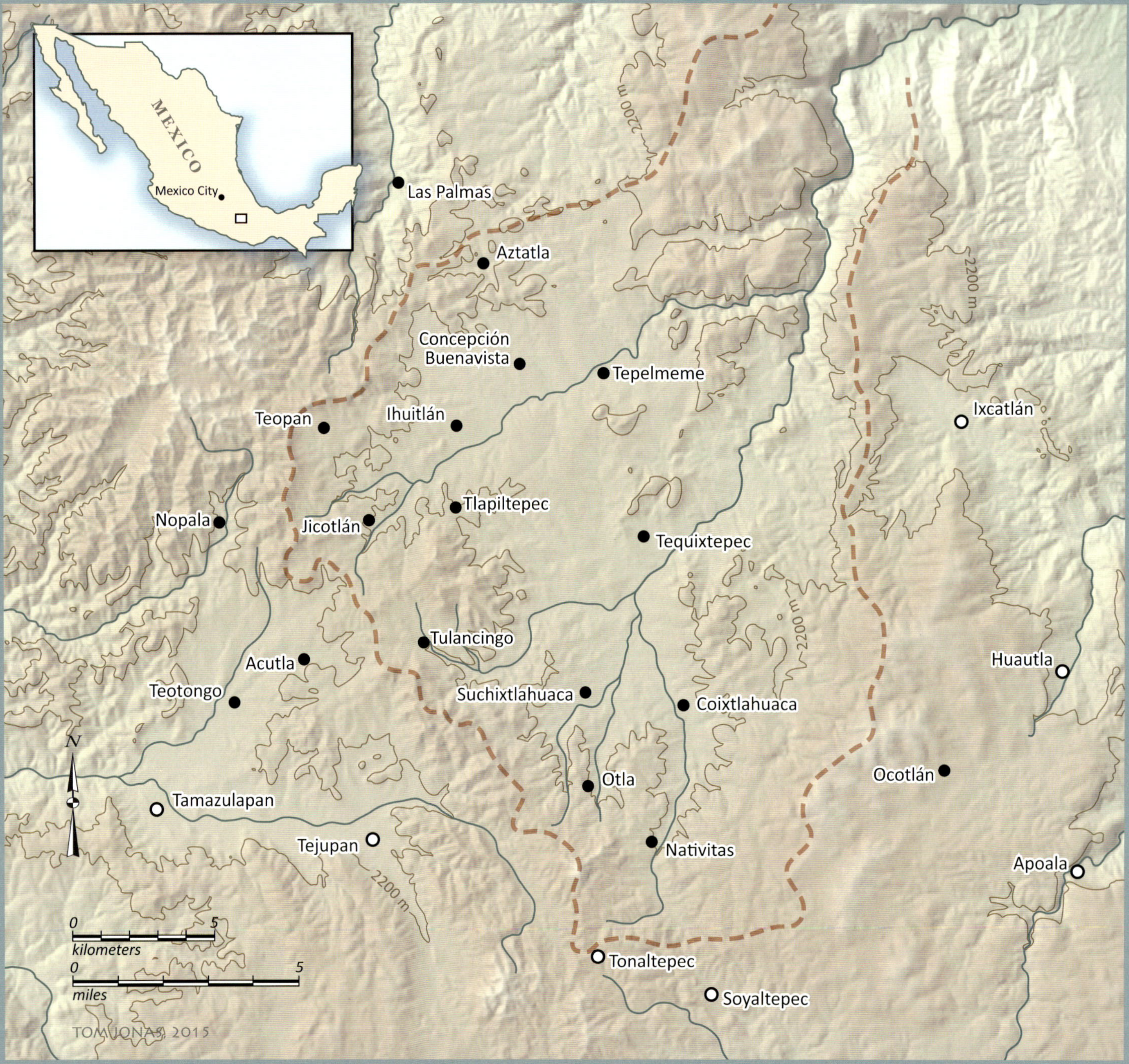

MAP 2.1. Coixtlahuaca Valley and adjacent areas. Black dots are towns with past or present Chocho (Ngiwa) populations. Contour lines indicate elevation of 2,200 meters above sea level. © 2015, University of Oklahoma Press.

CHAPTER 2

The Lienzo of Tlapiltepec

The Royal Historiography of the Coixtlahuaca City-State

BAS VAN DOESBURG

The Lienzo of Tlapiltepec, housed since 1919 at the Royal Ontario Museum in Toronto,[1] is a woven cotton cloth measuring 3.97 by 1.67 meters or 156.25 by 65.75 inches. It is covered with writing in the Postclassic pictographic, or semasiographic, script.[2] This type of writing was in use during what archaeologists have called the Postclassic and the early decades of the colonial period (AD 950–1600) in and around what is today the state of Oaxaca.[3] The lienzo dates, as best we can tell, from the middle of the sixteenth century and belongs to a group of at least thirteen coeval pictographic documents from the Coixtlahuaca Valley, a high, arid region in northern Oaxaca (map 2.1).[4] This remarkable Coixtlahuaca Group constitutes, together with the Mixtec pictorials, the most important corpus of texts that have survived of the indigenous literary tradition of central and southwest Mexico.

Like the Mixtec codices and lienzos, the contents of the documents of this group coincide considerably. All of the texts refer to the political history of small city-states that developed in the valley during the Postclassic era, and several places, people, and dates appear in more than one of the documents. Consequently, the comparison of the various documents and the identification of parallels and variations in the narratives recorded on them have proven to be the major tools for their decipherment.[5] Moreover, such an approach allows for the reconstruction of a narrative that is more complete than any contained in any single one of the documents.[6] This has allowed scholars to gain insight into the development of Postclassic polities that supplements what can be deduced from archaeology alone. For example, according to archaeologists, Postclassic culture inherited many general cultural constructs, ideas, and techniques from earlier periods, especially from the Teotihuacán horizon (150 BC–AD 700).

However, as the documentary record shows, Postclassic people did not preserve exact memories of these earlier cultural phases. The Classic to Postclassic transition was explained in terms of creation, when gods and spirits walked the earth and foreshadowed human social behavior through their actions. Traditions of prior horizons became the legends of the Postclassic (for example, the famous Quetzalcoatl cycle recorded in early colonial sources). The Postclassic period can thus be seen as a horizon in a continuous development of general cultural concepts and elements of material

FIG. 2.1, FACING. Lienzo of Tulancingo, now known to be from Ihuitlán. Woven cotton, 1.45 × 1.15 meters. Photo by Vittorio D'Onofri.

culture (the "external" view of archaeology), but also as a new creation in terms of a self-explaining and self-justifying political system that spanned the whole period and did not need explanation from earlier horizons (the "internal" view of philology). It is this last view that I will explore in this text.

The Lienzo of Tlapiltepec is perhaps the most complex of all Coixtlahuaca documents, offering to the beholder an ample panorama of the history of the Coixtlahuaca Valley, from the middle of the eleventh century until the early sixteenth century, on a surface of more than seventy square feet. As Ross Parmenter learned during his research in the 1960s and 1970s, the Lienzo of Tlapiltepec was kept in the village of Tlapiltepec in 1892, when it was seen and partially copied by a schoolteacher named Fidel López, a friend of the Oaxacan historian Manuel Martínez Gracida (1847–1924). It was probably stolen from that village around 1904 and sold to the British vice-consul in Oaxaca, Constantine Rickards, in 1907 (Parmenter 1982:22–27; Doesburg 1998b:59–66; see Brownstone, preface, this volume). Between 1908 and 1912 Rickards tried unsuccessfully to sell the lienzo to the Mexican state. During that time, in 1910, Eduard Seler, the well-known German scholar of Mexican antiquities, was able to copy it at Rickards's house. Finally, in 1919 Rickards sold the lienzo to the director of the Royal Ontario Museum in Toronto.[7] Since the publication of Parmenter's study on the late nineteenth and twentieth century collection history of the document, it has always been assumed that the lienzo was painted in Tlapiltepec.

However, circumstantial evidence drawn from the lienzo itself and external colonial documentation from Mexican archives suggest that the lienzo may have been painted in the royal palace of Coixtlahuaca by order of its lords. In this chapter, I present the arguments for this hypothesis and also explore the significance of colonial documentation in the study of the Coixtlahuaca lienzos as a group. I have not found documentary evidence that explains how the lienzo could have been moved to Tlapiltepec before 1892, but such moves are not uncommon, as can be demonstrated by the case of the Lienzo of Tulancingo, another Coixtlahuaca Group document (fig. 2.1), which originally came from Ihuitlán (Doesburg 2000).

CHARACTERISTICS OF COIXTLAHUACA HISTORIOGRAPHY

When the Europeans arrived in what is now Mexico, Coixtlahuaca was a major urban center, with perhaps as many as eighty thousand inhabitants.[8] Indigenous historical sources of this period from central Mexico mention Coixtlahuaca's importance as a commercial center where products from distant lands were traded. However, its great size was relatively recent: according to the limited archaeological data available, the city experienced a surprising territorial and population growth from the fourteenth century onward and seems to have blossomed in the late Postclassic period. It is precisely this process that can be followed in the pictorial record. The rich historical information from the Coixtlahuaca area itself and other areas in contact with it—especially what is now southern Puebla and central Mexico—allows for a reconstruction of its political development.

Around the middle of the fifteenth century, just before the Aztecs took power in the Coixtlahuaca region, several dynastic houses governed the city. The coexistence of multiple ruling houses in the city may be the reflection of a multiethnic society in which the communities were built up of so-called *parcialidades,* or ethnic

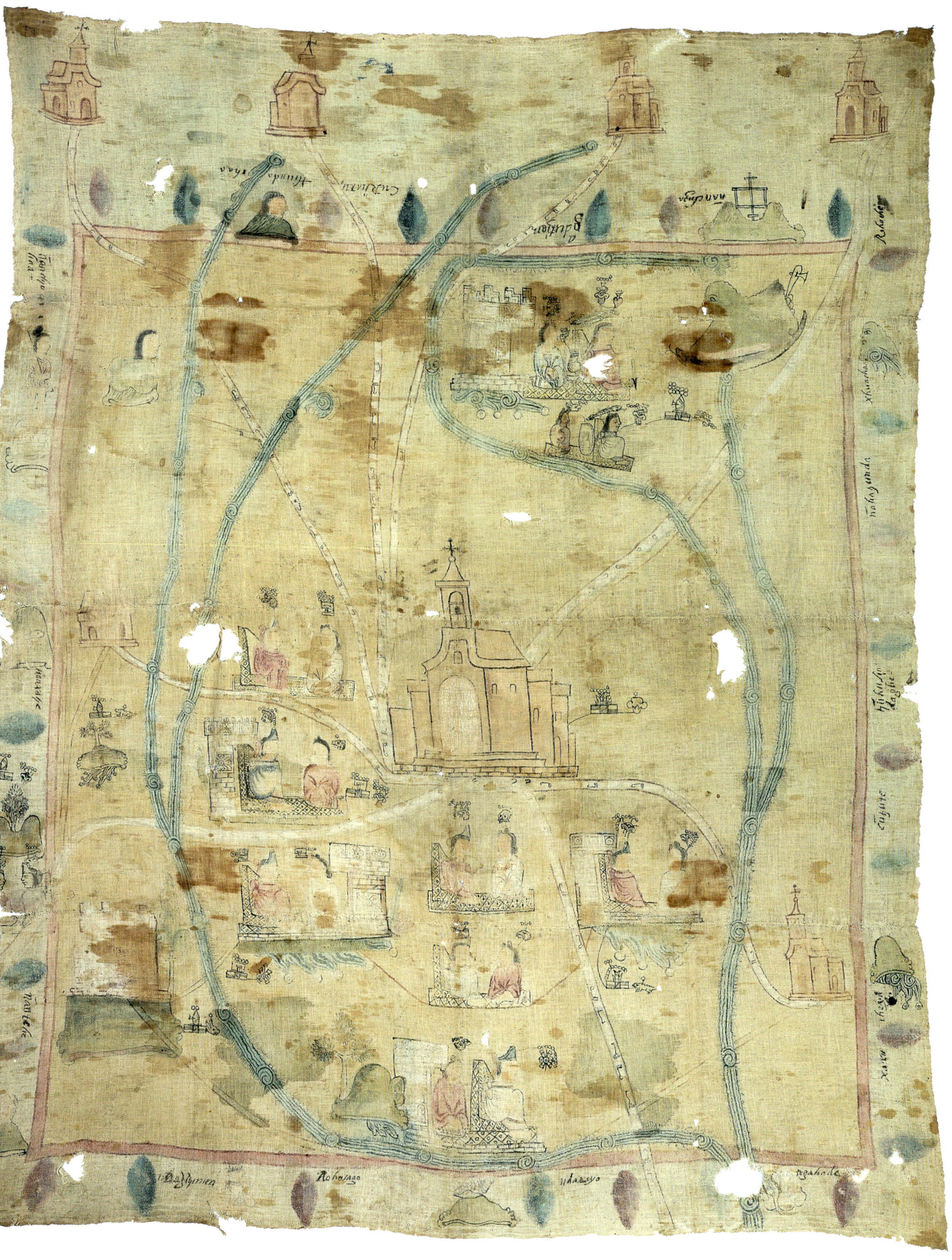

neighborhoods. Each parcialidad would maintain its own ethnic markers, including language, dress, gods and relics, origins and history, artisan specialties, and so forth. The parcialidades phenomenon is best documented in central Mexico in the works of Chimalpain (Chalco-Amecameca area), and in southern Puebla in the *Historia tolteca-chichimeca* (Kirchhoff, Odena Güemes, and Reyes García 1976), but it was clearly visible in neighboring Coixtlahuaca as well.[9] Together, the parcialidades would form a single community, although each dynastic house would maintain its own subjects and vassals, often located in discontinuous pockets throughout the landscape. In such an arrangement, personal and ritual ties between social groups and their rulers constituted the glue of society, with territorial unity secondary.

During the sixteenth century, the indigenous elite of the many independent polities that existed in the Mixteca produced a large number of painted cloths, today called lienzos. Here the elite recorded the villages, lands, boundaries, lineages, and sometimes, historical events related to their domains. The precise nature of their rule is still a matter of debate, but we can recognize two basic, partially overlapping, sociopolitical units: the community ("water-mountain" or "water and mountain" in the indigenous languages) and the *cacicazgo* ("mat-and-throne").[10]

The community represented an independent geopolitical unit, socially differentiated and stratified, that included gods, rulers, nobles, priests, administrators, artisans, traders, and farmers. This first type of sociopolitical unit was governed by a royal house and was held together by family ties, land, religious festivals, and tribute-service obligations. The second type of sociopolitical concept, cacicazgo, focused on the hereditary government, which was centered in the dynastic house (the palace), its sacred ancestors, the entailed lands—often the best ones in the region—and the land-bound farmers belonging to the palace. A royal couple, with both spouses supposed to be of direct royal descent, ruled the dynastic house. Daughters could hold and pass down ruling titles in the absence of a suitable male candidate. The distinction between the two structures blurred at the level of the royal couple, who functioned both as heads of the cacicazgos (of both spouses) and as rulers of the community.[11]

As I will seek to show, the distribution of pictographic documents through the Coixtlahuaca Valley reflects rather neatly the distribution and hierarchy of the mats-and-thrones, that is, the royal courts there. Because the city of Coixtlahuaca was the most important center of power in the valley, it should not surprise us that several lienzos relate to that city. Around 1890 Coixtlahuaca possessed at least three: the Lienzo of Coixtlahuaca I (now in the Museo Nacional de Antropología, Mexico City), the Lienzo of Coixtlahuaca II (or Seler II, now in the Ethnologisches Museum Berlin, former Museum für Völkerkunde), and the lost original of Lienzo A (a tracing was made around 1900). All of these left the village in the subsequent fifty years. Manuel Martínez Gracida sold the Lienzo of Coixtlahuaca II to Eduard Seler in 1897.[12] In 1901 the village still kept the two remaining lienzos in the municipal palace (Belmar 1901:124), but during the turbulent years of the Mexican Revolution these documents also disappeared.[13] In 1918 an inhabitant of the village found the Lienzo of Coixtlahuaca I in the possession of a soldier (Caso 1954:8; Parmenter 1970:189). It was acquired by Mexico's Instituto Nacional de Antropología e Historia in 1941 at a price of four hundred pesos and exhibited for several years at the Regional Museum of Oaxaca by orders of the Oaxacan governor, much against the will of Alfonso Caso, who favored centralizing these documents in Mexico City (see also Monroy 1946:31).[14] In 1955 it was borrowed by the National Museum in Mexico City but was never returned.[15] The third lienzo has never reappeared.[16]

Santiago Ihuitlán, a second major mat-and-throne in the Coixtlahuaca Valley, possessed two lienzos: the Lienzo of Ihuitlán and the Lienzo of Tulancingo. The Lienzo of Ihuitlán left the village in 1900 and is now in the Brooklyn Museum, New York. For unknown reasons, the second document ended up in the archive of San Miguel Tulancingo (Doesburg 2000).

San Miguel Tequixtepec, another major mat-and-throne in the Coixtlahuaca Valley, also had, and still has, two lienzos: the Lienzos of Tequixtepec I and II. Finally, the Lienzo of Nativitas and the Lienzo of Otla, both still in their villages of origin, cover the southern Coixtlahuaca region (Doesburg 2001; Rincón Mautner 2007; Ruiz Ortíz and Jansen 2009; Doesburg 2010b). Three more documents (leaving the Lienzo of Tlapiltepec aside for a moment) in the Coixtlahuaca Group are all of unknown provenience.[17]

In general, these lienzos selectively presented information to meet specific political or judicial objectives of the elite who commissioned them. The most complex ones illustrate the ancestry of the parties in royal marriage. Less elaborate ones might record the boundaries of a certain mat-and-throne, or community. Mixed formats also existed. Lienzos were most likely presented orally on special occasions when rulers, priests, and nobles gathered to reaffirm and construct the collective memory of the dynastic house or the community. An example of a genealogical document is the Lienzo of Ihuitlán (fig. 2.2), perhaps painted during the arrangement of a marriage between an Ihuitlán princess and a Coixtlahuaca prince (Doesburg 2004).

Documents that register the new colonial boundaries of a community or a cacicazgo show the place sign of the village, the church, or the lord's palace in the center of the lienzo, surrounded by boundaries, which are represented on the edges of the document. Settlements of secondary importance within the borders might be represented off-center and on a smaller scale or with less detail, to express the settlement hierarchy. An example of a community boundary document is the Lienzo of Coixtlahuaca I (fig. 2.3). The large topograph in the center is also accompanied by a short genealogy of the Coixtlahuaca lords, identifying them as the representatives of the community.

When the goal was to demonstrate the antiquity of the domain, these genealogies are often much longer. This is the case in the Lienzo of Tequixtepec I and the Lienzo of Nativitas (fig. 2.4), which both include complete genealogical lists of their respective lords as well as territorial maps delimited by boundaries. The genealogical lines sometimes reach back to the time of creation, when the first ancestors walked a primordial world in which the foundation of later rule was laid out. In these documents, the painter established a clear relation between the semidivine origin of the lords in antiquity—coinciding with the beginning of the Postclassic period—and the territory under the control of their descendants, creating in this way an effective ideological statement.

The selection of information also depended on the person or persons to whom the document was directed. In a document painted for the Spanish authorities or in the presence of a Spanish official, it was necessary to exclude any reference to the elements of pre-Hispanic religion and to underline support for the Spanish-Catholic cause.

FIG. 2.2, OVERLEAF. Lienzo of Ihuitlán. Woven cotton, 2.48 × 1.57 meters. Courtesy of the Brooklyn Museum, Carll H. de Silver Fund, 42.160.

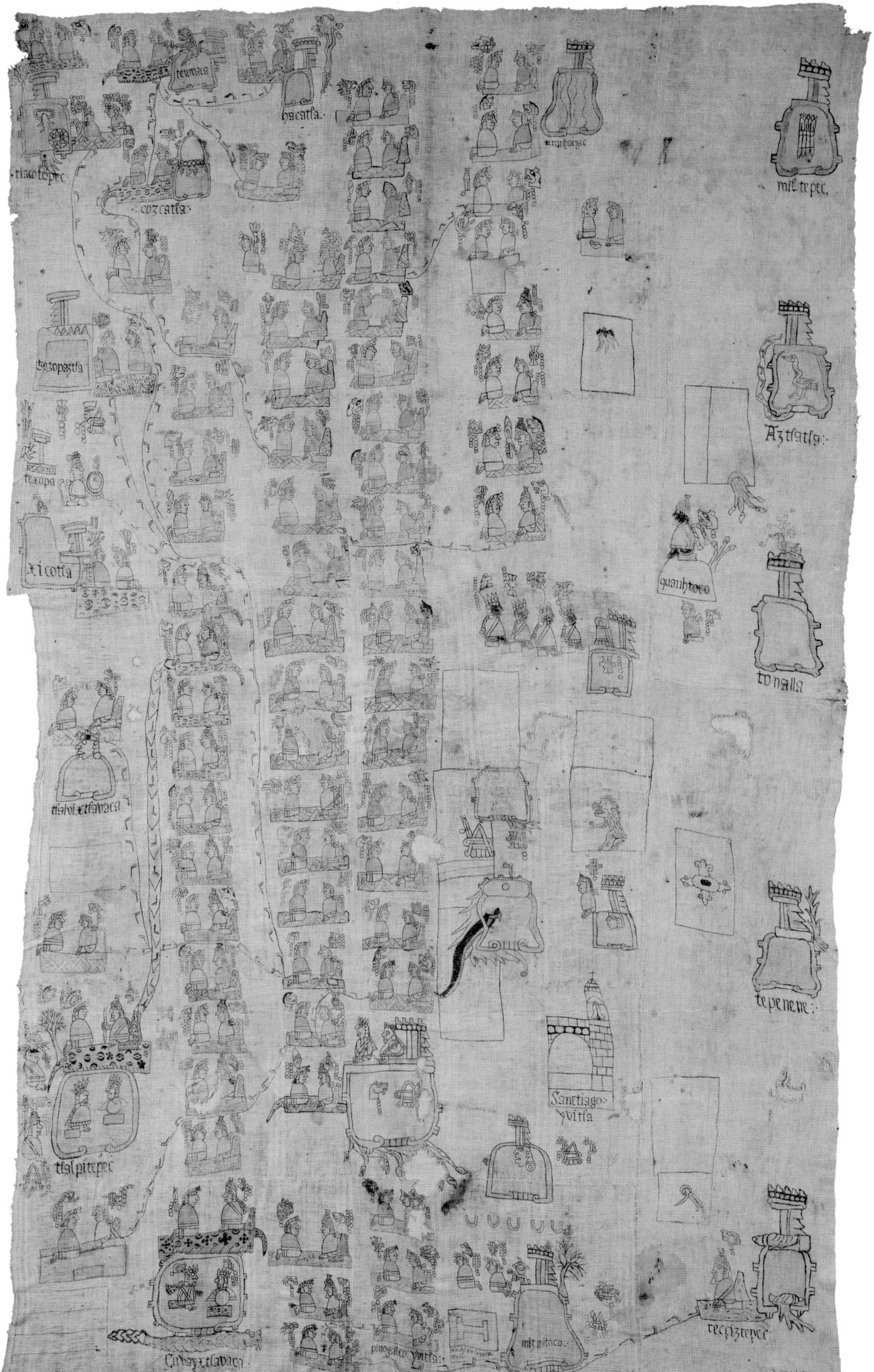

tlacotepec
hacatla
cozcatla
mil tepec
Aztatla
quauhtoco
tonalla
tepenene
Santiago yvitla
tlalpitepec
tecciztepec

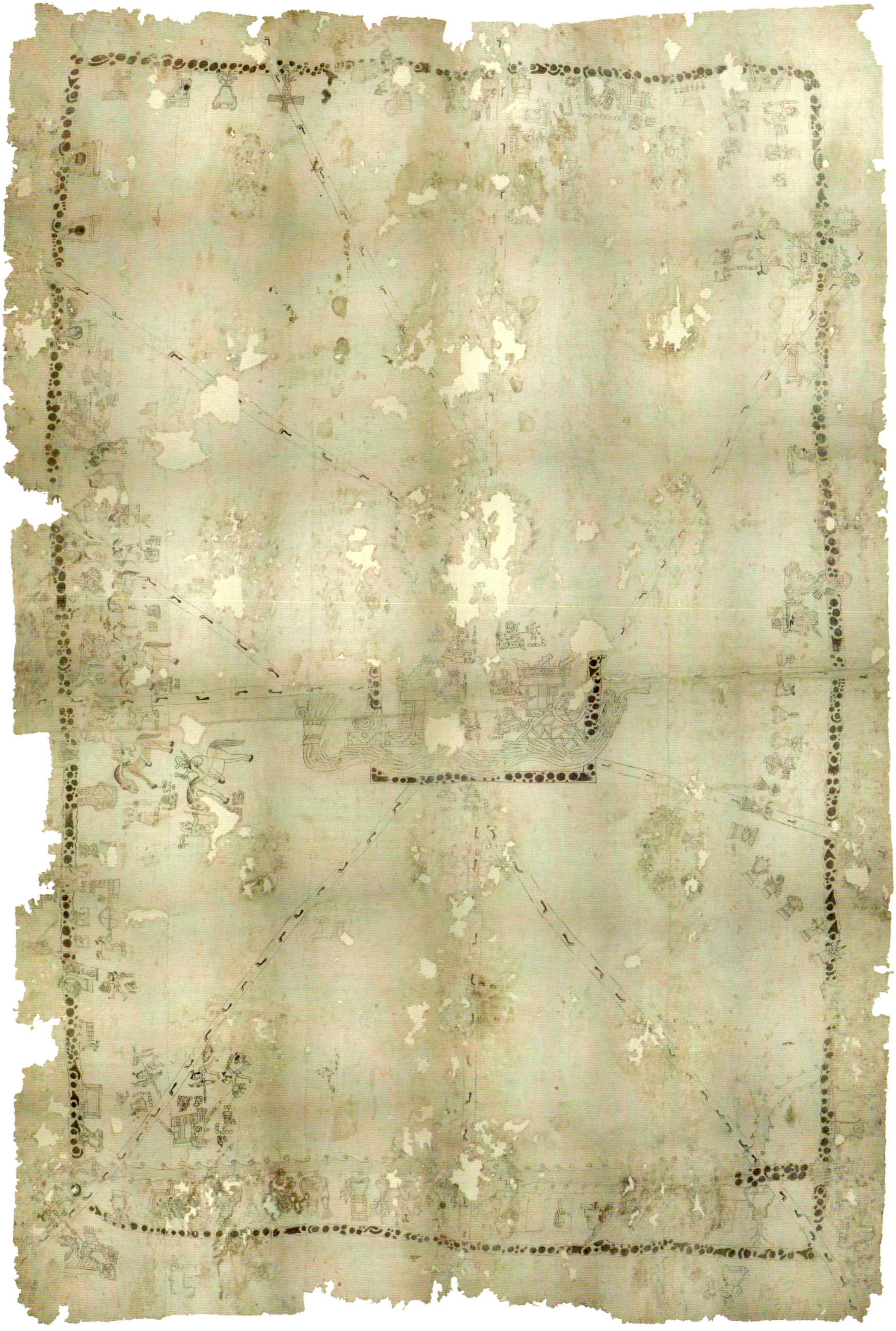

FIG. 2.3. Lienzo of Coixtlahuaca I. Woven cotton, 4.25 × 3.00 meters. Reproduction authorized by the Instituto Nacional de Antropología e Historia, Mexico.

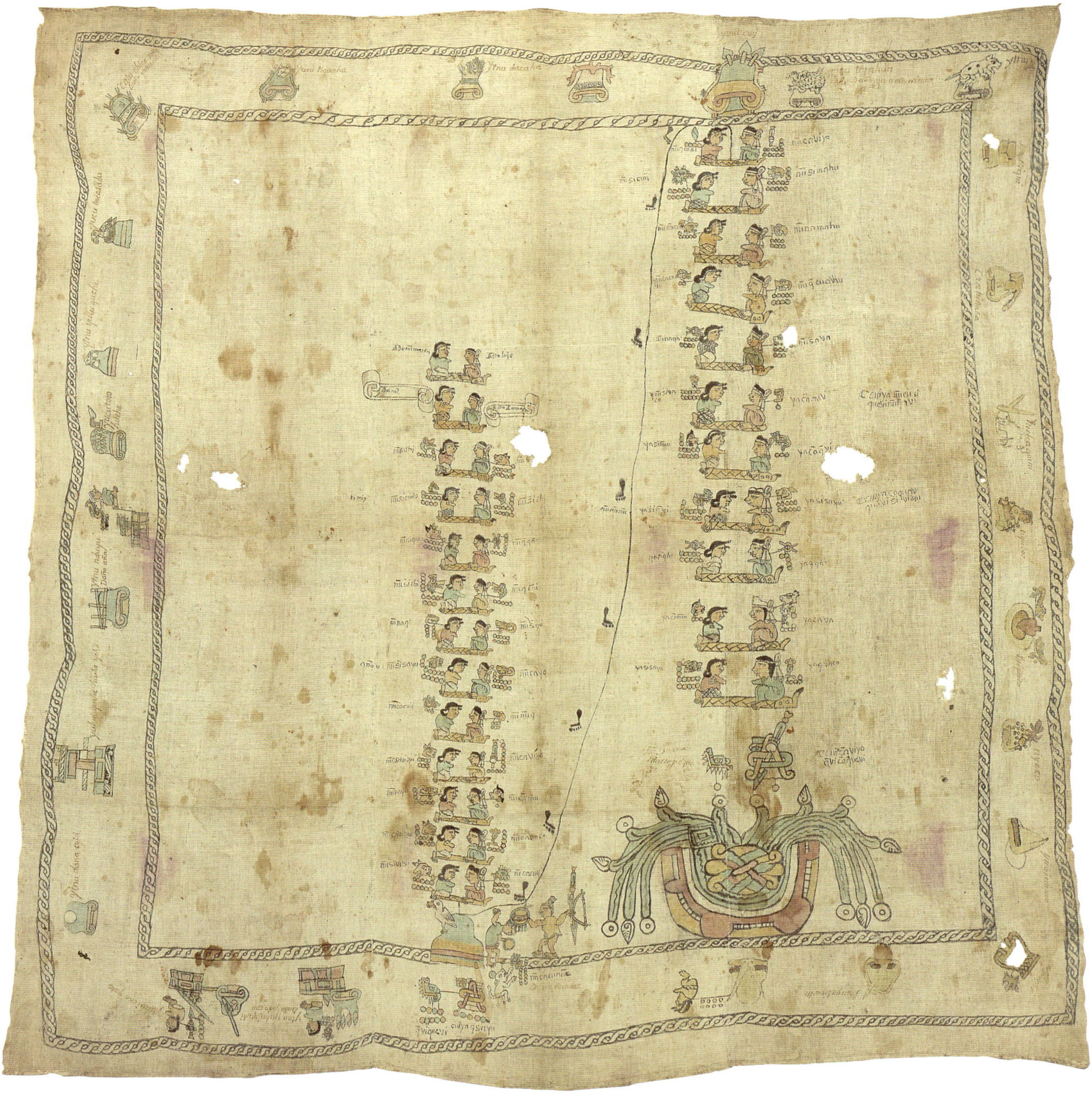

FIG. 2.4. Lienzo of Nativitas. Woven cotton, 1.73 × 1.75 meters. Photo by Vittorio D'Onofri.

The Lienzo of Coixtlahuaca II—in which the churches of Coixtlahuaca and Juquila are conspicuous—seems to be an example of such a document (Doesburg 2004). However, for an internal audience, the inclusion of pre-Hispanic ritual elements was important. The Lienzo of Ihuitlán, for example, shows the dynastic sacred bundles. These bundles concentrate the essence of the gods. The bundles originated during the transition from primordial to historical time and formed a strong link between primordial times and the living rulers, who were responsible for their cult.[18]

For documents without provenience, similar arguments about the presence or absence of certain geographical features or persons may lead to new hypotheses on their origins. For instance, the notable emphasis on the church and lands in Juquila on the Lienzo of Coixtlahuaca II suggests that the creation of this lienzo had to do with—among other issues—the conflict that took place in the 1570s between Coixtlahuaca and Zapotitlán over the control of Juquila.[19] Though this site was only a small settlement in the northern extreme of the Coixtlahuaca Valley, it produced some rare tropical products. Surely for this reason, the palace of Coixtlahuaca claimed to have patrimonial lands in the area, which must be the precise plots painted in the lienzo.

AT WAR WITH THE AZTECS (AD 1458–1462)

One of the best-known episodes in the history of Coixtlahuaca, the Aztec conquest of the city-state, is notably absent from the pictorial documents.[20] This lapse was no doubt due to ethnocentric considerations: it was seen as unnecessary to include this adverse event. Not surprisingly, our information about this conquest comes from central Mexican Nahuatl sources, which saw this conquest as a crucial moment in the Aztec rise to power. While this may make us wonder what other events were left out of the lienzos, in this case the existence of an external "Aztec" view of the late Coixtlahuaca city-state is a fortunate coincidence. I will summarize here what we know about this episode.

At the start of Aztec hostilities in AD 1458, the heads of the two most prominent houses in Coixtlahuaca were Lord 6 Water and Lord 6 Monkey. Both lords were backed by long and illustrious genealogies, but Nahuatl (Aztec) sources from central Mexico reveal that 6 Water (known in these sources as Atonal or Atonaltzin, not to be confused with his predecessor Atonal I)[21] was the main protagonist of Coixtlahuaca history. His legendary resistance to Aztec expansion is still known in the Coixtlahuaca region today. By the mid-fifteenth century, his lineage had acquired great prestige, and the Aztecs held Atonal in high esteem. Their stories attribute the origin of hostilities between them to the senseless killing of several Aztec merchants by people from Coixtlahuaca, but this seems highly improbable and was likely just an excuse. It seems more plausible that the Aztecs took advantage of an existing local conflict—just as they did in other conquests—and in reality arrived at Coixtlahuaca invited by one of the conflicting parties.[22] This party may have been Tlaxiaco, for one source states that Atonal had to fight Malinaltzin, the lord of Tlaxiaco, who is said to have been "on the side of the Mexicans" during the Aztec assaults.[23] If so, Malinaltzin's motive for inviting the Aztecs might have been the expansion of Atonal's demands for tribute: the same source says Atonal "had waged war against many of his neighbors and had made himself lord of many people." Other central Mexican sources suggest the same.[24] Tlaxiaco's people may have seen an Aztec intervention as a way to halt Atonal's political and economic ambitions. Other indications strengthen this reading of events: the pictorial documents hint at a temporary loss of power by the Atonal lineage during the four generations prior to the reign of Atonal's father, a man named 10 Serpent.

In the Lienzo of Tlapiltepec, the generations prior to 10 Serpent are depicted—without further explanation—seated in other locations (Tequixtepec and Tejupan) and not in Coixtlahuaca. Also, according to Lienzo A, 10 Serpent himself returned to the area from Chachoapan and ruled for fifteen years (AD 1405–20) at a border location on the southern frontier of the valley (fig. 2.5). In this same document he can be seen conquering the villages of Juquila and Eztepec in the extreme north of the area.

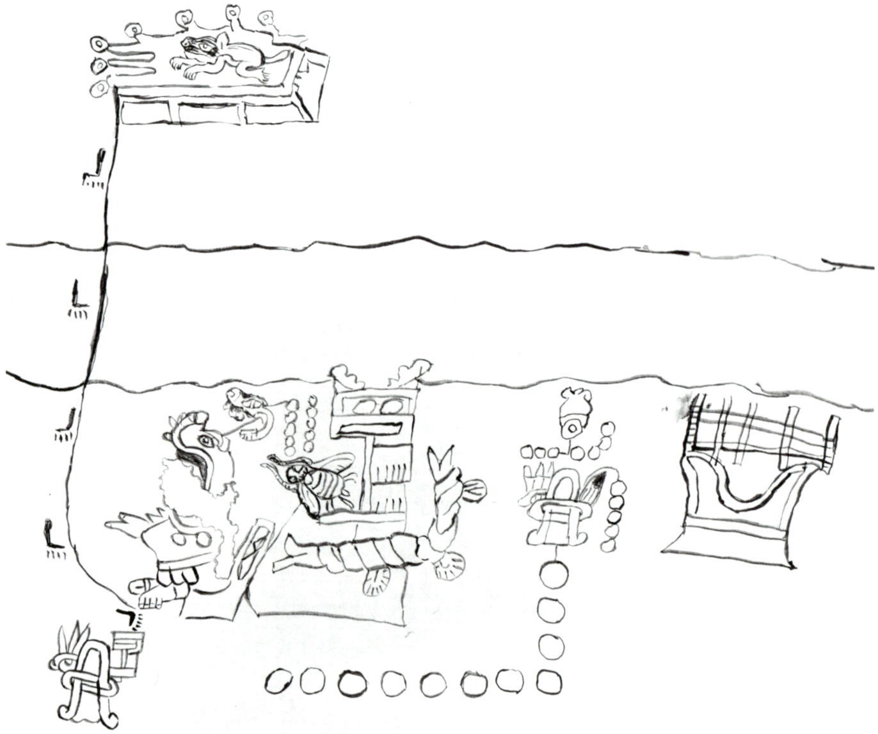

FIG. 2.5. Lord 10 Serpent arrives at the southern border of the valley from Chachoapan, "River of the Gopher," detail of Lienzo A. Damage to the original lienzo before copying apparently accounts for some loss of information. As can be deduced from comparison with the Lienzo of Coixtlahuaca I, there should be fourteen, not eleven dots, between the years [3] House and 5 Flint. The border locations "House of Rope" and "Slope with Fence" also occur on the Lienzo of Nativitas and are still known today with the same names. Courtesy of the Latin American Library, Tulane University, photo by Jason Kruppa.

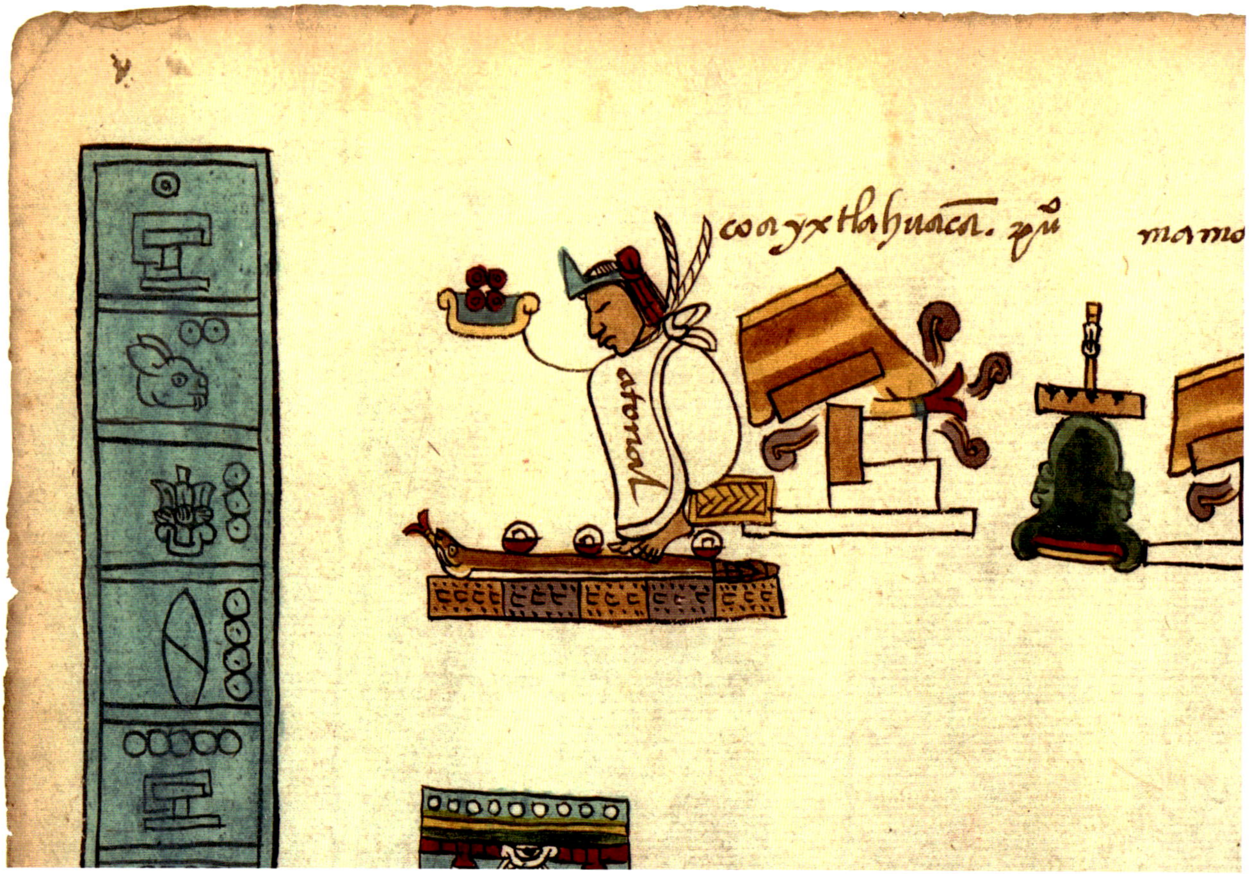

FIG. 2.6. The killing of Atonal by the Aztecs, detail of Codex Mendoza. Atonal's name glyph is composed of "water" and four red dots for *tonalli*, "day name." Courtesy of The Bodleian Library, The University of Oxford.

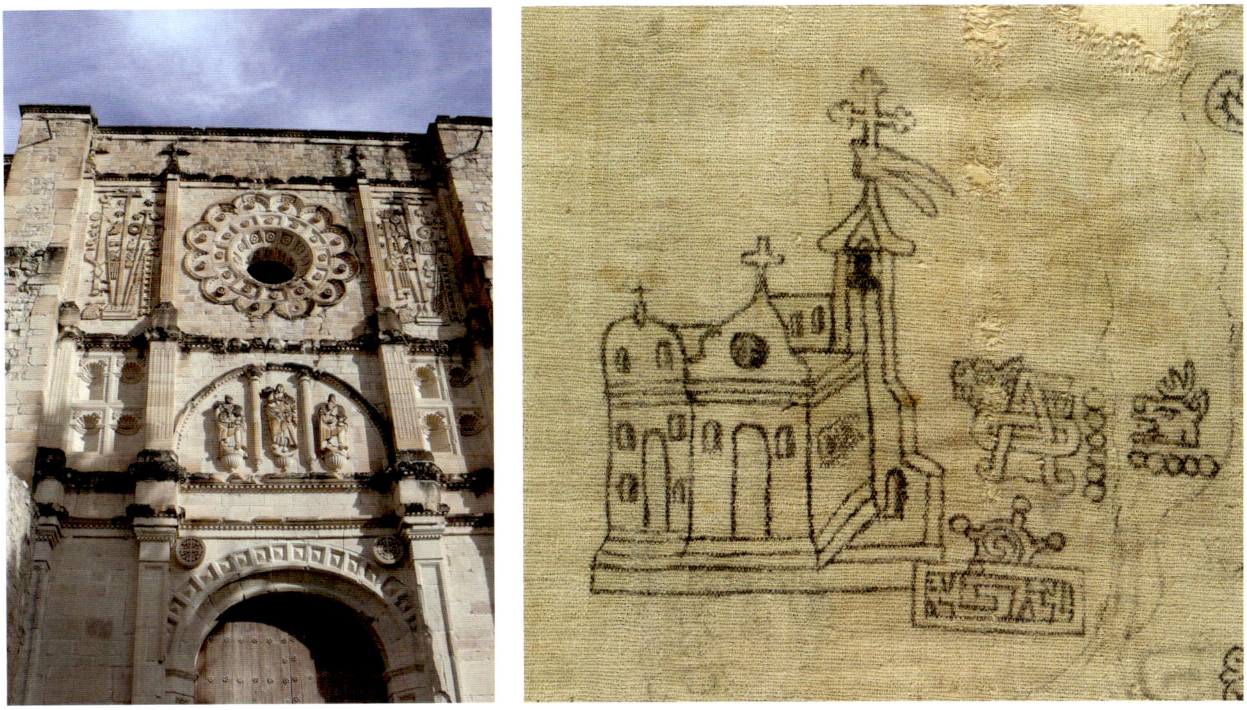

FIG. 2.7. *Left*, side door of Coixtlahuaca parish church. Photo by Nicholas Johnson Weitlaner. *Right*, church at Coixtlahuaca from Lienzo of Tlapiltepec. Courtesy of the Royal Ontario Museum, acc. no. 917.3, photo by Brian Boyle.

These bits combine to suggest that the recovery campaign by 10 Serpent and his son Atonal may have impinged on the interests of neighboring lords who then asked for the Aztec intervention mentioned above.

After several campaigns, Coixtlahuaca was conquered in AD 1462 and Atonal was killed (fig. 2.6). According to one source, his wife was led to Moctezuma's palace, but when the emperor tried to sleep with her, he found out that she was pregnant.[25] She was then sent back to Coixtlahuaca to oversee the periodic collection of tribute. Her child—the thus surviving daughter of Atonal—appears to have married the son of Lord 6 Monkey, and they became the first couple to rule the now subdued city-state. The new government was established in the Coixtlahuaca location called Eztepec[26] or Tineñe, "Little Place of Blood," which had been the seat of the lineage of 6 Monkey and was to be the place where, after the arrival of the Spaniards, the construction of a beautiful monastery was begun in 1544 (fig. 2.7).

TOLTEC ORIGINS

Atonal traced the origins of his lineage back to the time of the famous Toltec federation. The legendary Toltec civilization, somewhere around the tenth and eleventh centuries, was the first but short-lived attempt to bring order to the Postclassic political landscape. In later times, the Toltec—who should not be thought of as any particular ethnic group, but as peoples sharing a refined urban culture and, as part of that, a devotion to the sacred bundle of Quetzalcoatl—were credited with the invention of civilization, and their culture was seen as a model for later societies. The earliest historical memory of the Postclassic people harkened back to Toltec culture—or at least, to an amalgam of memories of early Postclassic revivals of Teotihuacán. The Toltecs were often portrayed as the first civilization after creation (that is, after the Classic to

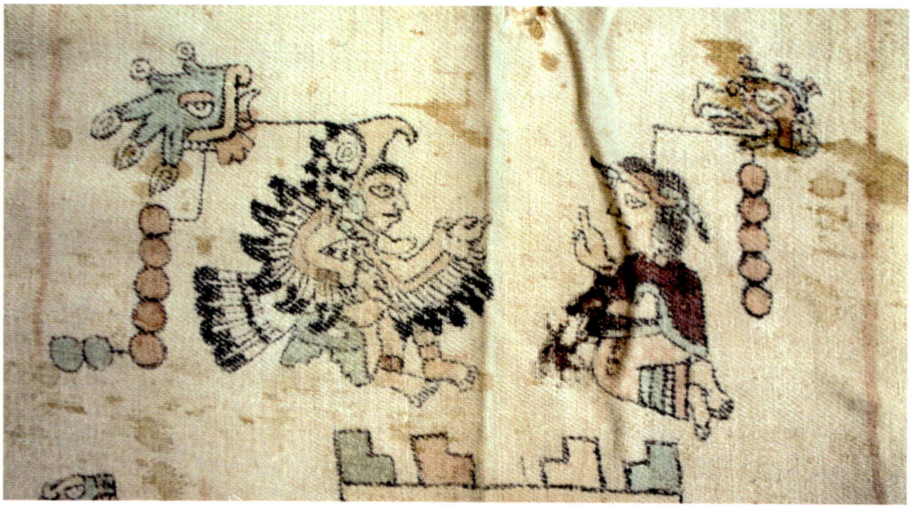

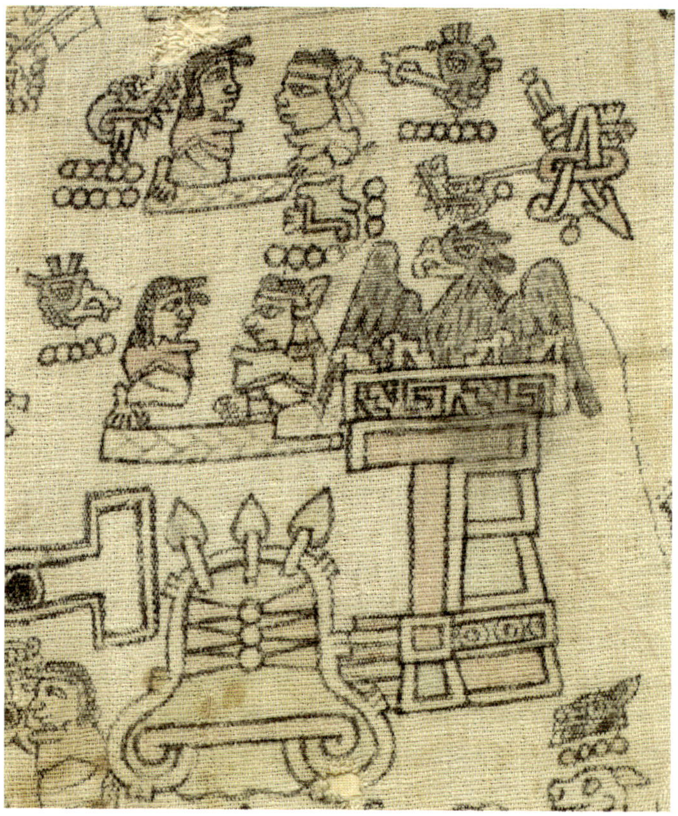

FIG. 2.8. *Top*, Lord 7 Water "Eagle" (Atonal I) from Lienzo of Tequixtepec I, photo by María de los Ángeles Romero Frizzi. *Bottom*, Lord 7 Water "Eagle" (Atonal I) from Lienzo of Tlapiltepec, courtesy of the Royal Ontario Museum, acc. no. 917.3, photo by Brian Boyle.

Postclassic transition). Several cities claimed Toltec ancestry. Archaeologically, Tula, in what is now the state of Hidalgo, is best known, but the ancient city of Cholula was also a respected Toltec center. The same stories of Toltec glory, however, also warn of the destruction of Tula as a result of the moral degeneration of its elite. The story of the rise and fall of Toltec society was taken as a moral role model for the elite, similar to the way in which the rise and fall of the Mixtec lord 8 Deer, whom several Mixtec lords claimed in their lineage, was interpreted by later generations in the Mixteca.

According to both Aztec and local sources, the house of Atonal was established eighteen generations before Aztec hostilities (that is, around the middle of the elev-

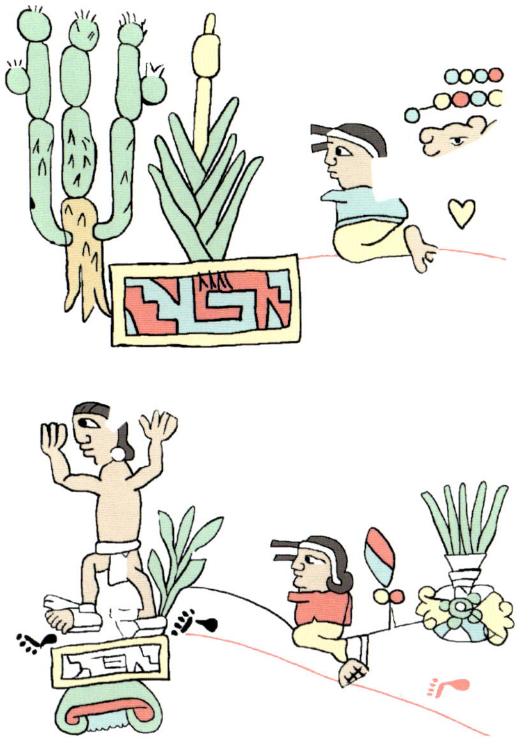

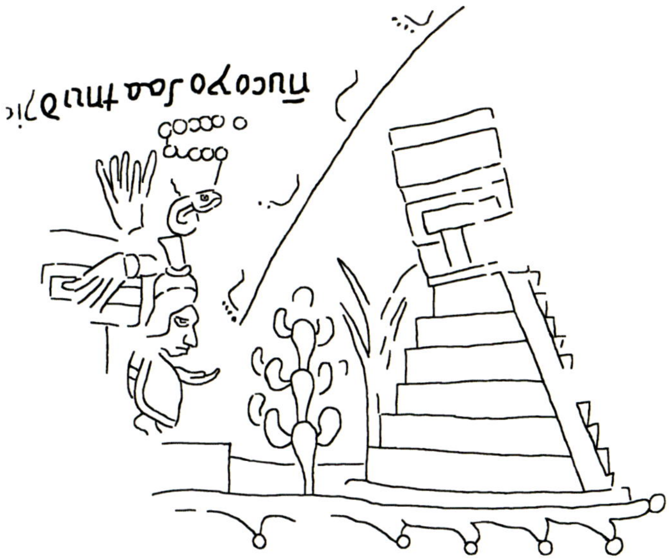

FIG. 2.9. Glyphs at left show the weddings of Atonal I's sisters on the Lienzo of Tlapiltepec. The glyph at right records the marriage of Lady 11 Serpent in Tenochtitlan on the Lienzo of Coixtlahuaca II. The painter may not have been sure of her gender, since in this representation she is drawn as a man.

enth century) by a man also named Atonal, or 7 Water in the Coixtlahuaca pictorials (we will refer to him as Atonal I) (fig. 2.8). According to the Aztec sources, Atonal I lived in the central Mexican basin during Toltec days and joined the migrating Toltec lords after the fall of the federation. This migration would bring him to Coixtlahuaca. His place of origin is given by one important Nahuatl source as Tamazólac, "At the Toad Pool," a high mountain in the Sierra de Guadalupe near Tultitlán, "Among the Cattail Reeds," located just north of Mexico City. This piece of information was possibly taken from a pictorial document, which would allow for an alternative interpretation: "Toad Hill" and "Reed Place" are also names for the important Toltec city of Cholula.[27] On the other hand, the pictorial lienzos depict Atonal I's origin place as two prominent mountains; in one representation (the Lienzo of Tequixtepec I) they are covered with snow, suggesting the volcanoes Popocatepetl and Iztaccihuatl.[28] Atonal I's great-grandparents are said to have been born from a legendary "River of Precious Stones and Quetzal Feathers" at the time of creation, which makes Atonal I the first historical person in the story.[29]

Two of his sisters were married in Tenochtitlan and Cholula, important centers on either side of the volcanoes (fig. 2.9). A third sister joined Atonal I in his journey south and married in a place, probably Tiltepec, near Yanhuitlán in the Mixteca Alta (fig. 2.10).[30] These very early marriages were undoubtedly part of an ideological statement that supported later claims about ties to these important places. At the time the Lienzo of Tlapiltepec was painted, the claim of a connection to pre-Aztec Tenochtitlan must have added to the prestige of the Coixtlahuaca royal court. The precision of this record—unusual for central Mexican standards, but shared with neighboring Mixtecs—probably also impressed the Aztecs and added to the dynasty's prestige.

Several short references in the documents connect the first three generations of the Atonal dynasty, living in the Coixtlahuaca area in the eleventh and twelfth cen-

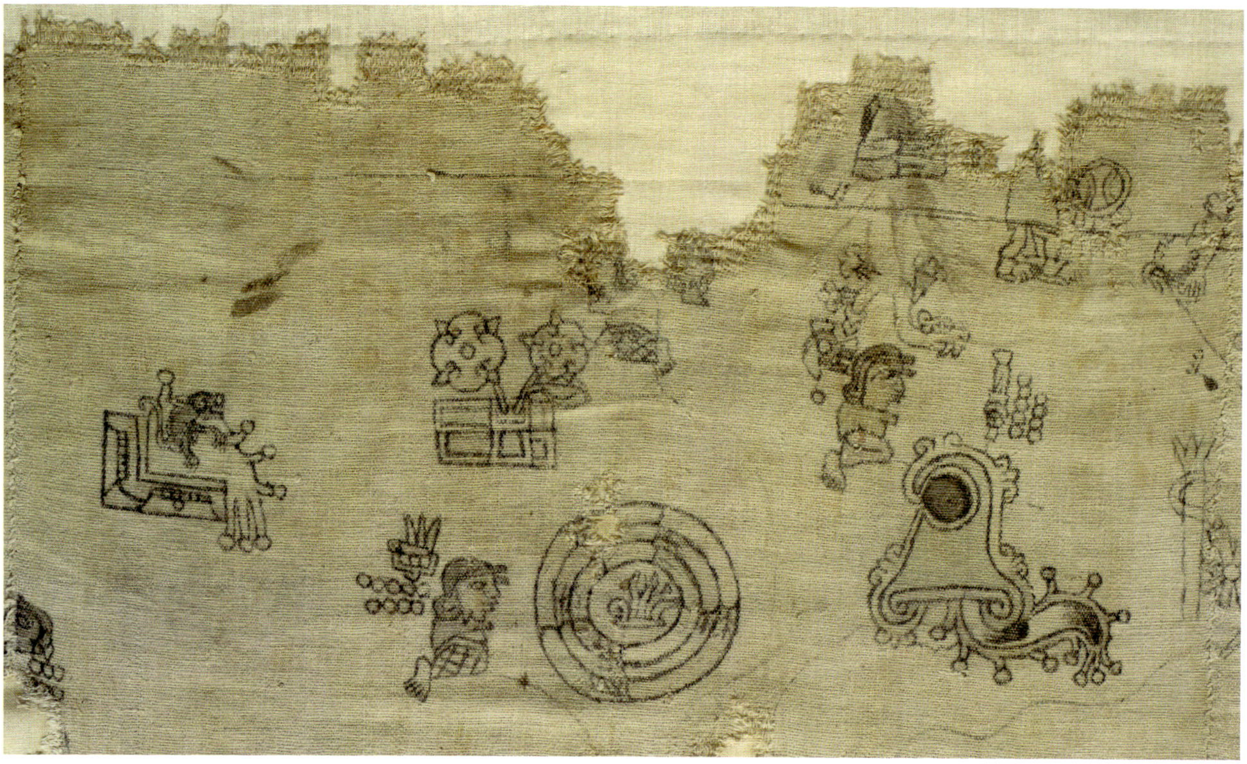

FIG. 2.10. Topograph of Tiltepec in the Yanhuitlán area, on Lienzo of Tlapiltepec (hill with black circle). Note similarity between the Chachoapan "River of the Gopher" topograph here and in figure 2.5. Courtesy of the Royal Ontario Museum, acc. no. 917.3, photo by Brian Boyle.

tury, with events on a wider geopolitical scale: a network between the Mixteca and the Olmeca-Xicalanca capital (and an important center of Toltec culture), Cholula. This was a time when the Mixteca was absorbed by the last florescence of the political network of Cholula (AD 700–1150), which had filled the void left by Teotihuacán's demise. A better control of the trade route toward the Guatemalan coast, which ran through the Mixteca, was high on Cholula's agenda. Mutual benefits of a Cholula-Mixteca alliance were obvious: while Cholula would be able to extend its control over long-distance commerce, the Mixtec allied lords would be able to take advantage of Cholula's great prestige as a center of religious power. In fact, famous early Mixtec lords of Tilantongo, such as 8 Deer "Jaguar Claw" (AD 1063–1115) and 4 Wind "Fire Serpent" (AD 1092–1164), also rose to power within this network. During the last quarter of the twelfth century, this alliance network came to an end with the arrival and subsequent takeover of power by the Nahuatl-speaking Teochichimec in the Cholula area. Political relations between the Mixteca and Cholula were broken off, but the trend toward further political consolidation in the Mixteca had been set. From that moment, the Mixteca experienced a relatively introverted period of development, until it reached out into Oaxaca's central valleys and southern Puebla again at the end of the fourteenth century.

In this big picture, the house of Atonal was one of the parties in Cholula's network. The marriage of Atonal I's sister in Cholula surely was no coincidence. His grandson 2 Flower, who had strong ties—and thus claims—to Tiltepec through his mother and his grandfather's sister, was recognized by the Cholulan Toltecs for his military service in some unspecified episode in the saga of 8 Deer and 4 Wind (fig. 2.11).[31] As a reward, he received the Toltec regalia, the most important of which was the blue-stone nose pin.

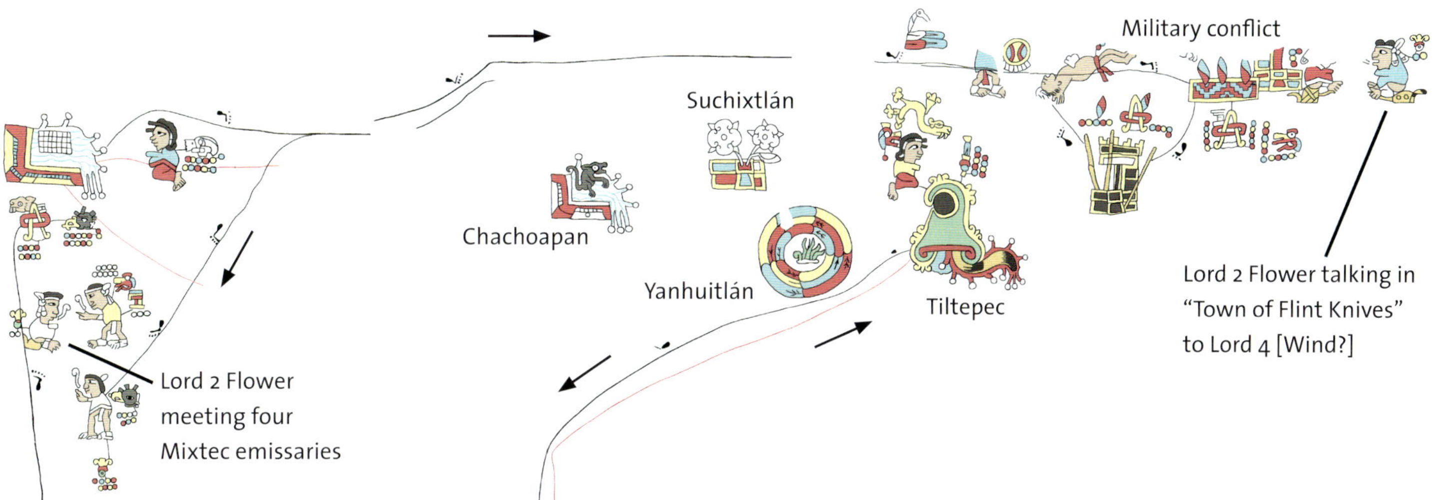

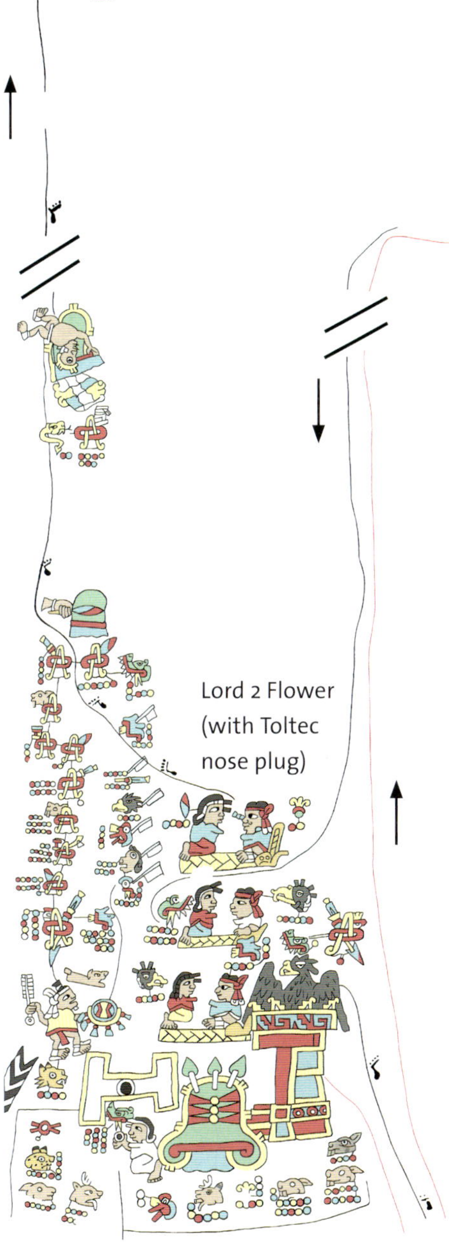

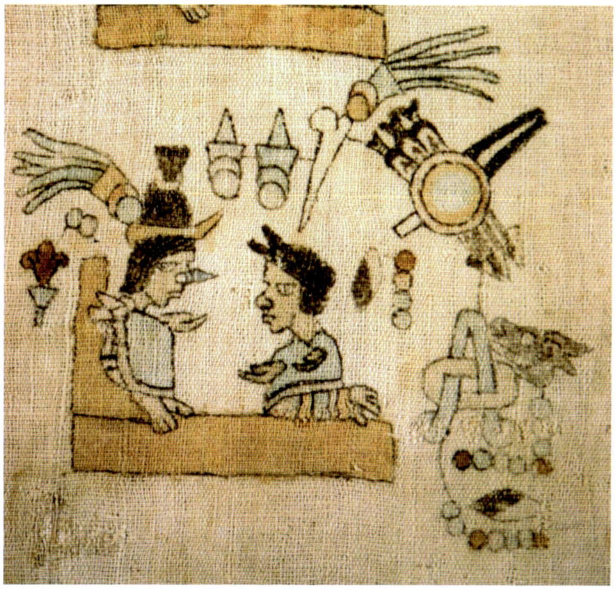

FIG. 2.11. Journey of Lord 2 Flower into the Mixteca on the Lienzo of Tlapiltepec. *Detail*: Lord 2 Flower in Atonal's lineage, on the Lienzo of Coixtlahuaca II. Lord 2 Flower wears the Toltec nose plug, a diadem, and a warrior's hairdo. The signs behind and above his wife 4 Flint can be read as: "day 7 Flint of the year 8 Rabbit there was war, the sharp bone [for piercing the nose] was used to bestow on him the two nose plugs." Courtesy of Ethnologisches Museum Berlin.

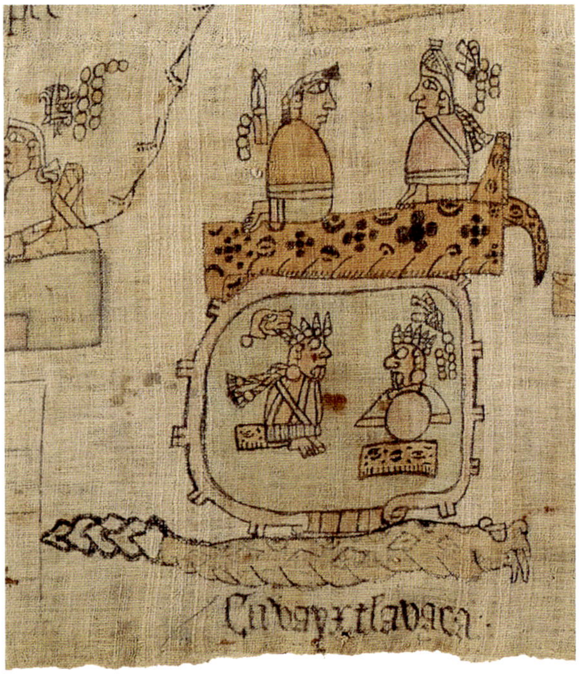

FIG. 2.12. Sacred bundle of 9 Wind in Coixtlahuaca on the Lienzo of Ihuitlán. Inside a cave on top of the Coixtlahuaca topograph, the sacred bundle of Quetzalcoatl—adorned with a mask—sits on a base covered with jaguar skin. Facing the bundle sits a guardian priest named 1 Lizard with earth spirit characteristics. On top of the cave sit the founders of the city of Coixtlahuaca, descendants of Atonal I. Courtesy of the Brooklyn Museum, Carll H. de Silver Fund, 42.160.

KEEPERS OF THE SACRED BUNDLE OF QUETZALCOATL

Descent from Toltec ancestry was not the only claim that lent prestige to the house of the later Atonal of the fifteenth century. The lineage also boasted of relations with early Postclassic Cholula in the religious sphere. Specifically, as seen in the pictorial documents, the house of Atonal was the keeper of the sacred bundle of 9 Wind, Quetzalcoatl (fig. 2.12).[32] This powerful bundle contained relics of Quetzalcoatl, perhaps a piece of the flint knife he was born from. It connected the Atonal lineage directly with one of the major gods of creation, venerated at Cholula, and infused the lineage with great prestige. The story of the arrival of this bundle finds a parallel in the Mixtec codices,[33] where it is the ruling house of the Mixtec capital of Tilantongo that receives the bundle of Quetzalcoatl (fig. 2.13). In the Mixtec codices, the event is situated at the very beginning of history, around the middle of the tenth century. Both the Mixtec codices and the Coixtlahuaca lienzos are vague about the links between the legendary priests responsible for the introduction of the sacred bundle and the first members of the ruling lineage. The bundle origin stories were more mythical in nature than the historical register of the ruling houses, which made it difficult to integrate both stories in one coherent narrative.

The Coixtlahuaca pictorials tell of the mythical journey of a group of people characterized by black eyes, a graphic convention meaning "Toltec," and bearing Toltec names.[34] They had emerged from Chicomoztoc, "Place of Seven Caves," the mythical cave of creation of the Teochichimecs and Toltecs (fig. 2.14). However, they seem distinct from Atonal I and his people and were not directly associated with him. Yet, their early arrival in the valley seems to have paved the way for Atonal I. They were the carriers of the sacred bundle of Quetzalcoatl. After traveling though primordial locations, they entered the human dimension near a place called Comoztoc, "At the Cave of the Pot," the rocky face of a canyon in what is today called La Huerta de Juquila or Jiquila in the northeastern extreme of the Coixtlahuaca area (fig. 2.15) where the Mixteca Alta descends into the Nahuatl-speaking Cañada.[35] Here they performed the ritual drilling of New Fire, the symbolic foundation act, and placed the bundle of Quetzalcoatl in his temple. His temple was represented by an enormous *coatepec*, or serpent mountain, the conceptual temple pyramid at the world axis, where primordial time and human time merged.[36] After the bundle was placed, a warrior with magical powers named 7 Death took possession of the Coixtlahuaca Valley through a series of ritual conquests. Several documents depict him traveling through a cloud serpent that emerged from Comoztoc. In some instances—such as the Lienzo of Tlapiltepec—he himself appears transformed into a fire serpent, the most powerful *nahual*, or supernatural double, of the Mesoamerican universe. These foundation rituals, also paralleled in the Mixtec codices, brought the political geography into existence and

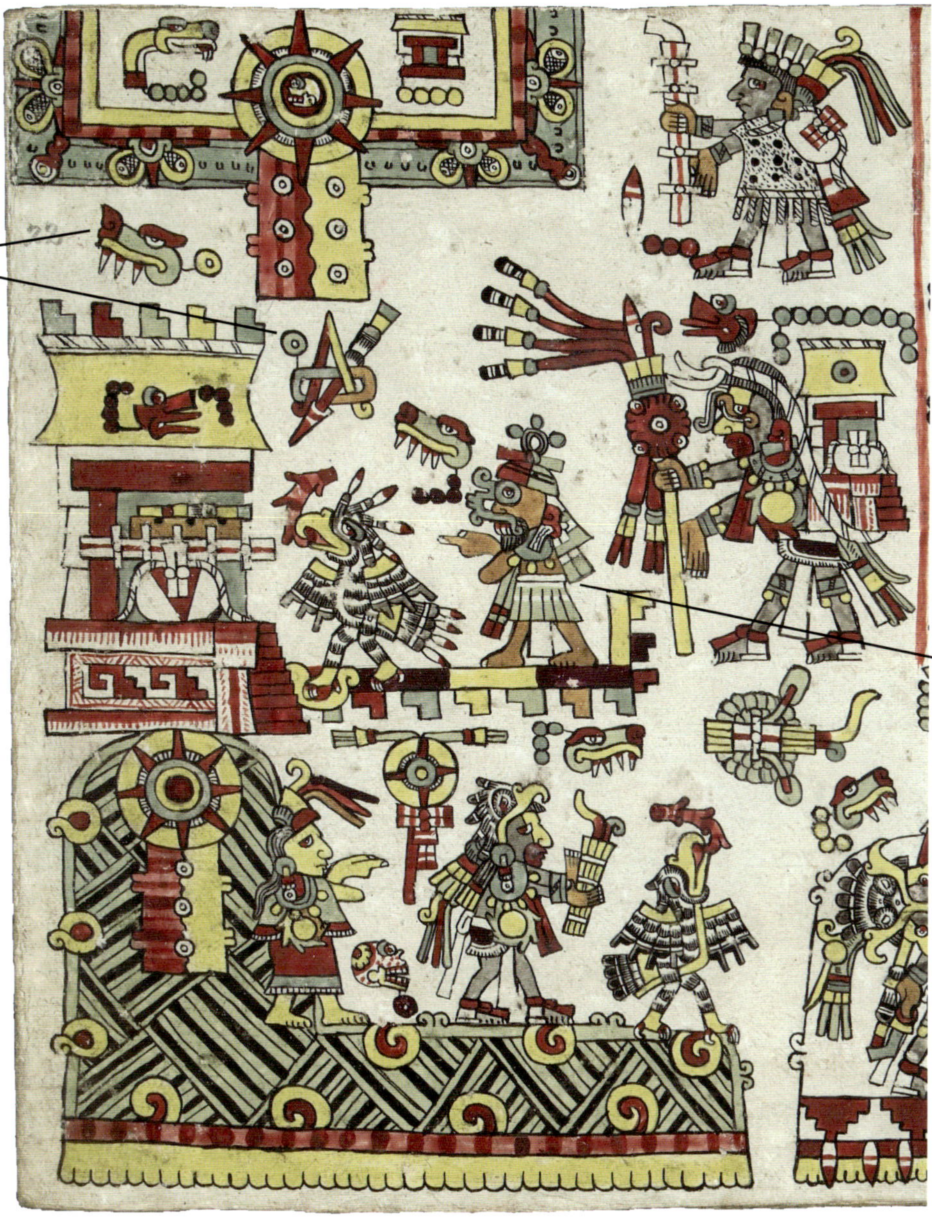

FIG. 2.13. Arrival of the sacred bundle of Quetzalcoatl at Tilantongo (detail Codex Zouche-Nuttall, p. 21). In the lower part of the scene, Lord 4 Alligator "Blood Eagle" and Lady 1 Death "Sun Fan" receive the priest 12 Wind, who enters from the middle right, at the "Mountain of Dawn." The priest arrives "carrying" the religious cult of 9 Wind "Quetzalcoatl." At first dawn and at the beginning of time, Lord 4 Alligator, center—now with the characteristics of the earth spirits—enters the temple where the bundle of 9 Wind "Quetzalcoatl" is deposited. Courtesy of The British Museum.

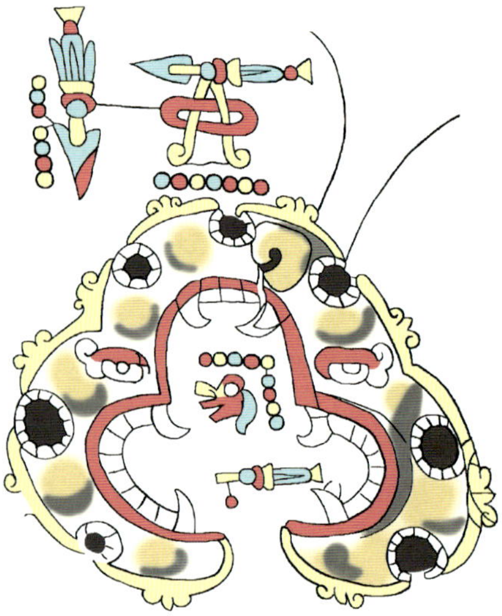

FIG. 2.14. Chicomoztoc, detail from the Lienzo of Tlapiltepec.

propelled the count of human "historical" time. In the impressive Lienzo of Coixtlahuaca II, the largest document of the group, the drilling of New Fire is represented at the center of a circle formed by the founding couples of the regional polities. One of the figures among the couples is Lord 7 Water, or Atonal I (fig. 2.16).

Some of the documents suggest the founders who carried the bundle came in groups of four. In the Lienzo of Tlapiltepec, four men perform the New Fire ceremony near Comoztoc (two are depicted, the other two are only mentioned by name). Four similar men, but with different names, reached Ihuitlán territory (see fig. 2.1) and another four founders are shown in the Codex Baranda (of unknown provenience) (fig. 2.17). Centuries later, people related to the bundle-carrying founders still lived in the area, but their relation to the house of Atonal is not clear. One of their lineages lived in Tequixtepec, where a member of the line painted the Lienzo of Tequixtepec II.[37]

FIG. 2.15. Coatepec, as represented on the Selden Roll. *Left*, the four founders rise up from an underground passage or cave. Priest 10 House carries the Quetzalcoatl bundle. *Center*, the large topograph of Coatepec, "Serpent Hill," on which the sacred bundle of Quetzalcoatl is deposited. *Right*, the warrior 7 Death on a cloud serpent departs to conquer the earth from Comoztoc, "Rock of the Pot." Courtesy of The Bodleian Library, The University of Oxford, MS. Arch. Selden A. See fig. 2.16 for a more naturalistic representation of Comoztoc in the Lienzo of Coixtlahuaca II.

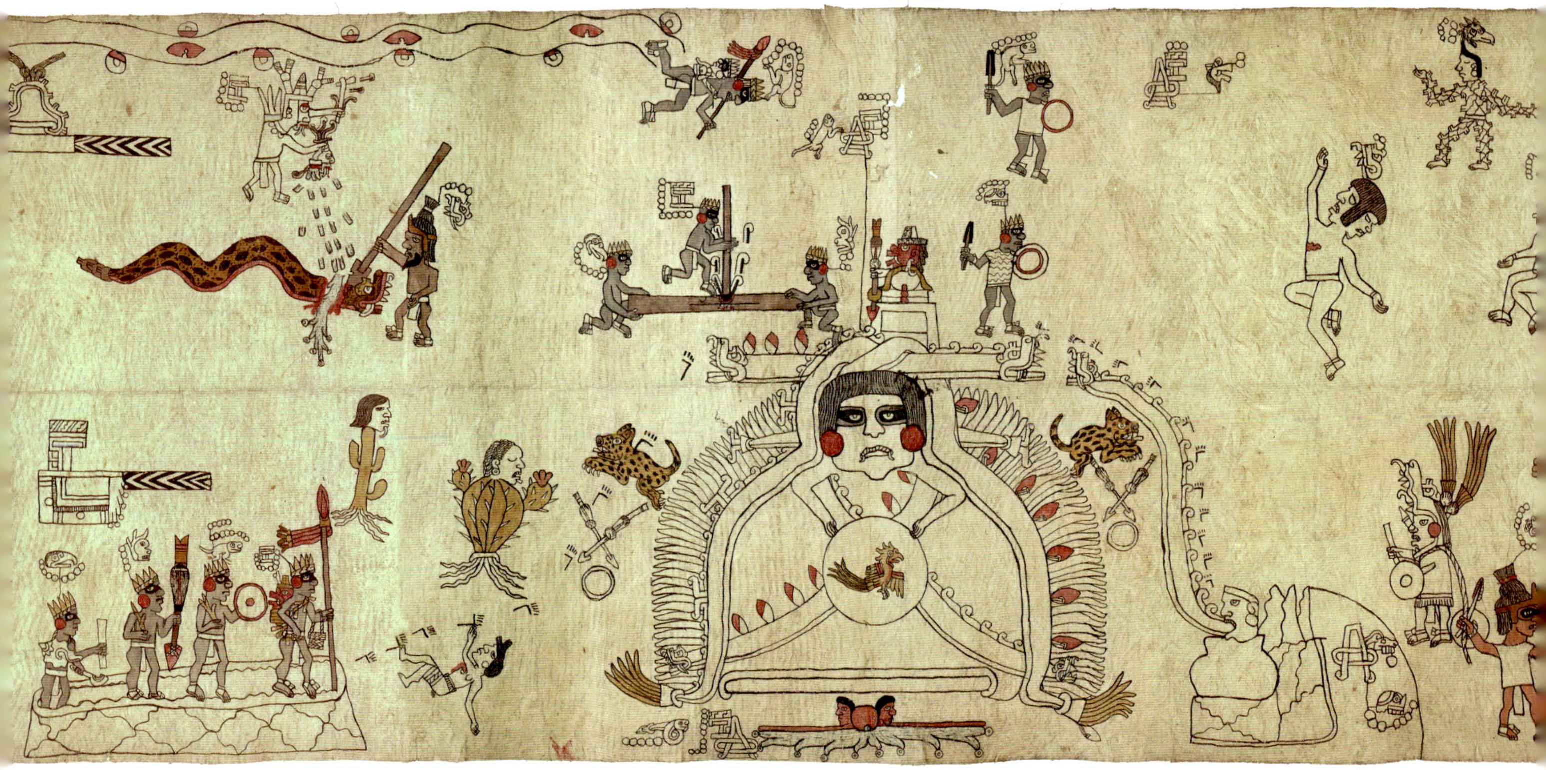

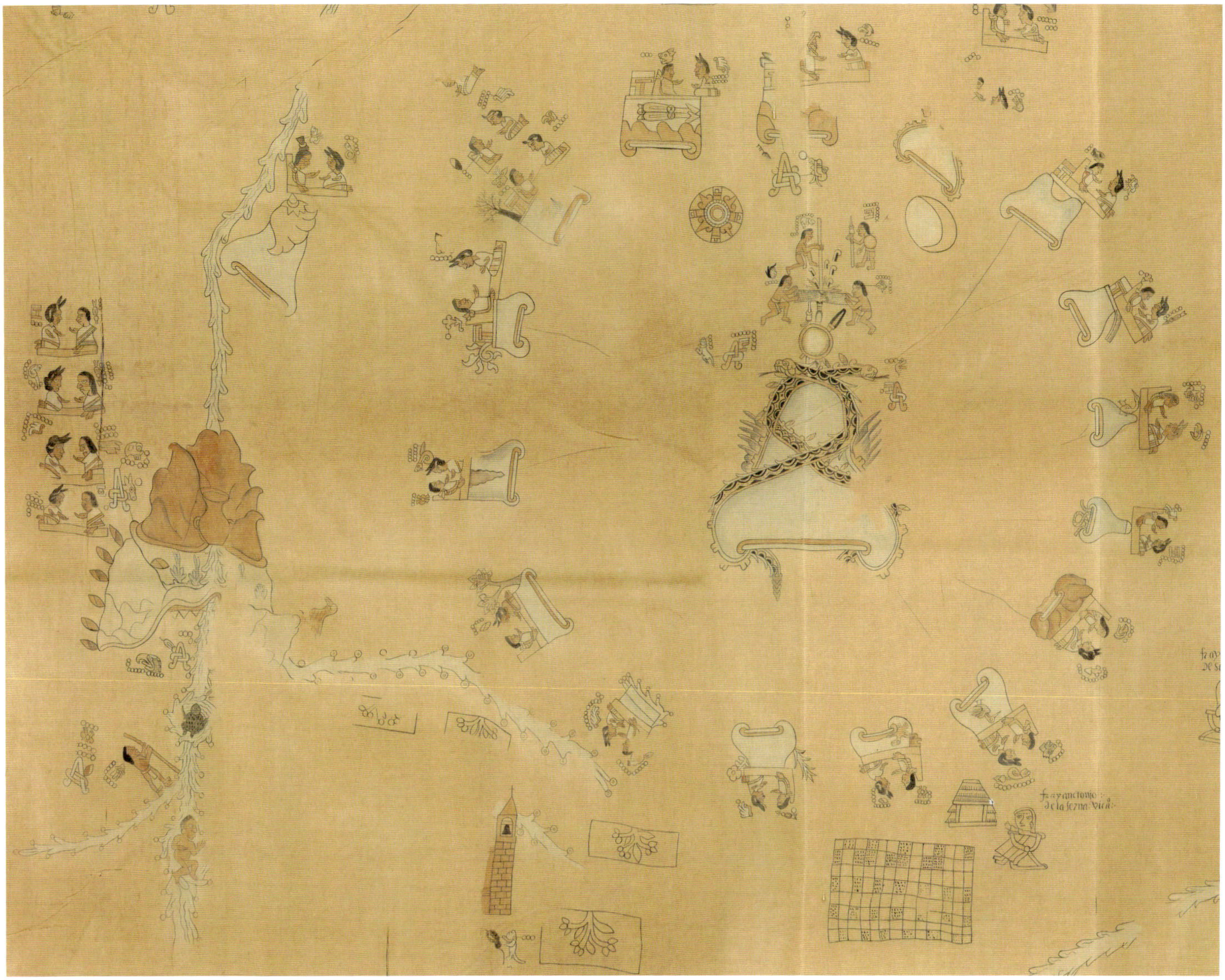

FIG. 2.16, ABOVE. Detail, New Fire ceremony at Coatepec, from Wilhelm von den Steinen's copy of Lienzo of Coixtlahuaca II, made for Seler in 1899, shows sixteen royal houses around Coatepec. *Top center*, the house of Atonal. *Left*, Comoztoc, "Rock of the Pot," on the Jiquila River. Courtesy of the Division of Anthropology, American Museum of Natural History, cat. no. MCAA/0975.

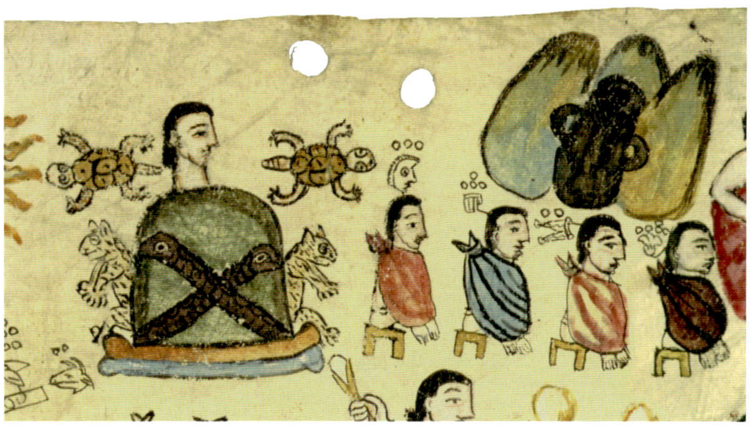

FIG. 2.17. A group of four founders near Comoztoc, "Rock of the Pot," and Coatepec, detail of Codex Baranda. Reproduction authorized by the Instituto Nacional de Antropología e Historia, Mexico.

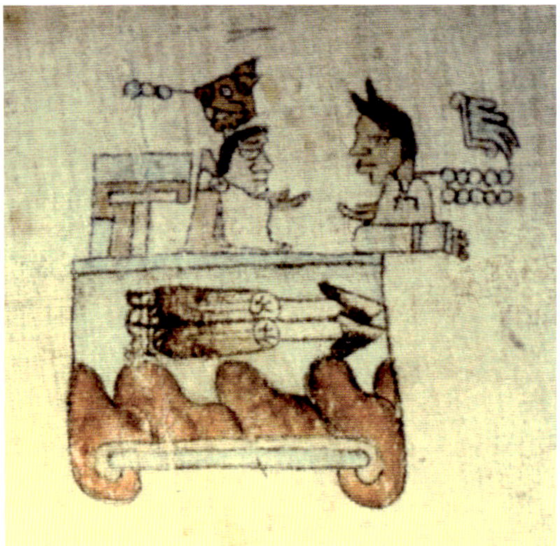

FIG. 2.18. "Mountain of the Arrows" on Lienzo of Coixtlahuaca II. Courtesy of Ethnologisches Museum Berlin.

FIG. 2.19, FACING TOP. Foundation rituals in Tula on Lienzo of Coixtlahuaca II. Detail of drawing by Wilhelm von den Steinen. Courtesy of the Division of Anthropology, American Museum of Natural History, cat. no. MCAA/0975.

FIG. 2.20, FACING BOTTOM. Founding of the city of Coixtlahuaca on Lienzo of Coixtlahuaca II. Detail of drawing by Wilhelm von den Steinen. Courtesy of the Division of Anthropology, American Museum of Natural History, cat. no. MCAA/0975.

THE FOUNDATION OF COIXTLAHUACA

As discussed above, the Mixteca was organized by two overlapping types of government: the community and the cacicazgo. Lord 6 Water (Atonal) and Lord 6 Monkey headed the two principal ruling houses of Coixtlahuaca during the Aztec conquest. The house of Lord 6 Monkey was founded by a man called 3 Jaguar at a still-unknown location called "Mountain of the Arrows" (fig. 2.18).[38] According to the Lienzo of Coixtlahuaca II, the grandson of 3 Jaguar participated with 2 Flower, Atonal's grandson, in the military service to Cholula and Tilantongo, though he was not awarded the Toltec regalia. However, we cannot be sure how politically important the 6 Monkey lineage really was: its inclusion in the pictorial documents may be due to its rise to dominance only after the death of Atonal. The palace of 6 Monkey became the site for the construction of the Dominican monastery around the mid-sixteenth century, while Atonal's palace compound, on the opposite side of the river, may have been demolished to furnish construction materials for the monastery.[39]

Around AD 1200 the descendants of Atonal I and of 3 Jaguar joined forces and founded the city of Coixtlahuaca, an act that involved a series of rituals at the altar of Tula (today Tulancingo), a sacred site with Toltec connotations (fig. 2.19).[40] Both lineages ruled the new city: The descendants of Atonal I ruled at "Stone/Mountain of the Heart" and, later, after the return of Lord 10 Serpent mentioned above, at Telyahualiuhcan, "Round Stone." The descendants of Lord 3 Jaguar ruled at "Stone of Tail and Footsteps"[41] and later at Eztepec (probably the site of modern Coixtlahuaca) (fig. 2.20). These places seem to have been parcialidades of Coixtlahuaca, but their precise geographical location remains a problem. The two ruling houses kept their own historical records, possibly spoke their own languages, and probably practiced their own cults.

Shortly after the foundation of the city, the Coixtlahuaca lords incorporated most of the Coixtlahuaca Valley into their realm through marriage and conquest. The house of Atonal founded secondary lineages in Ihuitlán and Tequixtepec that can be traced on their respective lienzos (Ihuitlán on the Lienzo of Ihuitlán and Lienzo of Tulancingo; Tequixtepec on the Lienzo of Tequixtepec I). The house of 3 Jaguar controlled the southern part of the valley, as seen in the Lienzo of Nativitas and the Lienzo of Otla.

THE EXPANSION OF THE COIXTLAHUACA LINEAGES INTO CUAUHTINCHAN AND TEPEXI

During the fourteenth century—and surely even earlier—the city-state of Coixtlahuaca expanded its influence north into the regions of Cuauhtinchan and Tepexi, towns in what is today the southern part of the state of Puebla. This northern consolidation culminated in AD 1398 with a takeover of power in the southern half of the Cuauhtinchan city-state (map 2.2). The increasing influence of Coixtlahuaca was expressed through the construction of strategically planned marriage alliances with cacicazgos in southern Puebla—often achieved in compensation for military support

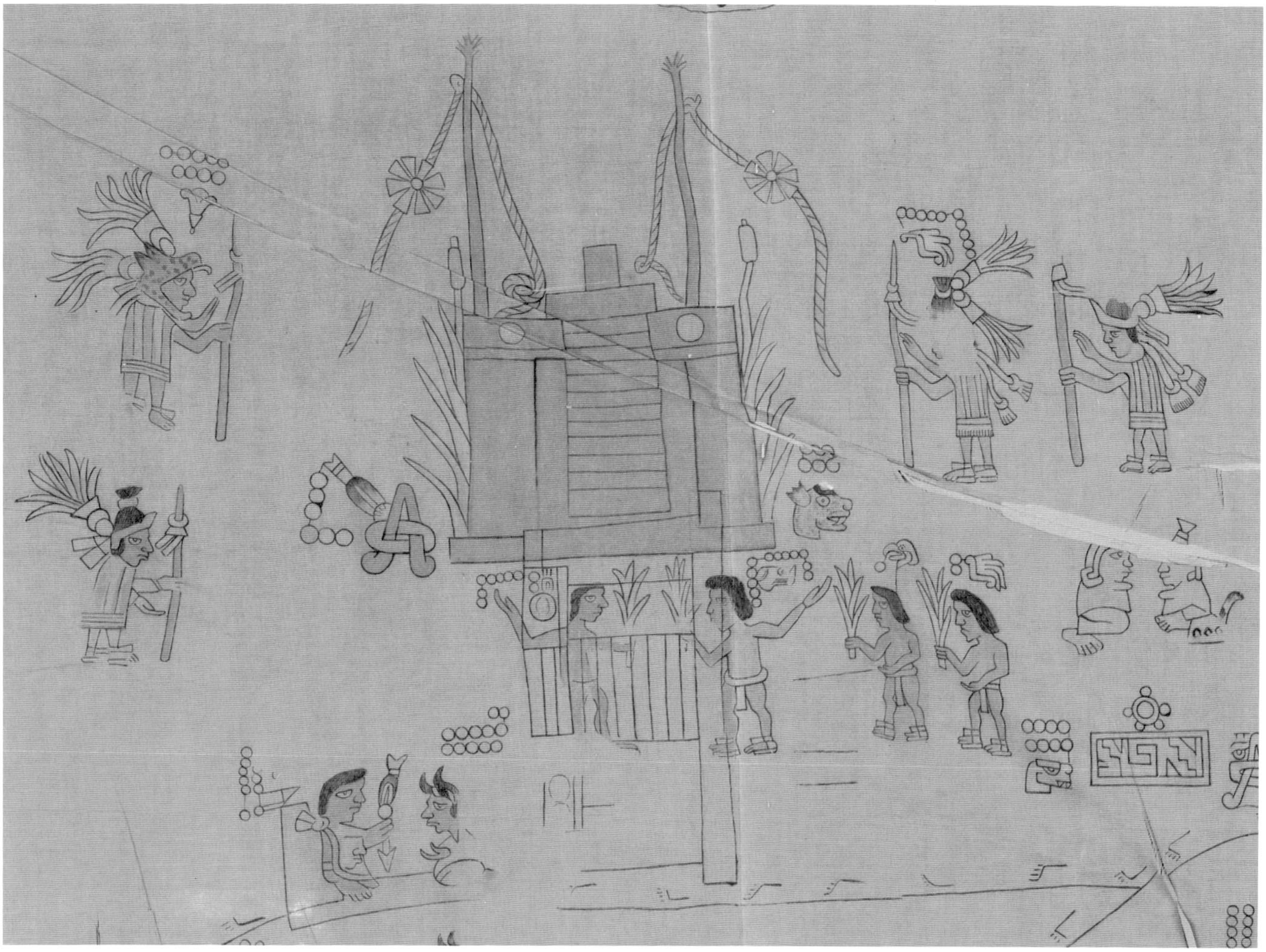

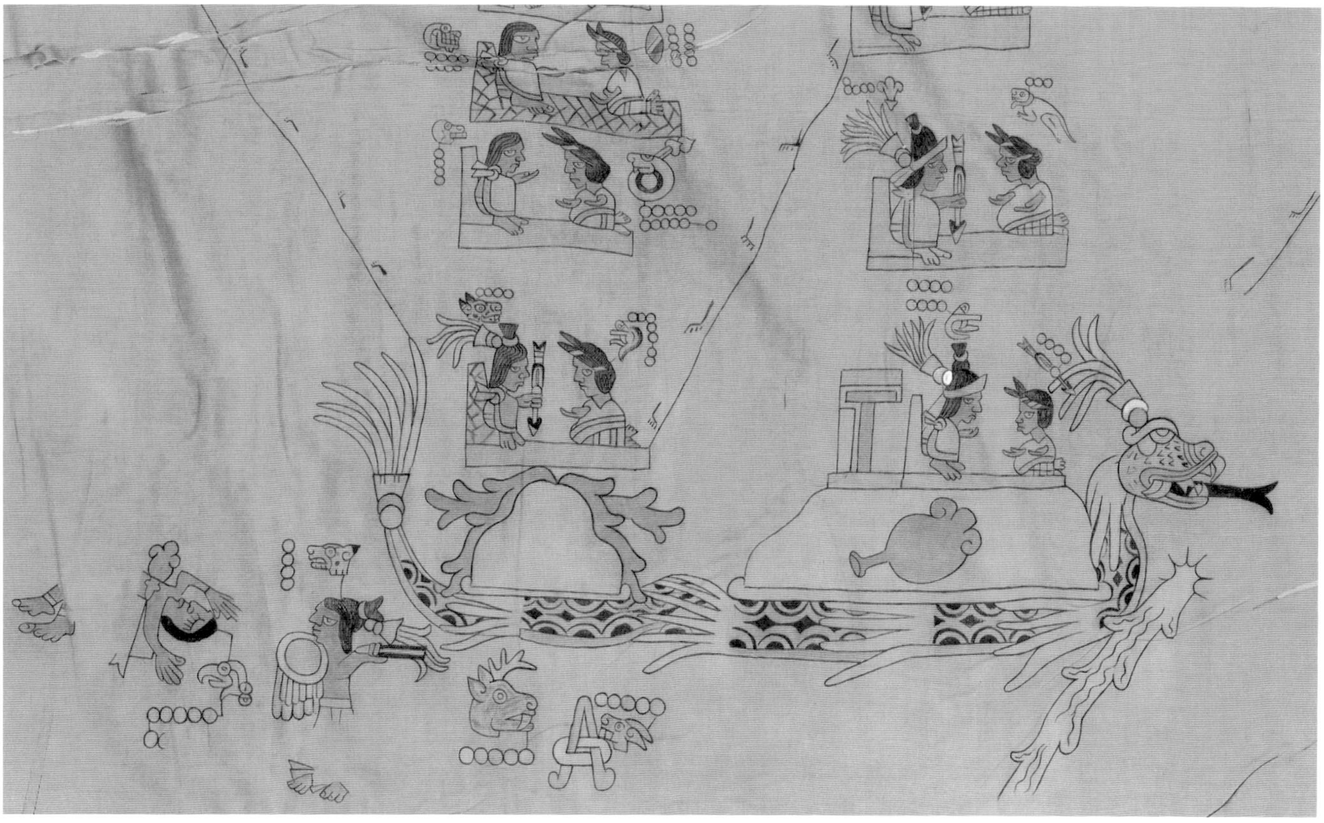

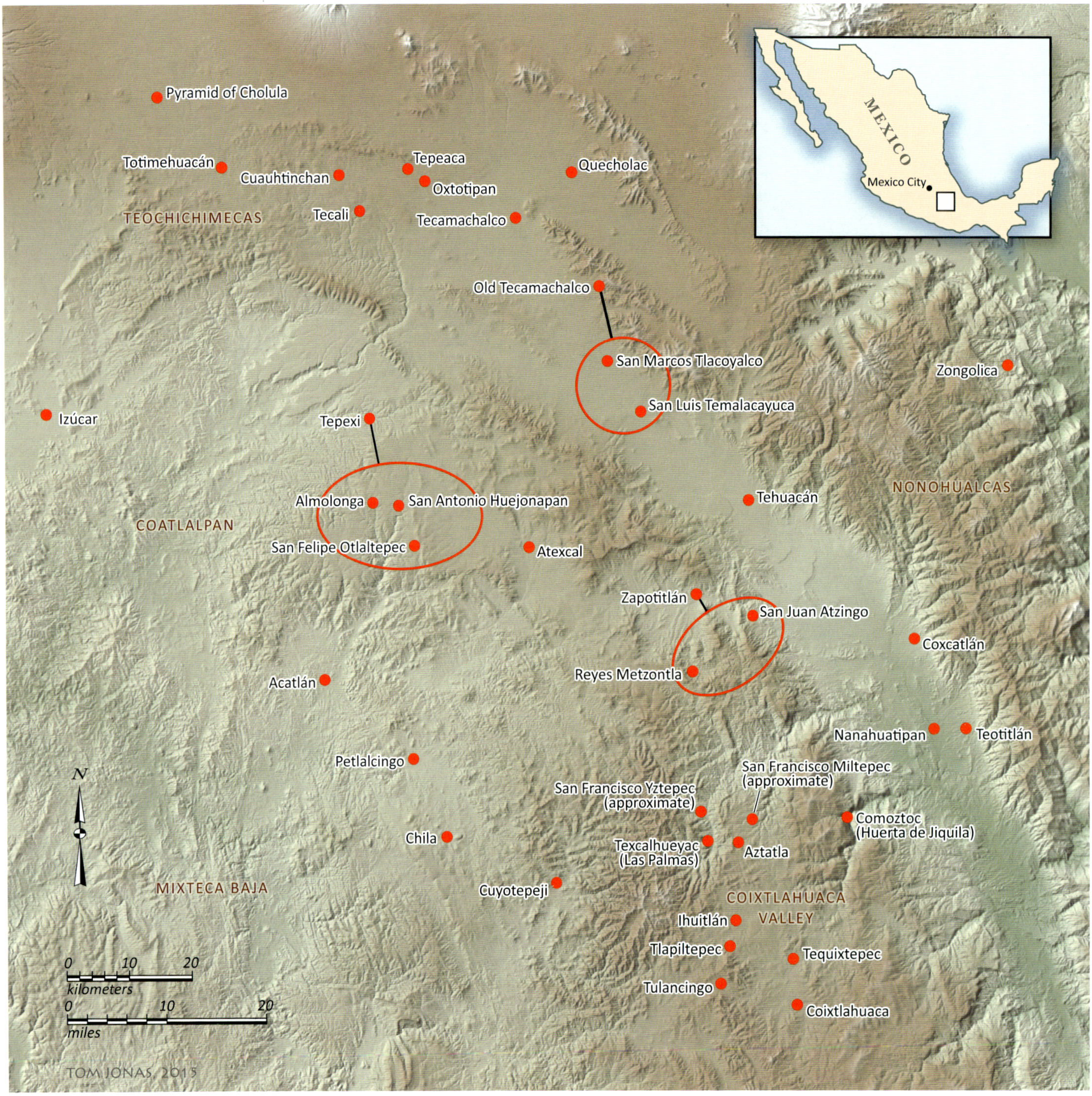

MAP 2.2. Chocho (Ngiwa) migrations into southern Puebla starting in the twelfth century. The three areas where Popoloca is spoken today are circled and connected by a line to their respective Popoloca head towns. © 2015, University of Oklahoma Press.

to the lords in the area—and later with the ruling families of Tlatelolco and Tenochtitlan in central Mexico.[42] The Nahuatl language sources call the incoming people from Coixtlahuaca the Pinome.[43] Pinome rule was defeated by a coalition of Teochichimec forces in AD 1441, when their capital Cuauhtepec (near modern-day Tecamachalco) was destroyed, but their nobles would continue to play a role in the area. In 1451, they controlled the area anew and founded Tecamachalco and Quecholac. Descendants of Coixtlahuaca lineages also gained prominence in neighboring Tepexi.

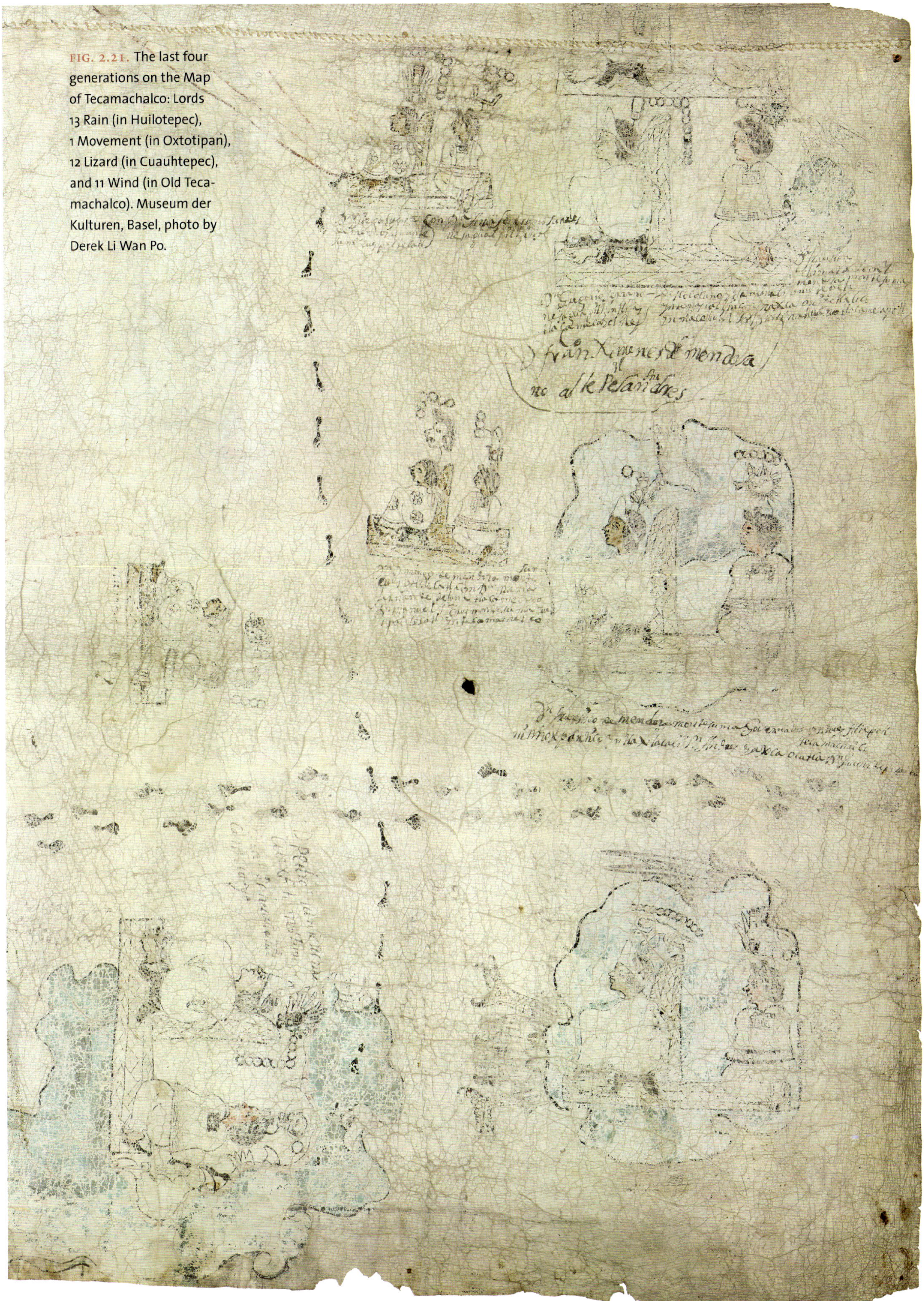

FIG. 2.21. The last four generations on the Map of Tecamachalco: Lords 13 Rain (in Huilotepec), 1 Movement (in Oxtotipan), 12 Lizard (in Cuauhtepec), and 11 Wind (in Old Tecamachalco). Museum der Kulturen, Basel, photo by Derek Li Wan Po.

FIG. 2.22. *Bottom*, Lord 3 Flint and his wife in the Tepexi genealogy on the Map of Tecamachalco. *Middle*, Lord 9 Monkey and Lady 13 Rabbit, descendants of Lord 3 Flint, were painted over on purpose, but because the later paint is flaking, the original can be seen again, as illustrated on the line drawing below. Museum der Kulturen, Basel, photo by Derek Li Wan Po.

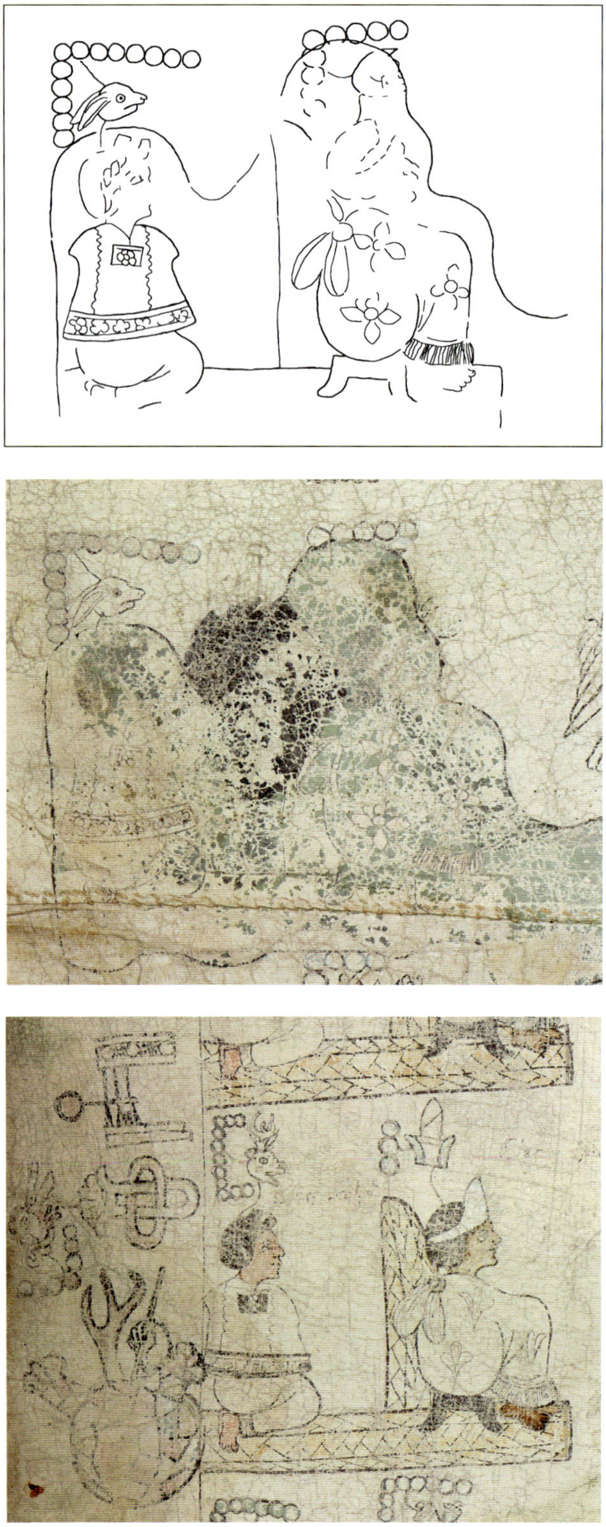

The arrival and the success of these Coixtlahuaca lineages can be traced in the Puebla area sources, most notably the Map of Tecamachalco (Museum der Kulturen, Basel). This map contains a complex series of layers added at different times, which makes interpretation difficult, but the oldest painting on it represents two lineages. The first is a long genealogical register that starts in Aztatla, a village in the northern part of the Coixtlahuaca area. The last four ruling couples, however, starting with Lord 13 Rain, have moved to localities in Tecamachalco (fig. 2.21). Their migration is also documented in the *Historia tolteca-chichimeca*: "And in this year it was that the Mixteca-Popolloca arrived: Matlactliomey Quiyauitl [13 Rain] and Tecpatzin [Flint], who had departed from Couayxtlauacan, Tlacpacalco, Aztacalco: the Colomochcatl [a Teochichimec lord] went to make them [Lord 13 Rain and Lord Flint] move when he had gone there [Coixtlahuaca]."[44] Though Lord 13 Rain probably arrived in Tecamachalco in the second half of the fourteenth century, the *Historia tolteca-chichimeca* projects their arrival far into the past (to be precise, in AD 1182). It is possible that Coixtlahuaca lords had offered military assistance on the earlier date, when the newly arrived Teochichimec lords of Cuauhtinchan subdued the native population.[45] The second lineage in the Map of Tecamachalco, which may have reached Tepexi, is shorter and ends with a Lord 9 Monkey (fig. 2.22).[46]

Both migrating lineages are also represented in the Lienzo of Tlapiltepec and the Lienzo of Coixtlahuaca II (fig. 2.23). In these documents, the painters represented in detail the Teochichimec lords' request for military support at the time of the foundation of Coixtlahuaca (around AD 1200), roughly coinciding with the 1182 date. Then, without temporal precision, but apparently jumping to the mid- or late fourteenth century, Lord 8 Movement (the son of 13 Rain) and Lord 9 Monkey are depicted in the southern Puebla area as founders of successful lineages. Still later pictorials, such as the Map of Ecatepec-Huitziltepec (private collection, Paris), follow the later descendants of Lord 13 Rain in the Tecamachalco area until 1593. Linguistically and archaeologically, it seems plausible that the current Popoloca-speaking population in southern Puebla, mainly concentrated in the former city-states of Tecamachalco and Tepexi, are the descendants of the farmers and artisans brought in by the lineages migrating from Coixtlahuaca.[47]

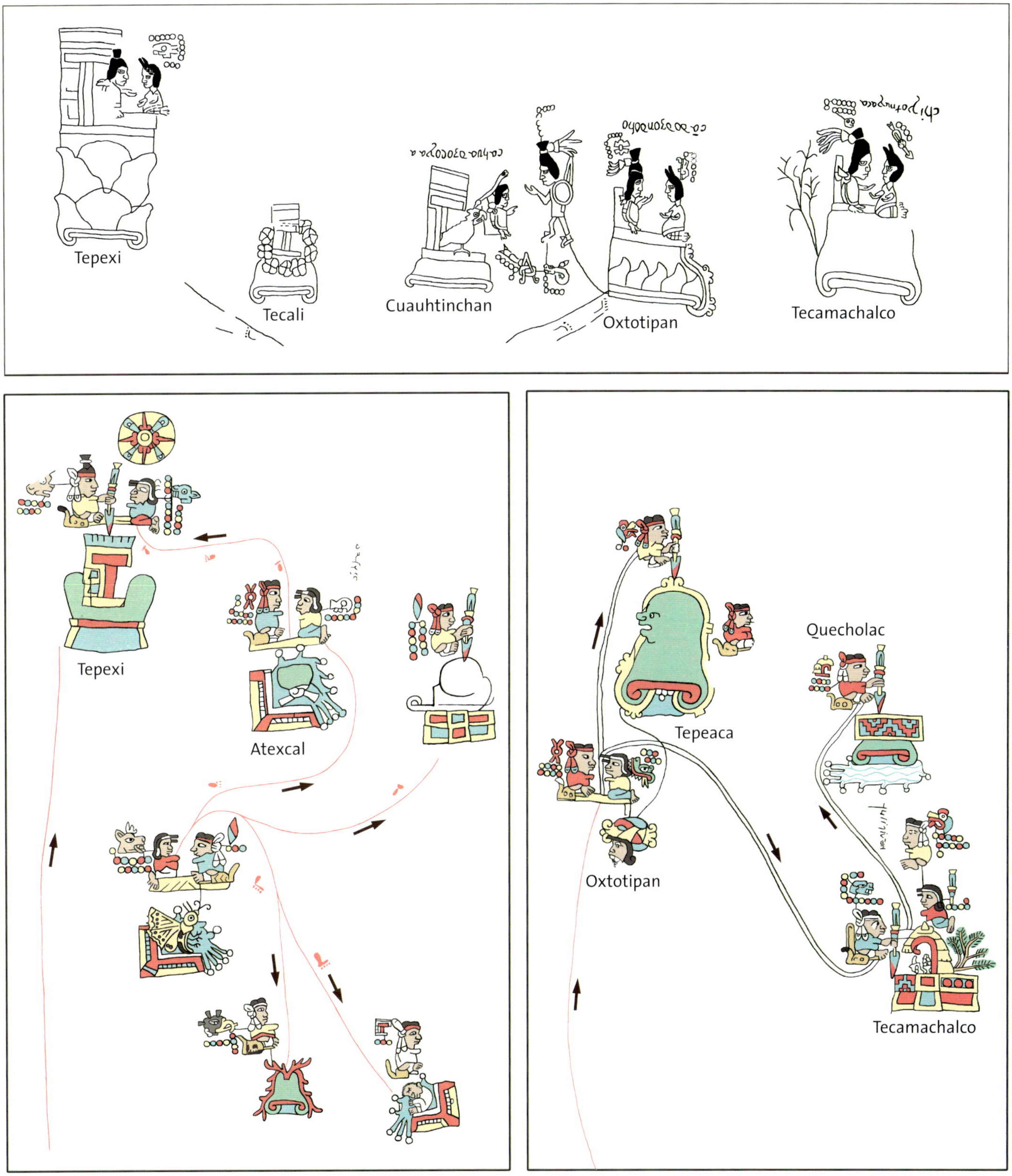

FIG. 2.23. *Top*, detail, Lienzo of Coixtlahuaca II, shows destinations of migrations into southern Puebla. Lord [9 Monkey] and his wife 13 Rabbit at Tepexi. She was a descendant of 3 Flint. *Bottom*, details, Lienzo of Tlapiltepec, also show destinations of migrations into southern Puebla.

LORD 11 VULTURE (COZCACUAUHTLI)

Aztec sources contain a second story, besides the ones about the conquest of Coixtlahuaca, relevant to our interpretation of the lienzo. This story, dating from when Coixtlahuaca was already an Aztec province, tells how Lord Vulture (Cozcacuauhtli in Nahuatl) was made ruler of Coixtlahuaca by the Aztecs after the rebellion of Sosola, which took place during the first decade of the sixteenth century. According to a well-known version of this story,[48] during the reign of Moctezuma II, a group of important Mixtec and Zapotec lords planned a rebellion against the Aztecs. The leaders were Cetecpatl (1 Flint) from Coixtlahuaca and Nahuixochitl (4 Flower) from Sosola. In accordance with the plan, Cetecpatl had organized a banquet for the lords of the Mixteca Alta, including the Aztecs of the garrisons in the area. Nahuixochitl had prepared an ambush in the narrow canyon of Sosola and killed most of the Aztecs on their way back from the banquet. The response was swift, but the armies of the Triple Alliance could not subdue the Mixtec defense.

During their second attempt, the Aztecs took a detour to reach Huauhtlan, where they found Vulture (Cozcacuauhtli), the brother of 1 Flint. Choosing to side with the central Mexican armies, he offered them his knowledge of the situation. When the Aztecs attacked again in Sosola, 4 Flower was in Tututepec asking for military assistance. Without their captain, his army in Sosola was forced to retreat to a mountain. By the time 4 Flower arrived with the Tututepec troops, it was too late. He was defeated and the Aztecs took 1 Flint prisoner, together with many men from Tututepec, Tehuantepec, and Yopitzingo. Four Flower escaped but was captured later. In reward for his aid, and his treason against his own brother, Vulture was installed as ruler of Coixtlahuaca. This famous war against Sosola is mentioned and represented—without the Coixtlahuaca connection—in several manuscripts from central Mexico as having occurred around 1506.[49]

However, it should be no surprise that the local version is quite different from the Aztec one. For example, 1 Flint is never mentioned in the Coixtlahuaca pictorials. But a Lord 11 Vulture, possibly the same person as Cozcacuauhtli from the Nahuatl sources, is depicted as the ruler of Coixtlahuaca two generations after the second Atonal (fig. 2.24, lower section). Lord 11 Vulture is depicted in the Lienzo of Coixtlahuaca I and Lienzo A receiving an Aztec emissary of war in the year 1503 (fig. 2.24, upper section). This meeting may have been related to the aforementioned relation between Cozcacuauhtli and the Aztecs. The 1503 meeting date would fit well with the date of the death, two generations earlier, of Atonal in AD 1462. In the Lienzo of Ihuitlán and the Lienzo of Coixtlahuaca II, Lord 11 Vulture is shown as a warrior, while his predecessor and descendant are not, suggesting he accomplished some important military feat, which may have been precisely the unconventional way he acceded to power.

HISTORICAL EVENTS CLOSE TO THE TIME OF CONQUEST

In the Lienzo of Tlapiltepec, 11 Vulture and his wife 3 Serpent are the last rulers depicted in the main genealogy. Being the last ones depicted, one would consider them the commissioners of the lienzo and patrons of the artist (Doesburg 2001:18). In this same scenario, the document would represent the claim of this patron-couple to the depicted community or cacicazgo.[50] Because of his unconventional accession to power, Lord 11 Vulture may have felt the need to make a strong claim to the political landscape of

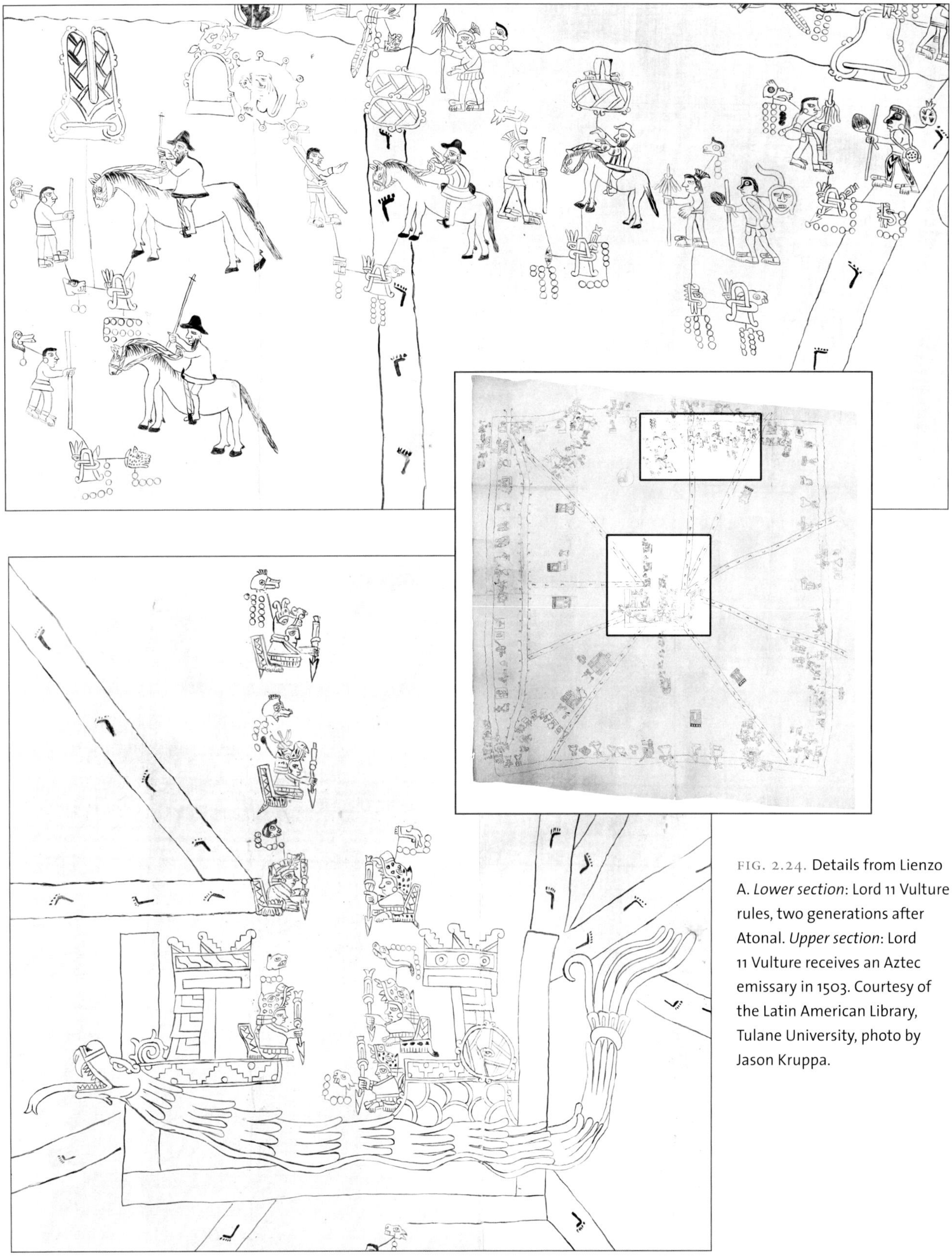

FIG. 2.24. Details from Lienzo A. *Lower section*: Lord 11 Vulture rules, two generations after Atonal. *Upper section*: Lord 11 Vulture receives an Aztec emissary in 1503. Courtesy of the Latin American Library, Tulane University, photo by Jason Kruppa.

Coixtlahuaca. However, a chronological problem arises: churches included here and there and three animal enclosures near Ihuitlán show that the lienzo must postdate the first decades of the colonial era.[51] The document depicts the monastery church of Coixtlahuaca and what appears to be the adjacent open chapel with what looks like its domed vault. The construction of this compound was started around 1544.[52] Other churches are depicted in Ihuitlán, "Valley of Feathers," and near Suchixtlahuaca. This last village and several others were "congregated" (resettled in a nucleated fashion) in 1556 or 1557 by the Spanish judge Luis Daza, which may have prompted the building of the churches.[53]

Chapels (so-called *visitas*, where friars of the Coixtlahuaca monastery said mass) are depicted in Texcalhueyac, "Large Rock," today called Las Palmas; Aztatla, "Stone of the Heron"; an unidentified place, "Hill of Maguey Stalk or Grass,"[54] near Tlapiltepec; and another unidentified place north of Tamazulapan. The images of these buildings on the Lienzo of Tlapiltepec seem to be highly generic: Ihuitlán features a square stone-walled church with a flat roof, a small gable with a cross, and a buttress with a bell tower to the back. This cannot have represented the real situation, since in the sixteenth-century archival documents from Ihuitlán, it is said that the chapel of Ihuitlán, prior to 1593, was just a simple shed with a thatch roof (see Appendix A, documents 11 and 15). In fact, both the Suchixtlahuaca and Coixtlahuaca churches on the lienzo are identical to the Ihuitlán church, confirming that the painter employed a generic image for all three. However, the addition of what may be a representation of the open chapel of Coixtlahuaca suggests the painting was done after 1545. This also accords with the representation of livestock in the area, since this enterprise was introduced around the same date.

If the lienzo postdates 1545 and Lord 11 Vulture was still alive, he must have been at least sixty years old (recalling that he received the Aztec war emissary in 1503, when he was probably at least eighteen years old). In support of this possibility, it should be noted that the Lienzo of Coixtlahuaca I and Lienzo A (made after 1552; see Doesburg 2004) also end with Lord 11 Vulture, in those cases more than sixty-seven years old.

Archival documents from the area, however, do not mention the existence of an old lord in Coixtlahuaca around these years. In fact, what we know of the early colonial lords is that sometime before 1535, the brothers Don Francisco and Don Diego were installed as tutors of Don Domingo, the young heir. In one letter from about 1543, the young Domingo is introduced as follows: "at the time his father expired from this present life, he stayed behind at the age of four or five, more or less. And because he was not of age, the said town had been governed by a Don Francisco, now deceased, and another who is named Don Diego, who is [currently] in the said town."[55] This situation is confirmed by several other documents.[56]

In other letters, young Domingo gives some additional but also enigmatic information. In one document from 1544 he presents his party as: "Don Domingo, cacique and minor of Coixtlahuaca, twenty-five years of age, and the council and justice of Coixtlahuaca as a town that has no cacique, nor principales, because all were sent to the mines by Your Majesty."[57] While this suggests a birthdate around 1519, a closer look suggests another reading. In his letter, Don Domingo invokes an important Spanish legal principle, which allowed a person under twenty-five (a minor) to ask for "restitución," that is, the cancelation of any disadvantageous contract relating to his inherited estate entered into by his curator.[58] The quote above should be understood as:

"Don Domingo, cacique of Coixtlahuaca and under twenty-five years of age." Indeed, in 1545 Domingo states: "[It is] fifteen years and more that the town of Coixtlahuaca has had no natural lord ("señor natural") and he who currently is, Don Domingo, is under twenty-five years of age." After writing this, the word "five" was crossed out, apparently to reveal his real age.[59] From this and other pieces of information we now know that Don Domingo was most likely born around 1524.[60] Because his sons Pedro and Juan were born around 1546, he may have married in 1545. He died young in 1552. His tutor and curator Don Francisco died in 1543, but his other tutor and curator, Don Diego, stayed active in town until at least 1562. While Don Domingo stated that Coixtlahuaca had been without a lord for fifteen years—possibly referring to his father's death—his own witnesses in the same year (1545) declared that Coixtlahuaca had been without a lord for two or four years (depending on the witness), probably referring to the death of Don Francisco.[61]

One hypothetical scenario has the tutors as the uncles of Domingo and has Don Francisco, the elder of the two, as the temporary successor of Domingo's father. Such a scheme has been documented for the contemporaneous case of Yanhuitlán (Jansen 2011:382, 469–74). In this scenario, the only candidate to be eventually identified with Lord 11 Vulture is Domingo's father, who may have died around 1529.[62] The Lienzo of Tlapiltepec may have been produced during the reign of Don Domingo and his tutor-curator Don Diego. If this was the case, then the unavoidable question is: why didn't Don Domingo (or Don Diego) include himself at the end of the main genealogy? At present, I believe no satisfactory explanation can be given.[63]

IHUITLÁN AND TLAPILTEPEC IN THE LIENZOS

At this point, we may want to focus on the role of Tlapiltepec within the Coixtlahuaca Valley. Because Tlapiltepec was a political subject of Ihuitlán during the colonial period, the two extant lienzos from Ihuitlán—in particular the Lienzo of Ihuitlán—acquire special importance in our analysis of Tlapiltepec's history. The Lienzo of Ihuitlán contains information about the incorporation of Tlapiltepec into the Ihuitlán polity during pre-Hispanic times. It shows how Tlapiltepec was first controlled through the marriage of Lord 2 Rabbit, one of the children of the Ihuitlán royal line, at Tlapiltepec around AD 1225 (see fig. 2.2).[64] Some eight generations later, sometime around AD 1420, Tlapiltepec was conquered again by Lord 3 Rain, a descendant of a second Ihuitlán line, apparently by order of 10 Serpent of Coixtlahuaca, the father of Atonal.[65] This conquest of Tlapiltepec may have been part of the recovery campaign of 10 Serpent mentioned above. Not surprisingly, this conquest is shown prominently on the locally oriented Lienzo of Ihuitlán. Lord 3 Rain's "warpath" starts at Coixtlahuaca and ends at a jaguar-spotted throne at "Mountain of the Tree" (Tlapiltepec, according to the gloss).[66] The conqueror, thrusting his spear into the throne (that is, taking possession), is dressed in a combination of priestly and warrior attire, which perhaps suggests that the Tlapiltepec lords had some special religious status. Indeed, inside the sign of Tlapiltepec, the relics of Quetzalcoatl are depicted. At Tlapiltepec, Lord 3 Rain marries Lady 6 Deer, his second wife and possibly the daughter of the conquered lord. The children of this couple would be legitimate rulers of Tlapiltepec through their mother, but loyal to Ihuitlán through their father. This situation of political dependency continued well into the colonial period.

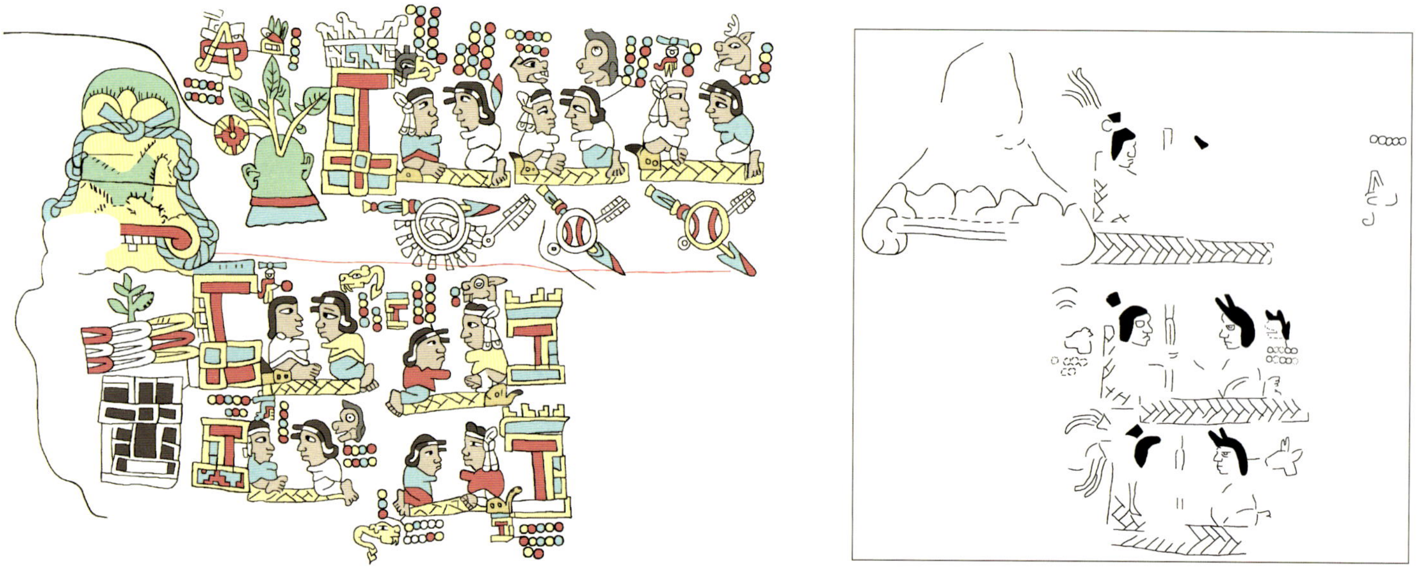

FIG. 2.25. *Left*, Tlapiltepec as depicted on the Lienzo of Tlapiltepec. *Right*, Ihuitlán conquerors in Tlapiltepec, redrawn from Lienzo of Coixtlahuaca II.

Turning now to the Lienzo of Tlapiltepec's version of history, the first feature that strikes us is the large geographical scale of the painting, in contrast to the local interest displayed in the Lienzo of Ihuitlán. Tlapiltepec and Ihuitlán are just two among many villages on the lienzo. No relation between the two is indicated, and if it were not for the Lienzo of Ihuitlán, we would not be able to piece the information together. The sign for Tlapiltepec, "Hill of the Knot," is easily identified as a hill surrounded by a knotted cord, halfway down the right side of the document (fig. 2.25).[67] Its interior is drawn as being "rocky," just as the real mountain stands out for its rocky surface. At the foot of this mountain we find, at "Valley of the Small Plant," four small palaces with couples in front. Among them are Lord 2 Rabbit, whom we already met in the Lienzo of Ihuitlán, and his wife 10 House. The relation of the other three couples to Lord 2 Rabbit and his wife is not clear. It seems this relation is not genealogical: the couples do not observe the typical vertical order used in genealogical registers, but each couple is seated in front of its own palace. They may have been the founders of other noble lineages in the Tlapiltepec area, much as the Lienzo of Otla represents five noble houses in the Otla area.[68]

The later reconquest of Tlapiltepec by 3 Rain is also depicted: to the right of Tlapiltepec mountain, near a second place-sign consisting of a "Hill with Ears and a Plant with Sun-Fruits" as Parmenter called them, we find another palace with three pairs of rulers in front.[69] Among these rulers are Lord 3 Rain and Lady 6 Deer, but the other two pairs remain unidentified. All three couples have weapons below their mats, indicating they came as conquerors. Several lines go out from this place, reaching seven conquered villages, among these perhaps Tehuacán and Asuchitlan, an important salt-producing village.[70]

This same group of people is represented on the Lienzo of Coixtlahuaca II (see fig. 2.25). Although badly faded, it is possible to distinguish the same three couples as shown on the Lienzo of Tlapiltepec, also beside a rocky hill.[71] However, in this case, the couples are arranged vertically, with 3 Rain sitting in the lower register, suggesting the couples form a short genealogy. The couples are also accompanied here by military symbols. The presence of these elaborate scenes on both lienzos indicates that the conquest of the Tlapiltepec area and the establishment of 3 Rain's lineage was an important event. Curiously, and despite its political importance, Ihuitlán seems to be absent from the Lienzo of Coixtlahuaca II.

IHUITLÁN AND TLAPILTEPEC IN SIXTEENTH-CENTURY RECORDS

In previous publications, the documents of the Coixtlahuaca Group have not been analyzed in relation to written sources in local and national archives. Most studies by Caso, Parmenter, and König focused almost exclusively on pictorial content, and early colonial written documents have only recently been brought to light (Doesburg 2002; Doesburg and Swanton 2011). But this documentation can shed considerable light on the political situation in the Coixtlahuaca Valley during the sixteenth century and thus improve our understanding of the histories depicted in the pictorial documents. For example, the apparent lack of hierarchy among today's thirteen municipalities in the Coixtlahuaca Valley does not reflect the historical situation of five centuries ago, when the valley was divided among a small number of ruler seats (or mats-and-thrones, mentioned above) under Coixtlahuaca's control. Ihuitlán was one of these seats, dominating the northwestern corner of the valley. The written documents also make it clear that Tlapiltepec was a small subject-community within the mat-and-throne of Ihuitlán, not the capital of an independent city-state.

Before turning to the colonial written documents, we need to briefly describe the context in which they were created. During pre-Hispanic times, the communities in the Coixtlahuaca region looked very different from their present-day counterparts: The population lived in dispersed hamlets, close to their cultivated lands. Administrative and religious functions were concentrated at special centers made up of temples, palaces, and other buildings. These centers were often located on some prominent low hill.

In 1563, the Spanish administration carried out an important resettlement program in the region. These programs, called *congregaciones*, were intended to better control the local population by concentrating it in nucleated villages around a Catholic church. Although several of these programs were carried out during the sixteenth century, the 1563 program in particular had a profound effect on Ihuitlán and Tequixtepec, the two major secondary mats-and-thrones in the valley.[72] Before congregación, nearby farmers protected the distant community lands. Resettlement left these lands unprotected, and soon concerns arose about their vulnerability to invasions of Spanish cattle. The viceroy Luis de Velasco ordered that the lands be protected:

> Letter of protection for the Indians of Ihuitlán, subject of Coixtlahuaca, over the lands they left because of resettlement.
>
> I, Don Luis de Velasco, viceroy, etc., insofar as I was told by the Indians of the village of Ihuitlán, subject to Coixtlahuaca, that they left some uninhabited lands within their borders, because they gathered at another place in congregación and good order. And for this reason some persons are entering these lands and taking and occupying them against their will, without right or permission to do so, for which reason they asked me to order them to be protected. And concluding in consideration of the aforementioned, I hereby, in the name of His Majesty, do protect and defend the Indians of the said village of Ihuitlán

> in the possession, use, and exploitation of all the lands that they have had and possessed and left behind within their borders due to having resettled, in order that, notwithstanding their absence, they enjoy them as if they personally lived on them. And I order the persons who have occupied and taken them to return them and give them back, over which the authorities of the mentioned village will do them justice and protect them as stated. Issued in Mexico, the 14th of December of the year fifteen hundred sixty-three. Don Luis de Velasco. By order of his lordship: Antonio de Turcios (Appendix A, document 01)

Apparently, the order was insufficient. In 1583, Ihuitlán asked the Spanish local judge (*alcalde mayor*) Fernando de Mújica, to grant it formal title to its lands. In order to do so, the judge walked—or claimed to have walked—across the territory of Ihuitlán together with most of the nobles and indigenous officials, visiting and recording each of the hamlets that were left abandoned during congregación.[73] The resulting description is of great value for the reconstruction of early colonial Ihuitlán history. The first place they visited was the old pre-Hispanic center of Ihuitlán:

> In the village of the above mentioned people, on the eighteenth day of the month of September of the said year of fifteen hundred eighty-three, the mentioned lord *alcalde mayor*, by petition of the said Don Francisco de Zárate and Don Diego del Castillo and Francisco Jiménez, Don Martín de Cuevas, Fernando Méndez, Domingo Gutiérrez, Don Miguel de Mendoza, Indian nobles of the head town of Santiago [Ihuitlán], left the mentioned village of Santiago, taking with him the grant, the said Pedro de Barrios, interpreter, and Don Joseph de Guzmán, governor of the village of Coixtlahuaca, and Don Miguel de Mendoza, *alcalde* of the said village, Francisco Jiménez, *alcalde*, and (. . .), and Alonso de San Pedro, *regidor*, and the Indians named above and many more nobles and commoners, walking the road that runs from the said head town toward the city of Veracruz about three quarters of a league, [we came] to a hill that is called Taximingo, and next to an arroyo, of which the said governor and *alcaldes* and the other Indians that were there (. . .) formally declared that it was the ancient site of the settlement called Ihuitlán, that today [they] stay and live in the mentioned head town of Santiago, and that the nobles of the said settlement are Don Francisco de Zárate, Don Diego del Castillo, and Don Diego de Aguilar; and there were many piles of stones and mulberry trees and zapote trees and in the said site there was a stockyard for small cattle, which was said to be that of Don Diego de Aguilar, and many cultivated cornfields and near the stream three or four Indian huts and nearby, at the distance of a harquebus shot, there was another yard, fenced with stone, also for sheep, that the mentioned Indians confessed to be lands and yard of Domingo de Santa María, noble of the settlement of Guautongo; and all the lands and the ancient site that were there, together with the streams, (. . .) and hills nearby were said to be lands of the Indians of the mentioned settlement Ihuitlán. (Appendix A, document 06)

This description can be correlated with a modern map of the region. Supposing the present church to be at the same spot where the sixteenth-century chapel stood, the pre-Hispanic center of Ihuitlán must have been on a hill four kilometers north of the church, that is, close to the arroyo called Ndaningu today.[74] This landscape is also rep-

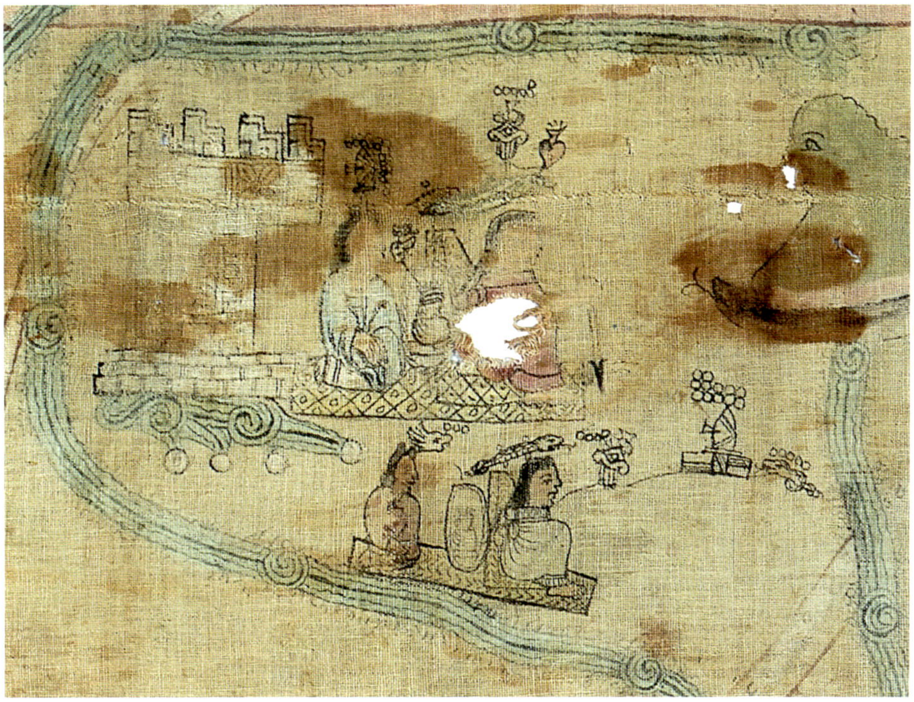

FIG. 2.26. Detail, Lienzo of Tulancingo, showing Lord 6 Rain and Lady 10 Flint, founders of Ihuitlán, at their palace. Between them is a sacred bundle with names 9 Wind and 1 Lizard. Below them are the parents of Lord 6 Rain, accompanied by the foundation date year 12 Flint, day 5 Serpent. The river that surrounds the palace is Ndaningu. Photo courtesy of Vittorio D'Onofri.

resented on the Lienzo of Tulancingo. Next to Ndaningu we find the first founders of Ihuitlán, Lord 6 Rain and Lady 10 Flint, in front of their palace and accompanied by the foundation date of pre-Hispanic Ihuitlán (Doesburg 2000:178–80). Here they installed the sacred bundles of 9 Wind and 1 Lizard, which they had received in Coixtlahuaca (fig. 2.26). Their palace might have served also as temple and shrine of the bundles of the sacred ancestors.[75] It may have been for this reason that the place was considered the pre-Hispanic center of Ihuitlán. This would also suggest that the three colonial lords who claimed this site in 1583, Don Francisco de Zárate, Don Diego del Castillo, and Don Diego de Aguilar, considered themselves descendants of the founding couple. Indeed, they appear in the colonial record as the most prominent lords of Ihuitlán. Of the three, Don Diego del Castillo appears frequently in documents between 1583 and 1594.[76] He was well educated, was able to write, and was frequently asked to translate in the local Spanish court. He apparently spoke Ngiwa, Mixtec, Nahuatl, and Spanish. It is possible that the three men descended from the lineages painted on the Lienzo of Ihuitlán, but since we do not know their calendrical names, it has not been possible to connect them with the last lords depicted on the lienzo.[77]

After visiting the old center, the committee turned to the other hamlets in the Ihuitlán territory (map 2.3). In each case, the judge described the place and recorded the names of the nobles who claimed it. From this, the following list can be extracted (Appendix A, document 06):

Ihuitlán	Francisco de Zárate, Diego del Castillo, and Diego de Aguilar
Cuauhtongo	Domingo de Santa María[78] and Juan de Santiago[79]
Tlapiltepec	Francisco Jiménez,[80] Fernando Méndez, and Juan García
Tlapixtlahuaca	Tomás de Rivera and Domingo Gutiérrez
Tzotzopaxtla	Miguel de Mendoza and Martín de Cuevas
Tlacotepec	Domingo Hernández[81] and Juan de Mendoza

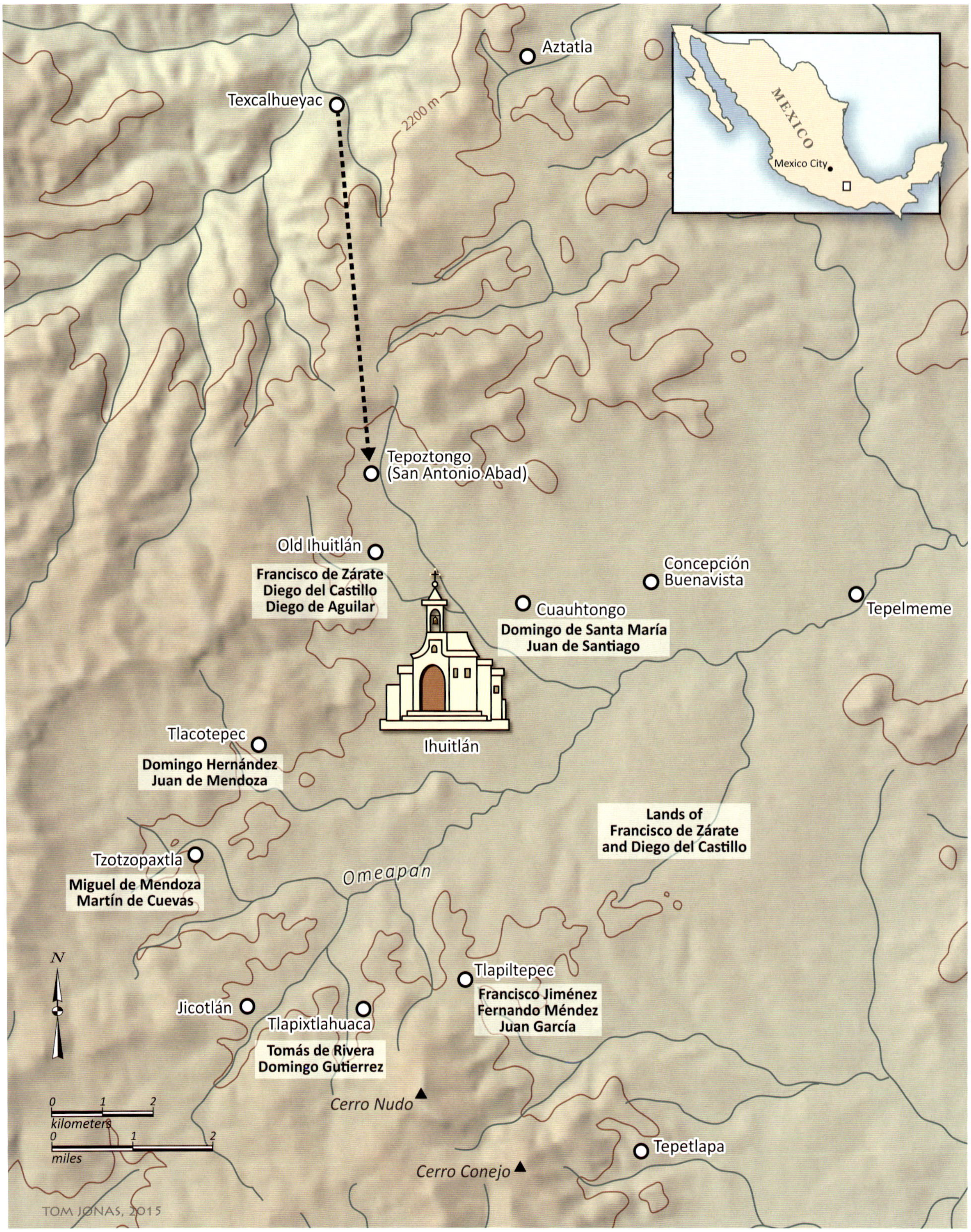

MAP 2.3. Ihuitlán region, ca. 1583. The map includes the relocation of the town of Texcalhueyac to the area known as Tepoztongo (now San Antonio Abad). The names of the Ihuitlán nobles living in 1583 are distributed over the map according to their hereditary lands. Contour lines indicate elevation of 2,200 meters above sea level. © 2015, University of Oklahoma Press.

One of the lords of Tlapiltepec, Fernando Méndez, crops up elsewhere in the historical record. In 1585, Fernando appeared as one of the witnesses in a case involving a cacique of Tepexi.[82] In his statement he declared that he was eighty years old and had witnessed the conquest of the Mixteca as a boy of fourteen, together with his father, Ocelotzin. According to much later documents, he had been granted a noble estate at the foot of Tlapiltepec hill in 1557 by the assembled nobles of Ihuitlán. This grant made it possible for the hamlet of Tlapiltepec to split off again in 1583 from the recent congregación:

> The Indians of the village of San Matheo Tlapiltepeque, after the said congregación, and by virtue of a dispatch of the Royal Audience, and of the license that was granted them in the year fifteen hundred eighty-three, moved to a slope and stream at the foot of a high hill, where their village is located today; (. . .) in this agreement and by virtue of a donation that the nobles and Indians of the village of Santiago Ihuitlán had made to Hernando Méndez, noble of the settlement of Tlapiltepec, in the year fifteen hundred fifty-seven, for all its Indians and commoners, of the lands, sites, and plots that were given and indicated to them in that place where they had established their settlement.[83]

Tlapiltepec still preserves today the sixteenth-century *tecpan*, or palace, at the center of town, built during its resettlement (fig. 2.27). The separation of Tlapiltepec from Ihuitlán took place almost at the same time as the issuing of the title of Ihuitlán:

> The Indians of Coixtlahuaca.
>
> I, Don Lorenzo Suárez de Mendoza, etc., make known to you, the *corregidor* of Coixtlahuaca, that it was made known to me by the Indians of the settlement of Santiago [Ihuitlán], subject of Coixtlahuaca, that they intend to go and live in the settlement of San Mateo [Tlapiltepec], also subject of the said village, with the approval and consent of its governor and nobles, and that thus by being in a better spot, place, and layout for their health, as well as because they will enjoy more and better lands for their crops and for other ends and regards useful to them, this move, which can be done easily and without harm to a third party, would do them good, and they ask permission to this effect. And because I want to be informed of the location of the one and the other settlement and everything else that might be useful in order to bestow the said license, I order that, once the Indians of the said village of Coixtlahuaca are summoned, and once their will is known and understood, you will inquire if by moving the said Indians from Santiago [Ihuitlán] to the said settlement of San Mateo [Tlapiltepec] there would come or might come harm or prejudice to a third party, and which [party] and in what, and the advantage of the spot, lands, water, and trees of the one they intend to occupy, and the shortages and needs of the place they will leave. And having seen the one and the other, and having spoken with the vicar of the said village, you will send before me, with your opinion and reasons, each and every particular in order that, once reviewed, I can decree that which is suitable. In the meantime, do not agree to do or allow any alteration to be done in anything. Issued in Mexico on the thirtieth day of the month of January of fifteen hundred eighty-three. El Conde de Coruña. By order of his lordship Martín López de Gaona. And likewise you

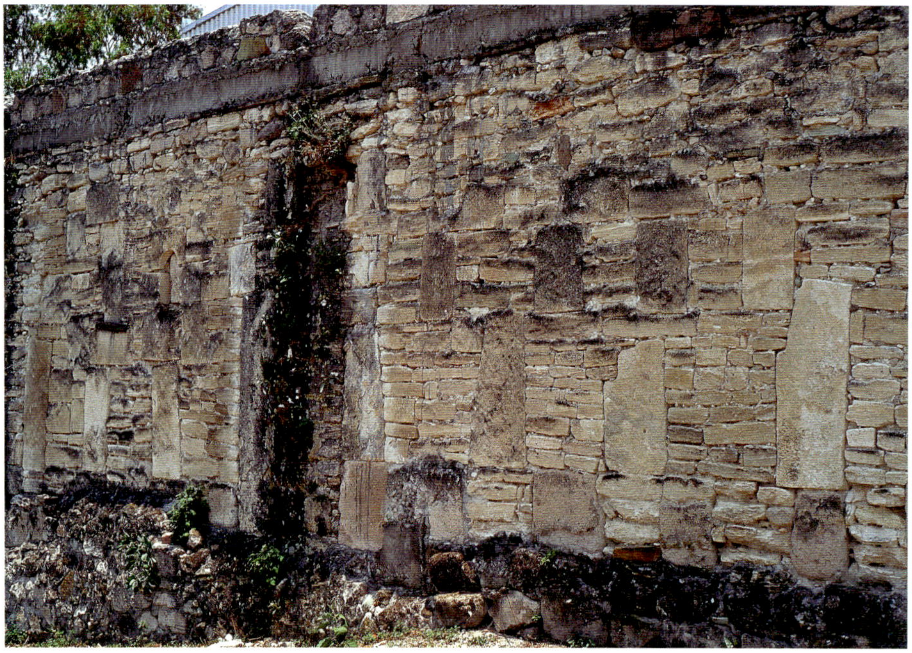

FIG. 2.27. An outer wall of the royal palace, or *tecpan*, of Tlapiltepec, showing stone work in pre-Hispanic style. Photo by author.

> will also inquire and inform me if the settlement under discussion is subject to Coixtlahuaca and if both settlements are equal in their service to the head town. (Appendix A, document 05)

Details about the place where, according to local tradition, the hamlet of Tlapiltepec was located before 1563 (the date of congregación) are preserved in a document from 1753. During a dispute with Magdalena Jicotlán the witnesses were asked specific questions about the congregación that had taken place some two centuries earlier. One witness stated:

> In the site that we call in our language Tunruyua, which in Nahuatl is called Jocotlan, some vestiges of there having been a village are found, as in fact this one of San Mateo [Tlapiltepec] was established there when it was a barrio of the village of Santiago Ihuitlán in those ancient times.[84]

Jocotlan coincides with a major Classic-period site (today called Cunatexa, "On Top of Small Tlapiltepec," on one of the protruding slopes of Tlapiltepec hill. Perhaps the site was still considered sacred during the Postclassic period, which would concur with Tlapiltepec's being depicted as a place of bundle worship in the Lienzo of Ihuitlán.[85] The scene of bundle worship is also a suggestive indication of the importance that Tlapiltepec may have had within the ideological geography of the valley.

LATE COLONIAL DEVELOPMENTS

Political developments leading toward the current situation—in which the valley is made up of thirteen municipalities—and toward the independence of Tlapiltepec, started in the seventeenth century, a period of changes in Oaxacan indigenous society. Around 1600 a new settlement arose in Ihuitlán territory: San Francisco Teopan, "Church of San Francisco." It is not clear why and how this village was created, but it might have been part of Tlacotepec.[86] During the first half of the seventeenth century, old noble families still controlled the region. In a document from 1628, we see how Ihuitlán (including Tlapiltepec and Teopan) took part in the Coixtlahuaca government. In that year, Don Gregorio de Aguilar, son of Don Diego, is mentioned as the cacique, but he does not occupy a post in the Coixtlahuaca *cabildo*. Don Tomás de Vera, a cacique from Santa María Nativitas, was governor. On his cabildo we find Don Joseph del Castillo from Ihuitlán, probably the son of Diego,[87] as *regidor*. Cristóbal Hernández was in charge of Ihuitlán's church matters as *fiscal*; Vicente de San Pedro was *alguacil mayor* or constable; while Juan López, Gerónimo Bautista, Cristóbal Hernández II, and Juan Hernández feature as nobles from Ihuitlán. At the same time, Juan García was *regidor* for Tlapiltepec; he may be the same Juan García mentioned in the list of land claimants above, but now forty-five years older. The *fiscal* Gabriel García took care of the church of San Mateo. Marcos Moreno and Sebastián Méndez appear as nobles. The latter may have been the son of Fernando Méndez, discussed above. Gabriel de Mendoza was the *regidor* representative for Teopan, while Juan de San Pedro was *fiscal*.[88] Despite this continuity, one major change had occurred: at the cabildo level there was no longer a clear hierarchical distinction between Ihuitlán, Tlapiltepec, and Teopan: all were represented through a regidor, increasing substantially the number of regidores in the Coixtlahuaca cabildo.

It becomes increasingly clear that the old structure of local and regional integration through marital ties between caciques and nobles and between the nobles was slowly abandoned. With the breakup of the internal hierarchy, originally kept in place by the complex marital alliance structure of the elite, the breakdown of the Coixtlahuaca polity after 1650 seemed inevitable. The elite families' loss of prestige, and their incapacity to monopolize the economy or create and maintain lines of political loyalty that determined the relation between the head town and its subject settlements, resulted in the rise of political pretenders and the rise of the communities as stronger economic and political entities.

Between 1678 and 1681 several villages tried to separate, without success, from their capital, Coixtlahuaca.[89] In 1718, Ihuitlán, in alliance with several nearby villages, launched a renewed effort to split off. By then, Tlapiltepec had outstripped Ihuitlán and manifested a population of 180 families against 120 for Ihuitlán. However, the allied villages proposed forming a new, independent community with Ihuitlán as its head town, "since this was the oldest of the said villages."[90] Although in the end the villages were not allowed to separate from Coixtlahuaca, each received permission to elect its own alcalde.[91] But Ihuitlán itself was also greatly affected by the shakeup, losing much of its original territory to the newly founded Concepción Buenavista[92] and San Antonio Abád,[93] the splitting off of Tlapiltepec and Teopan, and finally and most dramatically, the separation of Tlacotepec in the late nineteenth century.[94]

CONCLUSIONS

Images on the Lienzo of Tlapiltepec itself suggest that the document was drawn to tell the story of the royal house that ruled Coixtlahuaca in the early years of the sixteenth century. To the left, a long genealogical register of Coixtlahuaca rulers is painted, which starts in mythological times and ends in the first decades of the sixteenth century with the couple Lord 11 Vulture[95] and Lady 3 Serpent, rulers of Coixtlahuaca. As this is the only complete genealogical register depicted in the document, it strongly suggests a Coixtlahuaca origin for this lienzo. To the right, a cartographically arranged painting depicts many of the decisive historical events that resulted in Coixtlahuaca's powerful position in the region and beyond. This side of the document is devoted to the expansion of Coixtlahuaca's dominion, and the representations of Ihuitlán and Tlapiltepec have to be seen in this light. It shows the villages in the valley that were genealogically linked to the Coixtlahuaca rulers and it even indicates several villages in southern Puebla that were governed from approximately AD 1400 by descendants of these Coixtlahuaca rulers.[96] It depicts the two migrating lineages that ended up in the Tepeaca-Tecamachalco-Quecholac region and in the Tepexi area. These distant relations are painted without geographical detail and with only approximate directions and strongly "telescoped" distances. Combining these elements, it seems that the general message of the Lienzo of Tlapiltepec concerns an elaborate and powerful claim by Lord 11 Vulture and his wife to political power in the valley and beyond, based on an assertion of ancestral dominance there.

The cartographic portion of the lienzo contains other indications that Coixtlahuaca was the most important village for the painter. Significantly, the river basin of the Río Grande de San Miguel, which bisects the lands of Coixtlahuaca, is depicted in great detail, while the river basin of the Rio Grande de Tepelmeme, in which Ihuitlán is located, is not shown at all. Such details indicate that the accurate representation of Coixtlahuaca geography was more important to the painter than that of Ihuitlán. Moreover, the position of Tlapiltepec on the edge of the lienzo suggests that it is not the central topic of the lienzo either. While the Lienzo of Tlapiltepec does show several Tlapiltepec rulers, among them Lord 2 Rabbit and Lord 3 Rain and their wives, no Tlapiltepec lineage or genealogy is depicted. Nor does the lienzo give a complete lineage for Ihuitlán. Only the first five generations of its ruling couples appear, while the later generations are all absent from this sheet. This contrasts with the complete Coixtlahuaca lines.

The information recorded on the Lienzo of Tlapiltepec is indeed different from that of the more locally oriented lienzos from Ihuitlán, Tequixtepec, Otla, and Nativitas, the subject matter of which does not extend far outside their local territories. On the other hand, and not surprisingly, there are some striking similarities between the Lienzo of Tlapiltepec and the other documents from Coixtlahuaca, notably the Lienzo of Coixtlahuaca II. Most of the information registered in the latter is also found in the Lienzo of Tlapiltepec, except for a boundary list and an emphasis on the Juquila church, which can be identified as belonging to the specific message of the Lienzo of Coixtlahuaca II (Doesburg 2004).

However, the inclusion of Tlapiltepec in both the Lienzo of Tlapiltepec and the Lienzo of Coixtlahuaca II indicates that it must have been of some special importance to the rulers of Coixtlahuaca (just as elements of Nativitas history were included in the Lienzo of Coixtlahuaca I and Lienzo A; see Parmenter 1997; Doesburg 2001). In particular, Tlapiltepec's appearance on the Lienzo of Coixtlahuaca II without its head town of Ihuitlán suggests a special position, perhaps related to the famous mountain at its side. The painting of the "warpath" from Coixtlahuaca to Tlapiltepec on the Lienzo of Ihuitlán supports this special tie. Still, this special position does not align with the complex and far-reaching claims expressed by the Lienzo of Tlapiltepec.

In past studies, little attention has been paid to the internal political structure of the Valley of Coixtlahuaca during the sixteenth century. As I have tried to show above, colonial documents can give us a better insight into this structure and can help in resolving or identifying problems of interpretation in the lienzos. They give us the historical context in which the lienzos must be studied. Although there is no direct proof for the hypothesis advanced in this chapter, it has become clear that the Lienzo of Tlapiltepec is a Coixtlahuaca-centered document that focuses on the Coixtlahuaca lineages and the extent of their political influence. The fact that the city-state of Coixtlahuaca is depicted in great detail, both genealogically and geographically, and Ihuitlán-Tlapiltepec is not, seems to underscore this characterization. Moreover, Tlapiltepec was only a small, subordinate settlement dependent on Ihuitlán. The conclusion that the Lienzo of Tlapiltepec comes from Coixtlahuaca means that most of the documents in the Coixtlahuaca Group were produced in only five centers in the valley: the head town of Coixtlahuaca (four documents); the principal subjects of the house of Atonal, that is, Ihuitlán (two) and Tequixtepec (two); and the subjects of the secondary house at Coixtlahuaca, that is, Nativitas (one) and Otla (one). This conclusion reveals that the settlement pattern in the valley should not be perceived as a set of dispersed communities of more or less equal status, as it is today, but rather as a hierarchical system in which the royal palaces in Coixtlahuaca, Ihuitlán, and Tequixtepec were the main centers of power. Future studies of the colonial documentation can perhaps shed more light on the details of the historical-political context in which this lienzo was made and the important question as to why it was made.

Transcriptions of Sixteenth- and Early Seventeenth-Century Documents Related to Ihuitlán and Tlapiltepec

BAS VAN DOESBURG

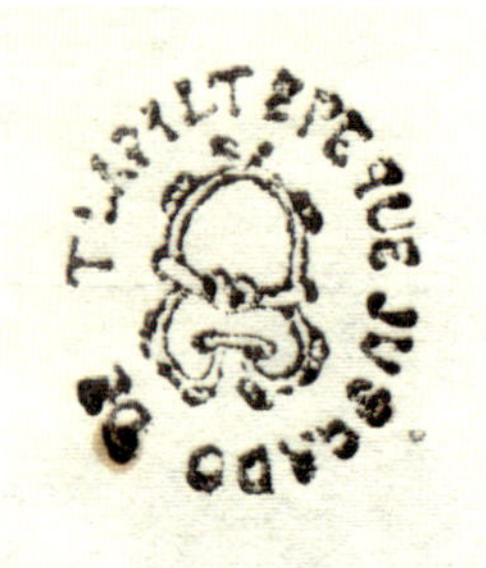

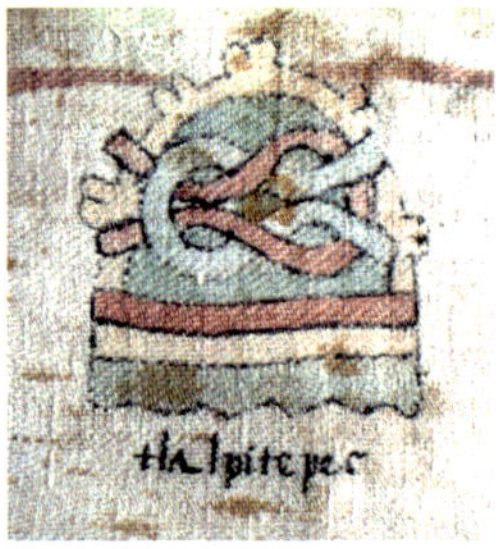

Ever since Alfonso Caso (1949) made his crucial identifications by comparing Mixtec pictographs against early colonial written documents, the study of these documents has been fundamental for contextualizing the pictographic manuscripts. In several instances, colonial documents have allowed us to identify the late pre-Hispanic or early colonial rulers depicted in pictographs. They also can be helpful in uncovering the sociopolitical circumstances that led to the creation of specific pictorials. But more important, they often help us identify places and features of the landscape—the geographic dimension—of the pictographic narratives, allowing us to reconstruct ancient political networks and trade routes with reference to modern maps. These places thus add realism to the pictorial narratives and anchor them to the actual landscape. In turn, this relation facilitates the connection of pictography with the current indigenous perception of cultural and social landscape, eventually creating new relations between the manuscripts and local identities.

For these reasons, the publication of archival transcriptions is useful for researchers, not only to access dispersed unpublished and often inaccessible materials, but also to indicate the existence of documentation that is often overlooked. The early colonial documents from San Miguel Tequixtepec, a neighboring community of Ihuitlán and Tlapiltepec, have been extensively published (Doesburg 2002). The following appendix compiles all known archival documents related to the Ihuitlán-Tlapiltepec polity prior to 1620. This appendix adds to the scholarly effort to publish all early colonial documentation of the Coixtlahuaca Basin.

In the transcriptions, I have followed the same criteria as those used in the Tequixtepec records. Reconstructed letters are in parentheses. Brackets are used to spell out abbreviations. Documents only known through later copies have been transcribed in modern Spanish spelling.

An indirect reference indicates the existence of an early 1574 document, now lost, which probably contained a copy of the text from 1557 that recorded the donation of lands to Fernando Méndez, noble of Tlapiltepec, mentioned in this chapter. In the Archivo General de la Nación (hereinafter AGN), Tierras, vol. 2787, f. 129, one reads:

> "Otro testimonio dado y autorizado por Jerónimo Ruiz Cabal, escribano público en esta ciudad, a veinte y cinco de octubre de mil setecientos y seis, a pedimento de los indios de San Mateo Tlaquiltepeque de la tran(sac)ción que hicieron en la estancia de Santiago, sujeto al pueblo de Custlahuaca de la Misteca, a siete de mayo de quinientos setenta y cuatro, ante Mateo de Pineda, escribano real, entre don Diego de Castilla y consortes, indios principales de dicha estancia, y don Hernando Méndez y consortes, también principales de ella, en que se desistieron del pleito que entre ellos había habido sobre las tierras que expresan, las que se dividieron entre todos igualmente y se les dio posesión con lo demás que se contiene en dicho testimonio, en f[oja]s. 24."

DOCUMENT 01

AGN, Mercedes, vol. 7, f. 241 (215 in the new page numbers) (1563). Letter of protection for the Indians of Ihuitlán.

El hordin[ari]o de anparo a los yndios de Yhuitlan subjeto de Cuestlauaca sobre las tierras que dexaron por la junta.

Yo don Luis de Velasco visorrei etc. por quanto por parte de los naturales del pu[ebl]o de Yhuitlan subjetos a Cuestlauaca me fue f[ec]ha rr[elaci]on que ellos dexaron en sus t[e]r[min]os algunas tierras ynabitables por averse juntado en congregaçion e puliçia a otras partes e que desta causa algunas personas no lo pudiendo ni deviendo hazer se entran en las d[ic]has tierras e las toman e ocupan contra su voluntad sobre lo qual me pidieron les mandase anparar e por mi bisto atento a lo suso d[ic]ho por la presente en nombre de su mag[estad] anparo e defiendo a los naturales del d[ic]ho pu[ebl]o de Yhuitlan en la posesion uso e aprovechami[en]to de todas las tierras que an tenido e poseido y dexado en sus t[e]r[min]os por averse juntado para que no enbargante el ausençia que hizieron las gozen como si personalmente las avitasen y mando a las personas que se las tienen ocupadas y tomadas se las buelvan y rrestituian en lo qual la just[ici]a del d[ic]ho pu[ebl]o les haga just[ici]a e anpare segun d[ic]ho es. F[ec]ho en Mex[i]co a xiiii de diziembre de mill e qui[nient]os e sesenta e tres a[ñ]os. Don Luis de Velasco. Por mandado de su señoria Antonio de Turçios.

DOCUMENT 02

Archivo General de la Nación, Indiferente Virreinal, caja 5480, exp. 18 (1578). Request for copy of permission to move from Ihuitlán to Jicotlán.

Los yndios na[tura]les de la est[anci]a de Xicotlan sujeta de Cuestlavaca dezimos que nosotros estavamos poblados en una est[anci]a llamada Santiago [Ihuitlan] y por ser tierra mui enferma donde se morian casi todos los na[tura]les pedimos a v[uest]ra ex[celenci]a nos mandase dar su m[andam]i[ent]o para pasarnos a la est[anci]a de Xicotlan que es donde al preessente estamos y v[uestra] ex[celenci]a nos dio su m[andam]i[ent]o para que la just[ici]a ynformase se seria util y probecho y aumento para los na[tura]les, la qual ynformo dello a v[uest]ra ex[celenci]a y se nos dio m[andam]i[ent]o para que librem[en]te pudiesemos estar en la d[ic]ha est[anci]a de Xicotlan y hazer en ella n[uest]ras casas e yglesia y estamos poblados en la d[ic]ha est[anci]a e se nos a perdido el m[andam]i[ent]o q[ue] teniamos de v[uest]ra ex[celenci]a el qual esta en libro asentado que paso ante el s[eñ]or Sancho Lopez de Rrecalde difunto.

A v[uest]ra ex[celenci]a pedimos y suplicamos nos la mande dar por duplicado pues es cosa util y provechosa y estamos en la d[ic]ha est[anci]a de Xicotlan de mas de tres a[ñ]os poblados en lo qual rreçibiremos bien y m[erce]d.

DOCUMENT 03

AGN, Indios, vol. 2, exp. 186 (1582). License for Juan de Santa María, principal of Cuauhtongo, to keep sheep.

Li[cenci]a a Juan de Santa Maria yndio prençipal del pu[ebl]o de Quautongo para traer en sus tieras doçientas obejas guardando las ordenanças.

Don L[orenz]o Suares de Mendoça, etc. por quanto Juan de Santa Maria yndio prençipal del pu[ebl]o de Quautongo me a fecho rrel[aci]on que el tiene en terminos del d[ic]ho pu[ebl]o un pedaço de tierra que llaman Con(d)aroa donde sin perjui[ci]o de terçero podra tener y traer algunas obejas de cuyos esquilmos y aprovechamientos sustente su casa, hijos y familia, pidiendo que para este efecto le mandase dar y diese li[cenci]a con declaraçion de la cantidad que hubiere de ser; por tanto atento a lo suso d[ic]ho por la presente doy l[icenci]a a el d[ic]ho Juan de Santa Maria para que libremente pueda tener y traer en las d[ic]has tierras hasta duzientas obejas y no mas con guarda y rrecaudo de manera que no hagan daño en las sementeras de los naturales y con esto y guardando las hordenanças no co(ns)tando [corrected as: cortando] cola ni oreja mando q[ue] por ninguna justiçia se le ynpida. Ff[ech]o en Mexico a diez y nueve dias del mes de nobienbre de mill y qui[nient]os y ochenta y dos años. El conde de Curuña. Por m[anda]do de su ex[celenci]a, M[art]in Lopes de Gaona.

DOCUMENT 04

AGN, Mercedes, vol. 11, f. 181v (1582–83). A copy from 1750 exists in AGN, Tierras, vol. 2787. Also in AGN, Mercedes, vol. 18, f. 181v. A grant of a sheep ranch to the hamlet of Ihuitlán.

M[erce]d a la est[anci]a de S[an]tiango Yuitlan sujeta a Cuestlabaca de un sitio dest[anci]a para ganado menor p[ar]a propios de su comunidad.

Don Lor[enz]o Suarez etc. por la p[resen]te en n[ombr]e de su m[agestad] hago m[erce]d a la est[anci]a de S[an]tiago Ybitlan sujeta del pu[ebl]o de Cuestlauaca de un sitio dest[anci]a de ganado menor para propios de su comunidad en t[e]r[min]os del d[ic]ho su pu[ebl]o en la p[ar]te que llaman: Cuseldarua lo qual por mi m[anda]do y comision fue a ver y bido Hernando de Muxica al[ca]lde mayor de Yanguitlan el qual aviendo hecho las dilig[enci]as y averiguaçiones conforme a lo que se le mando declaro y dio por paresçer estar sin ningun perjui[ci]o y poderseles haçer la d[ic]ha m[erce]d la qual le hago sin perjui[ci]o del d[e]r[ech]o de su m[agestad] y de otro qualquier t[e]r[cer]o con cargo y condiçion que dentro de un ano pueble el d[ic]ho sitio dest[anci]a con dos mill caveças del d[ic]ho ganado menor y en ningun t[iem]po ni por alg[un]a manera no lo puedan vender trocar ni enaxenar a pers[on]a alg[un]a so pena que por el mismo caso esta m[erce]d sea en si ning[un]a y de ningun valor y efeto y quede vaca para poder haçer m[erce]d della librem[en]te a otra p[er]s[on]a y con que el asiento que della hiçieren sea(. . .) medida de otra est[anci]a si oviere a su linde sin que quede tierra en medio y cumpliendo lo suso d[ic]ho e guardando las ordenanças que estan ff[ech]os sobre la dist[anci]a que a de aver de una est[anci]a a otra ques a la de ganado m[a]yor tres mill pasos de marca a la mas antigua y dos mill a la de menor la d[ic]ha est[anci]a sea suya y de la d[ic]ha comunidad para sienpre xamas y de la poss[esi]on q[ue] tomare mando que no sea despojado sin ser primeram[en]te oydo y por fuero y d[e]r[ech]o bençido ante quien y como deva. Ff[ech]o en Mex[i]co a v[ein]te y ocho de n[oviembr]e de mill e qui[nient]os y ochenta y dos. El conde de Curuna. Por m[anda]do de su ex[elenci]a Ju[an] de Cueva.

[Modernized spelling, copy from 1750]
Merced a la estancia de Santiago YnIhuitlán sujeta de Cuestlahuaca de un sitio de estancia de ganado menor para propios de su comunidad, testigo de asistencia.

Estando en la parte y lugar que se nombra Cuseldarua, término del pueblo de Santiago sujeto al de Cuestlahuaca, sábado veinte días que se contaron del mes de abril de mil quinientos y ochenta y tres años, ante el ilustre señor Fernando de Mújica alcalde mayor de la provincia de Yanhuitlán y de esta jurisdicción por su majestad, por ante mi el escribano y testigos yuso escritos, de pedimento de don Francisco de Zárate y don Diego de Aguilar y don Diego del Castillo, indios principales y naturales del barrio de YnIhuitlán del dicho pueblo de Santiago, mediante Pedro de Barrios, intérprete de su juzgado, pidieron a su merced les mande meter en nombre de la comunidad de dicho su barrio en la posesión que tenían del sitio de estancia para ganado menor que es en este dicho lugar nombrado Cuseldarua conforme a la merced a la dicha su comunidad fecha por el muy excelente señor visorey de esta Nueva España desotra parte contenida, y pidieron les mande amparar en ella y se los dé por testimonio para en guarda de su derecho; y por su merced visto dijo que en nombre de su majestad metía y metió en la dicha posesión del dicho sitio a los susodichos nombrado Cuseldarua para la dicha su comunidad, y en señal de posesión su merced los tomó de las manos y a cada uno de por si los metió por un rancho que en este dicho sitio tienen fecho a manera de ermita, y estando dentro los susodichos echaron fuera al dicho señor alcalde mayor y a otras personas que dentro estaban, y así mismo los metió de la propia manera en un corral que junto al dicho rancho está hecho de cerco de madera, y echaron fuera a los que dentro estaban, y luego este hizo pasear de una parte a otra, arrancando hierbas y tirando piedras y en señal de más posesión los susodichos pusieron y j(in)caron una cruz de madera gruesa frontero y junto a dicho rancho, la cual de dicha posesión tomaron por la manera dicha quieta y pacíficamente sin contradicción de persona alguna, presentes muchos indios naturales de dicho pueblo de Santiago y del pueblo de Tepenene y otras partes; y visto por su merced todo lo susodicho dijo que les amparaba y amparó a los susodichos y a la dicha su comunidad en la dicha posesión y tenencia del dicho sitio de estancia sin perjuicio del derecho de su majestad ni de otro tercero, y mandaba y manda que ninguna persona ni personas no sean osadas a perturbarles la dicha posesión ni de ella sean desposeídos hasta que primero y ante todas cosas sean oídos y por fuero y derecho vencidos, y mando se les dé por testimonio originalmente para en guarda de su derecho y por el dicho intérprete les fue dada a entender lo contenido en la dicha merced en cuanto a poblarla y no venderla, trocarla ni cambiarla ahora, ni en tiempo alguno, siendo presentes por testigos Pedro Sánchez, español residente en Cuestlahuaca, y Domingo de Villegas, alcalde del dicho pueblo, y don Francisco de Mendoza, principal del pueblo de Tepenene, y don Juan de Salazar y don Antonio de Mendoza, regidores de dicho pueblo de Tepenene, y don Miguel de Mendoza y Domingo de Cuevas y Fernando Méndez, naturales del dicho pueblo de Santiago, de otros barrios del, y lo firmó el dicho señor alcalde mayor y el dicho intérprete. Fernando Mújica, Pedro de Barrios. Doy fe de todo, Luis Gutiérrez, escribano de su juzgado.

DOCUMENT 05

AGN, Indios, vol. 2, exp. 431, f. 103 (1583). Order to investigate the move that the Indians of San Mateo desire.

Los n[atur]ales de Cuestlauaca

Don L[orenz]o Suarez de Mendoça etc. hago sauer a uos el correg[id]or de Cuestlauaca que por parte de los naturales de la estançia de Santiago [Ihuitlán], sujeto de Cuestlauaca, me a sido ff[ech]a rrelaçion que ellos pretenden pasarse a uiuir a la estançia de San Mateo [Tlapiltepec] asimismo sujeto del dicho pu[ebl]o con acuerdo y consentimiento del gouernador y prinçipales del y que asi por estar en mejor asiento, lugar y dispusiçion p[ar]a su salud como porque gozaran de mas y mexores tierras para sus sementeras y para otros fines y rrespetos de su utilidad les estara bien esta mudança que se puede hazer con façilidad y sin perjuizio de tercero pidiendo para este hefecto licençia. Y porque quiero ser ynformado del asiento de la una y otra estançia y de lo demas que conbenga para proveer la dicha liçençia os mando que çitados los n[atur]ales del dicho pu[ebl]o de Cuestlauaca, sauida y entendida su boluntad auerigueis si de mudarse los dichos naturales de Santiago [Ihuitlán] a la dicha estançia de San Mateo [Tlapiltepec] biene o podra benir dano o perjuizio a terçero y qual y en que y la bentaxa de[l] asiento, tierras, aguas y arboledas de la que pretenden ocupar y la falta y nessesidad de la que dexan, y bisto lo uno y lo otro y comunicado con el vicario del d[ic]ho pu[ebl]o enbiareis con su parezer y el v[uest]ro rrazon ante mi de todo y cada cosa en particular para q[ue] visto provea lo que conbenga. En el ynterin no consintais hazer ni se haga nouedad en cosa alguna. Ff[ech]o en Mexico a treynta dias del mes de hen[er]o de mil y quinientos y ochenta y tres anos. El conde de Curuna. Por mandado de su ex[elenci]a M[art]in Lopez de Gaona. Y asimismo aueriguareis y me ynformareis si (es) la misma estançia sujeta a Cuestlauaca y la una y otra estançia en una misma cosa en acudir a la cauecera.

DOCUMENT 06

AGN, Tierras, vol. 2787, f. 20v–31v. Copy (1750) of the title of 1583. Modernized spelling.

Don Felipe, por la gracia de Dios rey de Castilla, de León, de Aragón, de las dos Cecilias, de Jerusalén, de Portugal, de Navarro, de Granada, de Toledo, de Valencia, de Mallorca, de Sevilla, de Cerdeña, de Córdoba, de Córcega, de Murcia, de Jaén, de los Agarbes, de Algeciras, de Gibraltar, de las Islas de Canaria, de las Indias Orientales y Occidentales, islas y tierra firme del Mar Océano, Archiduque de Austria, Duque de Borgoña, Brabante y Milán, Conde [de] Habsburgo, de Flandes y de Tiról y de Barcelona, señor de Vizcaya y de Molina, etc. a vos, el mío alcalde mayor de la provincia de Yanhuitlán o a vuestro lugarteniente y a otras cualesquier justicias de la dicha provincia, salud y gracia. Sépades que ante el presidente y oidores de la nuestra audiencia y chancillería que reside en la Ciudad de México de la Nueva España pareció la parte de los indios naturales de las cabeceras [*sic pro*: estancias] de Santiago, Tlapiltepeque y Tlapoztlauaca y Zozompastla y Tlacotepeque, sujetas al pueblo de Cuestlavaca, y por petición que presentó nos hizo relación diciendo que ellos se habían congregado y pasado por mandado de un juez a una estancia, que asimismo está sujeta al dicho pueblo de Cuestlavaca, llamada YnIhuitlán, por ser tierra muy sana y en las estancias donde antes estaban habían dejado muchas tierras de que al presente se aprovechaban de sembrar morales que criaban para seda, y otras semillas donde pagaban sus tributos y se sustentaban, y se temían que algunos españoles se les entrarían en las dichas tierras y se las tomarían, y nos pidió y suplicó fuésemos servido de les mandar dar nuestra carta y provisión real para que ningún español ni otra persona alguna no se les entrasen en las dichas tierras, ni se las tomasen, o que sobre ello proveyésemos como la nuestra merced fuese; lo cual, visto por el dicho nuestro presidente y oidores, fue acordado de que debíamos mandar dar esta nuestra carta por la dicha razón y nos tuvímoslo por bien, por que vos mandamos que luego que vos fuere mostrada no consintáis, permitáis, ni deis lugar a que ningún español ni otra persona entren en las dichas tierras, ni las tome a los dichos naturales por ninguna vía ni manera, a los cuales ampararéis en la quieta y pacífica posesión que hasta aquí han tenido y tienen de ellas y *non fagades endeal* por alguna manera so pena de la nuestra merced y de cien pesos de oro para la nuestra cámara. Dada en la ciudad de México a treinta días del mes de Agosto de mil quinientos y ochenta y tres años. El Conde de Coruña, el Doctor Farfán, el Doctor Lope de Miranda, el Doctor Robles, yo Sánchez López de Agurto, escribano de Cámara de su majestad la hice escribir por su mandado y acuerdo de su presidente y oidores. Registrado Juan Serrano, por canciller Juan Serrano.

En el pueblo de Cuestlavaca en doce días del mes de septiembre de mil y quinientos y ochenta y tres años, ante el ilustre señor Fernando de Mújica, alcalde mayor de esta jurisdicción por su majestad, por ante mi el escribano público, parecieron presentes don Francisco de Zárate, don Diego del Castillo y Francisco Jiménez y don Martín de Cuevas, Fernando Méndez, Domingo Gutiérrez, indios principales de la cabecera de Santiago y barrios de la provincia de esta otra parte comendados [*sic pro:* congregados] que son en el dicho pueblo y cabecera de Santiago, y presentaron esta real provisión de su majestad y por lengua de Pedro de Barrios, intérprete de este juzgado, pidieron el cumplimiento de ella; y por el dicho señor alcalde mayor vista la tomó en sus manos y la cabeza descubierta la besó y puso sobre ella y dijo que la obedecía y obedeció como carta y provisión de su rey y señor a quien Dios nuestro señor deje vivir y gobernar por muy largos tiempos con acrecentamiento de muchos y mayores reinos y señoríos y en cuanto al cumplimiento esta pronto de hacer y cumplir lo que su majestad le manda y firmolo. Testigos Francisco de Montoya y Antonio de Villegas estantes en el dicho pueblo y el dicho intérprete. Fernando de Mújica, Pedro de Barrios. Ante mi Pedro González de Rueda escribano público.

En el pueblo de Cuestlavaca en once días del mes de Septiembre de mil y quinientos y ochenta y tres años ante el dicho señor alcalde mayor y por ante mi el dicho escribano parecieron presentes los dichos don Francisco de Zárate y don Diego del Castillo y Francisco Jiménez, regidor y don Martín de Cuevas, Fernando Méndez, Domingo Gutiérrez, todos indios principales del dicho pueblo y cabecera de Santiago sujeta a este dicho pueblo y por lengua de Pedro de Barrios intérprete pidieron y suplicaron al dicho señor alcalde mayor se parta al dicho pueblo de Santiago y los ampare e defienda por esta real provisión en todas las tierras baldías que tienen en los sitios antiguos que de antes tenían por que nadie se los pueda quitar y en los demás asientos antiguos y corrales u otras que son suyas y visto el dicho señor alcalde mayor dijo que está presto de se partir al dicho pueblo de Santiago y a la parte y lugar que los dichos indios señalaren tener sus tierras y obras y amararlos en ellas conforme a esta real provisión de su majestad y firmolo. Testigos Francisco de Montoya, Pedro de Vargas y el dicho intérprete. Fernando de Mújica, Pedro de Barrios. Ante mi Pedro González de Rueda escribano público.

En el pueblo de los susodichos en diez y ocho días del mes de septiembre del dicho año de mil e quinientos y ochenta y tres el dicho señor alcalde mayor de pedimento de los dichos don Francisco de Zárate y don Diego del Castillo y Francisco Jiménez, don Martín de Cuevas, Fernando Méndez, Domingo Gutiérrez, don Miguel de Mendoza, indios principales de la cabecera de Santiago, salio del dicho pueblo de Santiago llevando consigo la merced, el dicho Pedro [de Barrios, intérprete] y don Joseph de Guzmán gobernador del pueblo de Cuestlauaca y don Miguel de Mendoza alcalde de dicho pueblo, Francisco Jiménez alcalde [y . . . y Alonso] de San Pedro regidores y los indios arriba nombrados y otros mucho mas principales y macehuales yendo por el camino que va de la dicha cabecera hacia la ciudad de la Veracruz como tres cuartos de legua en una loma que se nombra Taximingo y junto a un arroyo de agua que los dichos gobernador y alcaldes y demás indios que allí estaban (. . .) en forma dijeron ser allí el sitio antiguo del barrio nombrado YnIhuitlán que ahora están y viven en la dicha cabecera de Santiago y ser los principales de dicho barrio don Francisco de Zárate, don Diego del Castillo y don Diego de Aguilar y había muchos montones de piedras y árboles de morales y zapotes y en el dicho sitio había un corral de ganado menor y dijeron ser de don Diego de Aguilar y muchas sementeras de maíz sembradas y en la quebrada tres o cuatro casillas de indios y allí junto como un tiro de arcabuz había otro corral cercado de piedra asimismo ganado menor que los dichos indios confesaron ser tierras y corral de Domingo de Santa Maria indio principal del barrio de Guautongo y todas las tierras y sitio antiguo que allí estaban con todas las quebradas y oyeras y montes allí cercanos dijeron ser tierras de los naturales de dicho barrio InIhuitlán y pidieron al dicho señor alcalde mayor los ampare en ellas y visto el dicho alcalde mayor dijo que en virtud de la dicha real provisión de su majestad que ante mi tienen presentada amparaba y amparó a los dichos indios en todas las tierras y sitio antiguo y árboles y quebradas como de antes lo tenían y gozaban para que lo labren y gocen sin que ninguna persona se lo impida con pena que el que se lo contradijere se procederá contra él con mucho rigor de justicia y de derecho y mando se guarde y cumpla la dicha real provisión de su majestad como en ella se contiene y firmólo de su nombre y los dichos intérpretes, siendo presentes por testigos Francisco de Montoya y Pedro de Vargas y otros muchos indios que allí estaban. Fernando de Mújica, Pedro de Barrios, Domingo Villegas. Pasó ante mi, Pedro González de Rueda escribano público.

E luego, incontinenti el dicho señor alcalde mayor juntamente con migo el dicho Pedro, saliendo del dicho sitio de InIhuitlán y atravesando el camino real que va a la Veracruz volviendo por una loma abajo hacia la cabecera de Santo Domingo como un cuarto de legua llegados a un corral de ganado menor que los dichos gobernador, alcaldes y demás indios dijeron ser el dicho corral y tierras del dicho barrio de InIhuitlán yendo prosiguiendo como media legua llegados a unas caserías viejas donde había muchos árboles de morales y tunales y muchas casas y algunas pobladas de indios que dijeron ser allí sitio antiguo del barrio de Guautongo y ser el principal Domingo de Santa Maria, Juan de Santiago, Domingo Luis y mas abajo hacia el pueblo de Tepenene como un tiro de arcabuz un corral cercado de piedra de ganados menor que era de la comunidad del dicho barrio y allí junto otro corral de Juan de Santiago indio del dicho barrio que el dicho sitio en las tierras y árboles y todas aquellas quebradas que cerca de allí estaban dijeron ser tierras del dicho barrio y visto el dicho señor alcalde mayor dijo que en virtud de la dicha real provisión de su majestad amparaba y amparó a los dichos indios naturales de dicho barrio en las dichas tierras y corrales para que lo tengan, gocen como de antes lo hacían y mandaba y mandó que por ninguna persona le sea puesto embargo e impedimento alguno con pena que se procederá contra él con mucho rigor de derecho y se guarde y cumpla lo mandado en la dicha real provisión de su majestad e firmolo de su nombre. Testigos los susodichos. Fernando de Mújica, Pedro de Barrios, Domingo Villegas. Pasó ante mi Pedro González de Rueda escribano público.

E luego incontinenti, el dicho señor alcalde mayor juntamente con migo el dicho Pedro y los demás indios principales y macehuales y gobernador, alcaldes, saliendo del dicho sitio de Guautongo atravesando el camino que viene del pueblo de Tepenene al de Santiago yendo por una loma arriba donde había muchas sementeras de maizales sembrados pasado un arroyo de agua pareció don Francisco de Zárate indio principal del barrio de InIhuitlán y señalo unos corrales y tierras que estaban hacia el pueblo de Tepenene que se nombraba dicho sitio en su lengua Coxinxa y todos dijeron ser suyo e las dichas tierras e mas arriba como un cuarto de legua hacia el camino que viene de Cuestlauaca al de Santiago en una loma pareció don Diego del Castillo indio principal del dicho barrio de YnIhuitlán que la dicha loma se nombra Texan(rh)irru [=Loma Palo Verde] y ser tierras de dicho Diego del Castillo y de sus antepasados y los demás que en una quebrada que allí junto estaba y todos confesaron ser así lo que dicho don Diego decía yendo por la dicha derecera pasando como tres cuartos de legua habiendo atravesado el dicho camino arriba nombrado yendo por una loma de tierra baldía y montuosa y bajando por una quebrada honda donde había muchas caserías viejas y antiguas y muchos árboles de zapotes y duraznos y sementeras de maíz y junto a ellas un corral de ganado menor que los dichos indios por las dichas lenguas dijeron ser tierras de los naturales del barrio de Tlapiltepeque y el dicho corral de la comunidad del dicho barrio antiguo y pidieron al dicho señor alcalde mayor los ampare en ellas y visto el dicho señor alcalde mayor en virtud de la dicha real provisión dijo que amparaba y amparó a los dichos indios en las dichas tierras y sitio antiguo para que lo tengan y gocen como hasta aquí lo han hecho y tenido y gozado y mandaba y mandó que de ellas ni de parte de ellas sean quitados ni despojados por ningunas personas so pena de que se procederá contra ellos conforme a derecho y los dichos indios lo pidieron por testimonio y el dicho señor alcalde mayor se los mandó dar. Testigos los dichos principales del dicho barrio, Francisco Jiménez, Fernando Méndez, Juan García, Fernando de Mújica, Pedro de Barrios, Domingo Villegas. Pasó ante mi Pedro González de Rueda escribano público.

E luego el dicho señor alcalde mayor juntamente con migo el dicho Pedro, gobernador, alcaldes y demás indios de suso nombrados saliendo del dicho sitio hacia la cabecera de la Magdalena[97] como un cuarto de legua llegado en una loma alta estaban unas caserías viejas e muchos árboles de morales y zapotes y muchas sementeras de maíz por todas aquellas quebradas que los dichos indios dijeron por las dichas lenguas ser el sitio antiguo del barrio nombrado Tlapistlauaca y ser suyas todas las tierras contenidas en el dicho sitio e quebradas que llegaban a un cerro alto que estaba hacia la cabecera de San Miguel sujeta al pueblo de Tamazulapa en las cuales dichas tierras y sitio antiguo que los dichos indios señalaron el dicho señor alcalde mayor en virtud de la dicha real provisión amparaba y amparó a los dichos indios para que las tengan y gocen como de antes las tenían y mandaba y mandó que de ellas no sean quitados ni desposeídos por alguna persona so pena de que se procederá contra ella por todo rigor de derecho y los dichos indios lo pidieron por testimonio y el dicho señor alcalde mayor se los mandó dar y lo firmó de su nombre juntamente con los dichos intérpretes, testigos los dichos insertos principales del dicho barrio: Thomas de Rivera y Domingo Gutiérrez. Fernando de Mújica, Pedro del Barrio, Domingo Villegas. Pasó ante mi Pedro González de Rueda escribano público.

Después de lo susodicho en la dicha cabecera de Santiago en diez y nueve días del dicho mes de Septiembre del dicho año el dicho señor alcalde mayor prosiguiendo en lo pedido por dichos indios y en cumplimiento de la dicha real provisión salió del dicho pueblo de Santiago por el camino que va a la Magdalena y llegado como una legua pequeña encima del dicho camino sobre mano derecha llegó a un término que se nombra Tanyngurro donde estaba hecho un corral para ganado menor que los dichos gobernador, alcaldes y demás principales que allí estaban dijeron ser de la cabecera de la Magdalena y llegar allí sus términos y desde allí abajo por una quebrada abajo donde había sementeras de maíz sembradas y subiendo un cerro arriba hacía el monte llegados en un sitio que todos dijeron nombrarse Dagazee y ser el sitio antiguo del barrio de Zozompastla donde había muchas casas viejas y árboles de zapotes y cerezos y morales y un corral cercado de piedra que era de la comunidad del dicho barrio y más abajo bajando por unas quebradas a las faldas de la sierra del monte como un cuarto de legua llegamos a un cerrillo alto donde estaba otro corral cercado de leña donde se nombra Codozaa que así mismo los dichos gobernador, alcaldes y los demás indios que allí estaban dijeron ser de la comunidad del dicho barrio de Zozompastla y todas las tierras que había en aquellas quebradas y montes que dicho señor alcalde mayor había andado y visto por vista de ojos eran del dicho barrio y naturales de el del cual era principal don Miguel de Mendoza, don Martín de Cuevas y visto el dicho señor alcalde mayor dijo que en virtud de la dicha real provisión los amparaba en ellas para que las tengan y gocen como hasta aquí lo han hecho y mandaba y mandó que de ellas no sean desposeídos ni quitados por ninguna persona so pena de que se procederá contra ella con mucho rigor de derecho y en todo se guarde y cumpla la dicha real provisión y firmolo de su nombre y los dichos Pedro de Barrios, Domingo Villegas intérpretes, siendo testigos Francisco de Montoya y los dichos intérpretes, y otros muchos indios que allí estaban presentes. Fernando de Mújica, Pedro de Barrios, Domingo Villegas. Paso ante mi Pedro González de Rueda escribano público.

E luego el dicho señor alcalde mayor juntamente con migo el dicho Pedro, gobernador y alcaldes y demás principales volviendo del dicho sitio arriba nombrado por una loma abajo hacia la dicha cabecera de Santiago como un cuarto de legua llegado a un término que se nombra Ninguiny Ninguil(joo) que los dichos gobernador, alcaldes y los demás indios por las dichas lenguas dijeron llamarse del dicho nombre y ser el sitio antiguo de Tlacotepeque y ser el principal Domingo Hernández e Juan de Mendoza donde parecía haber sido poblado y detrás de la dicha loma y de la sierra que junto allí estaba había casas caídas y todas aquellas tierras de los naturales y montes que había en las dichas quebradas dijeron ser tierras de los naturales del dicho barrio y visto el dicho señor alcalde mayor dijo que en virtud de la dicha provisión de su majestad amparaba y amparó a todos los dichos indios de los dichos seis barrios en la dicha provisión nombrados en todas las tierras corrales y árboles fructuosos y montes y quebradas como de antes los tenían y mandaba y mandó que por alguna ni algunas personas no les sean quitadas ni desposeídas de todo ello so pena de que se procederá con mucho rigor contra el que lo contrario hiciere guardando ante todas cosas lo mandado en la dicha real provisión y los dichos indios por las dichas lenguas lo pidieron por testimonio y el dicho señor alcalde mayor se los mandó dar y firmolo. Testigos los dichos. Fernando de Mújica, Pedro de Barrios, Domingo Villegas. Pasó ante mi Pedro González de Rueda escribano público.

Va enmendado o dice y do dice como todo vala hecho y sacado corregido y concertado en este dicho traslado con el original que se les dio a los indios del pueblo de Santiago por mandado del señor alcalde mayor con otros tres traslados que se les han dado a los dichos naturales en el pueblo de Cuestlavaca en diez días del mes de julio de mil quinientos y ochenta y tres años y esta cierto y verdadero, siendo testigos al ver corregir Pedro Sánchez Lucena y Pedro de Castro, estantes en el pueblo, y por donde hice aquí el tercero signo que va tal. En testimonio de verdad Pedro González de Rueda escribano público.

DOCUMENT 07

AGN, Mercedes, vol. 14, f. 188 (1589). Order to review the solicitation for a sheep ranch.

Acor[da]do don Fran[cis]co de Çarate.

En la çiudad de Mex[i]co a u[ein]te y seis dias del mes de henero de qui[nient]os y ochenta y nueue años se dio m[andamien]to acordado para que el correg[id]or de Quextlauaca vea vn sitio dest[anci]a p[ar]a ganado menor que pide don Fran[cis]co de Çarate yndio n[atur]al de S[an]tiago Yguitlan en t[e]r[min]os del d[ic]ho pu[ebl]o en la parte que llaman (Cosacatho) que son tierras patrimoniales suyas con que dentro de tres meses haga las diligençias y hechas dentro de treinta dias las (pres[ent]e).

DOCUMENT 08

AGN, Indios, vol. 4, exp. 632, f. 181v (1590). License for Diego de Aguilar to travel on horseback.

L[icenci]a a don Diego de Aguilar, caçique del pu[ebl]o de Yguitlan, para andar en un cav[all]o con silla y freno.

Don Luis de V[elas]co etc. por la pres[ent]e doy liçençia a don Diego de Aguilar caçique y prinçipal del pu[ebl]o de Yguitlan p[ar]a q[ue] librem[en]te en todas las partes y lugares q[ue] fuere y anduviere de la g[obernaci]on de esta d[ic]ha Nueva Spaña pueda andar en un cavallo con silla e freno no enbarg[ant]e la prohibiçion q[ue] esta hecha çerca de que los yndios no anden a cavallo y mando q[ue] en ello no le sea puesto enbargo ni contra[dicci]on algu[n]a. Ff[ec]ho en Mex[i]co a xxv de mayo de mill y qui[nient]os y noventa años. Don Luis de V[elas]co. Por m[anda]do del virrey Joan de Cueva.

DOCUMENT 09

AGN, Indios, vol. 4, exp. 633, f. 181v (1590). License for Juan de Santiago to travel on horseback.

Licencia a don Ju[an] de Sanctiago caçique del pu[ebl]o de Yaguitongo p[ar]a andar en un cavallo con silla y freno.

Don Luis de Velasco, etc. por la presente doy liçençia a don Ju[an] de Sanctiago, yndio caçique del pu[ebl]o de Yaguiztongo, para que libremente en todas partes y lugares que fuere y anduviere de la governaçion desta d[ic]ha Nueva España pueda andar en un cavallo con silla y freno no enbargante la proyviçion questa hecha çerca de que los yndios no anden a cavallo e mando que en ello no le sea puesto enbargo ni contradiçion alguna. Ff[ech]o en Mex[i]co a beinte y çinco de mayo de mill y qui[nient]os y noventa años. Don Luis de Velasco. Por mandado del virrey Joan de Cueva.

DOCUMENT 10

AGN, Indios, vol. 4, exp. 634, f. 18, (1590). License for Diego del Castillo to travel on horseback.

Liçençia a don Diego del Castillo, caçique del pu[ebl]o de Sanctiago, para andar en un cavallo con silla y freno.

Don Luis de Velasco etc. por la presente doy liçençia a don Diego del Castillo yndio caçique del pu[ebl]o de Sanctiago para que libremente en todas partes y lugares que fuere y anduviere de la governaçion desta d[ic]ha Nueva España pueda andar en un cavallo con silla y freno no enbargante la proyviçion questa hecha çerca de que los yndios no anden a cavallo y mando que en ello no le sea puesto enbargo ni contradiçion alguna. Ff[ech]o en Mexico a beinte y çinco de mayo de mill y qui[nient]os y noventa años. Don Luis de Belasco. Por mandado del virrey Joan de Cueva.

DOCUMENT 11

AGN, Indios, vol. 3, exp. 768 (1591). In order that the judge of Yanhuitlán inform about the church the Indians of Ihuitlán wish to build.

Para q[u]e el al[ca]lde mayor de Yanguitlan ynforme sobre la que piden los de la estançia de S[an]tiago Coax(s)tlauaca

Don Luis de V[ela]sco etc. hago saber a vos el al[ca]lde mayor de Yanguitlan q[ue] los naturales de la estançia de S[an]tiago Coaxstlauaca subjeto al pu[ebl]o de Coayxstlauaca me an hecho rrela[ci]on q[ue] ellos tienen una hermita de la adboca[ci]on de S[an]tiago la q[u]al esta cubierta de paja y tienen en ella hornamentos y rrecaudo p[ar]a çelebrar las fiestas q[ue] balen mas de ocho çientos p[es]os y podria por ser la yglessia de paja quemarse o subçeder alguna cossa en q[ue] lo viniessen a perder todo y para rremedio de ello me pidio mandasse darles liçençia para hazer la d[ic]ha hermita y acavarla pues hera muy convini[en]te rrespecto de estar distantes de la caveçera ocho leguas; y por mi visto por el press[en]te os m[an]do q[ue] luego que este mandami[en]to beais me ynformeis muy en particular q[ue] hermita es la que esta en la dicha estançia de la d[ic]ha voca[ci]on de S[an]tiago y el estado y traça de ella y si esta cubierta de paja y el rriesgo que podra correr por estarlo y si convendra cubrirla de vigas y terrado por escussar algun mal subçesso y q[uan]ta gente se podra ocupar en esto y si es de voluntad de los yndios o de fuerça y el tienpo que podra durar esta obra y la calidad y tamaño de ella y si acuden con servi[ci]o a otra parte y q[ue] cantidad y la que ay aora de gente por ultima tasa[ci]on e ynformado de todo me hareis rrela[ci]on con v[uest]ro paresçer jurado p[ar]a q[ue] visto provea lo q[ue] convenga. Ff[ec]ho en Mex[i]co a v[ein]te y dos de junio de mill y qui[nient]os y noventa y un a[ñ]os. Don Luis de V[ela]sco. Por m[anda]do del virrey Pedro de Campos.

DOCUMENT 12

AGN, Mercedes, vol. 18, f. 279 (1593). Order to review the solicitation for a sheep and goat ranch for Ihuitlán.

Acor[da]do a los yndios de Santiago Yguitlan.

En Mex[i]co a vein[t]e y nueve de novi[embr]e de mill y qui[nient]os y noven[t]a y tres a[ñ]os se dio mandam[ien]to acor[da]do p[ar]a q[ue e]l al[ca]lde m[ay]or de el pu[ebl]o de Yanguitlan bea un sitio de estan[ci]a para ganado menor y dos cavallerias de tierra q[ue] piden los naturales de el pu[ebl]o de Santiago Yguitlan subjecto a el de Cuestlauaca p[ar]a propias de su comunidad en termi[n]os de el d[ic]ho pu[ebl]o en la par[t]e donde dizen Cosaye no avi[en]doseles dado otro acor[da]do con q[u]atro meses de ter[mi]no.

DOCUMENT 13

AGN, Mercedes, vol. 19, f. 147 (1593). Order to review the solicitation for a sheep and goat ranch for San Mateo.

En este dia [September 6, 1593], se dio otro m[andam]i[ent]o acordado p[ar]a q[ue e]l d[ic]ho al[ca]lde m[ay]or dentro de q[u]atro meses haga las dilig[enci]as p[ar]a la visita de un sitio de est[anci]a q[ue] pide la comunidad del pu[ebl]o de S[an] Matheo subjeto de Questlauaca en ter[mi]nos del d[ic]ho pu[ebl]o en la p[ar]te que llaman Cotzachichiy.

DOCUMENT 14

AGN, Mercedes, vol. 18, f. 263 (1593). Order to review the solicitation for a sheep and goat ranch for San Mateo.

Acor[da]do a un sujecto de Cuestlauaca.

En Mex[i]co a vein[t]e y tres de agosto de mill y qui[nient]os y noven[t]a y tres a[ñ]os se dio mandam[ien]to acordado para q[ue e]l al[ca]lde m[ay]or de la provi[nci]a de Yanguitlan bea una cavalleria de tierra q[ue] piden los naturales de la estan[ci]a de S[an] Matheo Tlalpiltepeq[ue] sujecta a el pu[ebl]o de Cuestlauaca para propios de su comunidad en termi[n]os de la d[ic]ha estan[ci]a en la parte que dizen Thothi con q[u]atro meses de ter[mi]no.

DOCUMENT 15

Municipal Archive of San Miguel Aztatla (1593). Copy of the report of the visit of Francisco de las Casas to Ihuitlán during the program of congregations. Modernized spelling.

En la estancia de Santiago Yguitlan, y alias de las Plumas, sujeta al pueblo de Coixtlahuaca, a veinte y dos días del mes de abril de mil quinientos noventa y tres años, el dicho juez visitó y demarcó la dicha estancia, en la cual hizo parecer ante si a don Diego de Castillo, cacique principal, Juan de la Cruz [y] Domingo Ortíz, regidores, don Juan de Mendoza, Francisco de San Pedro, Martín Ortíz [y] Francisco de Santiago, indios mandones, y otros muchos naturales de la dicha estancia, a los cuales, mediante y por lenguas de los dichos intérpretes, les dio a entender como su Majestad mandaba que todos los naturales de esta Nueva España se juntasen y congregasen a pueblos formales y mayores y en partes a donde cada día de fiesta pudiesen oir misa y ser doctrinados con más cuidado, y que así era venido a este pueblo con una provi[c]ional comisión[98] del señor virrey para efecto de elegir sitio conveniente para su población; y que de parte de su Magestad demandaba tuviesen por bien y acudiesen a amirar[99] a los demás naturales y a juntarse y congregarse a donde se les señalare, los cuales, habiéndolo entendido, dijeron que lo oyen. Y luego el dicho juez les mandó citar para la visita y demás autos de estas diligencias y para que se hallen presentes a la publicación del sitio que se les diere y eligiese para su población; y mediante los dichos intérpretes fueron citados en forma. Y (lue)go el dicho juez les mandó digan y declaren la cantidad que tiene de tributos y el temple de este pueblo, si es frío o caliente, los cuales dichos indios declararon que en esta dicha estancia de Santiago había ciento y treinta casados tributarios de lengua cho(ch)a; que su temple era de tierra fría; la cual dicha estancia (está) fundada tres leguas de su cabecera de ésta en un repago[100] de una (lom)a rodeada de cañadas y valles que hacen unas lomas y cerrillos (. . .)ados que tienen alrededor, las casas de piedra y barro, con calles trazadas en policía; tienen un jacal para iglesia y casas de comunidad, van labrando iglesia nueva de buenos edificios de cal y piedra, que tienen levantadas paredes; el agua tienen bastante en fuentes y en un arroyo de agua que corre y pasa al raíz de las casas del pueblo hacia la parte de poniente, y otro arroyo de agua en su cercanía a la parte del sur, tienen muchos magueyales, nopaleras y muchas (. . .); que los naturales dicen que en tiempo antiguo había haber (sido) más pobla[c]iones, que los dueños de ellos[101] son los traídos a otros su(. . .) sementeras tienen en las cuadras del pueblo, y en las cañadas y valles que están en su cercanía hay muchas tierras baldías buenas para sementeras de maíz y trigo, y el sitio está muy acomodado para cualquier población, y el monte tiene a una legua del pueblo; más tienen muchos árboles morales (de) que crían seda; la comunidad tiene una estancia poblada con mil cabezas de ganados, obejas, para propios de ellos que está media legua del pueblo hacia la parte del norte, y los naturales declararon tener entre todos hasta la cantidad de dos mil cabezas, que es la principal granjería que tienen. Y en esta forma (fue) la dicha visita, estando presentes el dicho cacique y mandones de la dicha estancia y el gobernador, alcaldes y principales del pueblo y cabecera de Coixtlahuaca que respondieron y sa(tis)facieron en esta visita, a los cuales fueron preguntados; y lo firmó el dicho juez e intérpretes, siendo testigos el padre Cristóbal de Medina, Miguel de Casas y Gaspar de Mendoza estantes en este pueblo. Don Francisco de las Casas, Cristóbal Jiménez, Juan Mejía. Ante mi Alonso Vásquez, escribano real.

[Some remarks follow:]
Esto es un tanto de los autos y procesos originales que está[n] en el archivo de la comunidad de nuestra cabecera de Coixtlahuaca, que se trasuntó por mandado de don Pedro Hernández, gobernador de esta provincia en este presente año de 1732. [first copy]

Esta copia se hizo en treinta y uno de m(. . .) de mil setecientos y noventa años y para que conste firmé yo, Fabiman [*sic*] y Sebastián de la Cruz. [second copy]

En este pueblo de San Miguel Astatla, hoy día jueves a ocho días de enero del presente año de mil ochocientos siete, saqué yo, José Bernardo López, este traslado por tercera vez a según lo apercibí por su original; y deseo que esto sea a mayor honra y (gloria) de dios [y] bien, provecho y salva[c]ión de mi alma y de todas las personas que llegaren a ver este dicho traslado, para que re(visa)ndo su contenido no mueran inocentes para alguna co(. . .)ción por lo que pudiere suceder en lo sucesivo y para que (no los) cojan [de] tontos se dirigirán por esta comprención (. . .). [third copy]

DOCUMENT 16

Archivo de Notarías de Puebla, Tehuacán, caja 1, carpeta 4, f. 49–49v (1594). Power of attorney given by don Diego de Castillo to fray Jerónimo de Abrego, leaving for Spain. The lands he mentions coincide with mercedes transcribed in documents 04 and 12. This letter is part of a series of eight letters given to fray Jerónimo de Abrego just before the fleet sailed off to Spain. Among these letters are the written powers of Abrego himself, the cabildo of Coixtlahuaca, Francisco de Mendoza (lord of Tepenene, Coixtlahuaca), Miguel de Velasco (lord of Necustlatepeque, Coixtlahuaca), the cabildo of Tepexi, and the cabildo of Tehuacán.

En el pueblo de Teguacan en quatro dias del mes de mayo de mill e qui[nient]os e noventa e quatro años ante mi el escriv[an]o e testigos paresçio presente un yndio que mediante Miguel de Velasco ynterpete dijo llamarse don Diego del Castillo, caçique e prinçipal que dijo ser del pueblo de Cuestlabaca de la Misteca Alta, y señor natural de la estançia de Santiago Yhuitlan, subjeta al d[ic]ho pueblo, y como tal dijo tener en terminos de la d[ic]ha estançia muchas tierras de su señorio y caçicasgo heredadas de ynmemorial [tiempo] a esta parte de sus padres y aguelos y antepasados por linea rrecta en las quales an pretendido muchos españoles tomar caballerias de tierra e estançias e procurado se les haga m[erce]d dellas por los visorreyes que an governado esta Nueva España e porque no se les entren en las d[ic]has sus tierras [h]a pedido a los d[ic]hos visorreyes le hagan m[erce]d de dalle en ellas sitios de estançia no enbargante que son de su pattimonio las quales constandoles por diligençias q[ue] las justiçias a quien cometieron la bista de las d[ic]has tierras y aberiguaçion de si estaban en perjuisio de (. . .) persona que no lo estaban y ser suyas y de su patrimonio le hisieron m[erce]d de dos sitios destançia p[ar]a ganado menor las quales a mucho tienpo q[ue] las tiene pobladas con cabras y obejas llamadas la bna Cuxiedaroa y la otra Cuxaye de las quales tiene los titulos e mercedes de los d[ic]hos visorreyes e no enbargante lo susod[ic]ho y q[ue] las tiene y posee con el titulo que tiene declarado pretende que su Mag[esta]d del rrey don Felipe nuestro señor o los señores de su Rreal Consejo de las Yndias en su nonbre le confirmen las d[ic]has merçedes, titulos e rrecaudos que tiene de los d[ic]hos dos sitios de est[anci]a p[ar]a que el y todos sus herederos y subçesores presentes y por benir las tengan y gosen agora e para sienpre jamas como cossa suya propia, sin que por ning[un]a persona le puedan ser quitadas en ningun t[iem]po e porque p[ar]a poder conseguir la d[ic]ha m[erce]d tiene nesçesidad de que en su nonbre aya quien lo pida e porq[ue] ninguna persona mejor q[ue e]l muy rr[everen]do padre fray Jer[oni]mo de Abrego, rrelijioso de la orden del glorioso padre Santo Domingo, que al presente esta de camino p[ar]a los rreinos de Castilla en la flota que al presente esta surta en el puerto de San Ju[an] de Blua, a quien consta ser çierto lo contenido en esta carta, y sabe y conosçe las d[ic]has tierras, por tanto otorgo e dixo que daba y dio todo su poder cunplido tal qual de d[e]r[ech]o en tal casso se rrequiere e mas puede y debe baler al d[ic]ho fray Jer[oni]mo de Abrego q[ue] esta presente, espeçialmente p[ar]a que por el y en su nonbre y como el mismo rrepresentando su propia persona pueda pedir a su Mag[esta]d le confirme todas las merçedes e titulos que tiene de las d[ic]has estançias p[ar]a que agora ni en ningun tienpo le puedan ser quitadas por ninguna causa ni rrazon que sea, y asimismo p[ar]a que en las d[ic]has tierras de la d[ic]ha est[anci]a de Santiago ni en las de su caçigasgo ningun visorrey ni otra persona pueda hazer ninguna m[erce]d de tierras ni estançias a ninguna persona atento a que son pocas e muy nesçesarias p[ar]a los naturales para las senbrar e tener fruto dellas p[ar]a su sustento y de sus mugeres e hijos e paga de sus tributos, y asimismo pueda pedir a su Mag[esta]d se s(irv)a de le hazer nuebas merçedes por la orden q[ue] lo tiene tratado y com[un]icado con el d[ic]ho fray Jer[oni]mo de Abrego; y en todo haga aquello quel haria siendo presente que quan cun[p]lido y (bast[ant]e) poder es neçessario p[ar]a el d[ic]ho hefeto otro tal y ese mismo le dio con libre e general administraçion y con cargo de q[ue] lo puede sostituir en bn procurador, dos e mas, y los rrebocar y otros nonbrar; en testi[moni]o de lo q[u]al otorgo esta carta ante mi el d[ic]ho escriv[an]o e testigos e lo firmo de su nonbre con el ynterprete siendo testigos Alonso Prieto de Bonilla y Alvaro Alonso Prieto y el capitan Luis P[ere]z de Bargas, v[ecin]os deste pueblo.

Don Diego del Castillo
Miguel de Velasco
Ante mi Cosme de Tuesta escriv[an]o de su Mag[esta]d

DOCUMENT 17

AGPJO, Teposcolula, caja 2, doc. 217 (1616). Registration of shepherds in Ihuitlán. Gregorio de Aguilar and Gabriel de Mendoza also appear, together with Francisco de Santiago, as lords of Ihuitlán in Archivo General de Indias, México, leg. 141, ramo 3, no. 50 and 50a (1623). There is an early mention of San Francisco Teopan as a "barrio" of Ihuitlán.

En el pu[ebl]o de Santiago Yguitlan en beynte dias del mes de jullio de mill y seisçientos y diez años, Bartolome Sanchez theniente por don Gaspar de Bera Rrodriguez alcalde mayor del pu[ebl]o y prouinçia de Yanguitlan por su mag[esta]d dixo que por quanto los naturales deste d[ic]ho pueblo contrabiniendo a lo mandado por los señores birreyes y rreal audi[enci]a desta Nueba España tienen corrales de ganado menor dentro de las casas del d[ic]ho pueblo y solares en mas cantidad de las treçientas cabeças que se les permite a cada uno y muchos dellos les cortan las orejas a las obejas que asi tienen y atento a que la ordenança manda que tengan el tal ganado un quarto de legua del pu[ebl]o y apartado de las simenteras con guarda mandaba y mando a don Greg[ori]o de Aguilar rregidor y prinçipal deste d[ic]ho pueblo luego presente la memoria de todos los yndios e yndias que tienen corrales dentro del d[ic]ho pu[ebl]o y la cantidad que tiene cada uno y con que señal para mandarles lo que deban haçer con aperçibimi[en]to que si ocultaren alguno se proçedera conforme a der[ech]o y asi lo proueyo m[an]do e ffirmo.

Bart[olo]me Sanchez
Ante mi Manuel Lopez [e]scriu[an]o n[ombra]do

Notificación

E luego el dicho dia, mes y año yo el escriuano en pres[enci]a del d[ic]ho teniente y por lengua de Fr[ancis]co Rrodriguez ynterp[ret]e y de Çacarias Lopez alcalde del pu[ebl]o de Cuestlabaca ley y notifique el auto de atras a don Greg[ori]o de Aguilar contenido en el y auiendolo entendido dixo que cunplira lo que se le manda y lo ffirmo de su nonbre con el teniente e ynterpetes.

Bart[olo]me Sanchez
Don Greg[ori]o de Aguilar
Fran[cis]co Rrodriguez
Çacaria Lopez
Ante mi Manuel Lopez [e]scriu[an]o n[ombra]do

E luego el dicho dia beynte de julio del dicho don Gregorio en cumplimiento de lo que se la mando parecio ante el dicho teniente y exsibio una memoria firmada de su nonbre en que pareçe ay treynta y seys corales de ganado menor y numerado cada persona las obejas que tienen en que entran algunas cabras y declaro por lengua de los ynterpretes que todos estan dentro deste dicho pueblo de Santiago excepto dos que son el del dicho don Gregorio de Aguilar que tiene quatroçientas cabeças de cabras y obejas y el de don Grabiel de Mendoça prinçipal del bario de San Françisco [Teopan] que este tiene quatroçientas y treçe cabeças todas de bientre que estos dos corales esta[n] apartados deste dicho pu[ebl]o junto a unas milpas y que la dicha memoria fue asi presenta(do e)s çierta (y ver)dadera y que no ay mas corales dentro d(es)te d(icho pueblo) y sin estos ay otros dos corrales apartados deste dicho p[uebl]o el uno con duçientas y sesenta obejas y el otro conduçientas y çinquenta y çinco cabras y questaran el uno apartado del otro como un quarto de legua los quales declaro el dicho don Gregorio de Aguilar ser de la yglesia deste dicho pu[ebl]o y que sin estos ay otros dos corrales con quatroçientas y quarenta obejas y çiento y sesenta cabras que asimismo declaro ser todas de la comunidad deste dicho pu[ebl]o todo lo qual declaro debajo de juramento y lo firmo con los ynterpretes y tiniente.

Bart[olo]me Sanchez
Fran[cis]co Rrodriguez
Don Greg[ori]o de Aguilar
Çacaria Lopez
Ante mi Manuel Lopez [e]scriu[an]o n[ombra]do

Auto

En el pueblo de Santiago Yguitlan en beynte dias del mes de julio de mil y seysçientos y diez y seys años el dicho teniente abiendo bisto la memoria presentada por el dicho don Gregorio de Aguilar mando pareçer ante si a todos los contenidos en la dicha memoria exçepto a don Grabiel de Mendoça a (lo)s quales mando se les notifique a cada uno declare si es çierta la dicha memoria y siendolo presenten las liçencias, decretos y mandamientos que tubieren para poder tener los corrales y ganado dentro deste dicho pueblo y abiendo(. . .) juntado los yndios e yndias dueños de los dichos corrales yo el escribano les notifique lo mandado por el dicho teniente mediante los dichos ynterpretes los quales cada uno de por si dijeron que la dicha memoria es çierta y berdadera y que no tienen ninguna liçençia ni mandamiento ni decreto para poder tener las dichas obejas y corrales en el pu[ebl]o donde los tienen y esto dieron por rrespuesta y firmolo el dicho don Gregorio e ynterpretes.

Bart[olo]me Sanchez
Fran[cis]co Rrodriguez
Don Greg[ori]o de Aguilar
Çacaria Lopez
Ante mi Manuel Lopez [e]scriu[an]o n[ombra]do

Observations on the Glosses of the Lienzo of Tlapiltepec

MICHAEL SWANTON AND BAS VAN DOESBURG

In his classic study of the Lienzo of Tlapiltepec, Alfonso Caso observed that several early glosses were written in the map section of this remarkable pictographic document (1961:272–73). He attempted to transcribe five of the glosses but was unable to determine their meaning or the language in which they were written. Since then there has been no advance in the interpretation of these glosses, which have remained a mystery. In this short appendix, we offer a general description of the glosses and provide tentative interpretations for some of them.

Ten single-word glosses appear on the Lienzo of Tlapiltepec. They form two groups based on their geographic distribution and the orientation of the writing. Four glosses, which we number 1 to 4, appear in the map section of the lienzo that corresponds to the northernmost villages of the Coixtlahuaca Valley (fig. 2.28). These glosses are to be read from the north or lower end of the map; that is, they are upside-down from the perspective of the neighboring topograms.[102] A second group of six glosses, which we number 5 to 10, appears in the section of the lienzo that depicts a swath of what is now southern Puebla at the lower right of the lienzo. These glosses are oriented at a right angle to the neighboring topograms so as to be read from the west or right-hand side of the map.

The glosses were written in a Chocho-Popoloca language, a branch of the Popolocan language family.[103] As we shall see, there is evidence that the specific language is Chocholtec, also called Chocho. The annotations are toponyms, some of which can be interpreted to gloss adjacent topograms. We suspect that all of the glosses fulfill this function. Table 2.1 provides tentative transcriptions of nine of these ten difficult-to-read glosses.

In Popolocan languages, toponyms are generally endocentric compounds in which a noun functioning as a toponymic class term precedes a qualifier, also often a noun. The toponymic class term specifies what type of geographic feature is being named. This structure can be discerned in many of the glosses appearing in the Lienzo of Tlapiltepec. Gloss 1 begins with *tho-*, apparently meaning "hill." In gloss 3, the initial constituent, *ña-*, "mountain," is visible, though its qualifier is not. Glosses 6, 8, and 9 begin with the class term *da-*, meaning "river" or more generally "water." This constituent would have been prenasalized (i.e., *nda*) even though this feature was not written. Gloss 7 begins with the term *tza-*, probably meaning "ravine."

A second type of toponymic construction in Popolocan languages involves the use of spatial adpositions to indicate relative position. This may be the case in gloss 10 with the initial element *ca-* that could mean "on top of." Gloss 5 begins with a constituent *quii-* that can be interpreted either as the class term meaning "plain, flatland" or as the adposition meaning "below." As with the term *da-*, *quii-* would have been prenasalized.[104]

TABLE 2.1. Glosses of the Lienzo of Tlapiltepec

1	*thotzo*	6	*daroo*
2	*tox(.)o*	7	*tzachee*
3	*ña(...)*	8	*daradze*
4	[illegible]	9	*dasuçe*
5	*quiiquiza*	10	*cava*

Note: Dots indicate missing (unreadable) letters.

Tentative interpretations of the qualifying constituent can be proposed for some of the glosses. In gloss 9, the toponymic classifier *da-* is followed by *suçe*. The constituent *suçe* appears to be related to the word for "mirror." In Atzingo Popoloca today

FIG. 2.28. Location and orientation of glosses on map section of Lienzo of Tlapiltepec.

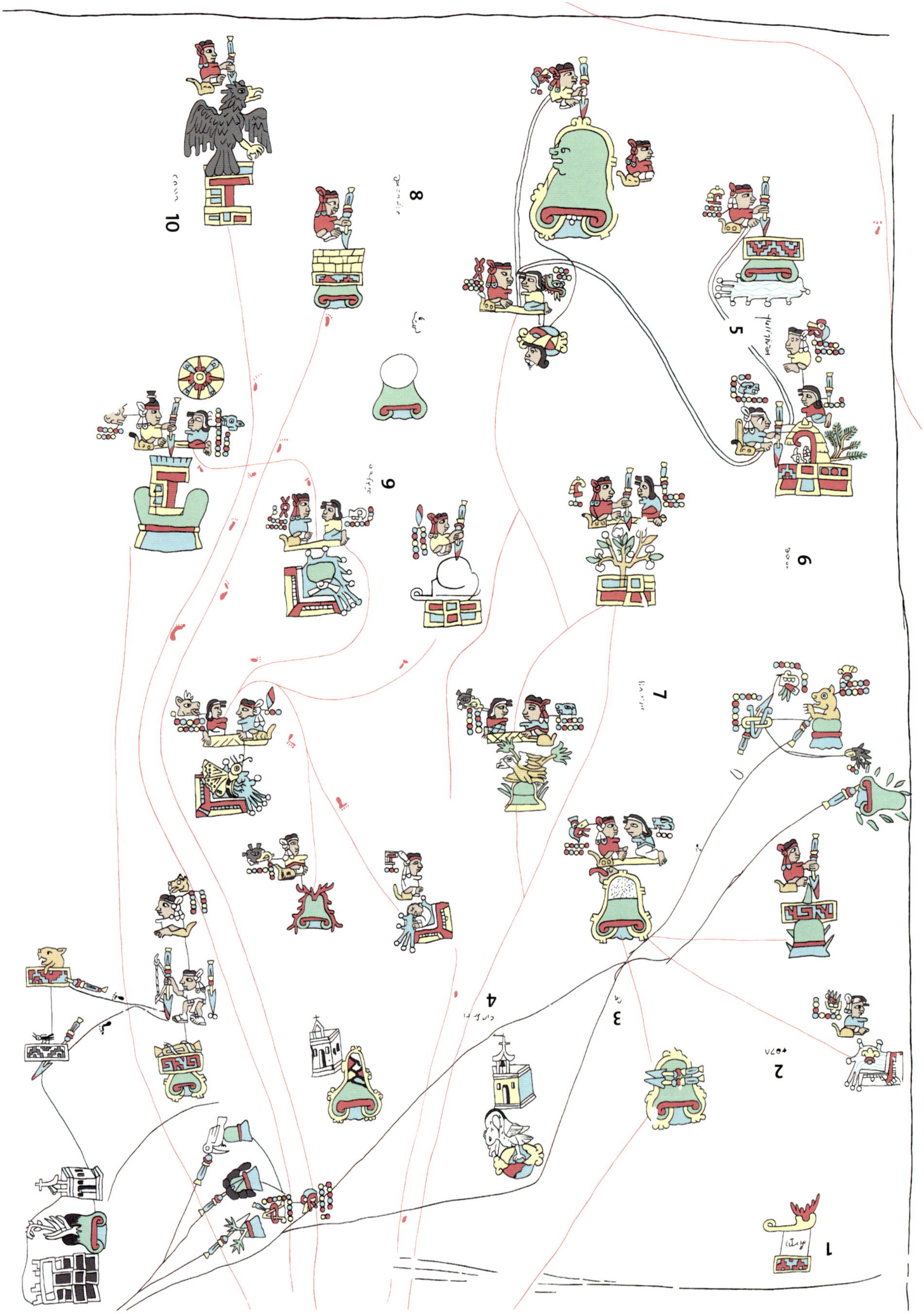

ʂu^1*se*^{1}*nda*^{1} means "mirror" or "glass," while in Otlaltepec Popoloca the cognate form *ʂuʔseʔndaʔ* refers to the stained-glass windows of the church.[105] This word also appears in a handwritten *doctrina* in Old Chocholtec, written *xuçenda*, where it refers to a mirror.[106] This noun is itself a compound, in which the head is *ʂu*^{1} (orthographically, *xu* or *su*), meaning "stone." We speculate that the form *se*^{1}*nda*^{1} (orthographically, *çenda*) is etymologically bimorphemic and that the second constituent, *nda*, originally meant "obsidian." This now obsolete morpheme for "obsidian" is attested in the Old Chocholtec toponym for the Tequixtepec "barrio" of Izapa: Ndanda. Izapa (in Nahuatl) and Ndanda (in Chocholtec) both mean "obsidian river."[107] This would mean that *suçe* would be some sort of mirror or reflector, and *xuçenda* would have originally specified an obsidian mirror.

Gloss 9 appears adjacent to a topogram that Doesburg has proposed to be Atexcal. The Nahuatl etymology for Atexcal, which means "lake," is "water mirror." The topogram depicts a hemispherical pyrite mirror that indigenous lords also wore as adornment, passing a leather strap through a hole in the convex back surface. These mirrors are well known by archaeologists and are sometimes depicted in pictography.[108] Although we have not been able to identify the present-day name for Atexcal in any Popolocan language, the close semantic relation of our interpretation of the gloss with both the Nahuatl etymology and the topogram leads us to propose that gloss 9 is the Chocho-Popoloca name for Atexcal.

We are less sure of our transcription of gloss 6: *daroo*. What we have transcribed as <r> may actually be <z>. However, if it is indeed <r>, the gloss can be read as "crag river." This gloss appears just beneath the topogram of Tecamachalco.[109] Although the present-day Chocholtec name for Tecamachalco is unknown, its name in Otlaltepec Popoloca is well attested as *ndaʔt*^{j}*huʔ*. The etymology of this toponym is "crag river."[110] By regular sound changes, proto-Popolocan **t*^{j} was innovated to Chocholtec *r* and was retained as *t*^{j} in Popoloca. This would mean the anticipated Chocholtec cognate would have had the approximate form **ndaɽhu*, closely corresponding to the gloss *daroo*.[111] We therefore propose that gloss 6 labels the accompanying topogram of Tecamachalco. The consequence of our interpretation, if correct, is that the language in which the gloss is written is indeed Chocholtec, not Popoloca.

Between these two glosses appears gloss 7 (*tzachee*). As mentioned above, *tza-* probably means "ravine." A possible interpretation of the second element is *ʧhè*, (in modern orthography, *chjè*) a classifying noun that appears both alone and as the head of a compound for various non-citric fruits. Next to gloss 7 appears a topogram of a platform with a zapote tree on top. When considering this topogram's geographic location relative to other topograms on the map section of the lienzo, a plausible identification would be Zapotitlán Salinas.[112] Unfortunately, we do not have a toponym for this village registered in any Popolocan language.[113] Since one of the fruits classified as *ʧhè* is the zapote, we suggest that gloss 7 is the toponym for Zapotitlán.

The orthography used to write in Chocholtec on the Lienzo of Tlapiltepec leaves out both prenasalization and, frequently, aspiration. Combined with the gothic-derived script, this suggests that the glosses date to the sixteenth century. It is not clear why these particular topograms were glossed in Chocholtec, but two other Coixtlahuaca Valley lienzos—the Lienzo of Coixtlahuaca I and the Lienzo of Coixtlahuaca II (Seler II)—also include Chocholtec glosses of topograms that depict localities to the north of the valley.

NOTES

1. Personal communication, Adam Sellen. Parmenter thought the sale of the lienzo to the Royal Ontario Museum took place in 1917.
2. Although some may question the use of the words "writing" and "script" in relation to the Postclassic semasiographic system, I prefer them since there are important formal and social similarities between writing systems in the strict sense (i.e., predominantly sound-based systems) and the Postclassic system. Both include, for instance, the use of books and paper, writing in "lines" [in books], and detailed historical and economic record-keeping.
3. See Johnson, this volume, chapter 1, note 7, on the measurements of the lienzo.
4. The Coixtlahuaca Group manuscripts are: Lienzo of Coixtlahuaca I, (Mexico), Lienzo of Coixtlahuaca II or Seler II (Berlin), Lienzo A (New Orleans), Lienzo of Ihuitlán (Brooklyn), Lienzo of Tulancingo (Tulancingo), Lienzo of Tlapiltepec (Toronto), Lienzos of Tequixtepec I and II (both in Tequixtepec), Lienzo of Nativitas (Nativitas), Lienzo of Otla (Otla), Gómez de Orozco Fragment (location unknown), Selden Roll (Oxford), and Codex Baranda (Mexico).
5. For the decipherment and the analysis of the Mixtec pictographic writing, see Caso (1949, 1960, 1966); Smith (1973a, 1983); Anders, Jansen, and Pérez Jiménez (1992b); Jansen (1992, 1994); Boone (2000b); Jansen and Pérez Jiménez (2000, 2011).
6. Alfonso Caso (1954, 1958, 1961) wrote valuable first commentaries on Gómez de Orozco Fragment, Codex Baranda, and the Lienzos of Tlapiltepec and Ihuitlán. Ross Parmenter (1961, 1970, 1982, 1993, 1994, 1997) added ideas, discovered more documents (the two Lienzos of Tequixtepec and the Lienzo of Tulancingo) and did important work on the identification of places and the history of the documents. Mary Elizabeth Smith (1973a) and Alfonso Caso (1979) gave general descriptions of these documents. Maarten Jansen (1982b, 1992) made several crucial identifications in the Lienzo of Tlapiltepec and Coixtlahuaca II. Viola König (1984) and her colleagues from Hamburg analyzed the Lienzo of Coixtlahuaca II in detail. Other works on documents of the Coixtlahuaca Group are Johnson (1994a, 1997) and Rincón Mautner (1994, 1997, 2000, 2007). See also Doesburg (1998a, 1998b, 2000, 2001, 2002, 2004, and 2010b).
7. According to Seler, Rickards acquired the lienzo at a price of 2,000 pesos (personal communication, Eckehard Dolinski), but Parmenter (1982) mentions a price of 800 pesos. A reconstruction of events between 1904 and 1919 can be found in Doesburg (1998b). The original sales contract states that the lienzo was sold for 400 pesos. A commentary by Abraham Castellanos states: "Este lienzo fue vendido en una cantidad insignificante al Lic. Constantino Rickards, de esta ciudad, por un tinterillo de la Mixteca. El lienzo salió de manos del Lic. Rickards, y fué rescatado por mí, en México, en momentos de hacerse una transacción mercantil. Después de un incidente judicial en el que intervino el Lic. Adolfo Fenochio, logré devolver el Lienzo a su legítimo dueño, quien lo posee actualmente. Posteriormente, logré localizar la procedencia, y confirmé que era de la región mixteca, perteneciente al pueblo de Tlapiltepec, Distrito de Coixtlahuaca" (*El Heraldo de Oaxaca*, undated clipping [1915?] in the Manuel Brioso y Candiani collection of the Francisco de Burgoa Library, Oaxaca).
8. Population estimates for Coixtlahuaca are according to preliminary results from Steve Kowalewski's (University of Georgia) archaeological survey project currently underway. Durán (1984:185) and Anales de Cuauhtitlán (in Velázquez 1975) give us sparse information. Sixteenth-century administrative documents repeatedly report the importance of Coixtlahuaca as an Aztec military post and tribute-collecting center.
9. Several colonial documents mention Mixtec and Chocho "parcialidades" (called "barrios" in the documents). In an undated text (ca. 1700) from the archive of Santa María Nativitas, "*la tepad* (from *tecpan*, 'palace') *de Tineñe, que es vn barrio segundo de los mistecos*" is mentioned. The same text mentions a "*barrio de los chochos, primer barrio Tlanepatlan Ytlaguaca.*" In another undated text from the same period, reference is made to the tequitlatos (administrators) of the Mixtec and Chocho "barrios." Finally, a Mixtec note written on the inside cover of a choral book from Coixtlahuaca also mentions Mixtec and Chocho barrios: *Barrio xitin tzicaha* and *Barrio xitin ngihua*.
10. The Nahuatl term for community was *altepetl*, "water mountain" or *in atl in tepetl*, "water and mountain." This appears sporadically in Mixtec as *yucunduta*. The Nahuatl term for cacicazgo, "mat-and-throne," was *in petlatl in icpalli*. This appears as *yuhuitayu* in Mixtec and *ñiñasitnau* in Chocho.
11. For a detailed study of the sociopolitical structure in the Mixteca region, see Terraciano (2001). Though that book is focused on the Mixtecs, abundant historical evidence suggests there was no notable difference from the situation in the Coixtlahuaca region, inhabited by both Mixtecs and Chochos. A detailed study of Chocho sociopolitical organization can be found in Doesburg and Swanton (2011). It was not uncommon to have more than one royal house in a community.
12. It is possible that the "Plano de Coixtlahuaca" that Antonio Peñafiel showed to the visitors of the International Congress of Americanists in 1895 (Glass and Robertson 1975:110) was the Lienzo of Coixtlahuaca II. A detail of the Lienzo of Coixtlahuaca II was included in the illustrations that Martínez Gracida commissioned for his monumental unpublished work (1910) on Oaxacan indigenous history and archaeology.
13. Another reference to the Lienzo of Coixtlahuaca I and the lost original of Lienzo A is from Louis Forsyth, who, perhaps in 1906, went to Coixtlahuaca, where he met a certain J. Cano, "a merchant of Coitlahuaca [sic]." Forsyth also notes in his 1912 article: "There are several old maps in Coixtlahuaca; one with numerous painted hieroglyphs and another showing the villages of the ancient district of Coixtlahuaca" (p. 269). Michael Swanton generously passed me this reference.
14. As Michael Swanton kindly told me, documents related to the acquisition of the Lienzo of Coixtlahuaca I can be found in the Archivo Histórico de la Dirección del INAH, vol. 19, exp. 12 (fols. 213–15) and vol. 24, exp. 13 (fols. 228–32). Monroy describes the exhibition in the Oaxacan museum as follows: "En el entrepaño de un muro hay un códice de Coixtlahuaca, pintado en el siglo XVI, se distingue por el jeroglífico del lugar que significa Llano de Culebra. En la parte superior tiene la llegada de los españoles, a la izquierda una banda azul del río que bordea la población, en cuanto a las fajas son huellas de caminos. En otros lugares del lienzo se reproducen las batallas de los conquistadores, en su recorrido por la mixteca, pues hay nombres de pueblos representados por sus jeroglíficos."
15. Archivo Histórico del Museo Nacional de Antropología, vol. 169, exp. 46, fols. 251–53.

16. Lienzo A exists only in the form of a copy, now at Tulane University, which was reportedly made by Nicolás León (Parmenter 1970:183) together with a copy of the Lienzo of Coixtlahuaca I and a copy of the Lienzo Abraham Castellanos / Javier Córdoba. Elsewhere (Doesburg 2001:30 n. 7 and 2010a) I have argued that Francisco Belmar made all three copies.
17. The Codex Baranda contains the image of a church with the sacred date of year 1 House, day 12 Alligator. Unfortunately, no other documents that refer to a church or temple have this date. There must have been documents from the northern kingdoms as well, such as Aztatla and Texcalhueyac, but these have not survived, with the exception of a heavily damaged and therefore unreadable cloth from Aztatla.
18. Sacred bundles, holding the symbols or remains of the gods and primordial ancestors, played a crucial role in Mesoamerican religion. They were considered the containers of divine power, and as such, essential in the protection of the community. They were also considered animated beings, holding their own calendar names. They are often represented adorned with a mask of the earth spirits with whom the ancestors were identified. Communication with the bundles was achieved through elaborate rituals involving trancelike experiences.
19. The written records of this conflict are preserved in Archivo General de Indias (hereinafter AGI), Escribanía, 160B, no. 4.
20. There may be one exception: In the left-hand margin of the Lienzo de Ihuitlán, a warrior is seated in front of a palace glossed Texopa, the name of the town called Tejupan today. However, the glyph behind the palace represents a cattail reed, which suggests that the Aztec capital, Tenochtitlan, was meant. Footsteps lead from the warrior toward Lord Atonal. The accompanying date, year 7 House, is 1461.
21. Atonaltzin means "Revered One with the Day-Name Water." Nahuatl sources generally do not mention the numbers in the translation of Mixtec or Chocho day names. We will see another example of this later on, in the case of a man named 11 Vulture in the Coixtlahuaca lienzos and Vulture (Cozcacuauhtli) in Nahuatl sources.
22. To give some examples of this scheme: the Aztec incursion into Cuauhtinchan territory in 1398 AD was in fact due to an invitation of the Pinome (or Chocho-Popoloca) lords of Cuauhtinchan (Reyes García 1977:83), who felt oppressed by the Chichimec lords, and the conquest of Tepeaca in 1466 was again the result of an invitation by the Pinome lords, this time suffering the pressure of Tepeaca. Older examples of this scheme can also be given: the Mixtec lord 8 Deer was probably invited to the coast by Juquila's Chatino lords in order to protect Juquila from the increasing chaos produced by the disintegration of the Río Viejo site (Joyce et al. 2004).
23. Torquemada 1986, 1:160. Torquemada even suggests there may have been an Aztec garrison in Tlaxiaco at this time.
24. Anales de Cuauhtitlán (in Velázquez 1975), par. 189.
25. According to the note in the previous source, the emperor found a "jewel" incrusted in her "nature." In a metaphorical sense, "jewel" (*chalchihuite*) refers to the fetus. I would like to thank Michael Swanton for this illuminating insight.
26. This Eztepec is different from the Eztepec previously mentioned. The names Eztepec (or Yeztepec) and Tiñeñe come from a series of interesting documents kept in the local archive of Santa María Nativitas (Doesburg 2001:45).
27. The names "Toad Hill" and "Reed Place" can be seen in the *Historia tolteca-chichimeca* (Kirchhoff, Odena Güemes, and Reyes García 1976, folio 14). See Graulich (2002:101–102) for the toad name of Cholula. Also, "Toad Pool" is a name for Teotihuacan in Codex Xolotl (Dibble 1996, plate 1).
28. In the Lienzo of Tlapiltepec, one of the mountains—also covered with snow, as Nicholas Johnson (personal communication) noted—is marked by a fishnet, the other by a flowering maguey with what looks like a bird's nest. The Mapa of Cuauhtinchan 2 (Yoneda 1981) locates an identical "Fishnet Mountain" close to Tultitlán.
29. "Precious Stone and Quetzal Feather" is a metaphor for offspring. A well with this name (Huicolli Chalchihuitli Quetzali, "Vase of Jade and Quetzal Feathers") is mentioned near Tehuacán in the Anales de Tepeteopan (Lara Tenorio, Celestino Solís, and Pérez Alemán 2009)
30. This place sign with its hill marked with a black circle and swirl of water occurs frequently in Codex Selden (pp. 5-III, 9-IV, 10-IV, 14-II, 15-III, 19-IV) and has tentatively been identified as Tiltepec by Jansen (2000:121). It is also depicted in Codex Bodley, p. 7v (compare Lord 8 Rain "War Eagle" in this painting and in Selden, p. 9). The same place, "Black Mountain–Swirl of Water," may be represented in Codex Vindobonensis, pp. 38 and 1. Tiltepec was an important cacicazgo during the Postclassic period and during the sixteenth century, when it had close ties to the dynasty of Yanhuitlán.
31. The Lienzo of Coixtlahuaca II and the Lienzo of Tlapiltepec show 2 Flower with the Toltec nose ornament. The Lienzo of Tlapiltepec also represents his journey to and conversations at "Town of Flint Knives," today the archaeological site of Mogote del Cacique, near Tilantongo (Jansen 1982b:275–76).
32. The Lienzo of Ihuitlán depicts the two sacred beings in the "mountain" or rock that is part of the glyph of Coixtlahuaca. The bundle called 9 Wind, wearing the mask of the earth spirit, has been put on a small throne. One Lizard, represented as a priest figure with the characteristics of the earth spirit, is sitting in front of the bundle. In the Lienzo of Tulancingo, these entities—the 9 Wind bundle and 1 Lizard—are depicted between Ihuitlán's founding couple. They are depicted as wrapped dead bodies (ancestors) bearing the same two names. Nine Wind is one of the names of Quetzalcoatl, an important primordial hero in the Mixtec creation story told in the Codex Vindobonensis. This Quetzalcoatl bundle is also prominent in the origin story told in the Selden Roll (Burland 1955).
33. The 9 Wind bundle is especially important in Codex Nuttall, pp. 14–22. See Jansen and Pérez Jiménez 2007:107–113, for a commentary.
34. The patches of black paint around the eyes represent the name "Burned Eyes," which is registered in sixteenth-century Mixtec language sources as a name for Toltecs. In the Lienzo of Tequixtepec II, the names of the bundle-carrying founders (Totepeuh, Chalchiuhtona, and Cuauhtlix) are identical to several of Culhuacán's early kings (Doesburg 2002:19). For example, the "Relación de la genealogía" (García Icazbalceta 1891:265, 270) mentions Totepeuh, Chalchiuhtlatonac, and Cuauhtlix among the Culhuacán kings. This is not to say these persons are the mentioned kings, but only that they carry names from the Toltec tradition. Culhuacán was a famous Toltec center in the central Mexican basin.
35. The identification of this place of origin as La Huerta de Juquila was first published by Rincón Mautner (1999:296 n. 70). The identification of this same place as the cliff called Comoztoc, in La Huerta, was first published by me in Castañeda de la Paz and

Doesburg (2008:178 n. 41), based on a document from the AGI in Seville.

36. According to several sources, the central Mexican temple pyramids were called Coatepec, "Serpent Hill." See also Matos Moctezuma, Broda, and Carrasco (1987) for the Mexica main temple as Coatepec, and Castañeda de la Paz and Doesburg (2008) for a comparison with Coatepec in the Coixtlahuaca documents.
37. These founders are represented in the Selden Roll, the Lienzo of Tequixtepec II, and the Lienzo of Ihuitlán wearing a specific type of crown. In the Selden Roll, one of the four founders carries a secondary bundle adorned with a similar crown. Some warriors appearing on the Coixtlahuaca lienzos, e.g., 8 Water and 12 Lizard, also wear this same type of crown. The Quetzalcoatl bundle and the accompanying priest 1 Lizard wear the same crown in the Lienzo of Ihuitlán and in the Lienzo of Tulancingo. Rincón Mautner (personal communication) has noted that four of the first five generations in the Lienzo of Tequixtepec II coincide with the four generations depicted next to Comoztoc in the Lienzo of Coixtlahuaca II, indicating that this Tequixtepec lineage had its origins in Comoztoc.
38. This "Mountain of the Arrows" (Miltepec in Nahuatl) may be the large archaeological site of El Despoblado, formerly known as Miltepec, "At Arrow Hill," northeast of Aztatla. This identification was made by Olivier van Buren and is based on a document from the Archivo Judicial de Teposcolula (Doesburg 2001:43 n. 19). In it, an abandoned settlement close to Rancho Los Naranjos is called Miltepec. Edgar Mendoza called my attention to a map in the Archivo Judicial de Teposcolula in which the location of Miltepec is clearly shown (Archivo Judicial de Teposcolula, Civil, Caja 1, Coixtlahuaca, 1887: *"Diligencias de posesión de terrenos de Rancho los Naranjos solicitadas por Justino Díaz"*). Its location coincides with the position of "Mountain of the Arrows" on the lienzos, especially on the Lienzo of Tlapiltepec, where it is east of Aztatla.
39. Personal communication, Steve Kowalewski, 2009.
40. In the early sixteenth century, Tulancingo was called Tula or Tulateopan, "Tula Temple." Lord Don Diego of Coixtlahuaca described this place (the border between Tamazulapan and Tequixtepec-Coixtlahuaca) as "a hill called Tulateupa in the Indian tongue, since at the foot of the said hill flows a stream that has tule and it grows in there" (*un çerro que se llama en lengua de yndios Tulateupa por quanto al pie del dicho çerro pasa vn arroyuelo de agua que tiene tule y se crya en el*), Archivo General de la Nación (hereinafter AGN), Civil, vol. 726, exp. 7 (1546–50), f. 41v. Other witnesses called it Tula in 1545 (Doesburg 2002:106, 108–11). It does not seem to have been still inhabited in the sixteenth century, but, as the Tulateopan name indicates, it surely was a religious site. Current Tulancingo seems to be the result of a congregación in the mid-sixteenth century.
41. Because of its location on the western side of the river, Telyahualiuhcan, "Round Stone," was probably the site Bernal excavated in the 1940s. The name Telyahualiuhcan is preserved in two archival documents; see Doesburg (2001:58 n. 27). In earlier publications I suggested that the "Stone of Tail and Footsteps" glyph consisted of the hindquarters of a jaguar drawn over a round stone. The Lienzo of Otla reveals this is not the case. What look like jaguar spots appear as footprints on the Lienzo of Otla. Maybe the glyph combination can be read as "Behind the Market."
42. The expansion of Coixtlahuaca's political influence into southern Puebla is treated in some detail in Doesburg and Buren (1997). This expansion was probably related to an attempt to control the important commercial route that led through the Puebla area.
43. *Pinome* is the plural of *pinotl*, the name for a speaker of a Popolocan language.
44. Kirchhoff, Odena Güemes, and Reyes García (1976:205). Translation by author.
45. Indeed, Torquemada (1986, 1:269) counts the Chochones and Pinomes among the confederates after the establishment of the Teochichimecs.
46. This Lord 9 Monkey may be the same as Lord Ozomatli of Tepexi-Atexcal who appears in several Nahuatl-language sources: the *Historia tolteca-chichimeca* (Kirchhoff, Odena Güemes, and Reyes García 1976:214, par. 351), the Anales de Cuauhtitlán (Velázquez 1975:31, par. 129), and the Anales de Tepeteopan (Lara Tenorio, Celestino Solís, and Pérez Alemán 2009:31). The first two sources put his defeat at the hands of the lord of Tehuacán as early as 1351.
47. Linguists suggest the Chocho and Popoloca languages may have started to separate during the twelfth century (Hopkins 1984:42–43, 53).

    This separation coincides with the date of the first arrival of Pinomes in southern Puebla according to the lienzos and alphabetic sources. Moreover, Popoloca is currently spoken in three discontinuous areas that coincide with the city-states that absorbed the Pinome migration according to the same sources: (1) San Marcos Tlacoyalco and San Luis Temalacayuca in the former city-state of Tecamachalco; (2) San Felipe Otlaltepec, Almolonga, San Antonio Huejonapan, Santa Inés Ahuatempan, San Vicente Coyotepec, and Natívitas Cuauhtempan in the former city-state of Tepexi; and (3) San Juan Atzingo and Los Reyes Metzontla in the former city-state of Zapotitlán. Massive population movements organized by ruling lineages were not uncommon during the late Postclassic. A well-known example is the movement of people from the central valleys of Oaxaca into the Isthmus of Tehuantepec during the fourteenth century (Zeitlin 1990:32).
48. Torquemada 1986, 1:207–209.
49. The Anales de Tlatelolco (Tena 2004:98–99) date the Aztec conquest of Sosola to 1505. Torquemada himself puts the event in the fifth year of the reign of Moctezuma (i.e., 1506). The *Historia de los mexicanos por sus pinturas* (Garibay 1979:63) puts the conquest 184 years after the founding of Tenochtitlan (i.e., 1506). The Anales de Cuauhtitlán (Velázquez 1975:59) have the conquest in 1506; In his seventh Relación, Chimalpain (2003:184–85) mentions the captives of Sosola sacrificed during the New Fire ceremony of 1507. However, Codex Telleriano Remensis mentions a rebellion in Sosola in 1509. Durán (1984:436–37) also tells the story of the uprising of 1506 (without specifying the date), but locates it in Yanhuitlán and Sosola.
50. Following Smith (1973a), scholars have normally interpreted pictographic lienzos with genealogical registers as having been made to show to the Spanish administration. Although this might be true for some documents, I consider it more likely that most were made for internal purposes (Doesburg 2004).
51. The churches are drawn by the same hand as the other drawings (personal communication, Arni Brownstone), indicating the lienzo was painted after churches were established.
52. Vences Vidal (2000:181); Gerhard (1986:295). The important monastery at Tamazulapan (shown as "Hill at Frog Pond") was built after 1555 (Reyes Gómez 1998:39). At first glance, this could indicate the document was painted between these two dates, but ethnocentric reasons might also explain this situation: Tamazulapan did

not belong to Coixtlahuaca, which might be the reason to exclude the monastery. This might also explain why no chapel was depicted at Tequixtepec, which became independent from Coixtlahuaca at an early date (Doesburg 2002). Early documents from Yanhuitlán state that people from Coixtlahuaca had to walk to Yanhuitlán to hear mass in 1541, indicating that at that time there was still no church in Coixtlahuaca.

53. Doesburg (2010a:82, 98).
54. On the Lienzo of Ihuitlán, "Hill of Maguey Stalk or Grass" is located more or less in the direction of Jicotlán. However, this town was founded only in 1575 (see appendix A, document 02; the "Merced" from 1562 preserved in the Archivo Histórico of the Registro Agrario Nacional in Oaxaca may be a forgery). Five of the towns depicted on the Lienzo of Tlapiltepec ("Hill of Maguey Stalk or Grass," Ihuitlán, Tequixtepec, Tlapiltepec, and a unidentified place close to the Nudo Mixteco) are related to black pre-Hispanic temples.
55. *"Al tiempo que su padre fallecio desta presente vida, el quedo de hedad de hasta quatro o çinco anos poco mas o menos, e que por no ser de hedad avia gouernado el dicho pueblo un don Francisco, ya difunto, e otro que se dize don Diego, questa en el dicho pueblo"* Archivo Antiguo de San Miguel Tequixtepec (hereinafter AAT) (AAT-55a, f. 24). This letter bears the date 1540, but other documents related to the case indicate that this is probably a copyist's error for 1543. The letter was directed to the corregidor of Tejupan. The case was investigated by the corregidor Juan Núñez Sedeño (active in Tejupan in 1543), and in January 1544 Tequixtepec contested the results. Therefore the original accusatory letter was most likely from 1543. In earlier publications (e.g., Doesburg 2002, 2004) I had not yet realized the chronological contradictions in the letter.
56. AGN, Jesuitas, vol. 1-14, exp. 107, undated; AAT-31, undated.
57. *"Don Domingo, caçique e menor de hedad de Cuestlabaca, de beynte e çinco a[ñ]os, y el conçejo e justiçia de Cuestlavaca como pueblo que no tiene caçique ni prinçipales por estar todos echados a las minas por su magestad"* (AGN, Indios, vol. 101, exp. 1, f. 10v, 1544).
58. This is according to part VI, title 19, of the famous "Siete Partidas." Since at 25, Don Domingo cannot be a minor, the word "menor" (which can mean both "minor" and "less") in the Spanish phrase is out of place.
59. *"Quinze años e mas tiempo a quel pueblo de Cuestlavaca no tiene señor natural e el ques agora ques don Domingo es menor de beynte e çinco años" (afterward the scribe crossed out the word "çinco")* (AGN, Civil, vol. 726, f. 76, 1545).
60. In an earlier publication (Doesburg 2004), I reconstructed the year of his birth as 1519, based on the statement by Don Domingo himself that he was 25 years old in 1544. I had not yet recognized the possibility of a more coherent reading in legal terms.
61. AGN, Civil, vol. 726, f. 76.
62. Again, I here adjust the date I published earlier (Doesburg 2004). From this follows that the hanged man in the Lienzo of Coixtlahuaca II is not Domingo's father, as I earlier thought.
63. Two other documents more or less contemporary with the Lienzo of Tlapiltpec—the Lienzo of Coixtlahuaca II and the Lienzo of Ihuitlán—show two additional generations after 11 Vulture, though they differ on the identity of the first generation after him. Does this mean there was a dispute between Coixtlahuaca and Ihuitlán about succession after 11 Vulture?
64. The reader interested in more detailed information on the lineages of Ihuitlán may consult Caso (1961) and Doesburg (2000).
65. Neither Caso nor Parmenter noted that Lord 3 Rain is also seated among the rulers of the second Ihuitlán lineage on the Lienzo of Ihuitlán. It is possible that the reason for the painter of the Lienzo of Ihuitlán to highlight Lord 3 Rain's (i.e., Ihuitlán's) service to the father of Atonal (i.e., Coixtlahuaca) can be found in the function of the lienzo as a document accompanying marital negotiations between Ihuitlán and Coixtlahuaca.
66. It is not clear why the place glyph shows a tree instead of the knot representing the *tlalpilli*, "knot," part of the name Tlapiltepec. The mountain with tree perhaps corresponds to the "Hill with Ears and a Plant with Sun-Fruits" depicted in the corresponding scene on the Lienzo of Tlapiltepec.
67. In 1851, Tlapiltepec used a municipal seal that represented a "Hill of the Knot," although it differs from the one painted on the Lienzo of Tlapiltepec. Details indicate it is a sixteenth century design, and it may have been copied from an unknown document. See illustration on page 74.
68. Doesburg 2010b.
69. This hill with ears also appears in the Lienzo of Tulancingo. Perhaps it is related to the place Santa María Magdalena Necustlatepeque (from *nacaztli*, "ear"?), an "estancia" of Coixtlahuaca mentioned in the Archivo de Notarías de Puebla, Tehuacán, caja 1, carpeta 4, f. 50, 50v. Jicotlán also has María Magdalena as its patron, but the relation between these two towns is not clear.
70. The town of Asuchitlan, "Among the Water Flowers," is mentioned in the Relación Geográfica of Cuzcatlan (Acuña 1985, 5:98–99). In the accompanying maps it is represented as a market town. The nearby river is represented in pictography as "Flower River."
71. On the Lienzo of Coixtlahuaca II, the lady in the middle register is named Monkey (10 Monkey in the Lienzo of Tlapiltepec), and the lady in the lower register is named Deer (6 Deer in the Lienzo of Tlapiltepec).
72. Earlier congregación programs were carried out by the Spanish judge Luis Daza around 1556 (AGN, Indios, vol. 5, exp. 279 (1591), AGI, Escribanía, 160B); later programs took place during the last years of the sixteenth century. The Lienzo of Otla shows the change from the dispersed pattern—with noble houses spread through the area—to the nucleated village. The drawing of the congregated town was clearly added later to the document.
73. Tequixtepec went through the same process: it congregated in 1563, and it obtained its title in 1582, one year before Ihuitlán (Doesburg 2002).
74. Ndaningo might derive from *nda-xri-ningo*, "water-animal-bat," which is possibly the underlying form of the toponym Taximingo.
75. The Lienzo of Ihuitlán shows the two sacred figures, this time without names, seated inside the palace-temple of Ihuitlán.
76. Appendix A, documents 06 and 10. Archivo Municipal de San Miguel Aztatla, 1593, calls Diego del Castillo "cacique principal." Archivo General del Poder Judicial de Oaxaca (hereinafter AGPJO) Teposcolula, Penal, leg. 3, exp. 45, calls him "cacique." In 1594 he identifies himself as "cacique y principal" of Coixtlahuaca and "señor natural de la estancia de Santiago Yhuitlan," appendix A, document 16. For Diego as a translator, see AAT 23 (1585) and AAT-53 (1592), where he appears with Francisco de Zárate, principal of Ihuitlán. In the early seventeenth century, Gregorio de Aguilar, born 1587, perhaps the son of Diego de Aguilar, appears as lord and translator. Both Aguilars served as alcaldes in Coixtlahuaca. For Diego de Aguilar, see appendix A, document 08; for Diego de Aguilar as alcalde, see AAT-23, f. 45 (1585). For Gregorio de Aguilar

as a translator and alcalde, see AAT-45 (1617); for Gregorio de Aguilar as regidor, see AGPJO, Teposcolula, Civil, leg. 8, exp. 14, 1616, and also Penal, leg. 12, exp. 7, 1628, where he is called "cacique." For Francisco de Zárate, see appendix A, document 07.

77. This recurrent problem—the lack of calendrical names in archival documents in the Coixtlahuaca area—has made it difficult to connect pictographic documents with the alphabetic records (Doesburg 2004). The Lienzo of Ihuitlán depicts four distinct Ihuitlán lineages, ending respectively in Lord 1 Vulture and Lady 8 Deer, Lord 9 Lizard and Lady 6 Eagle, Lord 4 Reed and Lady 1 Rain, and Lord 2 Rabbit and Lady 13 Grass. The Lienzo of Tulancingo represents couples from only two of these lineages (first and third).
78. In appendix A, document 03, a noble of Cuauhtongo named Juan de Santa María, is granted a license to keep sheep. Although his first name is different, he is probably the same person.
79. In appendix A, document 09, Juan de Santiago is called cacique of Yaquiztongo, an unidentified place.
80. Francisco Jiménez was the regidor of Ihuitlán in the cabildo of Coixtlahuaca in 1582 ("Título de Santa Cruz Capulalpan," Archivo Histórico Agrario, Registro Agrario, 276.1/2743[1]) and 1583 (appendix A, document 06). He should not be confused with Francisco Jiménez, noble of Octla (AGN, Indios, vol. 5, exp. 1115, 1591; AGPJO, Teposcolula, Criminal, caja 1, doc. 52, 1596), part of Suchixtlahuaca, who was alcalde in the cabildo of Coixtlahuaca in 1583 (appendix A, document 06). It seems that at this time the two alcalde posts in the cabildo of Coixtlahuaca were divided between nobles from Coixtlahuaca and Suchixtlahuaca; Ihuitlán participated only at the level of *regiduría*.
81. Domingo Hernández appears in AGI, Escribanía 160B, no. 4, f. 928v, as a witness. In 1572 he was 35 years of age.
82. AGI, Patronato 245, no. 10, f. 277.
83. *"los naturales del pueblo de San Matheo Tlapiltepeque, después de dicha congregación y en virtud de despacho de la Real Audiencia y de la licencia que se les concedió por el año de mil quinientos y ochenta y tres, se mudaron en una ladera y quebrada al pie de un cerro alto donde hoy se halla su pueblo; (. . .) en esta conformidad y en virtud de una donación que por el año de mil quinientos cinquenta y siete hicieron los principales y naturales del pueblo de Santiago Yguitlan a Hernando Méndez, principal de la estancia de Tlapiltepec, para todos sus naturales y macehuales, de las tierras, sitios y solares que les fueron dados y señalados en aquel lugar donde tenían poblada su estancia"* (AGN, Tierras, vol. 384, exp. 1. Also Tierras, vol. 2787, f. 92 and f. 125).
84. *"en el paraje que decimos en nuestra idioma Tunruyua, que en mexicano se dice Jocotlan, se hallan unos vestigios de haber habido alli pueblo, como que efectivamente alli estuvo fundado este de San Matheo cuando fue barrio del pueblo de Santiago Yguitlan en aquellos tiempos antiguos"* (AGN, Tierras, vol. 384, exp. 1). Jocotlan means "Place of Fruit."
85. In the Lienzo of Ihuitlán, the representation of two sacred beings in the glyph of Tlapiltepec is very similar to the depiction of the bundle of 9 Wind and the priest 1 Lizard in the glyph of Coixtlahuaca. Unfortunately, no names are given. It may be that the absence of names means these names were the same as the Coixtlahuaca ones.
86. In later documents Teopan and Tlacotepec are mentioned as part of the cacicazgo of the Esquivel family from Acatlán. In the early seventeenth century, Teopan was ruled by a noble named Gabriel de Mendoza. He may have been the son of Don Juan de Mendoza, noble of Tlacotepec.
87. In later documents we find mentioned a Don Juan de Castillo, cacique of Ihuitlán, living around 1670 (AGN, Tierras, vol. 242). He may be the son of Joseph.
88. AGPJO, Teposcolula, Penal, leg. 12, exp. 7.
89. AGN, Indios, vols. 25 and 26, several files.
90. AGN, Indios, 42, exp. 9.
91. AGN, Indios, vol. 42, exp. 126.
92. Concepción was founded by people from Coixtlahuaca in the late sixteenth century on the border between Ihuitlán and Tepelmeme. AGN, Tierras, vol. 242. It is mentioned as early as 1593 in AGN, Mercedes, vol. 18, f. 279, as Santa María de la Concepción.
93. Concepción Abád was founded by people from Texcalhueyac (today Las Palmas) during a rather conflictive process between approximately 1675 and 1710. AGN, Tierras, vol. 242, Indios, vol. 33, exp. 279; Indios, vol. 36, exp. 411. The main reason seems to have been the difficult access of the original location. The priests of Coixtlahuaca, especially Fray Sebastián Ramos, fostered the move. The identification of Texcalhueyac was first published in Doesburg (2000:171). An interesting archaeological site just above Las Palmas marks the location of pre-Hispanic Texcalhueyac.
94. The fragmentation process is full of details and complexities, many not yet understood. Edgar Mendoza is currently doing useful research on the political breakup of the Coixtlahuaca Valley. Here, I only present some general elements of the process.
95. The destroyed name is reconstructed on the basis of the lienzos of Ihuitlán, Coixtlahuaca I and II, and Lienzo A.
96. The Lienzo of Tlapiltepec shows Ihuitlán and Tequixtepec, which were linked to the house of Atonal, but it does not show Nativitas, which was linked to the house of Lord 3 Jaguar. Securely identified villages in southern Puebla on the lienzo are "River of the Mirror" (Atexcal), "Valley" (Tepexi), "Head of the Rock" (Oxtoticpac), "Face of the Mountain" (Tepeaca), "Altar of the Coscomate and Tree" (Tecamachalco), "Town on the Mountain of Water" (Quecholac), "Mountain of Town of the Wall" (Tecali), and "House of the Eagle" (Cuauhtinchan). The identification of Atexcal was first published in Doesburg (2001:19 n. 2).
97. This is a curious statement, since Santa María Magdalena Jicotlán was a *sujeto* of Coixtlahuaca.
98. Probably an error for "provisión real y comisión."
99. Possibly an error for "mirar."
100. The word "repago" does not exist in Spanish. Perhaps "regazo" is meant.
101. It is not clear to what this refers, since "poblaciones" is feminine.
102. For this reason, it appears that Caso read the glosses here labeled 1 and 2 upside-down.
103. See Campbell (1997) and the references therein.
104. Regarding the structure of toponyms in Popolocan, see Fernández de Miranda (1961).
105. Austin Krumholz, Kalstrom Dolson, and Hernández Ayuso (1995). The Otlaltepec Popoloca data is from Swanton's field notes. To facilitate comparison, both forms are presented using the International Phonetic Alphabet.
106. Regarding this Chocholtec Christian *doctrina*, see Doesburg and Swanton (2008).
107. Doesburg (2002:24).
108. Mirrors of this kind are preserved in the collections of the Pitt Rivers Museum (Oxford), the Museé du Quai Branly (Paris), and the Museo Civico (Turin), to name just a few. A similar mirror is represented in the "Genealogie von 33 Personen" preserved in the Berlin State Library.

109. Jansen (in Jansen and Gaxiola 1978:15); Doesburg and Buren (1997:129); Jansen and Pérez Jiménez (2000:153–54).
110. The form presented here comes from Swanton's field notes. Compare with Williams and Pierson (1950:32) and Fernández de Miranda (1961:445). The phones [o] and [u] are non-contrastive in Popoloca, and in this phonological context /u/ is pronounced as [o].
111. Gudschinsky (1959).
112. Jansen and Pérez Jiménez (2000:154) proposed that the topogram represented Ixcaquixtla. However, we agree with Caso (1979, 2:79, 306) that it is a zapote that is represented. The Zapotitlán identification is also more in accord geographically with the identification of the topogram for Atexcal nearby.
113. The Atzingo Popoloca word for Zapotitlán provided in Austin Krumholz, Kalstrom Dolson, and Hernández Ayuso (1995) is *tha*^{1}*hna*^{1} and originates from a Popoloca calque of the Nahuatl word *altepetl* (literally, "water mountain"), meaning "town." Compare with the Otlaltepec Popoloca word for Tepexi, which is tha?hna?.

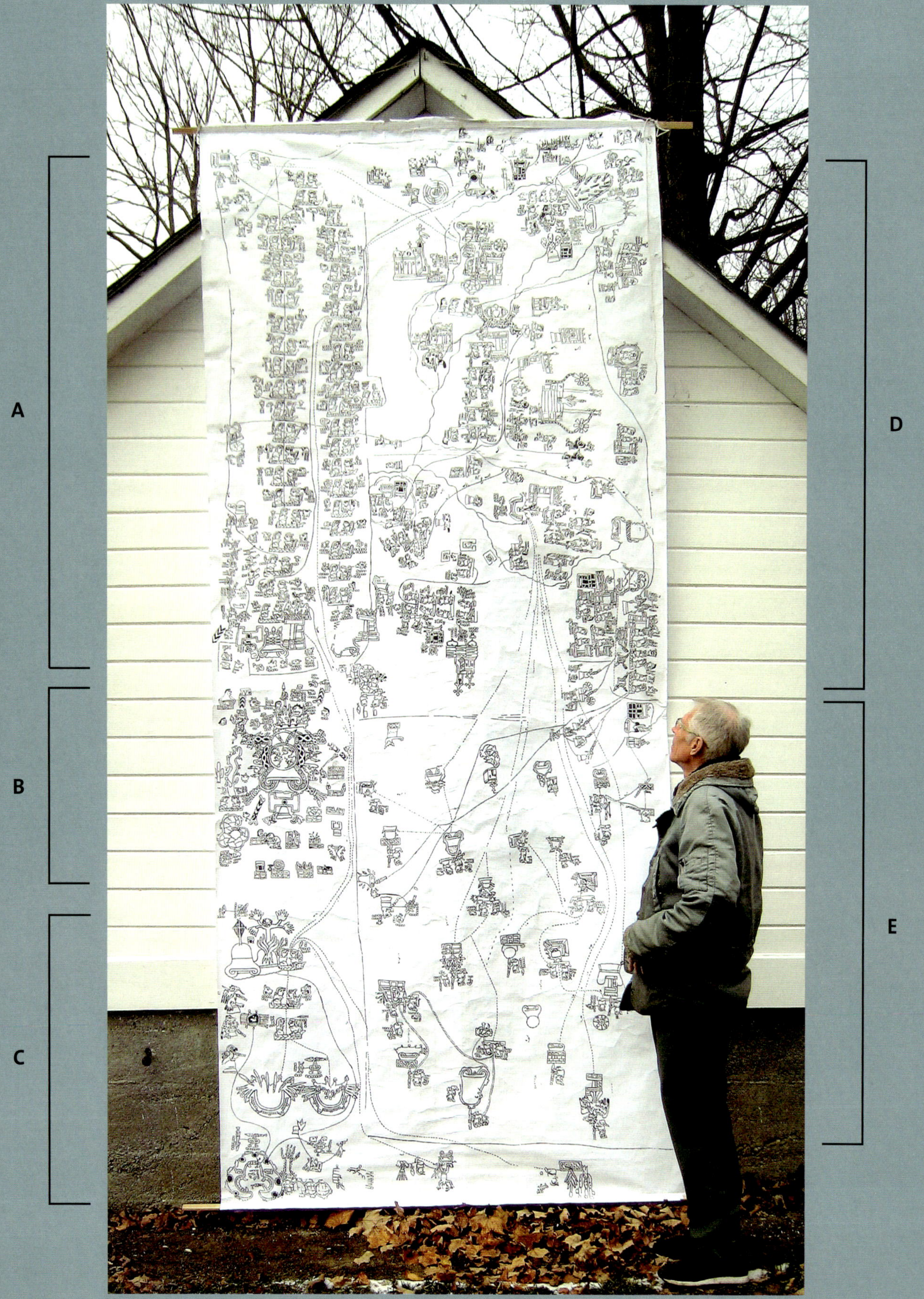

FIG. 3.1. Full-size tracing of Lienzo of Tlapiltepec, with author Nicholas Johnson included for scale. Photo by Ian Johnson.

CHAPTER 3

The Language of Lines on the Lienzo of Tlapiltepec

NICHOLAS JOHNSON

As seen from the perspective of a viewer standing before it, the Lienzo of Tlapiltepec is a broad column of white cloth covered with small drawings, reaching into the sky (fig. 3.1). When a full-size copy of the Lienzo of Tlapiltepec is hung vertically on the end wall of a one-story, pitched-roof building, its lower end touches the ground and its upper end nearly surpasses the roof peak. A thick black vertical line from the base of the lienzo almost to the top, one-third of the way from its left edge, divides the broad column into two narrower columns. To the left of this line and toward the top of the lienzo, stacks of human couples represent generation after generation of Coixtlahuaca's pre-Hispanic rulers (fig. 3.1, A).

Below the human figures and at about the eye level of a tall viewer, a large hill is prominent. A priest on top of the hill, surrounded by a cluster of details, makes fire by twirling a stick (fig. 3.1, B). This important ritual fire-drilling signifies the founding of the Coixtlahuaca lineages. Below the hill scene, still to the left of the dividing line and near the bottom of the lienzo, are sacred ancestors and their ancient places of origin: a pair of rivers and below it, a cave at the base of the lienzo (fig. 3.1, C).

The area to the right of the vertical line that divides the lienzo is devoted to a map of the Coixtlahuaca Valley and neighboring regions. This column is the wider of the two demarcated by the black line. The upper and more crowded half of this map corresponds primarily to the Coixtlahuaca Valley (fig. 3.1, D). Clusters of towns, rulers, and historical events are crisscrossed by connecting lines. For a viewer standing or sitting in front of the lienzo and looking up at it, the greater density of this section is partly an effect of distance and the angle of sight, although, in fact, the top half of the lienzo contains nearly twice as many figures as the lower half.

The more sparsely painted lower right side of the lienzo shows towns located north of the Coixtlahuaca Valley. A major system of red lines fans out from a point in the upper, Coixtlahuaca, section of the map and leads to the towns of the lower, northern, section, as if to buds at the ends of branches (fig. 3.1, E). This area of the lienzo is brighter and more open than the densely painted areas above and to the left of it. It contains a high proportion of white space. The eye is drawn to this more open area at the lower right and is directed to it by the red lines and footprints that lead into it.

This section of the map, situated at the base of the vertically displayed lienzo, is closer to the viewer than the areas above it. Extending from the ground up to about the eye level of a standing person, this section is even the approximate size of a viewer. Looking at the lienzo thus vertically displayed, the system of red lines that leads into this section swells dramatically to its maximum width, and the lines reach their destinations directly in front of the viewer.

The vertically displayed lienzo as a whole has the shape of a tall, bent-over tree. The cave and rivers of origin at the lower left form the roots, with the tree reaching upward on the left and sweeping downward on the right, terminating with its branches of red lines almost touching the ground at the lower right.

LINES IN MIXTEC MANUSCRIPT PAINTING

Mesoamerican manuscript painting is an art of lines. Fine black outlines frame individual motifs and set them off from the white space that surrounds them. As in stained glass windows, additional black lines separate the areas of bright color that internally compose each motif (Robertson 1994:16). Then there are dividing lines, connecting lines, and guidelines, as well as imaginary lines implicit in the arrangement of the motifs, such as in rows or columns. These lines structure the ensemble of motifs and relate to the coherence of the whole rather than to the definition of the parts.

In the screenfold genre of pre-Hispanic Mixtec manuscripts, figures are closely spaced in chronological sequence in interconnecting channels of space demarcated by red guidelines. The red lines are drawn horizontally in some manuscripts and vertically in others. The reader's path through the densely painted pages of the Mixtec genealogical-historical screenfold is, as a result, a single continuous line that weaves its way rhythmically back and forth across the pages and without interruption through the length of the manuscript (fig. 3.2).

In cartographic lienzos, in contrast, figures are often widely separated, rather than closely spaced, and there may be multiple paths for the reader instead of only one. Lines useful and important in this context are connecting lines. Connecting lines differ from guidelines and dividing lines in that they are not merely structural devices but also frequently part of the manuscript's signifying pictorial contents.

Connecting lines on the Lienzo of Tlapiltepec help indicate to the viewer the order in which the dispersed figures and place signs are to be read. At the same time, the lines tell of the migrations, expeditions, and changes of location of the lienzo's protagonists and signify genealogical ties among the rulers of various towns. On the Lienzo of Tlapiltepec these ligatures are merely lines, or lines accompanied by hu-

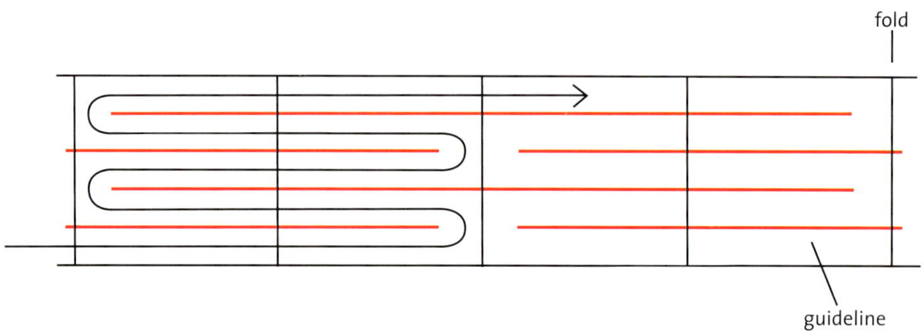

FIG. 3.2. Diagram of registers separated by red guidelines. Example here is based on the Mixtec screenfold Codex Bodley. Arrow indicates reading path from register to register and page to page.

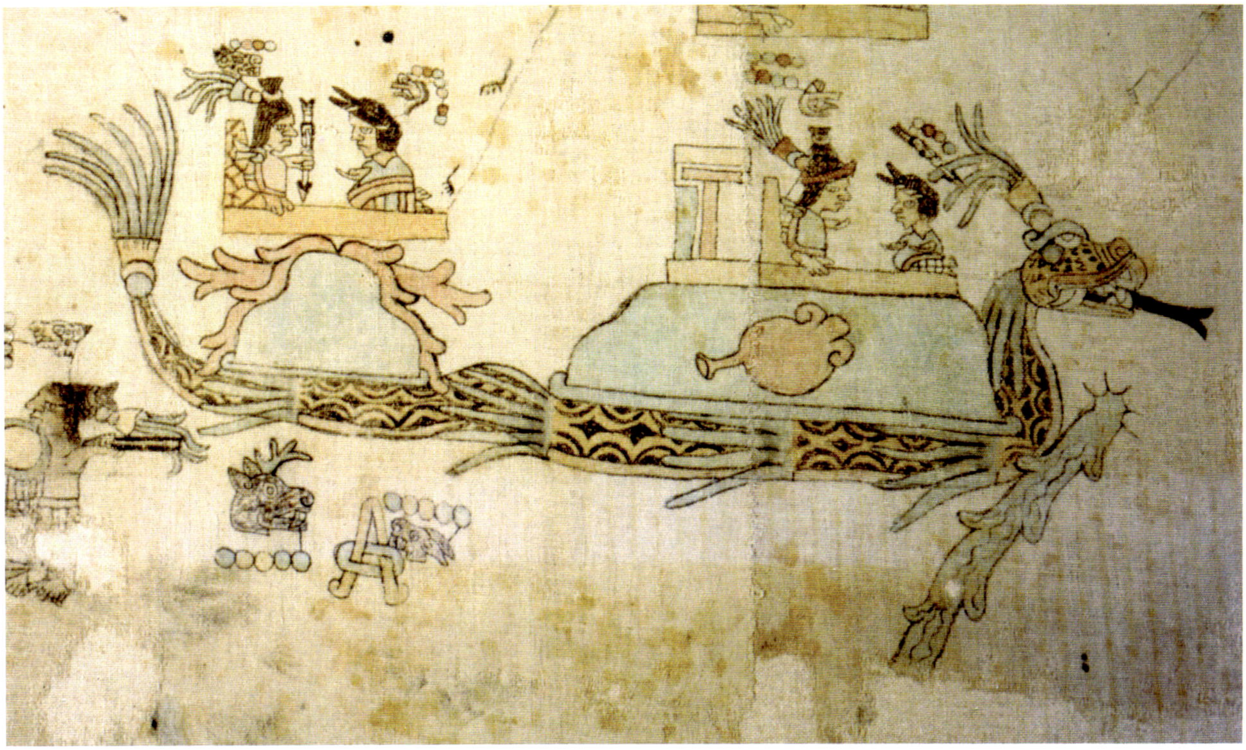

FIG. 3.3. Feathered serpent representing the town of Coixtlahuaca on Lienzo of Coixtlahuaca II (Seler II). Courtesy of Ethnologisches Museum Berlin.

man footprints—simple graphic traces—but they take many different forms in other manuscripts, from roads, ropes, and rivers to umbilical cords and streams of blood. These are motifs that derive pictorially from things of the world that are linear or elongated in shape and they function in a variety of ways to link, group, or lead between elements. Connecting "lines," thus broadly defined, are a vital, characteristic, and distinctive feature of the visual syntax of Mesoamerican pictographic writing and storytelling.

An example is the band-like plumed serpent that represents Coixtlahuaca at the center of Lienzo A and the Lienzo of Coixtlahuaca I as well as on the Lienzo of Coixtlahuaca II, also known as Lienzo Seler II (fig. 3.3). Supporting on its back a pair of place signs with their respective palaces and ruling couples, the Coixtlahuaca serpent, in this usage, in addition to naming the town, becomes a symbol of the joining of forces of the two ancient lineages that came to dominate the Coixtlahuaca area.

Another "connecting line" that is not merely a line is the reed mat, rendered as a narrow, yellow, weave-patterned rectangle that on the Lienzo of Tlapiltepec and many other manuscripts supports and joins together figures of husbands and wives. Marriage was a central institution of Mixtec political life. Symbolized by two figures facing each other on a woven mat, marriage united ruling families from different towns, with men and women alike holders of hereditary positions and power, traceable back to sacred ancient ancestors and generating networks of social-political alliances (Spores 1974; Terraciano 2001:158–97; Pohl 2003).

Other narrow rectangles, variously patterned, similarly link or group together the figures they support and are a common structural configuration in the manuscripts. Elongated and marked with human footprints, the rectangle becomes a road; with a chevron design, it signifies "enemy," the road is a "warpath." Decorated with a row

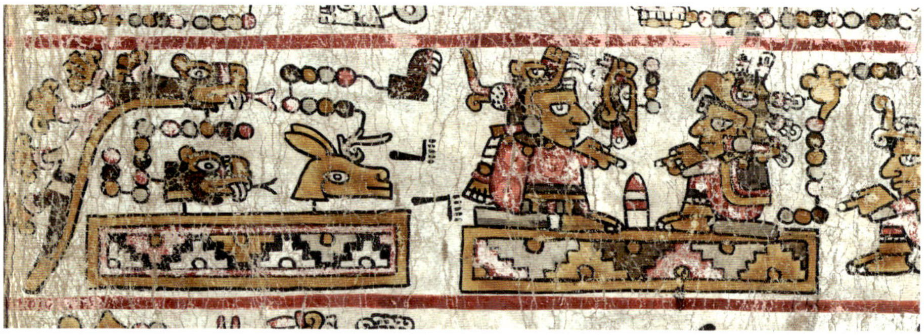

FIG. 3.4. Detail, Codex Bodley, p. 30. *Right*, ruler and wife seated on place sign of their town. *Left*, names of ruler's parents and place sign of their town. Courtesy of The Bodleian Library, The University of Oxford, MS. Mex. D.1.

of stars, the rectangle is the sky. With a pattern of stepped pyramids or interlocking frets, the rectangle turns into an architectural frieze that signifies "town" (Smith 1973a:38–39). In genealogies found in the pre-Hispanic Mixtec screenfold known as Codex Bodley, closely spaced mats and friezes that sustain husbands and wives comprise a near continuum of color and design. They form a geometrically patterned baseline that underpins the human figures and the details of their names (fig. 3.4).

Underlying many of the elaborate pictorializations of relationships and continuities in the pre-Hispanic Mixtec screenfolds is the politically important custom of ruling-class men and women to marry within their class but outside their own communities. In Codex Bodley, for example, the ruling couple is routinely followed by the place sign of the town and names of the parents of whichever member of the couple originated from elsewhere. An abbreviated trail of human footprints indicates that he or she came from this other place and was the son or daughter of its named rulers (fig. 3.4).

On the Lienzo of Tlapiltepec, connecting lines to wives or husbands make the same statement of the individual's family and town origins. Simple connecting lines are rare in the extant pre-Hispanic Mixtec screenfold manuscripts, and lines accompanied by footprints, common on the Lienzo of Tlapiltepec, are nonexistent. Their equivalents in the genealogies of the pre-Hispanic screenfolds are footprints without lines, and in some cases, footprints within colored bands, or roads. Roads, as opposed to footprints alone, highlight the journey, rather than merely indicating the change of location of the wife- or husband-to-be. Roads suggest that the journey that led to the union of the man and woman was in itself an important or storied event.

The longest painted road in Codex Bodley, and of any of the Mixtec genealogical-historical screenfold manuscripts—indeed, the longest painted "line" apart from red guidelines in these manuscripts—tells of the journey of an ancestral personage named 5 Reed. It is his journey from his own village to the village of the woman he marries. The road, a gray-blue band animated with footprints, runs flush with the red guideline from right to left across three and one-third pages of Codex Bodley. Above the road—underlined by it, as it were—are scenes of events related to the instigation and carrying out of the journey, followed by the parents and place of origin of 3 Serpent, the woman 5 Reed marries at the end of his journey (fig. 3.5).

One other important "line" in the genealogies of Codex Bodley is the human umbilical cord. Umbilical cords frequently link the figures to their birthdates. In the initial phases of the genealogies, which pertain to the era of origins, umbilical cords connect venerated ancient ancestors to the earth, mountain, tree, or river from which they were born, or to the place sign of their hometown. Thus, in the above-mentioned example from Codex Bodley, looping red and purple umbilical cords tie 3 Serpent's

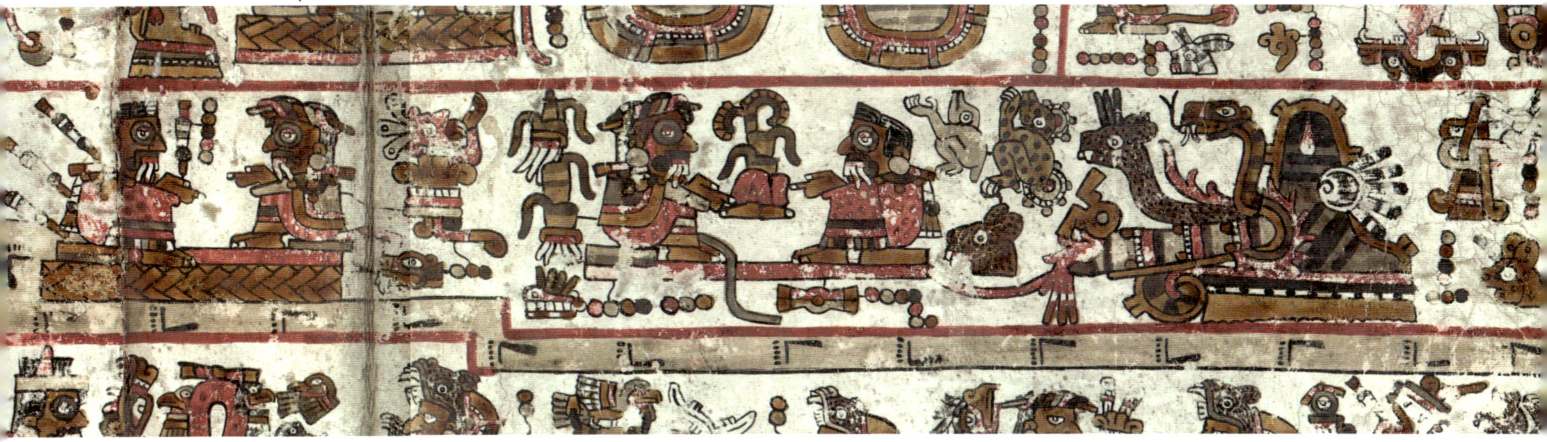

FIG. 3.5. Marriage of 5 Reed "Arrows," Codex Bodley, pp. 38–37. Courtesy of The Bodleian Library, The University of Oxford, MS. Mex. D.1.

father, 7 Movement, and implicitly her mother, 7 Grass, to the sign of their town (see fig. 3.5). In the long, narrow registers of Codex Bodley—the most detailed of all Mixtec genealogical-historical manuscripts—and in the Mixtec screenfold manuscripts generally, connectors such as trails of footprints, roads, umbilical cords, reed mats, and architectural friezes are linear components of an intricately patterned linear whole.

There are no umbilical cords on the Lienzo of Tlapiltepec, and with one exception, no roads. This is partly attributable to the simplified genealogical-historical content of the lienzo. For example, there are no statements of birth as there are in the screenfold manuscripts, hence no umbilical cords. Figures and dates that record the births of rulers' offspring in the screenfolds have been omitted on the lienzo. The hometowns and parents of those members of the Coixtlahuaca ruling couples who came from other places also have mostly been left out. The profusion of figures and place signs notwithstanding, history on the Lienzo of Tlapiltepec, in comparison with the pre-Hispanic screenfold manuscripts, has been greatly abridged.

There is also a notable tendency in the Lienzo of Tlapiltepec to employ ligatures of graphically simplified or pared-down form even where more elaborate alternatives might be justified. Rivers linking some of the place signs on the Lienzo of Tlapiltepec are represented by simple black undulating lines. In contrast, on other sixteenth-century native maps such as the Lienzo of Coixtlahuaca II, rivers are commonly depicted as either wholly or partly pre-Hispanic-style streams of blue, flowing water (fig. 3.6). Some events of travel on the lienzo are represented by simple black connecting lines, lacking footprint indicators of movement and direction, and often lines that do have footprints are only sparsely supplied with them.

Post-conquest dilution of pre-Hispanic forms under the influence of European cartographic examples or colonial mapmaking practices might explain this type of paring down. Rivers reduced to wavy black lines on the lienzo are reminiscent of the sketchy depictions of rivers in some of the many maps made at the request of Spanish colonial authorities, often by native artists and in partly pre-Hispanic styles, to show the location of viceregal land grants.[1] Graphic simplifications of this type may also be related to the format and purpose of the manuscript. On the Lienzo of Tlapiltepec, which summarizes expansive genealogical-historical development through time and across geographical space, it is the course and configuration of the lines, and the pattern as a whole, rather than their elaboration as full-fledged depictions of flowing water or roads, that is important.

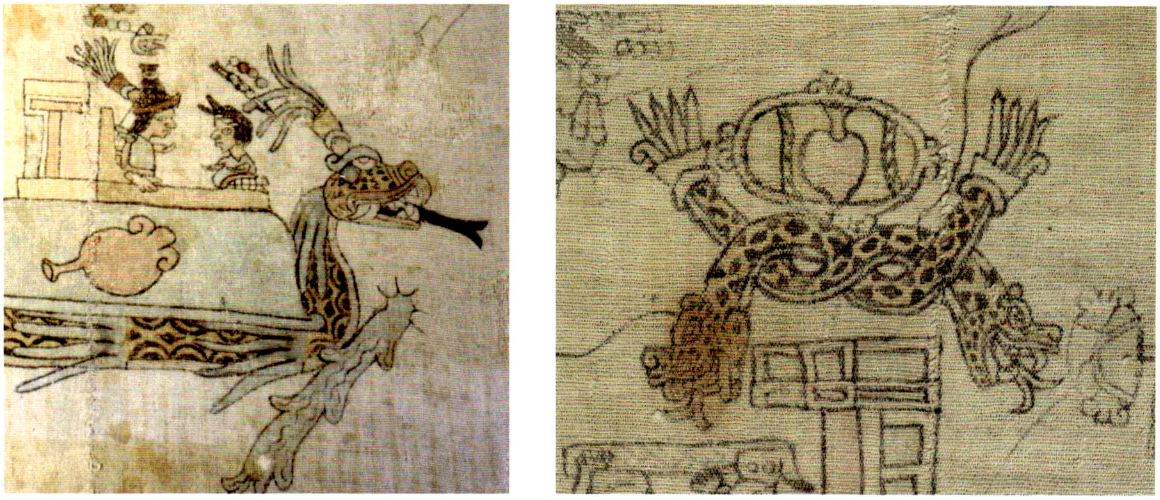

FIG. 3.6. River at Coixtlahuaca represented by blue stream on Lienzo of Coixtlahuaca II, *left*, and by undulating line on Lienzo of Tlapiltepec, *right*. Courtesy of Ethnologisches Museum Berlin and the Royal Ontario Museum, acc. no. 917.3, photo by Brian Boyle.

THE LIENZO MAP: CORE AND MARGINS

The Lienzo of Tlapiltepec contains a map of towns and other sites of historical importance, many of which continue to exist (Parmenter 1982:34–38).[2] While some native maps of the sixteenth century and beyond show mountain ranges and comprehensive networks of roads and rivers, these features are absent from the Lienzo of Tlapiltepec. On this lienzo, the connecting lines and footprints leading from one town to another may signify travel between the towns but do not represent specific roads linking them. Rivers are the exception. Undulating black lines represent some, though not all, of the rivers of the Coixtlahuaca Valley. The Lienzo of Tlapiltepec is also not a map of community land boundaries, as many of the native maps of the colonial period are.[3]

This map is selective. That is, not all towns of the area encompassed by it are shown. The lower right half of the lienzo, for example, contains place signs of towns located in a large area of Oaxaca and Puebla north of Coixtlahuaca, but only towns with which Coixtlahuaca had important ties. Other towns located there do not appear on the map. The map is a map of locations but not distances. Place signs tend to be evenly distributed in the space of the lienzo regardless of how far apart the towns are in the actual geography. Distances are especially compressed along the edges of the lienzo.

The map is oriented with south at the top and north or northwest at the bottom. The distance spanned by the lienzo from top to bottom is approximately 275 km as the crow flies. The map extends from towns located south of Coixtlahuaca in the heart of the Mixteca of southern Mexico, to Tenochtitlan, forerunner of Mexico City, far to the northwest in the Valley of Mexico. This span extends from a pre-Hispanic Mixtec settlement whose place sign is a frieze with flint blades—now an archaeological site called Mogote del Cacique—at its upper, southern edge, to Tenochtitlan and Cholula at its lower, northern edge (fig. 3.7). From side to side, the distance encompassed by the map at its widest is probably less than 100 km.

The lienzo map may be described as consisting essentially of a core and its margins. The map's core occupies the upper right half of the lienzo (fig. 3.8). The core consists of place signs of Coixtlahuaca and several other sites. It also includes associated scenes of pivotal events related to the founding of the town of Coixtlahuaca and the launching of the regime that came to dominate the local Coixtlahuaca Valley area, and to the spread of its influence into other regions.

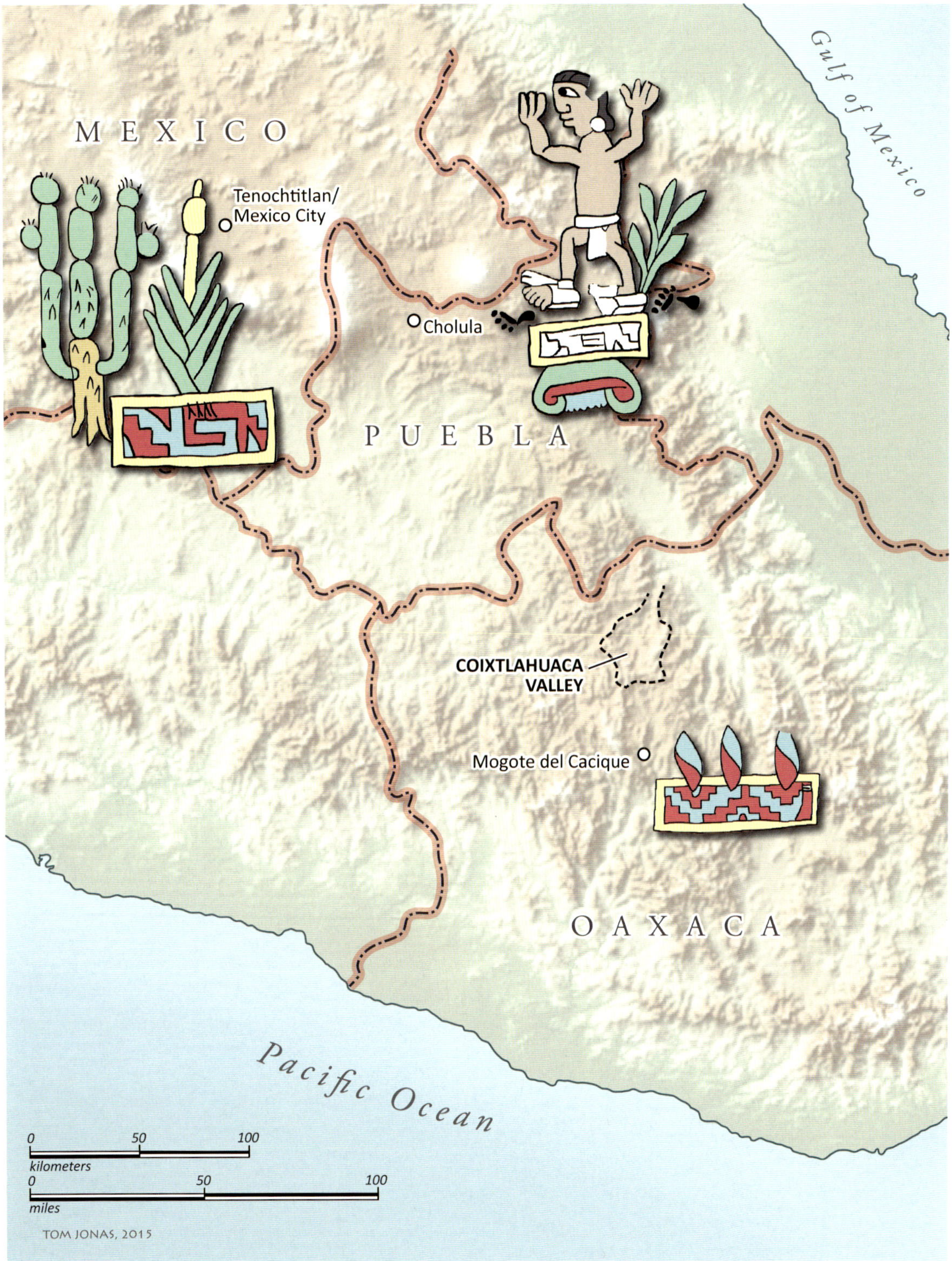

FIG. 3.7. Towns represented on northern end (Tenochtitlan and Cholula) and southern end of the Lienzo of Tlapiltepec. "Town of Flint Knives" is now the archaeological site Mogote del Cacique. © 2015, University of Oklahoma Press.

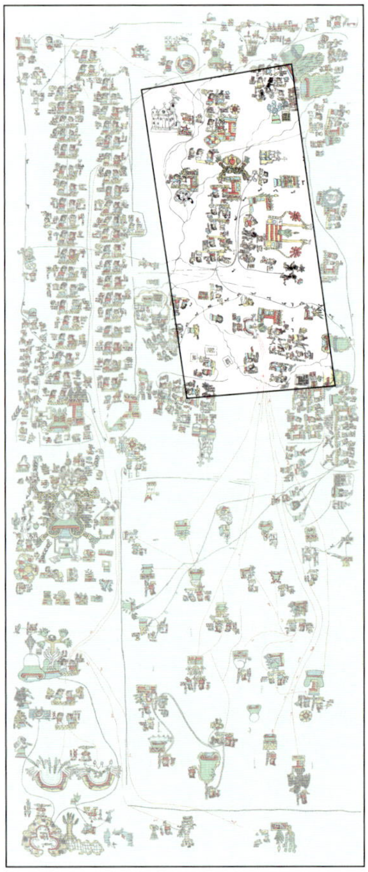

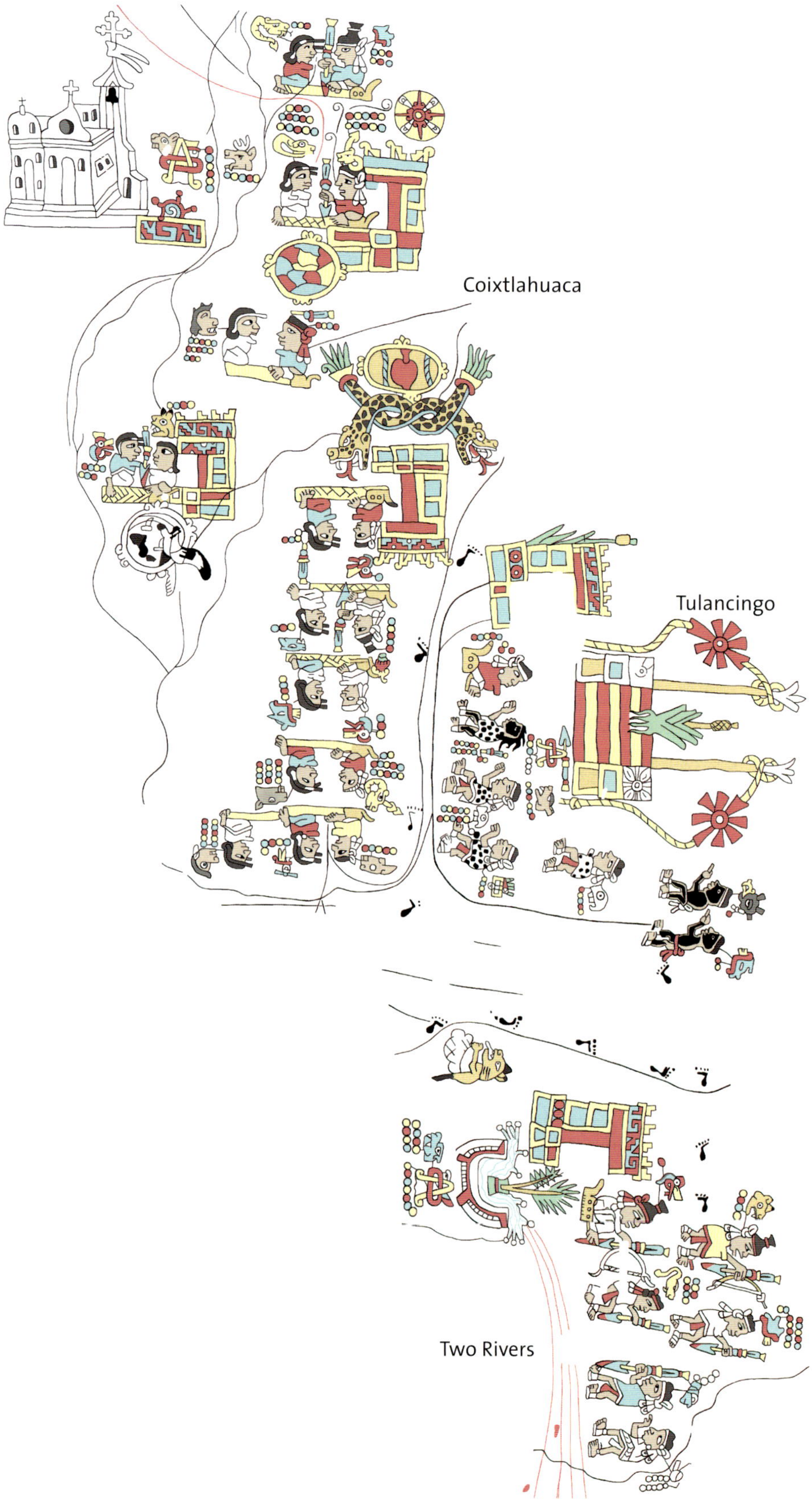

FIG. 3.8. Core area of map on upper right side of Lienzo of Tlapiltepec.

The margins of the map surrounding this core contain place signs of towns, some of which were subjects of Coixtlahuaca located in the Coixtlahuaca Valley, but many of which were outside the territory controlled by Coixtlahuaca and located in neighboring valleys of the Mixteca and farther afield. The majority of these more distant towns are south and especially north of the valley, rather than east or west of it. The entire lower right half of the map pertains to areas north of Coixtlahuaca, and to some extent north of the Mixteca altogether. The margins of the map are defined visually by the "centrifugal" orientation of these place signs, most of which, along with their accompanying figures, buildings, and dates, are arranged with their bases facing inward toward Coixtlahuaca.

Place signs on the upper edge—or southern margin—of the map refer to locations generally south of the Coixtlahuaca Valley and outside Coixtlahuaca territory (figs. 3.10, 3.11, *overleaf*). Among those that have been identified are several sites that figure importantly in the genealogies and stories of the pre-Hispanic Mixtec historical screenfold manuscripts, which originate from this more southern area.

Prominent within this southern margin is a trio of hill signs clustered together like a small mountain range and set at an angle across the upper right corner of the lienzo (fig. 3.9). One of these hills, with three green leaves protruding from its top, is

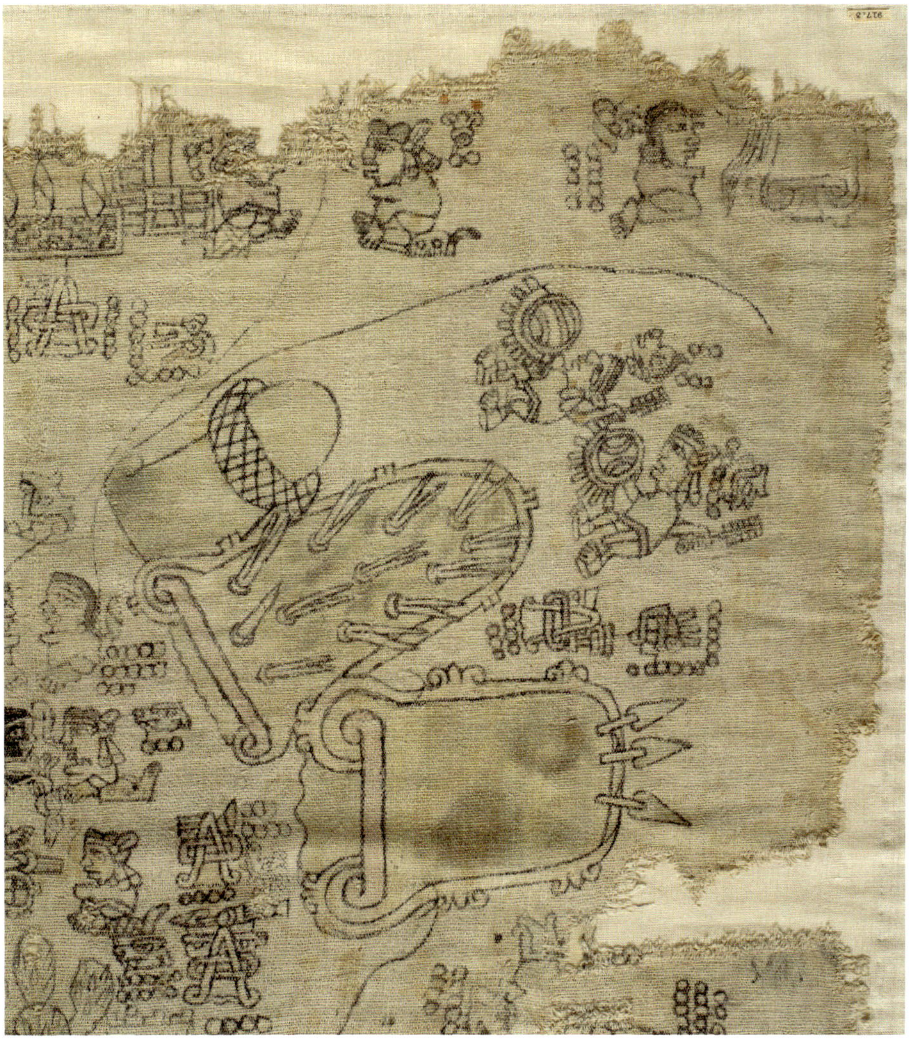

FIG. 3.9. Monte Verde (the hill with leaves on top) and two other mountains, detail from upper right corner of Lienzo of Tlapiltepec. Courtesy of the Royal Ontario Museum, acc. no. 917.3, photo by Brian Boyle. See figure 3.12 on page 106.

FIG. 3.10. Places in core and on south, east, and west margins of map on upper right side of Lienzo of Tlapiltepec. See also fig. 3.11.

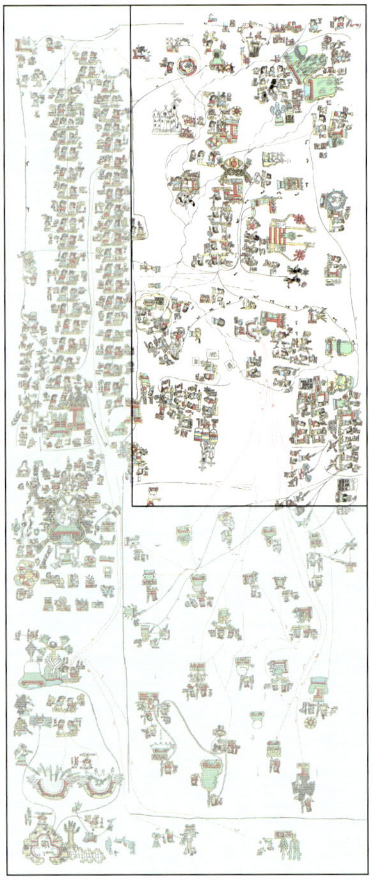

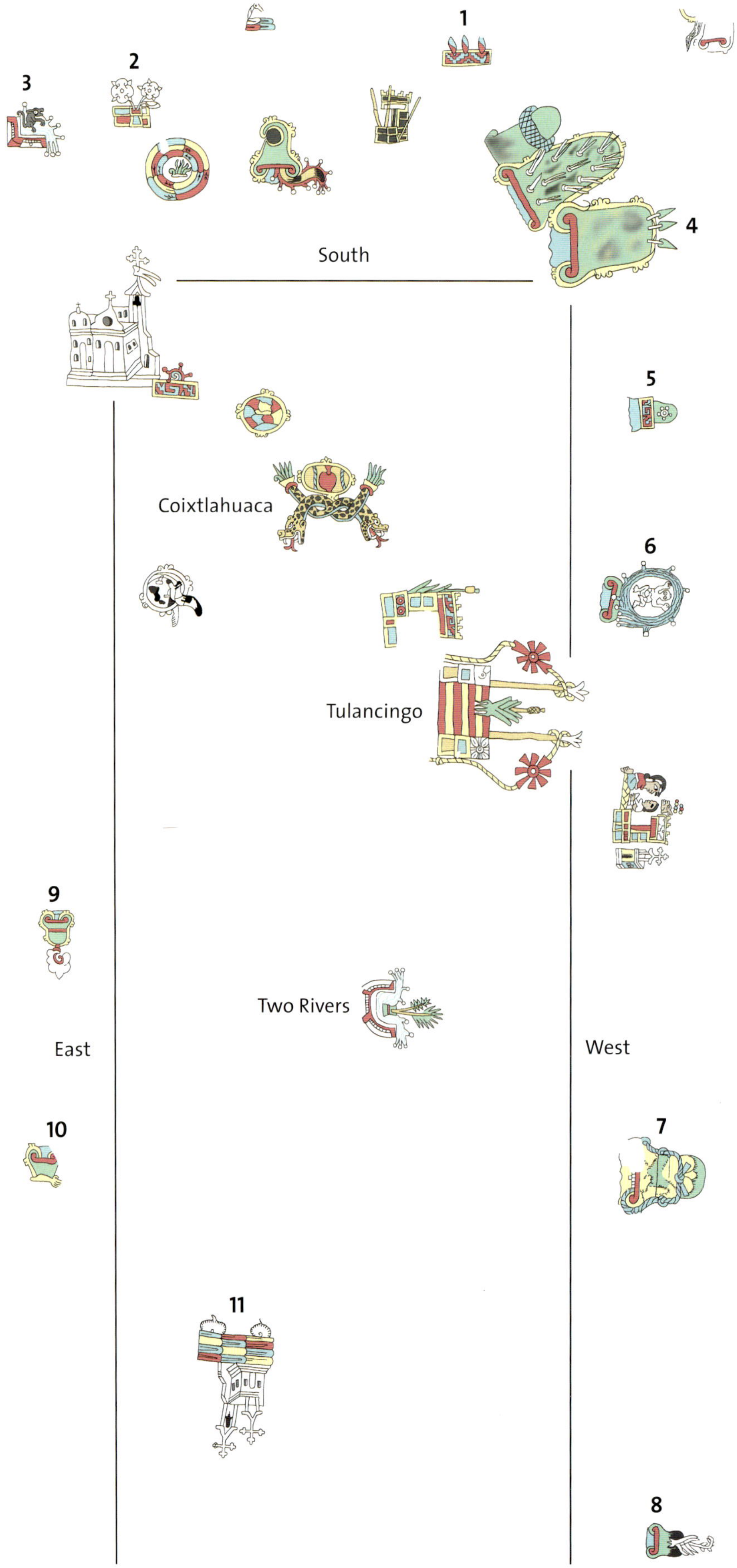

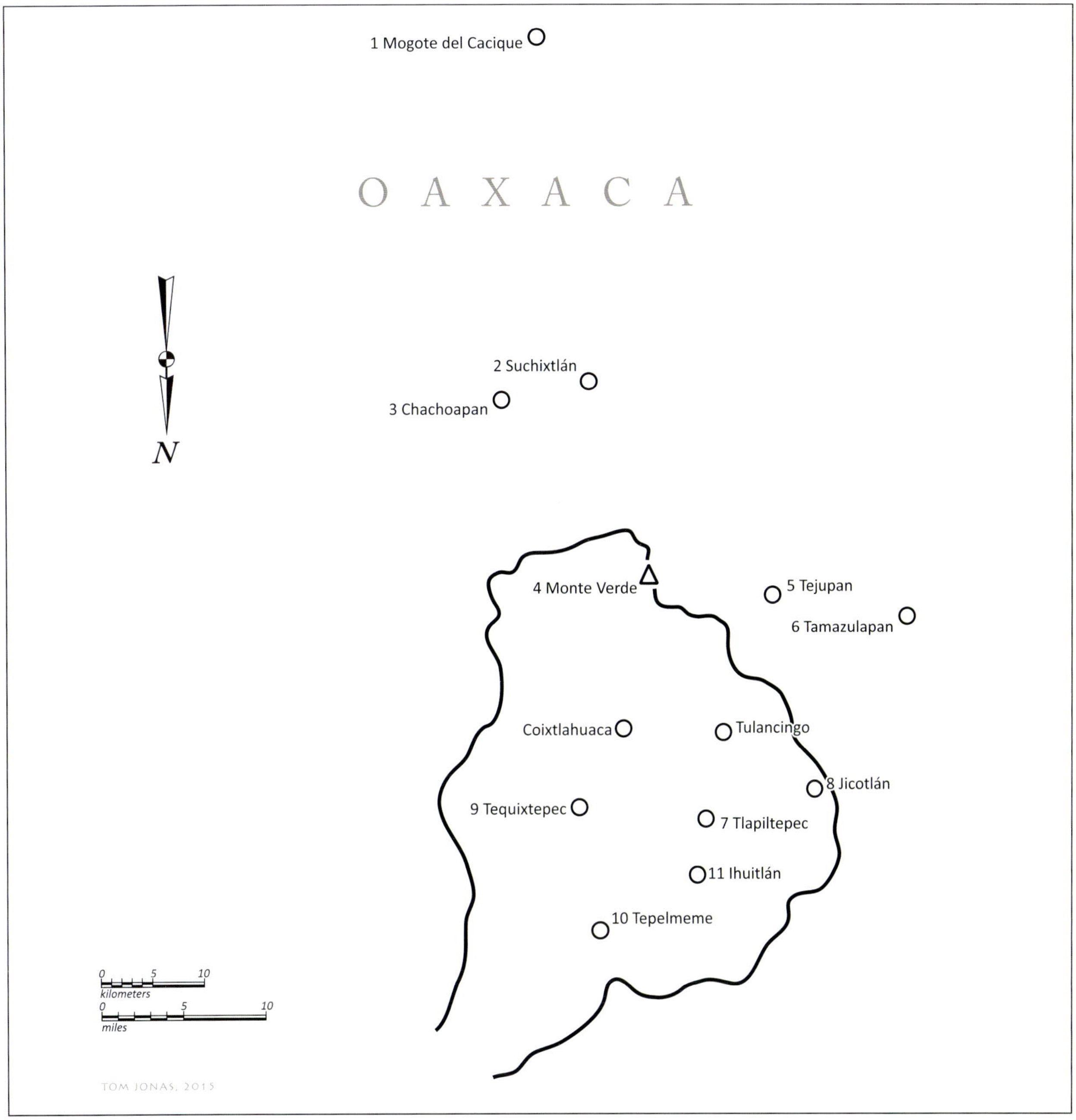

FIG. 3.11. Coixtlahuaca Valley (outlined) and area south, showing some towns from map on upper right side of Lienzo of Tlapiltepec. Based on map, "The Coixtlahuaca Valley," by Cecil R. Welte. See also fig. 3.10.

Monte Verde (*Yucucuy* in Mixtec), meaning green hill or mountain (Caso 1961:251, 259–60). Rising to a height of approximately 2,800 meters, Monte Verde is the tallest mountain in the Mixteca. It is a landmark in the actual landscape of the southwest corner of the Coixtlahuaca Valley, as in its corresponding location on the southwest corner of the lienzo map (fig. 3.12).

Place signs on the western margin, or right side of the map, include Tlapiltepec, "Hill of the Knot," halfway up the right edge of the lienzo, and above it, Tamazulapan and Tejupan, located in valleys just west of the Coixtlahuaca Valley. The sparsely occupied eastern margin, or left side of the map, contains the Coixtlahuaca Valley towns of Tequixtepec, Tepelmeme, and Ihuitlán.

Ihuitlán, represented on the lienzo by a Christian church combined with a feather-

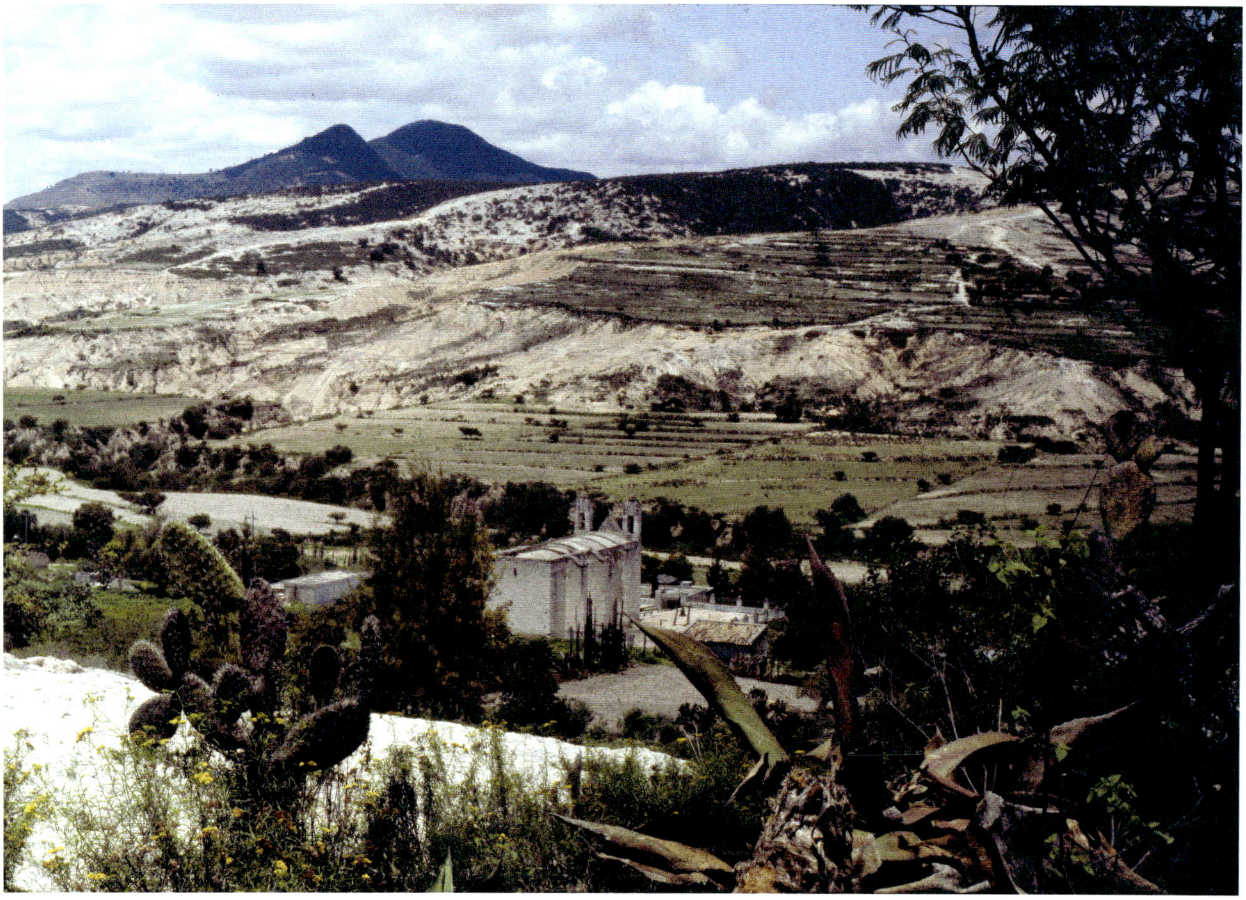

FIG. 3.12. Monte Verde (most distant peak), southwest of Coixtlahuaca. Coixtlahuaca's sixteenth-century Dominican church and monastery in foreground. Photo by Nicholas Johnson.

carpet place sign (11 on figs. 3.10–3.11), is in reality located north of Tlapiltepec, farther west than is shown on the lienzo. Ihuitlán has been shifted on the lienzo to create a central passageway of open space. This passageway is framed on the right by blocks of figures and place signs associated with Tlapiltepec and on the left by those associated with Ihuitlán (fig. 3.13). The purpose of this opening is to make way for red lines that originate from inside the core of the map above Ihuitlán and Tlapiltepec. The red lines pass through this corridor as they fan out to the many place signs that comprise the wide northern margin of the map below them.

CORE EVENTS ON THE LIENZO

History on the Lienzo of Tlapiltepec centers on the genealogy of the rulers of Coixtlahuaca, their ancient ancestors, and the related rulers of other towns. The ancestors appear on the lower left of the lienzo, surmounted by the rulers listed in two tall columns at the upper left, starting from the earliest at the base of the columns and ascending chronologically to the most recent at the top (fig. 3.14). The earliest rulers probably lived in the eleventh or twelfth century, and the most recent, some twenty-one generations and four to five hundred years later, around the time of the Spanish conquest of Mexico of 1519–21.

Although the lienzo records the collaboration of these two parallel lineages of Coixtlahuaca rulers, much of the detail of the manuscript concerns only the left-hand

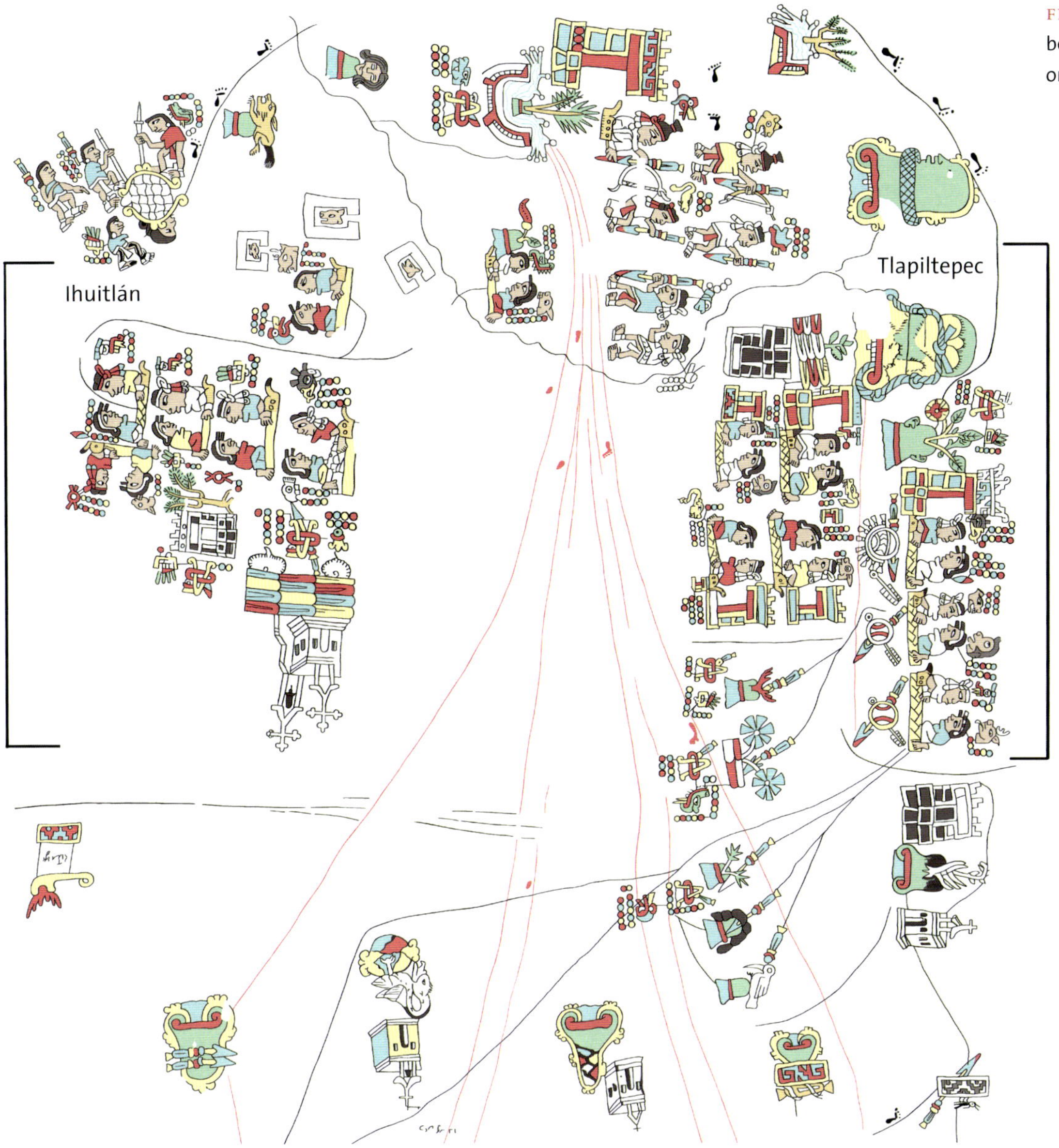

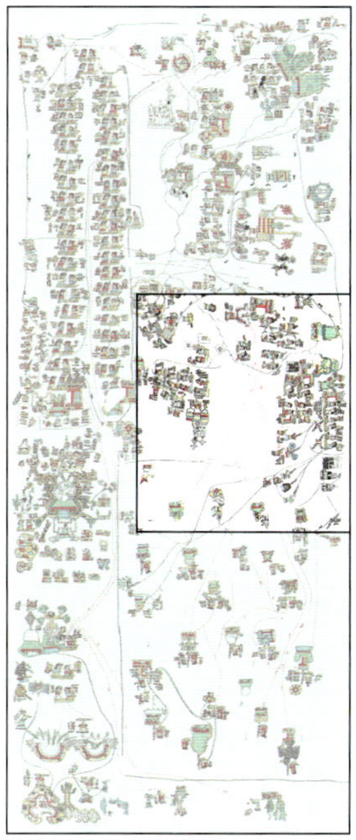

FIG. 3.13. "Corridor" of red lines between Ihuitlán and Tlapiltepec on Lienzo of Tlapiltepec.

lineage. The ancestors depicted at the lower left, below the columns of rulers, were ancestors exclusively of this lineage, and it is the historical development of this lineage that is emphasized in the map on the right side of the lienzo. The lienzo indicates that the two lineages were originally founded not at Coixtlahuaca but at two other Coixtlahuaca Valley locations; only later did they join forces at Coixtlahuaca.

The place sign that accompanies the earliest, or founding, rulers at the base of the important left-hand column of rulers is a hill with protruding green leaves (fig. 3.14, A; 3.15). Like the similar hill clustered with two other hills in the upper right corner of the lienzo, this place sign refers to the mountain known as Monte Verde or Yucucuy, located at the southwest corner of the Coixtlahuaca Valley (see fig. 3.9). This implies that the left-hand lineage was first established at or near Monte Verde.

The place sign that appears at the base of the right-hand column, although partly effaced, can be reconstructed as a hill crossed by arrows (fig. 3.14, B). This is thought

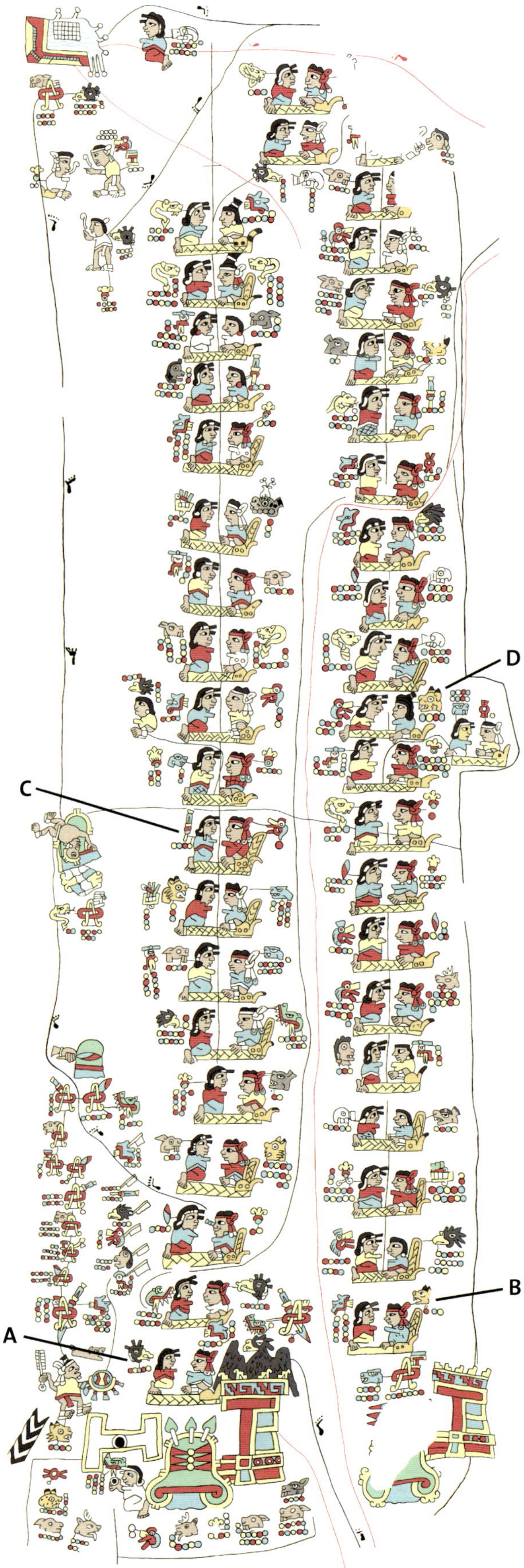

FIG. 3.14. Coixtlahuaca's two ruling lineages, detail from upper left side of Lienzo of Tlapiltepec. Left column is the Monte Verde lineage; right column is the Miltepec lineage.

by Doesburg and Buren to refer to a now-disappeared settlement known as Miltepec that was located near the north end of the Coixtlahuaca Valley, distant from Monte Verde at the south end (Doesburg 2001:43–44 n. 19; also chapter 2 of this book).

There is evidence that the founder of the important left-hand, or Monte Verde, lineage, named 7 Water "Eagle" on the lienzo, was not from Coixtlahuaca, or from the Mixteca at all, but from the Valley of Mexico. In the sixteenth-century historical account known as the Annals of Cuauhtitlán, 7 Water is called Atonal (I) and is described as the leader of a southeastern migration of Toltecs, legendary predecessors of the Aztecs in the Valley of Mexico. Some of them settled in the Coixtlahuaca area.[4]

For some eight generations, or two centuries, the two lineages apparently continued to reside respectively at Monte Verde in the south and Miltepec in the north of the Coixtlahuaca Valley. Their joint move to the town of Coixtlahuaca in the south-central valley, either as co-founders of the town or displacers of previous rulers there, consolidated their power in the area and launched the political regime that made Coixtlahuaca an important center in late pre-Hispanic Mexico. Their joint move took place in the mid-to-late thirteenth century.

The transition from Monte Verde and Miltepec to Coixtlahuaca occurred during the lifetime of the ninth ruler of Monte Verde in the left-hand column, 1 Wind, and his contemporary from Miltepec in the right-hand column, 4 Jaguar (see fig. 3.14, C and D). While nothing in the two columns of rulers marks this transition, the map on the right side of the lienzo centers around it. Place signs and events comprising the map's core are directly related to this transition, and other developments prominent on the right side of the lienzo follow from it.

Coixtlahuaca is represented on the right side of the lienzo by four different place signs arranged in pairs (fig. 3.16). One of the pairs names the two specific sites or sectors of the town that were established or newly occupied by 1 Wind and 4 Jaguar (fig. 3.16, lower pair). The appearance of the figures of 1 Wind and 4 Jaguar and their wives in conjunction with these place signs signifies the founding of rulerships at Coixtlahuaca by these members of the Monte Verde and Miltepec lineages. The second pair of Coixtlahuaca place signs names two other sites or sectors of the town of Coixtlahuaca, established in nearby locations, by much later members of the two Coixtlahuaca lineages.

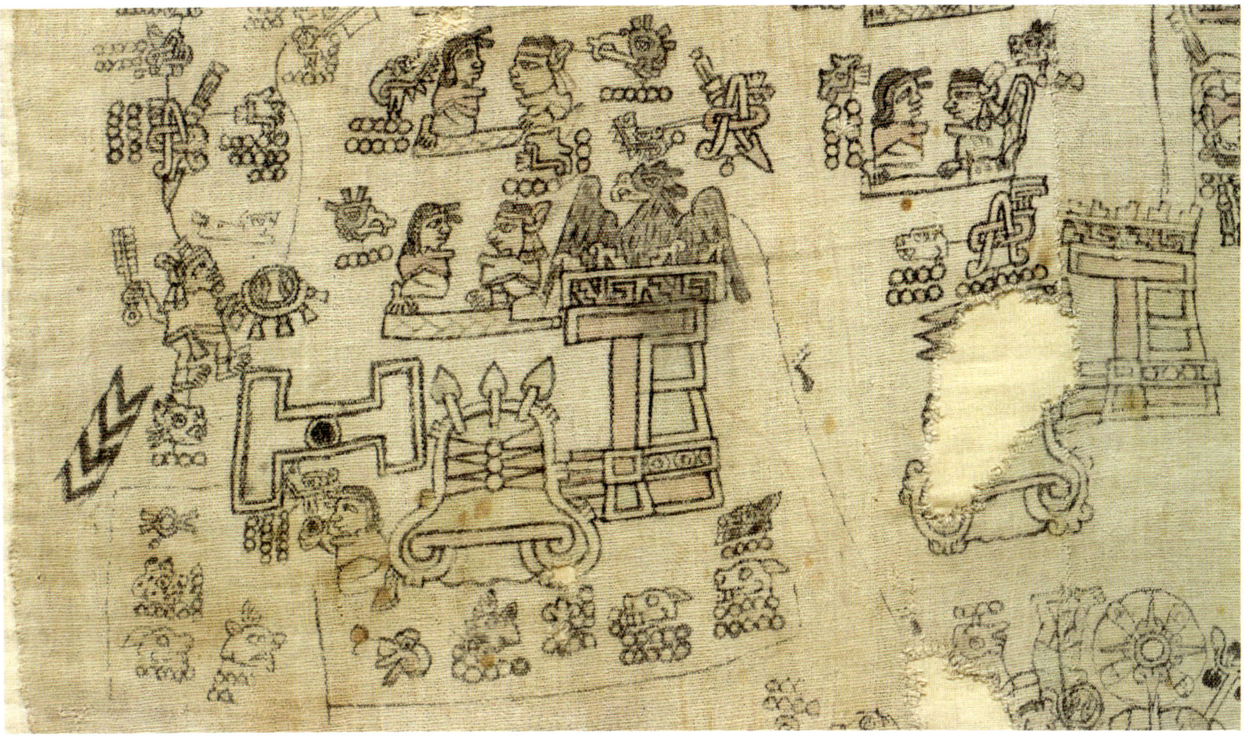

FIG. 3.15. *Left*, Monte Verde, and *right*, Miltepec, at base of columns of Coixtlahuaca rulers on Lienzo of Tlapiltepec. Courtesy of the Royal Ontario Museum, acc. no. 917.3, photo by Brian Boyle.

The place sign that accompanies 1 Wind and his wife on the right side of the lienzo consists of entwined serpents signifying Coixtlahuaca, plus an oval rock containing a heart and lengths of rope or thread; this second component of the place sign names the particular Coixtlahuaca site ruled by 1 Wind and his successors. The place sign that accompanies 4 Jaguar, identifying the site ruled by him and his successors, consists of a round rock combined with the spotted tail of a jaguar and the fringed tail of a coyote or similar animal. Within the rock are jaguar-claw lip plugs and, identified by Doesburg (2010a:91 n. 56), smudged but visible, at least one human footprint.

In addition to their prominence as the first rulers of Coixtlahuaca, 1 Wind and 4 Jaguar appear a second time on the right side of the lienzo at a meeting of two groups of warriors (fig. 3.17). The location of this meeting, shown as a river visually cleaved in two by a small hill and palm fronds, is uncertain. On other Coixtlahuaca lienzos that depict this meeting, the place sign explicitly includes a pair of rivers, and for purposes of this book I will refer to the site of this important meeting as Two Rivers.[5] On the Lienzo of Tlapiltepec, the seated host at this gathering is 1 Wind, accompanied by the standing figure of 4 Jaguar, both of whom are armed with bows and arrows.

From Two Rivers, red lines with red footprints, now badly faded, fan out to many of the place signs that compose the lower, or northern, half of the lienzo map. The implication of the Two Rivers scene of the two confronting groups is that a military alliance was formed for the purpose of launching an expedition into areas north of Coixtlahuaca, if not also for installing 1 Wind and 4 Jaguar at Coixtlahuaca. The origins of the warriors with whom 1 Wind and 4 Jaguar made this arrangement are not explained on the Lienzo of Tlapiltepec, nor on the Lienzo of Coixtlahuaca II, which contains versions of these same events.[6]

Closely associated with the gathering of warriors hosted by 1 Wind and 4 Jaguar at

FIG. 3.16. The four Coixtlahuaca place signs from upper right side of Lienzo of Tlapiltepec. Founding rulers 1 Wind and 4 Jaguar and their wives are next to the lower pair of place signs. Courtesy of the Royal Ontario Museum, acc. no. 917.3, photo by Brian Boyle.

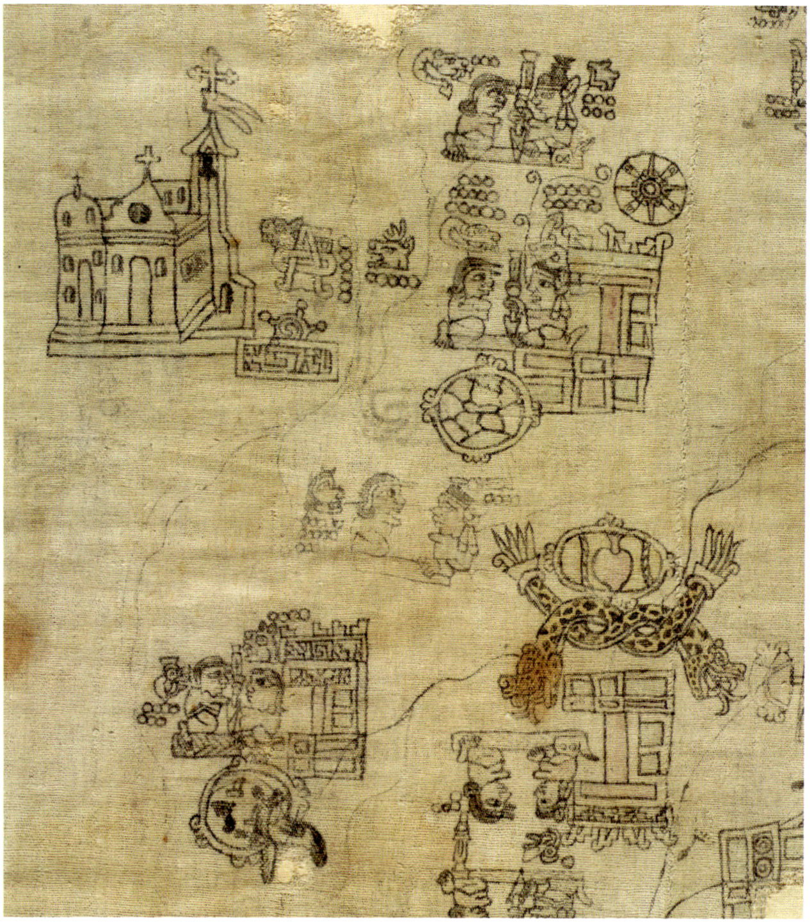

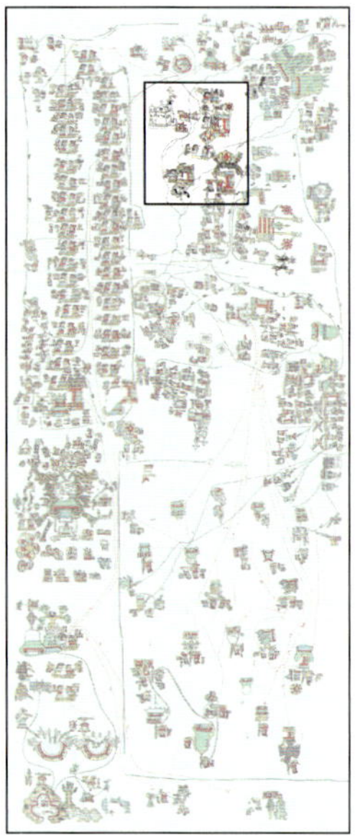

FIG. 3.17. Meeting of two warrior groups hosted by 1 Wind and 4 Jaguar (with bows and arrows) at Two Rivers on Lienzo of Tlapiltepec. Courtesy of the Royal Ontario Museum, acc. no. 917.3, photo by Brian Boyle.

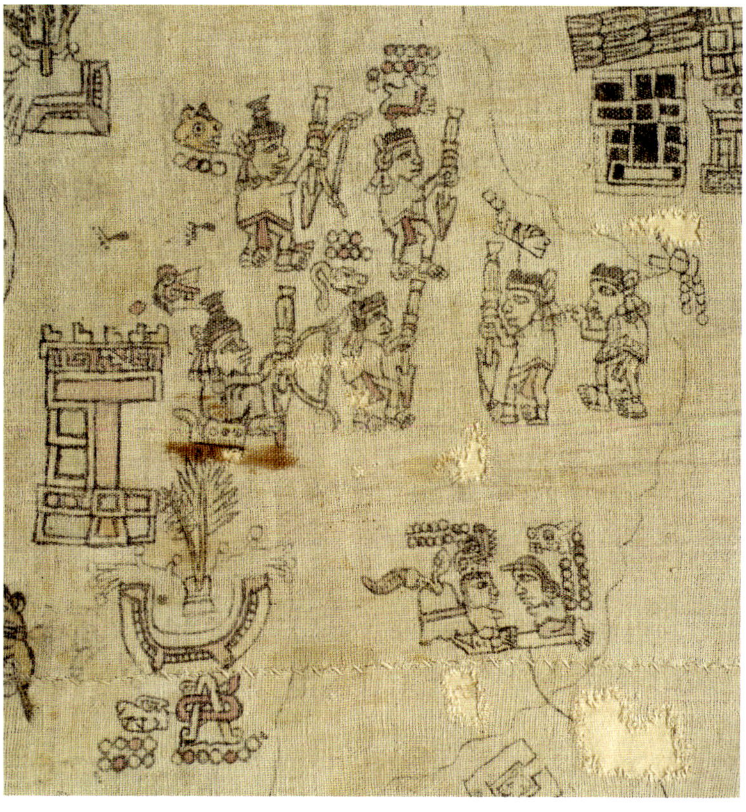

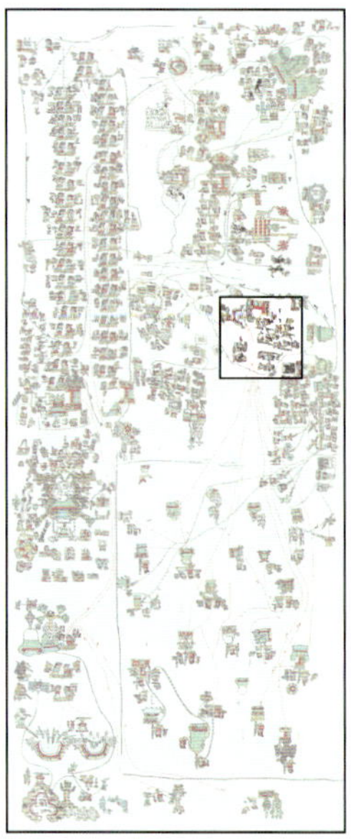

Two Rivers and with the founding of their rulerships at Coixtlahuaca is a scene of six priests. The priests, identifiable as such by their black body paint and black-spotted garments, are visiting a seated ruler near a large temple platform (fig. 3.18). Cattail reeds affixed to the side of the ruler's house identify the village where this took place as Tulancingo, a few kilometers west of Coixtlahuaca. The adjacent temple platform also has a cattail on top, meaning that this structure stands for a ceremonial site likewise located at Tulancingo. A thick, black line brackets the Tulancingo scene on the lienzo and helps separate it from surrounding material.

Combining the evidence from the Lienzo of Tlapiltepec and Lienzo of Coixtlahuaca II, it seems that important ceremonial activities took place twice at Tulancingo around this time, first before the meeting of warriors at Two Rivers, and second after this meeting and before the installation of 1 Wind and 4 Jaguar at Coixtlahuaca.[7] While neither 1 Wind nor 4 Jaguar is among those present at Tulancingo on the Lienzo of Tlapiltepec, the fathers of both men, their predecessors in the ruler lists, visit the Tulancingo temple in the version of these ceremonies depicted on the Lienzo of Coixtlahuaca II.

Approximately nine generations after the pivotal careers of 1 Wind and 4 Jaguar and eighteen generations after the original founding of the lineages by 7 Water "Eagle," known also as Atonal (I), at Monte Verde, and his contemporary at Miltepec, the Coixtlahuaca lineages moved to a new location at some time in the first half of the fifteenth century. The move is indicated on the lienzo by the second pair of Coixtlahuaca place signs, positioned above, or south, of the first pair (fig. 3.16, top).

The fifteenth-century successor of 1 Wind who reestablished his lineage at the new location was named 10 Serpent. He and his wife are seated near the top center of

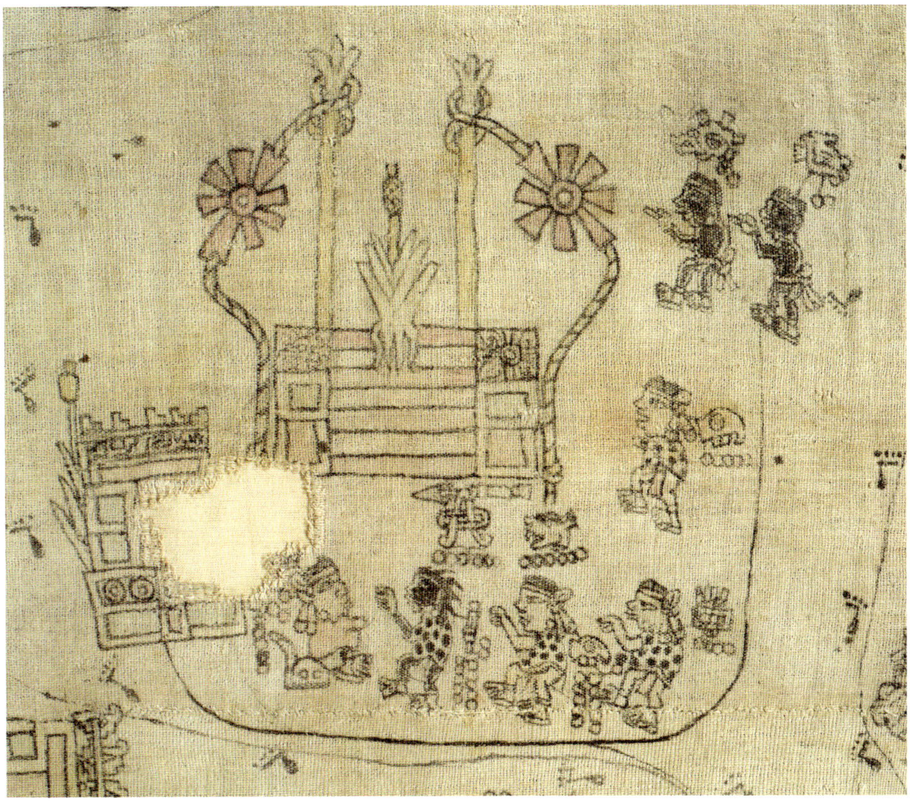

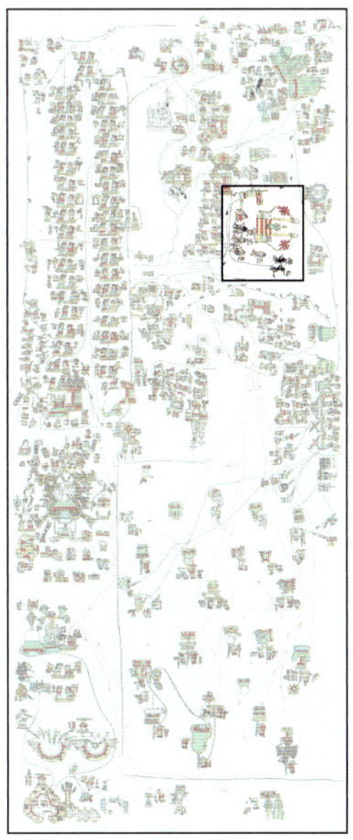

FIG. 3.18. Priests assembled at Tulancingo on Lienzo of Tlapiltepec. Courtesy of the Royal Ontario Museum, acc. no. 917.3, photo by Brian Boyle.

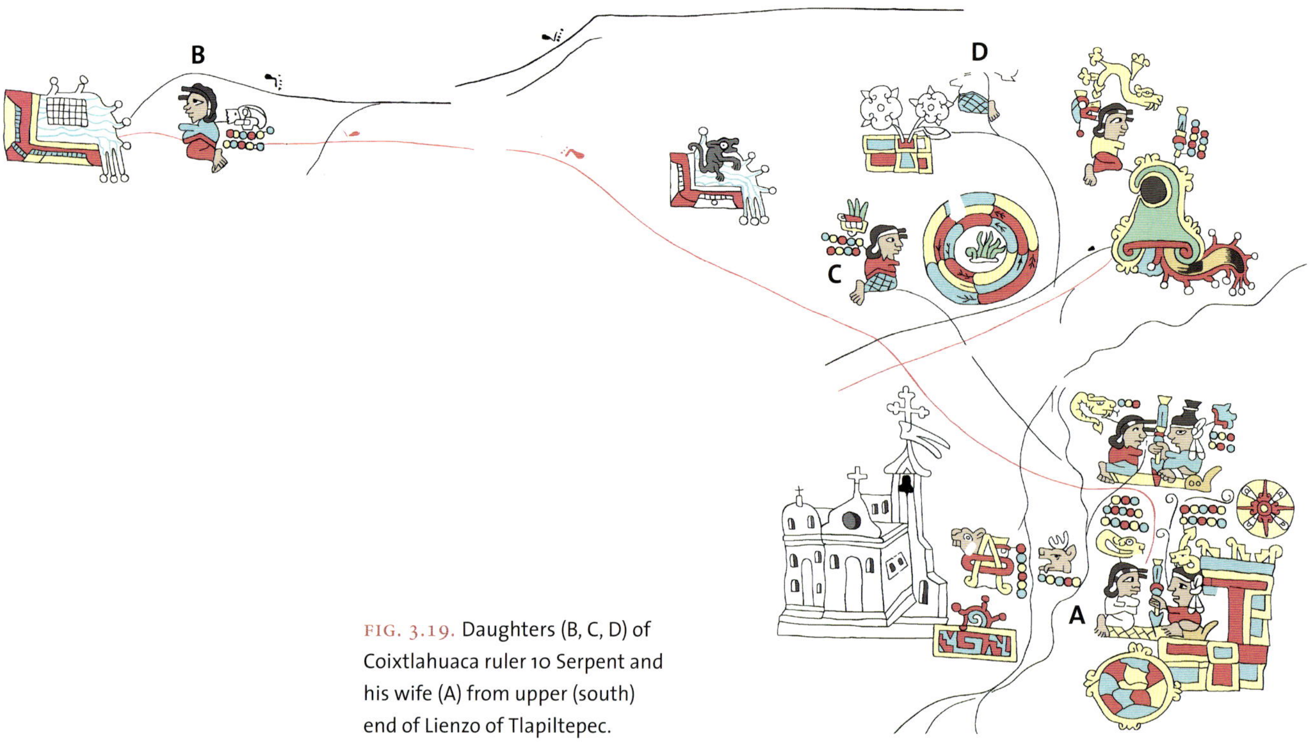

FIG. 3.19. Daughters (B, C, D) of Coixtlahuaca ruler 10 Serpent and his wife (A) from upper (south) end of Lienzo of Tlapiltepec.

the lienzo. The Coixtlahuaca site that 10 Serpent ruled is represented by a round rock (fig. 3.19, A).[8] The couple is succeeded there by the only other ruler of this site, their son 6 Water, who is known from various sources to have been killed by the Aztecs during their defeat of Coixtlahuaca in 1458–62. Six Water was known to the Aztecs as Atonal, like the founder of his lineage, 7 Water "Eagle," Atonal (I).[9]

Connecting lines, one red and two black, branch out from 10 Serpent and his wife to their three daughters, sisters of the ill-fated 6 Water; they apparently married into ruling families of towns located farther south in the Mixteca (fig. 3.19, B–D).[10] These lines suggest an expansion of Coixtlahuaca's ties and its southward influence, related to the reestablishment of the lineage in a new location in the fifteenth century. The lines mirror, on a smaller scale, the larger system of red lines that leads north from Two Rivers at the time 1 Wind and 4 Jaguar first established their rulerships at Coixtlahuaca some two centuries earlier.

In the columns of rulers on the left side of the lienzo, eight couples separate 1 Wind and his wife from 10 Serpent and his wife, and most of these intervening couples reappear on the right side of the lienzo in the core area of the map. There the first four of these couples are stacked in a short column above 1 Wind at Coixtlahuaca, but the fifth and sixth couples appear on the map as rulers of two other local towns: Tequixtepec, north of Coixtlahuaca, and Tejupan, in a valley west of Coixtlahuaca.

This genealogical-geographical sequence on the right side of the lienzo forms a connecting loop that begins at Coixtlahuaca, circles around Tequixtepec and Tejupan, and returns to Coixtlahuaca (fig. 3.20). From the successors of 1 Wind at Coixtlahuaca, a black line leads to their son at Tequixtepec. A trail of black footprints then winds its way through the crowded middle of the map to this Tequixtepec ruler's own son at Tejupan on the western edge of the lienzo. Finally, another black line leads back into the center of the map, to the Tejupan ruler's son at Coixtlahuaca. In addition, two

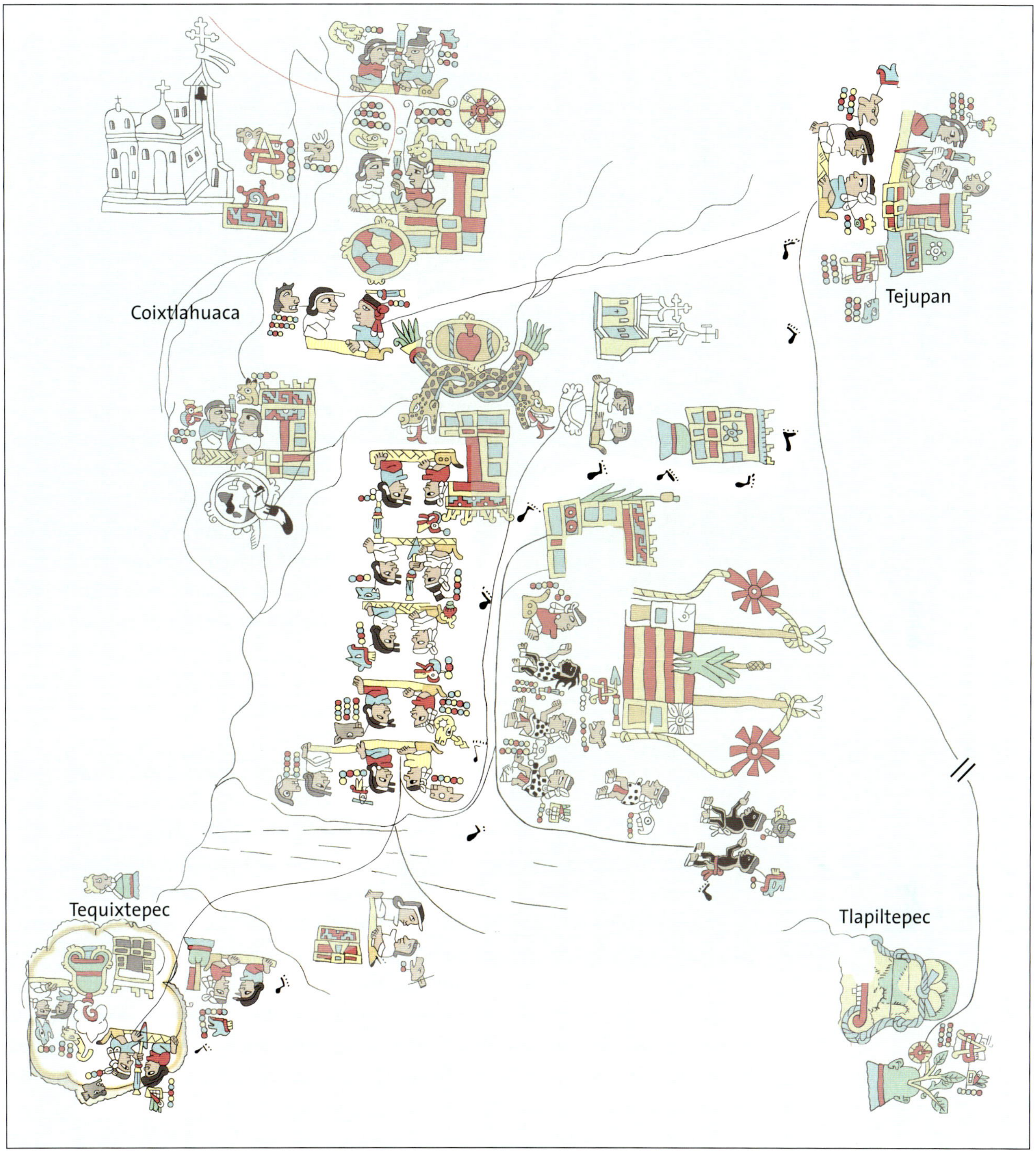

lines represent secondary offshoots of this sequence. One leads to the rulers of an unidentified place located near Coixtlahuaca in the center of the map and the other to a settlement at Tlapiltepec—and implicitly to the rulers of this Tlapiltepec site—on the western edge of the map.

FIG. 3.20. Descendants of Coixtlahuaca ruler 1 Wind at Tequixtepec and Tejupan, detail of Lienzo of Tlapiltepec.

The corresponding sequence of ruling couples descended from 1 Wind's contemporary, 4 Jaguar, of the Miltepec lineage listed on the left side of the lienzo, does not reappear on the map. Nor does the fifteenth-century member of the Miltepec lineage who, along with 10 Serpent of the Monte Verde lineage, reestablished Coixtlahuaca in a new location. A prominent place sign names the site of this resettlement, but its rulers are not identified. This is the fourth of the quartet of Coixtlahuaca place signs on the right side of the lienzo, paired with the "Round Stone" sign of 10 Serpent. The sign consists of a geometric frieze and whirlpool which, although very faded, appears originally to have been red in color and to represent blood rather than water (Doesburg 2010a:93).[11] The frieze and spiral are accompanied by the lienzo's largest depiction of a Christian church (see fig. 3.16). This site later became the Spanish colonial and present-day town of Coixtlahuaca. A large Dominican monastery, which now functions as the parish church, was built here beginning in the 1540s. The "Round Stone" site to its right, established at the same time and ruled by 10 Serpent and ultimately by his son 6 Water, located on a hill across the Río Culebra from the present town, is now reduced to archaeological traces (Bernal 1949).

With the death of 10 Serpent's son 6 Water during the Aztec invasion of Coixtlahuaca, the lineage of Coixtlahuaca rulers whose history and genealogy are featured on the Lienzo of Tlapiltepec—the Monte Verde lineage—comes to an end. The genealogy concludes at the top of the columns on the left side of the lienzo, where a daughter of the final ruler 6 Water, from the left-hand column or Monte Verde lineage, marries a man from the right-hand column or Miltepec lineage (see fig. 3.14, top). With this marriage, the Miltepec lineage henceforth, and into colonial times, becomes Coixtlahuaca's sole ruling line, based at the site represented by the swirling current of blood and the large Christian church.

THE NORTHERN MAP

The web of lines on the Lienzo of Tlapiltepec has a core, corresponding to the area around Coixtlahuaca, and a fringe of extensions. We have looked at lines of the core. Some of the lines that extend out from this core lead south into the heart of the Mixteca, but the lines lead most prominently north and northwest into transitional and non-Mixtec areas of what is today south and central Puebla.

Most of the lines leading north are red, extremely faded, and sparsely accompanied by red footprints.[12] The red lines originate from the unidentified Coixtlahuaca Valley site referred to here as Two Rivers, where warriors from Monte Verde and Miltepec, who co-founded a regime at Coixtlahuaca, met with a second group of warriors about whom little is known (see fig. 3.17). At their point of origin there are three red lines, and as they funnel between Tlapiltepec and Ihuitlán and out onto the northern map they divide into six lines, which lead to five or six place signs, and ultimately a total of ten place signs and their rulers, spread out over this section of the lienzo (figs. 3.21, 3.22; numbers in following section refer to these figures).

Of the six lines, three lead to a single place sign each, the farthest of which consists of an eagle on top of a house, known to represent Cuauhtinchan in central Puebla (**1**).[13] Near Cuauhtinchan on the lienzo, as in reality, and the sole destination of its red line, is Tecali, represented by a hill and wall of blocks (**2**). The third of the individual destinations is a hill with two peaks and a house between them, representing Tepexi in central southern Puebla (**3**).

A fourth of the six red lines originating from Two Rivers leads to two intermediate place signs before continuing on to its destination, represented by an oval stone and a woman's face in profile. This is Oztoticpac, present-day Santa María Oxtotipan (Reyes García 1977:59), east of Cuauhtinchan and Tecali (4). From the rulers of Oztoticpac, black roads without tracks lead in turn to their children and grandchildren at nearby Tepeaca, represented by a hill with a human face (5); Tecamachalco, represented by a platform, thatched building, and plant (6); and Quecholac, by a frieze, hill, and current of water (7).

The course of a fifth branch of the Two Rivers system is not entirely certain. This line appears to lead to a sign that consists of a man with closed eyes in an L-shaped container of water. Or the line may merely pass close to this sign, before apparently merging with the red line that leads to Oztoticpac and the family of rulers linked by black roads.

The sixth red line, the shortest of the system, leads first to a hill crossed by arrows (8). This is the same place sign that appears at the base of one of the two columns of rulers on the left side of the lienzo (see fig. 3.14), and that is believed to represent a former town called Miltepec, ancient home of the second of the lienzo's two Coixtlahuaca lineages, located near the north end of the Coixtlahuaca Valley. From Miltepec, red lines continue to three other place signs.

In addition to the red lines leading from Two Rivers, this lower section of the lienzo includes a second system of red lines, one of whose branches converges with the Tepexi branch of the Two Rivers system but is otherwise independent of that system and is contained entirely within the northern section of the map. This second system of red lines originates from the rulers of an unidentified town represented on the lienzo by a yellow and black swallowtail butterfly and L-shaped container of water, positioned near the edge of the map. From these rulers, four red lines fan out to three sons and a daughter at four other locales. A further segment of red line leads from the daughter and her husband to their daughter, wife of the ruler of Tepexi (3). In other words, the ruler of Tepexi, who came from Coixtlahuaca or was descended from someone who did, married the granddaughter of the rulers of "Butterfly Water," located, judging from the lienzo map, somewhere in southwestern Puebla or northern Oaxaca.[14]

Also found on the northern section of the map are a number of place signs outside of the two red-line systems and for which no rulers are shown. Some of these places are pierced by arrows, signifying they were conquered. Black lines, attached harpoon-like to the conquest arrows, cross the map diagonally and connect several such place signs to rulers of Tlapiltepec. A hill with a jaguar or mountain lion, quite possibly representing Tehuacán, northeast of Coixtlahuaca (Jansen 1983:13), was one of the Tlapiltepec conquests (9). Towns conquered by a man named 2 Reed on the western edge of this section of the lienzo are possibly Cuyotepeji, in the Mixteca Baja, represented by a jaguar and frieze (10) (Jansen 1983:13), and another, unidentified site located somewhere south of Cuyotepexi, represented by an insect and frieze.

Also included on the northern map are a number of isolated place signs, attached neither to red lines nor to black lines and conquest arrows. Several of these are accompanied by small Christian churches. One of these place signs, centrally positioned at the south end of the northern map, and consisting of an egret or heron perched on a rock, stands for Aztatla, located at the northern extreme of the Coixtlahuaca Valley (11). Nearby, a hill with a rocky peak and small church is thought to stand for a village formerly called Texcalhueyac (now Las Palmas), west of Aztatla (12; Doesburg 2000:170–72). The small churches attached to both of these signs, simpler in design

FIG. 3.21. "Northern map" from lower right side of Lienzo of Tlapiltepec. Note: detail area is flipped upside-down from lienzo. See also fig. 3.22.

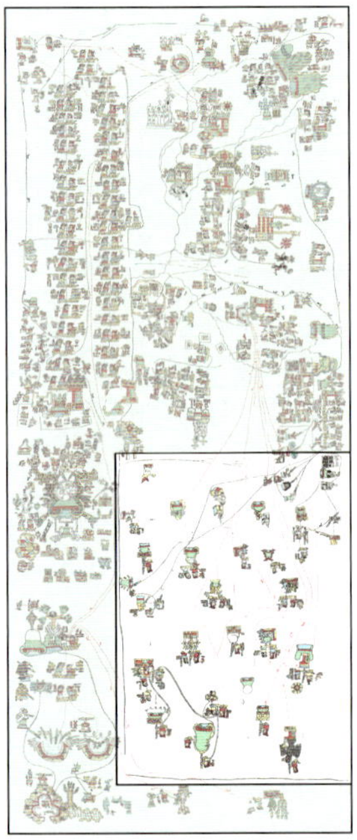

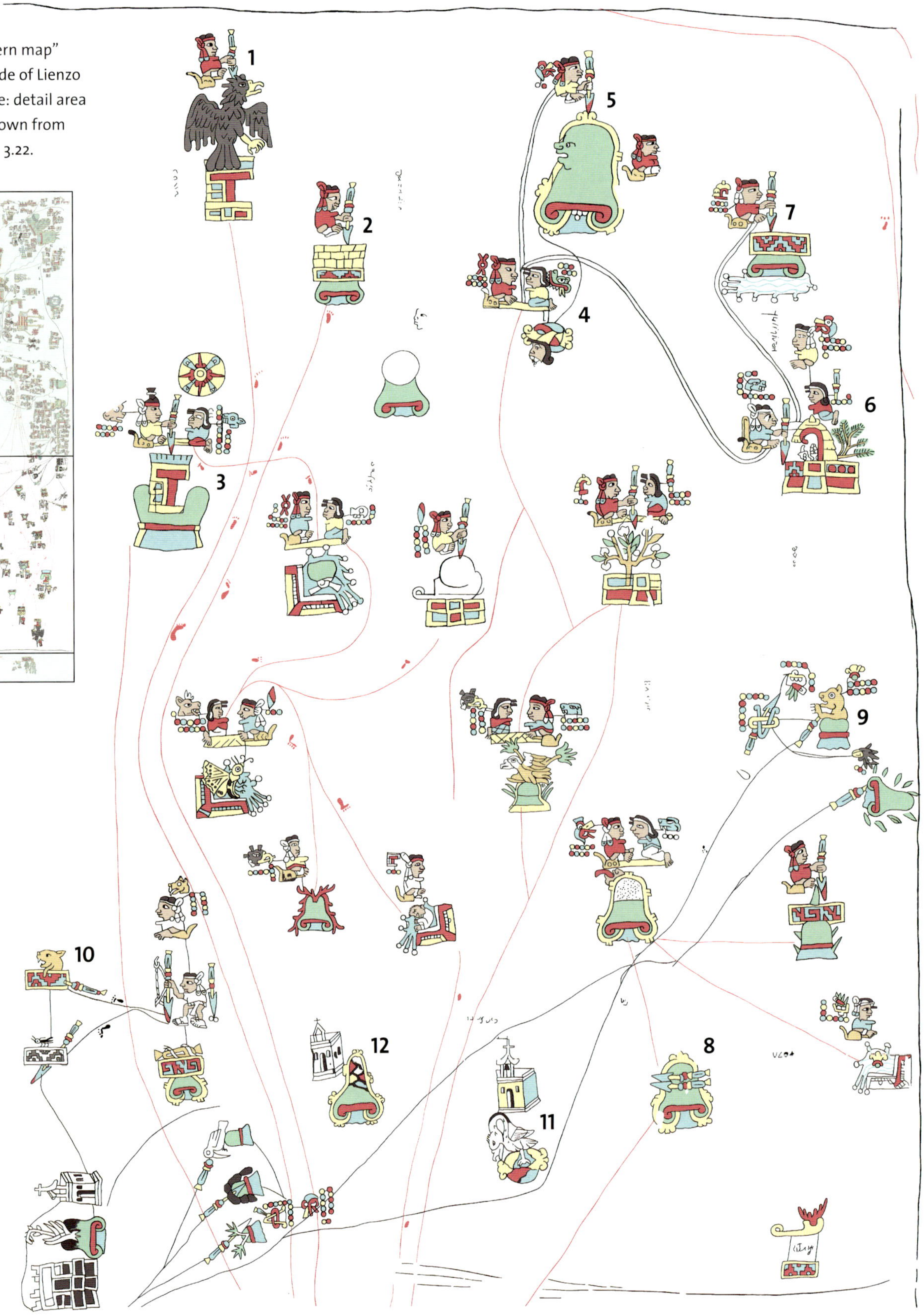

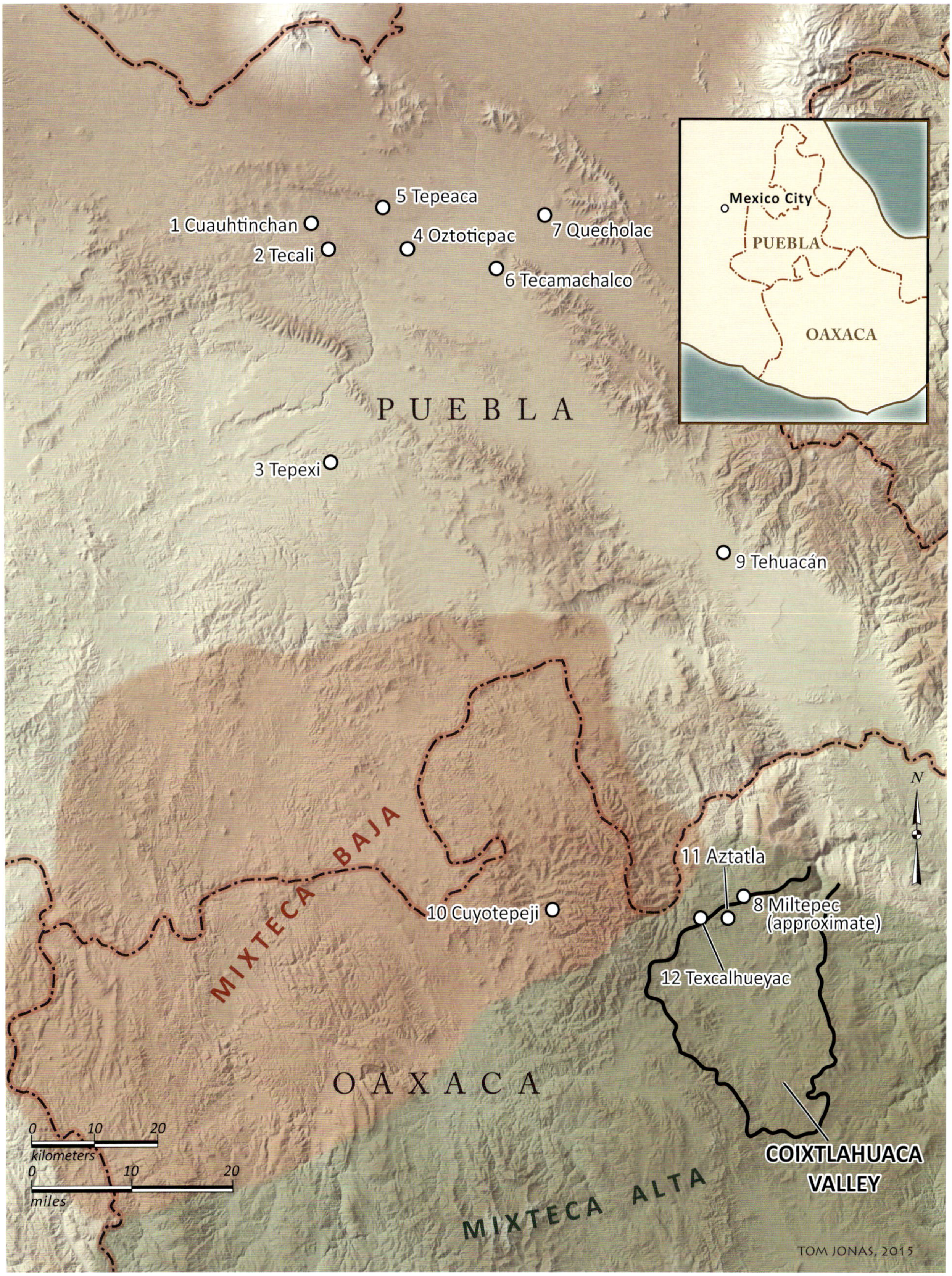

FIG. 3.22. Some towns from lower right side of Lienzo of Tlapiltepec. See also fig. 3.21.

than churches in the core of the map, suggest these villages were northern outposts, or *visitas*, of the Dominican parish established at Coixtlahuaca in 1544.

The northern section of the map—the bottom right of the lienzo—is a visually compact block of place signs, separated from the southern core by a gap and from other material on the east and north by black dividing lines. In real life, the towns represented by the northern place signs are unevenly distributed over a large and geographically varied area. Cuauhtinchan and Tecamachalco, for example, and others near them on the lienzo, are clustered on the plains of central Puebla, in the vicinity of the important pre-Hispanic city of Cholula, just across the volcanoes Popocatepetl and Iztaccihuatl from the Valley of Mexico. Aztatla, with its small church, on the other hand, is in the Coixtlahuaca Valley, albeit at its north end.

Still other towns in this northern section—such as Cuyotepeji—belong to the Mixteca Baja, the mountainous region partly in Oaxaca and partly in Puebla. Tehuacán, on the opposite edge of the map from Cuyotepeji, is contained in the long trough of the Tehuacán Valley, in the lee of the massive Sierra Madre Oriental, while Tepexi is situated in the more sparsely populated center of the southern Puebla region. The area encompassed by the northern half of the map on the Lienzo of Tlapiltepec is known as a transitional zone linking the peoples and cultures of central Mexico with those of southern Mexico. It is an area that tends to be overshadowed because of our better knowledge of these other regions.

The best understood part of this section of the lienzo is the small group of northern rulers and place signs linked by distinctive double black lines, or roads, discussed above (**4–7**). The reason for this is that the same group is referred to in some detail in sixteenth-century pictographic and alphabetic sources from Puebla and the Valley of Mexico. According to the manuscript known as the *Historia tolteca-chichimeca* from Cuauhtinchan, Puebla, and other sources, this particular family of rulers rose to power in the late fourteenth century. They were identified as "Mixteca-Popolocas" originally from "Couayxtlahuacan (Coixtlahuaca), Tlacpacalco, Aztacalco," and ruled in the area of east-central Puebla until then dominated by Cuauhtinchan.[15]

With the help of an Aztec group from the Valley of Mexico, the Mixteca-Popolocas defeated the Nahua rulers of Cuauhtinchan and in 1398 established their own dynasty, first at Oztoticpac (represented on the lienzo by the oval stone with a woman's face in profile, **4**), and subsequently at Tecamachalco (platform with thatched building and plant, **6**) and Quecholac (hill and frieze with current of water, **7**).[16] The Mixteca-Popolocas were themselves displaced by other local factions and their own Valley of Mexico allies in 1441.

Cuauhtinchan, represented on the lienzo by an eagle on top of a house and the figure of an unnamed male ruler, is the sole destination for one of the six red lines originating from Two Rivers in the Coixtlahuaca Valley (**1**). According to the *Historia tolteca-chichimeca*, it was the rulers of Cuauhtinchan who received the Mixteca-Popolocas when they first arrived in the area, which suggests that this red line might refer to the original migration of Mixteca-Popolocas from Coixtlahuaca into Cuauhtinchan territory.

In the Puebla sources the founder of the Mixteca-Popoloca dynasty at Oztoticpac is said to have been the son or descendant of one of the original migrants from Coixtlahuaca. On the lienzo there is no connection between Cuauhtinchan and Oztoticpac or their rulers. They belong to different branches of the Two Rivers red-line system.

TWO RIVERS ON THE LIENZO OF COIXTLAHUACA II

The Lienzo of Coixtlahuaca II, which may show evidence of the same artist's hand as the Lienzo de Tlapiltepec, includes some of the same scenes and can thus illuminate and enrich our understanding of the latter. On the Lienzo of Coixtlahuaca II, as on the Lienzo of Tlapiltepec, one group of armed men representing the lineages of Monte Verde and Miltepec meets with a second group of armed men at Two Rivers (fig. 3.23). The rulers of Monte Verde and Miltepec are on the verge of establishing themselves at Coixtlahuaca. In the Lienzo of Coixtlahuaca II version, the rulers from Monte Verde and Miltepec are not 1 Wind and 4 Jaguar, but their fathers. This scene on the Lienzo of Coixtlahuaca II is badly damaged, leaving the figures of the second contingent of warriors, aligned in the right-hand column directly beneath the Two Rivers place sign, only partly and faintly visible.

A road on the Lienzo of Coixtlahuaca II consisting of parallel black lines containing black footprints originates not from the Two Rivers place sign, like the red lines on the Lienzo of Tlapiltepec, but more particularly from the second group of warriors and extends to the right (fig. 3.24, A).[17] The road crosses the ribbon of jaguar spots and boundary signs that indicate the territorial limits of Coixtlahuaca on this lienzo, onto the lienzo's right hand, or northern, margin. There it divides into two branches, one of which leads downward to Oztoticpac and the other upward to Tepexi.

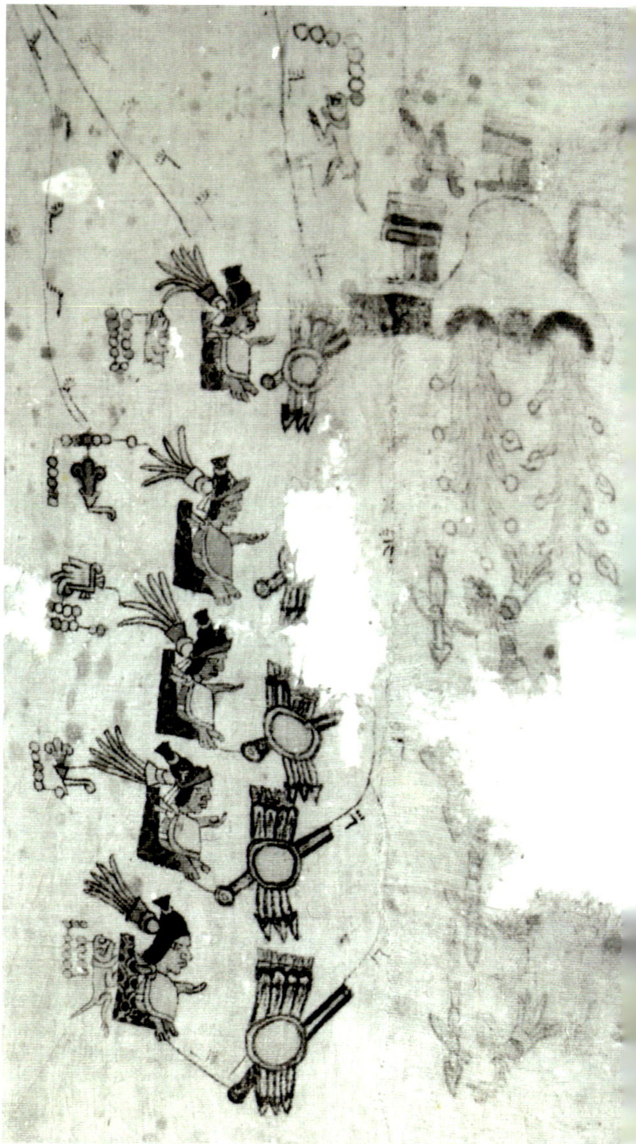

FIG. 3.23. Meeting of two warrior groups at Two Rivers on Lienzo of Coixtlahuaca II. Courtesy of Ethnologisches Museum Berlin.

These two towns also appear on the Lienzo of Tlapiltepec, but many other towns of the northern map that are the destination of red lines do not appear on the Lienzo of Coixtlahuaca II. Conversely, other towns connected with Two Rivers on Coixtlahuaca II are not mentioned on the Lienzo of Tlapiltepec. Cuautinchan, the town represented by an eagle, is present on the Lienzo of Coixtlahuaca II as the site of a confrontation between the Nahua ruler of Cuauhtinchan and the Mixteca-Popoloca ruler of Oztoticpac who displaced him, but no independent road or line leads to it.

While the two lienzos contain similar versions of Coixtlahuaca history, they vary in many details. Each contains or emphasizes some material that is not on the other, reflecting different purposes and priorities. Most notably, the Lienzo of Coixtlahuaca II, unlike the Lienzo of Tlapiltepec, is a map of Coixtlahuaca's boundaries. It is nearly square in shape and divided concentrically into a large central area that stands for lands controlled by Coixtlahuaca and a narrow perimeter of surrounding areas, demarcated by boundary place signs and the symbolic ribbon of jaguar markings. The Lienzo of Coixtlahuaca II is designed as an image of territorial dominance rather than a narrative of historical development.

Relations with Oztoticpac and Tepexi and possibly other towns located north of Coixtlahuaca, arising from the gathering at Two Rivers, are important on the Lienzo of Coixtlahuaca II, but they are not the culminating focus of attention that they are on the Lienzo of Tlapiltepec, nor are they the only outcomes of the Two Rivers gathering on this lienzo. On the Lienzo of Coixtlahuaca II, lines radiate outward from Two Rivers to the east, west, and south as well as north; consequences of the meeting of the two groups of warriors are more completely accounted for. Coixtlahuaca II also has more to say about the second, outsider, group of warriors and their role in these events. They are a larger group than on the Lienzo of Tlapiltepec, they are distinctively armed, and their alignment beneath Two Rivers suggests they, rather than the Coixtlahuaca contingent, might have been the hosts of the encounter.

A black line accompanied by black footprints leads diagonally down from Two Rivers toward five or six place signs and their rulers grouped together outside Coixtlahuaca's boundaries on the lower right corner of the Lienzo of Coixtlahuaca II (fig. 3.24, B). Of this line, only faint traces of some segments now survive and others are missing altogether. The place signs are also faded and damaged, and it is not clear which of them are actually the line's destinations.

Presumably these unidentified place signs—which may or may not correspond to any of those found on the northern map of the Lienzo of Tlapiltepec—represent towns located somewhere north or northeast of Coixtlahuaca.[18] This northern or northeastern pathway like the first road to Oztoticpac and Tepexi, may originate specifically from the second group of warriors, those in the poorly legible right-hand column.

Three other black lines accompanied by black footprints radiate outward from Two Rivers and lead to destinations located within as well as beyond Coixtlahuaca's boundaries. These lines appear to originate from the left-hand column of armed men in the Two Rivers scene, the group that includes the fathers of 1 Wind and 4 Jaguar from Monte Verde and Miltepec. One of these lines originates specifically from these two senior Monte Verde and Miltepec men (fig. 3.24, C). Following the lines, we see their movements after the Two Rivers meeting and come to the installation of their sons 1 Wind and 4 Jaguar at Coixtlahuaca. Extending diagonally left from Two Rivers, the line leads first toward the ceremonial site of Tulancingo at the upper center of the Lienzo of Coixtlahuaca II. There this same pair of Monte Verde and Miltepec individuals appears, along with their wives, in Monte Verde and Miltepec ruler lists just below the Tulancingo temple platform. Parallel lines lead from the two couples to their sons, 1 Wind and 4 Jaguar, seated side-by-side with their own wives on the Coixtlahuaca feathered serpent sign. Above each of the two ruling sons is a column of their successors. Two other lines derive from Two Rivers on the Lienzo of Coixtlahuaca II. One leads down toward the lower, generally eastern edge of the lienzo. Its destination is a ruler whose place sign, located within Coixtlahuaca's boundaries, consists of a hill and flower (fig. 3.24, D).

The second line originates specifically from the lower two or three of the warriors in the left column at the Two Rivers meeting, extends upward, and divides into at least two branches (fig. 3.24, E). One branch leads to a place sign that includes an egret or heron, a house containing a throne, and a hill, inside Coixtlahuaca's boundaries and near the upper, western, edge of the lienzo (fig. 3.25). The egret sign represents Aztatla, which, in spite of its western location on the Lienzo of Coixtlahuaca II, is in reality situated at the far north end of the Coixtlahuaca Valley. The second branch of this line crosses the lienzo's western boundaries to a damaged place sign that appears to consists of a frog or toad in a current of water, and almost certainly stands for Tamazulapan, located in a neighboring valley west of Coixtlahuaca. Arrows held point-down by the rulers of both of these sites suggest they were acquired by conquest.

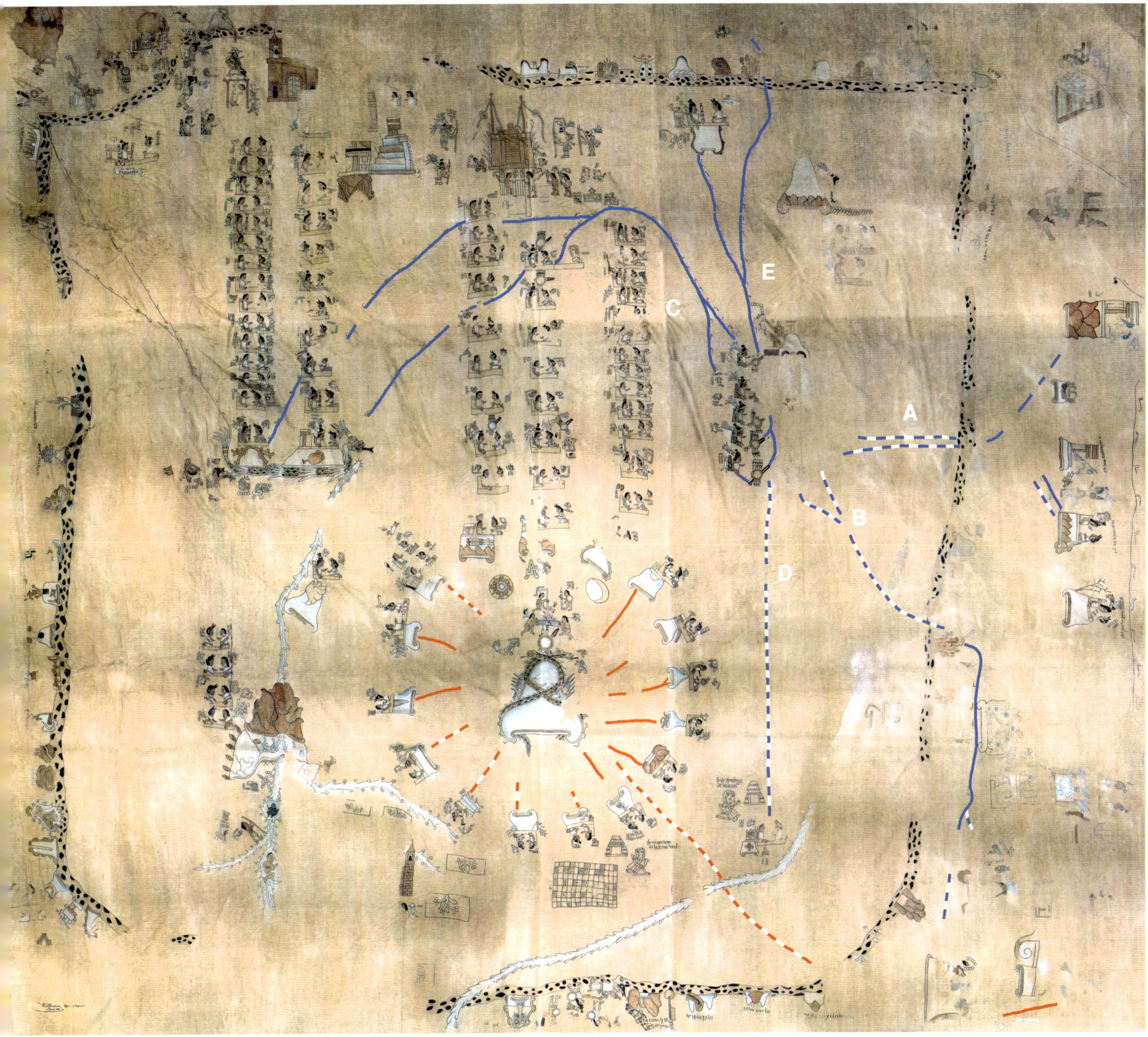

FIG. 3.24. Copy of Lienzo of Coixtlahuaca II (Lienzo Seler II) by Wilhelm von den Steinen, 1899. Woven cotton, 3.85 × 4.35 meters. Close cropped to painted passages and electronically retouched. Lines faintly visible on the original lienzo but missing from the copy are indicated as dashed lines. Red highlights the lines surrounding the large hill and is also the color of these lines on the original. Lines A–E, highlighted in blue, are black on the original. For more on the von den Steinen copy and its origins, see note 17, this chapter. Courtesy of the Division of Anthropology, American Museum of Natural History, cat. no. MCAA/0975.

FIG. 3.25. Aztatla on the Lienzo of Coixtlahuaca II, *left*. Courtesy of Ethnologisches Museum Berlin. Aztatla on the Lienzo of Tlapiltepec, *right*. Courtesy of the Royal Ontario Museum, acc. no. 917.3, photo by Brian Boyle.

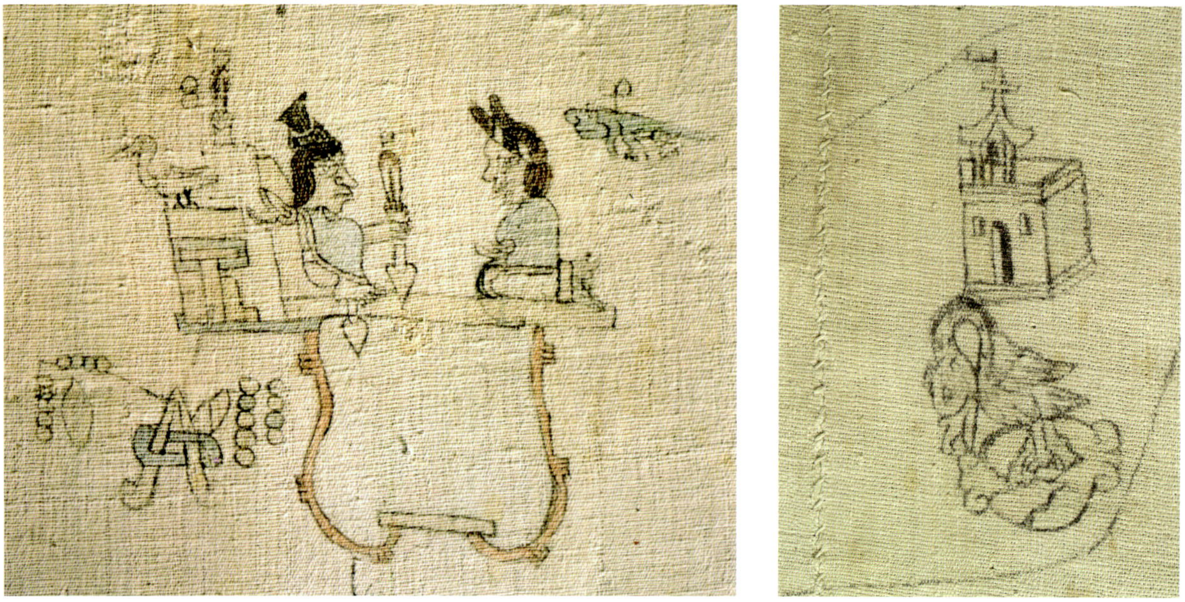

FIG. 3.26. Aztatla (A) and its warrior ruler 2 Reed (B) on Lienzo of Tlapiltepec. Note: detail area is flipped upside-down from lienzo.

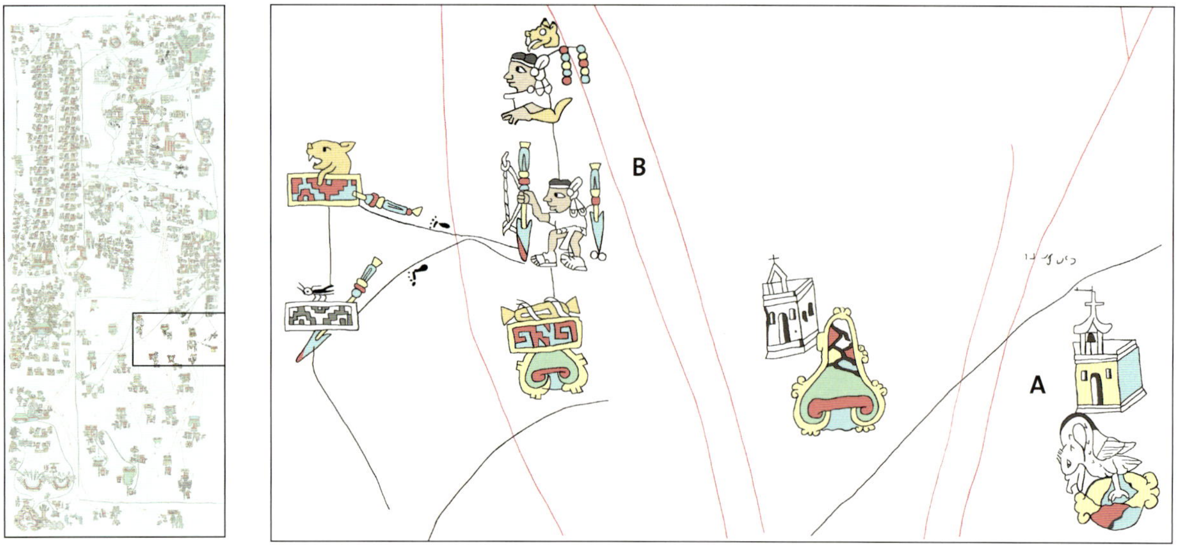

Aztatla and its ruler 2 Reed are also found on the northern map of the Lienzo of Tlapiltepec, but not together, nor are they directly linked, as here, to the meeting of warriors at Two Rivers (fig. 3.26). The egret-rock sign of Aztatla on the Lienzo of Tlapiltepec is not a destination for any of the red lines from Two Rivers nor is a ruler shown with it (fig. 3.26, A). Two Reed is armed with a bow and arrow and is depicted as the conqueror of two other towns, not of Aztatla (fig. 3.26, B). While 2 Reed does not appear at Two Rivers on the Lienzo of Tlapiltepec, the bow and arrow he carries is a sure sign of his association with the leaders of the Coixtlahuaca contingent at that gathering: One Wind and 4 Jaguar are both armed with bows and arrows, and no other warriors on the lienzo carry this weapon.

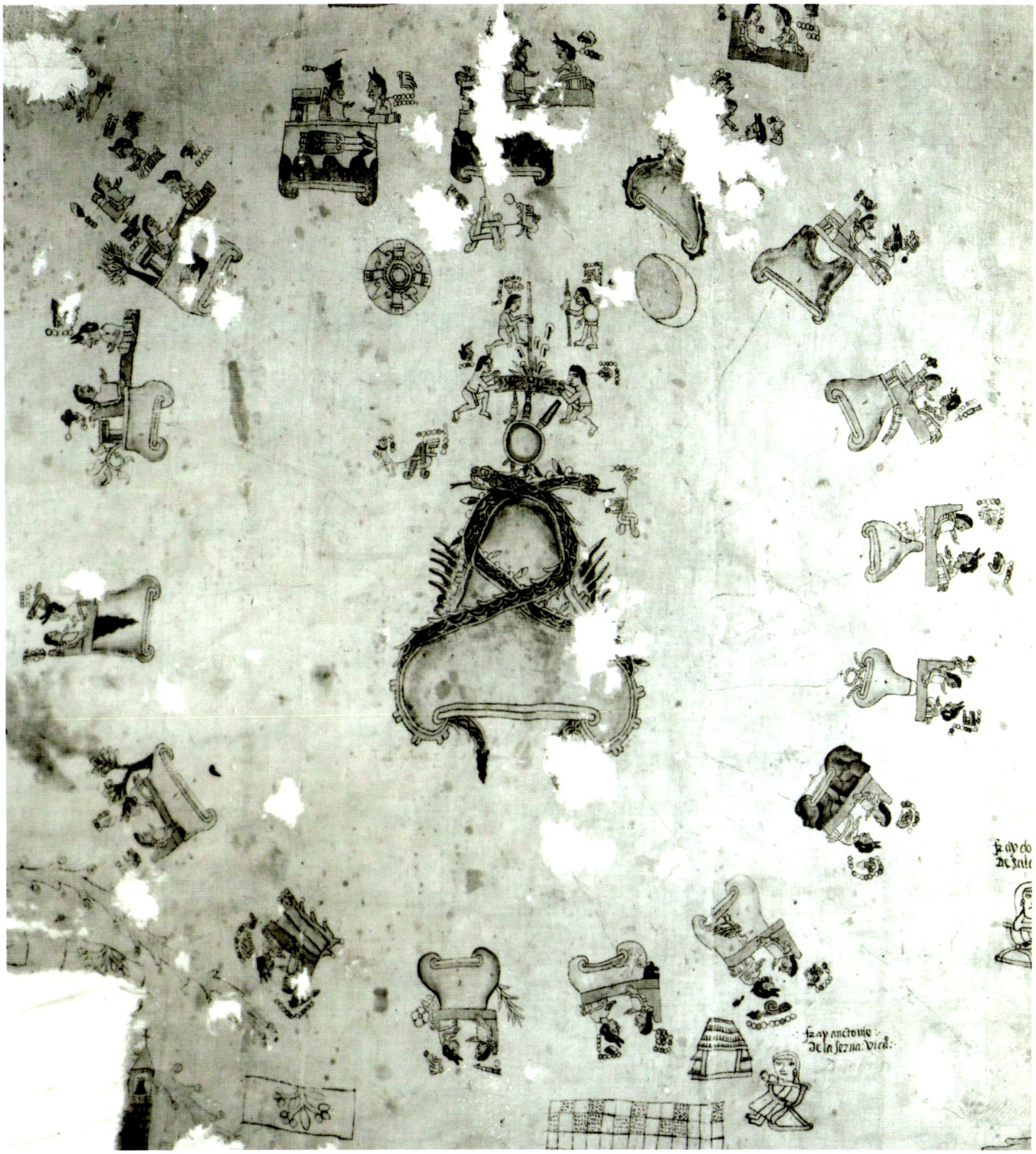

FIG. 3.27. Fire-making ritual atop a mountain of the Coixtlahuaca Valley and surrounding circle of place signs on Lienzo of Coixtlahuaca II. Courtesy of Ethnologisches Museum Berlin.

Aztatla is placed within Coixtlahuaca's territorial boundaries on the Lienzo of Coixtlahuaca II. On the Lienzo of Tlapiltepec, a small church accompanying the egret-rock sign locates Aztatla implicitly within the reach of the Dominican parish and the underlying political jurisdiction of Coixtlahuaca, but its position on the lienzo suggests some separation from Coixtlahuaca and association with other towns located farther north in central and southern Puebla, that compose the northern section of the lienzo map.

Aztatla's ties to these other northern communities are not explained on either lienzo but are abundantly confirmed in the Puebla sources. The *Historia tolteca-chichimeca*, for example, states that the "Mixteca-Popolocas" who migrated north to

Cuauhtinchan originated from "Aztacalco" (Aztatla) as well as "Couayxtlahuacan" (Coixtlahuaca) and an as yet unidentified "Tlacpacalco."

Especially important for the history of Aztatla is the pictographic manuscript known as the Map of Tecamachalco, or Lienzo Vischer I.[19] The Mixteca-Popolocas who rose to power and created a dynasty at Oztoticpac and Tecamachalco in the late fourteenth to mid-fifteenth centuries, and who are represented on the northern section of the Lienzo of Tlapiltepec as a family connected by double black lines, or roads (see figs. 3.21, 3.22, **4-7**), are shown as descending from rulers of Aztatla in the genealogies of this painted history from Tecamachalco, Puebla. Furthermore, Aztatla's early ruler 2 Reed, shown conquering Aztatla around the time of the meeting at Two Rivers on the Lienzo of Coixtlahuaca II and other towns on the Lienzo of Tlapiltepec, appears on the Map of Tecamachalco as an ancestor of this much later Oztoticpac-Tecamachalco dynasty.[20]

The egret place sign of Aztatla appears twice on the Lienzo of Coixtlahuaca II. As we have seen, 2 Reed takes over the town following the gathering at Two Rivers and around the time the lineages of Monte Verde and Miltepec establish themselves at Coixtlahuaca. Aztatla appears a second time in a much earlier context: at the lower center of the lienzo, it is one of a circle of towns surrounding the fire-making ritual that marks the original founding of the Monte Verde lineage. The place sign is accompanied there by a man and woman identified on the Map of Tecamachalco as Aztatla's very first rulers. The place sign of Monte Verde occupies the twelve o'clock position in this circle of place signs, partly effaced but with its identifiable first ruler, 7 Water "Eagle," and his wife 5 Vulture affixed to it, and the egret sign of Aztatla is at three o'clock (fig. 3.27, A and B).

ORIGINS AND BEGINNINGS

The ring of ancient towns and earliest rulers on the Lienzo of Coixtlahuaca II is the beginning of history. Before that is the time of semi-mythical origins. In this circle of towns, Monte Verde is located at almost the exact center of the square space that stands for territory controlled by Coixtlahuaca, its edges framed by boundary markers and the ribbon of jaguar spots. This positioning is not cartographic, since the real "Hill with Green Leaves" is located at the southwest corner of the Coixtlahuaca Valley, not in the middle of the territory. The central placement of Monte Verde reflects its importance as the starting point for the history that is spread out concentrically around it.

On the Lienzo of Tlapiltepec, the "Hill with Green Leaves" sign of Monte Verde appears twice, first, in the upper right corner of the lienzo, corresponding cartographically to its southwest location in the Coixtlahuaca Valley landscape, and second, midway along the lienzo's left edge. Stacked above the Monte Verde sign on the left edge of the lienzo are its rulers and the Coixtlahuaca rulers who are their descendants, and below it, as on the Lienzo of Coixtlahuaca II, is the fire-making ritual that marks the founding of the Monte Verde–Coixtlahuaca lineage. Farther below the fire-making ritual on the Lienzo of Tlapiltepec are the ancient ancestors born from a pair of rivers, and at the bottom left corner of the lienzo, a seven-chambered cave (fig. 3.28).

The same primordial cave, rivers, and ancestors appear on the Lienzo of Coixtlahuaca II but not in the center of the sheet. Rather, they are located in the lower right corner, outside the ribbon of jaguar spots and perimeter of boundary place-signs.

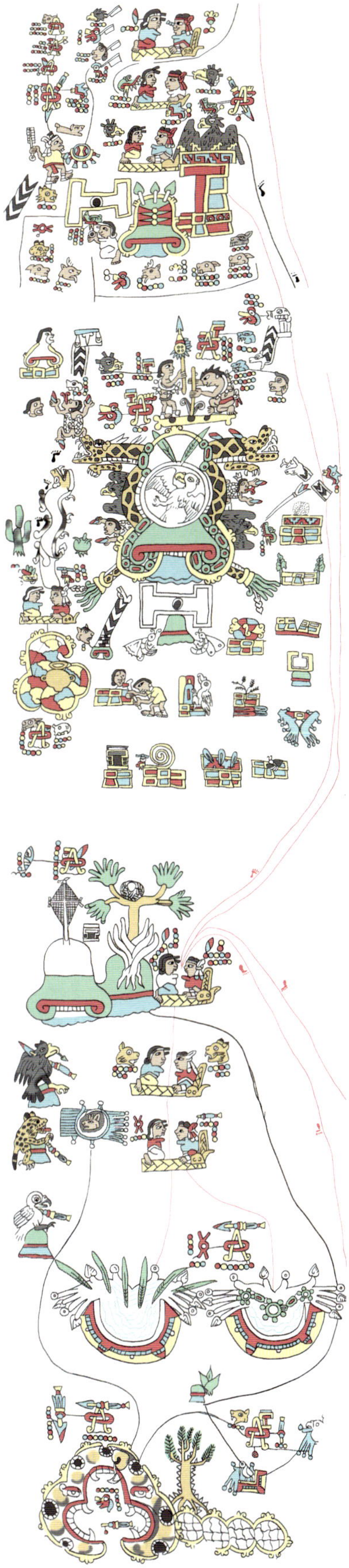

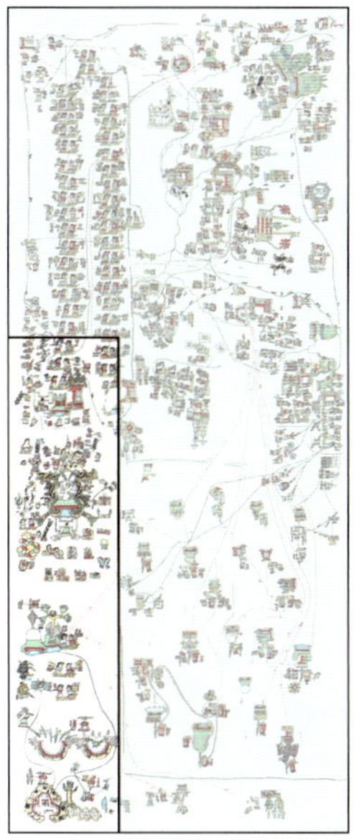

FIG. 3.28. Origins and beginnings, detail from lower left side of Lienzo of Tlapiltepec.

Thus, while the fire-making ritual presumably took place inside the territory that would eventually belong to Coixtlahuaca, these other ancient sites were understood by the authors of the Lienzo of Coixtlahuaca II to exist somewhere north or northeast of this territory.

The Lienzo of Tlapiltepec does not show Coixtlahuaca's boundaries, nor does it tell us anything about the geographical distance that separates the cave and rivers from the fire-making ritual, but it agrees with the Lienzo of Coixtlahuaca II about the direction of the cave and rivers. Adjacent to the large, lower right section of the Lienzo of Tlapiltepec that pertains to areas north and northwest of Coixtlahuaca, the positions of the cave and rivers of origin at the lower left signify their north or northeastern locations.

The main place signs in this section of the Lienzo of Tlapiltepec related to origins and beginnings are larger and more elaborate than most of those elsewhere on the lienzo, highlighting the importance of this part of the story. Side-by-side rivers from which the ancestors originate are shown as bowl-shaped cross-sections of flowing streams, the water painted white with blue ripple lines (fig. 3.29, right). The left river in this pair is decorated with green or blue quetzal feathers; the right river with a string of jade beads with red centers. In other Coixtlahuaca Valley manuscripts that contain versions of this prelude to Coixtlahuaca history, the two rivers are conflated into a single river containing both quetzal feathers and the precious blue-green stone.

Red lines, now barely visible, on the Lienzo of Tlapiltepec extend from the rivers to a husband and wife seated on a straw mat above the rivers. In other Coixtlahuaca Valley manuscripts, the male of this earliest ancestral couple is depicted physically stepping out of the quetzal-jade river (fig. 3.29, left). This must be the implication of the red lines on the Lienzo of Tlapiltepec as well: he, or both he and his wife, were born from the river.

A red line continues up from this first ancestral couple through two more generations. The third and final couple sits next to a compound place sign representing

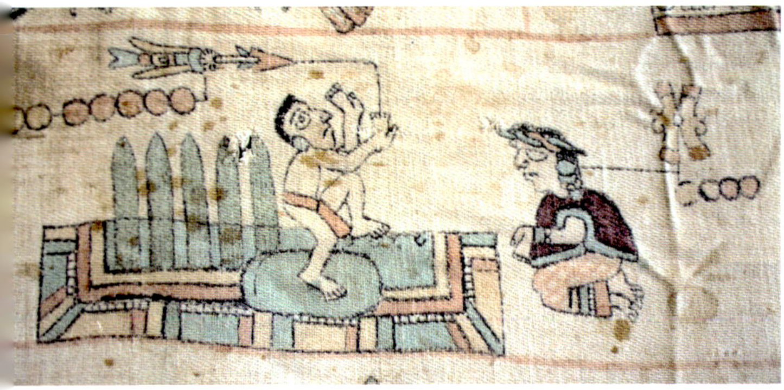

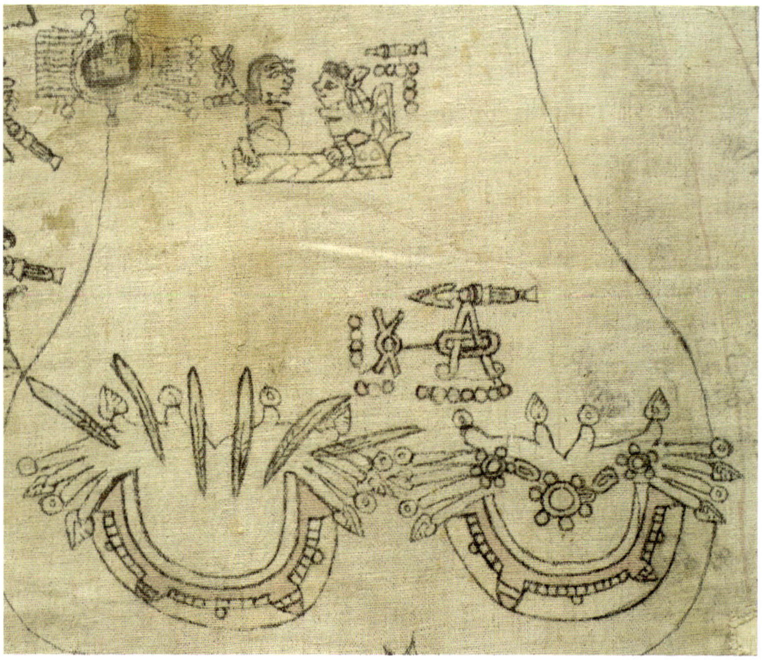

FIG. 3.29. *Left*, birth of ancestor from river of quetzal and jade on Lienzo of Tequixtepec I. Photo by María de los Ángeles Romero Frizzi. *Right*, corresponding scene on Lienzo of Tlapiltepec. Photo by Brian Boyle, Courtesy of the Royal Ontario Museum, acc. no. 917.3.

the ancestors' geographical home: a green hill with a white peak surmounted by a diamond-shaped net; joined to a hill with a flowering maguey, or combination of tree and maguey, with a bird's nest in its branches (see fig. 3.28). Between the hills is a small black house or temple. The white peak of the first hill suggests a location near one of Mexico's landmark snowcapped volcanoes, such as Popocatepetl, southeast of Mexico City on the edge of the Valley of Mexico, or further east at the same latitude, the Pico de Orizaba.[21]

Four long, red lines accompanied by red footprints branch out from the third ancestral couple to their son and three daughters at four other locations on the lienzo. One of the lines is directed up (south) to the ancestral couple's son, 7 Water "Eagle," or Atonal (I), as he is called in the Annals of Cuauhtitlán from the Valley of Mexico, seated with his wife above the place sign of Monte Verde as the first in its long list of historical rulers. A second line threads its way up between the columns of Monte Verde and Miltepec rulers to the top, or extreme south, end of the lienzo. It terminates near a daughter of the ancestral couple, named 1 Wind "Flower Serpent," an early ruler—or perhaps wife of an early ruler—of an as yet unidentified but evidently important southern site.[22] Its complex place sign comprises a hill with a hooked-over top enclosing a black circle, at its base an animal tail with black markings, sheathed in a swirl of flowing liquid which, though extremely faded, appears to be red (fig. 3.30).

Two more red lines lead down to two other daughters on the lower, or northern, end of the lienzo, in conjunction with place signs for the important towns they or their husbands ruled. A sign consisting of a hill, a frieze, a running or jumping man, and a plant stands for the Toltec city of Cholula in central Puebla. A frieze, cattail, and cactus represent the Aztec city of Tenochtitlan, or its forerunner, in the Valley of Mexico (fig. 3.30).

A black line drawn horizontally across the lienzo separates these early northern connections from the later expansion into areas north of Coixtlahuaca that occupies a large section of the lienzo directly above them, and groups them with other

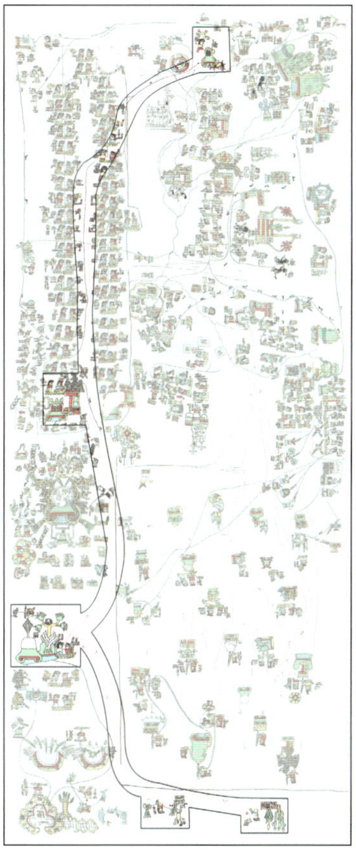

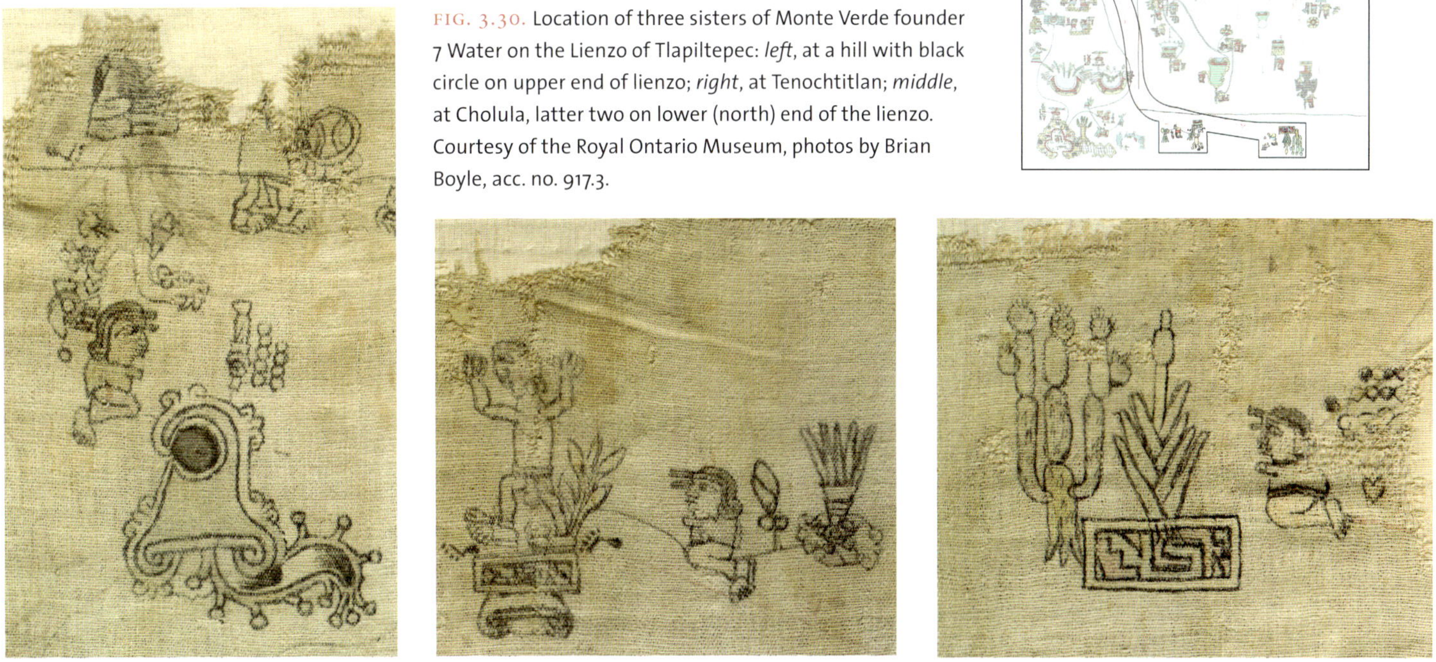

FIG. 3.30. Location of three sisters of Monte Verde founder 7 Water on the Lienzo of Tlapiltepec: *left*, at a hill with black circle on upper end of lienzo; *right*, at Tenochtitlan; *middle*, at Cholula, latter two on lower (north) end of the lienzo. Courtesy of the Royal Ontario Museum, photos by Brian Boyle, acc. no. 917.3.

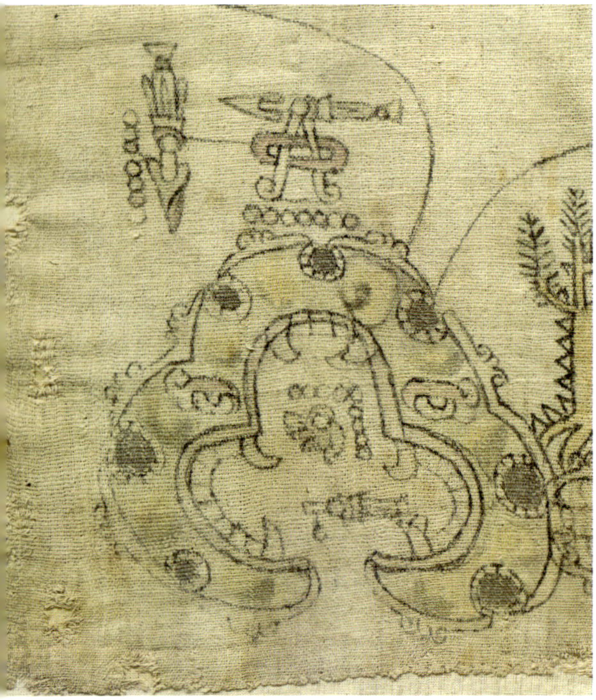

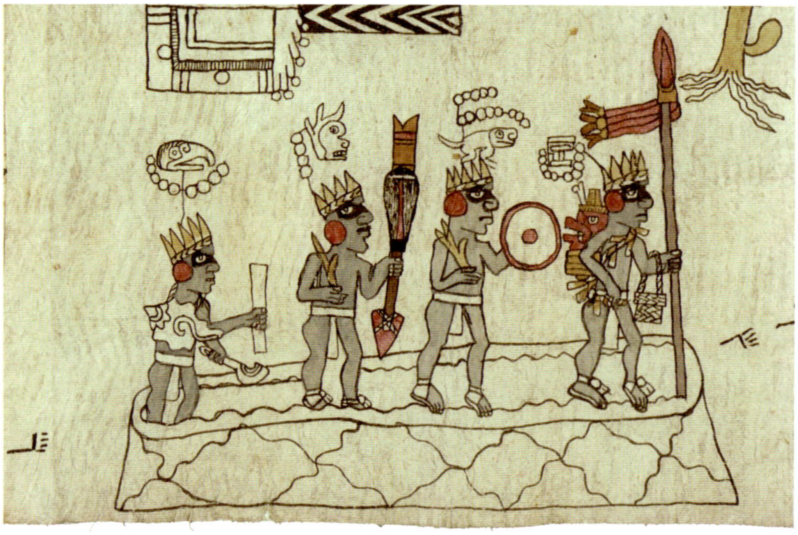

FIG. 3.31. Chicomoztoc on lower left corner of the Lienzo of Tlapiltepec. Courtesy of the Royal Ontario Museum, acc. no. 917.3, photo by Brian Boyle.

FIG. 3.32. Priests transporting image of 9 Wind "Quetzalcoatl" on Selden Roll. Courtesy of The Bodleian Library, The University of Oxford, MS. Arch. Selden A.

early northern material such as the seven-chambered cave and quetzal-jade rivers. The cave, which appears at the bottom left corner of the lienzo of Tlapiltepec, combines the features of a hill, mottled yellow and gray, and an animal jaw lined with teeth (fig. 3.31). Seven black discs or orifices set into the hill's edges identify this motif as a variant of Chicomoztoc, as it is known in the Nahuatl language of the Aztecs, meaning "Place of Seven Caves."

Chicomoztoc is a featured place of origin in central Mexican historical traditions. The presence of Chicomoztoc here and on other manuscripts from the Coixtlahuaca Valley in the northern Mixteca may in part be a reflection of central Mexican cultural influence.[23] In most Mixtec genealogical histories, earliest ancestors are born from trees, rivers, or the earth, as they are on the Lienzo of Tlapiltepec.

In central Mexican traditions, Chicomoztoc is a place from which the ancestors emerge, but this does not appear to be its role at the beginning of Coixtlahuaca history. Rather, in the Coixtlahuaca manuscripts, Chicomoztoc is a place of primordial human encounter with the Mixtec god 9 Wind, close counterpart of the Aztec god Quetzalcoatl.

The pre-Hispanic Mixtec Codex Vindobonensis depicts 9 Wind as a figure with many powers and talents. He oversees a series of ritual and generative activities that systematically lay the foundations for organized Mixtec life. In the Coixtlahuaca Group manuscript known as the Selden Roll, and more succinctly on the lienzos of Tlapiltepec and Coixtlahuaca II, 9 Wind appears to occupy a similarly authoritative position at the dawn of Coixtlahuaca history.[24]

In the Selden Roll, trails of footprints tell of the pilgrimage of a group of priests to the Place of Seven Caves and of their contact with 9 Wind, seated above the cave on a platform of stars in the sky. The priests depart from the cave with an image of 9 Wind carried on the back of their leader and eventually arrive at the summit of a large hill framed in the coils of entwined serpents (fig. 3.32). There the priests place the image of 9 Wind on an altar, and in front of the altar they perform the fire-making ritual that is depicted with similar prominence on the lienzos of Tlapiltepec and Coixtlahuaca II.

On the Lienzo of Tlapiltepec these events are greatly abbreviated. The presence of the god 9 Wind at Chicomoztoc is indicated only by the inclusion of his name within the central maw of the Chicomoztoc motif. Two priests drill fire on top of the hill of entwined serpents, but the relationship of this rite to 9 Wind is not explicitly indicated. Nor are the priests shown making the journey and transporting the sacred objects from Chicomoztoc to this Coixtlahuaca Valley site. The travels of the four priests are represented minimally on the lienzo by a pair of curving black lines without footprints, neither of which extends fully from Chicomoztoc to the hill with intertwined serpents (fig. 3.33; see also fig. 3.28).

Circling around the rivers of quetzal and jade, one of these black lines connects Chicomoztoc to a place sign composed of the head of a deer, a black circle, and a stream of water. As Boone has suggested, this line may lead *to* Chicomoztoc rather than away from it. "Deer River" may have been the starting point for the priests' pilgrimage to Chicomoztoc.[25]

The second line loops through several other locations before circling around the quetzal and jade rivers and terminating at the compound place sign that may represent either Popocatepetl or the Pico de Orizaba. This sign with its white peak and diamond-shaped net, and its hill with a plant with a bird's nest in its branches, accompanies the final generation of ancestors derived from these rivers. This second black line would represent the priests' journey south, away from Chicomoztoc, bringing with them the image of 9 Wind.[26] The lienzo implies that the priests traveled first to the home of the ancient ancestors and from there to the hill of entwined serpents in the Coixtlahuaca Valley. Perhaps we are meant to understand that the priests made this second stage of their southward journey in the company of 7 Water, son of the ancestors, who became the first ruler at Monte Verde.

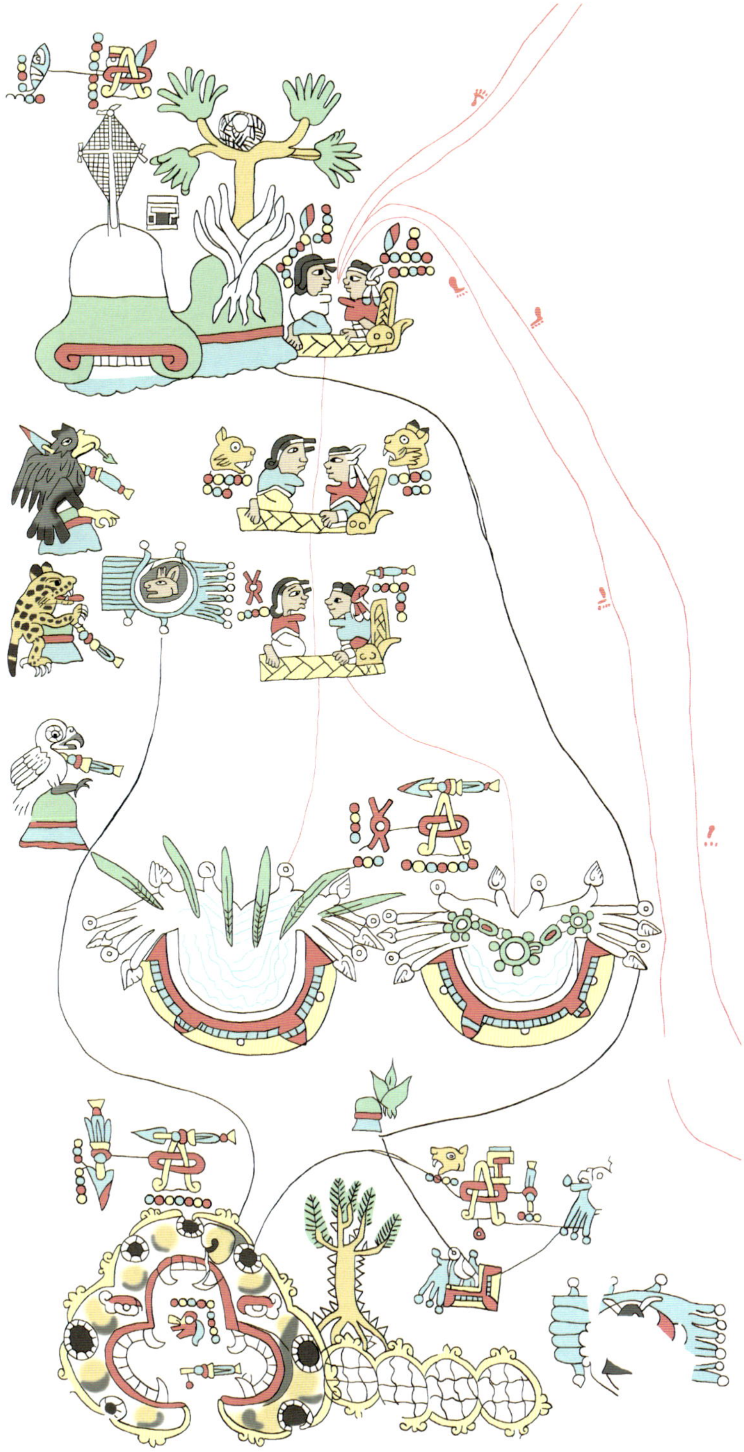

FIG. 3.33. Lines to and from Chicomoztoc on Lienzo of Tlapiltepec.

FIG. 3.34. Fire-making ritual surrounded by signs of cardinal directions on Lienzo of Tlapiltepec. Courtesy of the Royal Ontario Museum, photos by Brian Boyle, acc. no. 917.3.

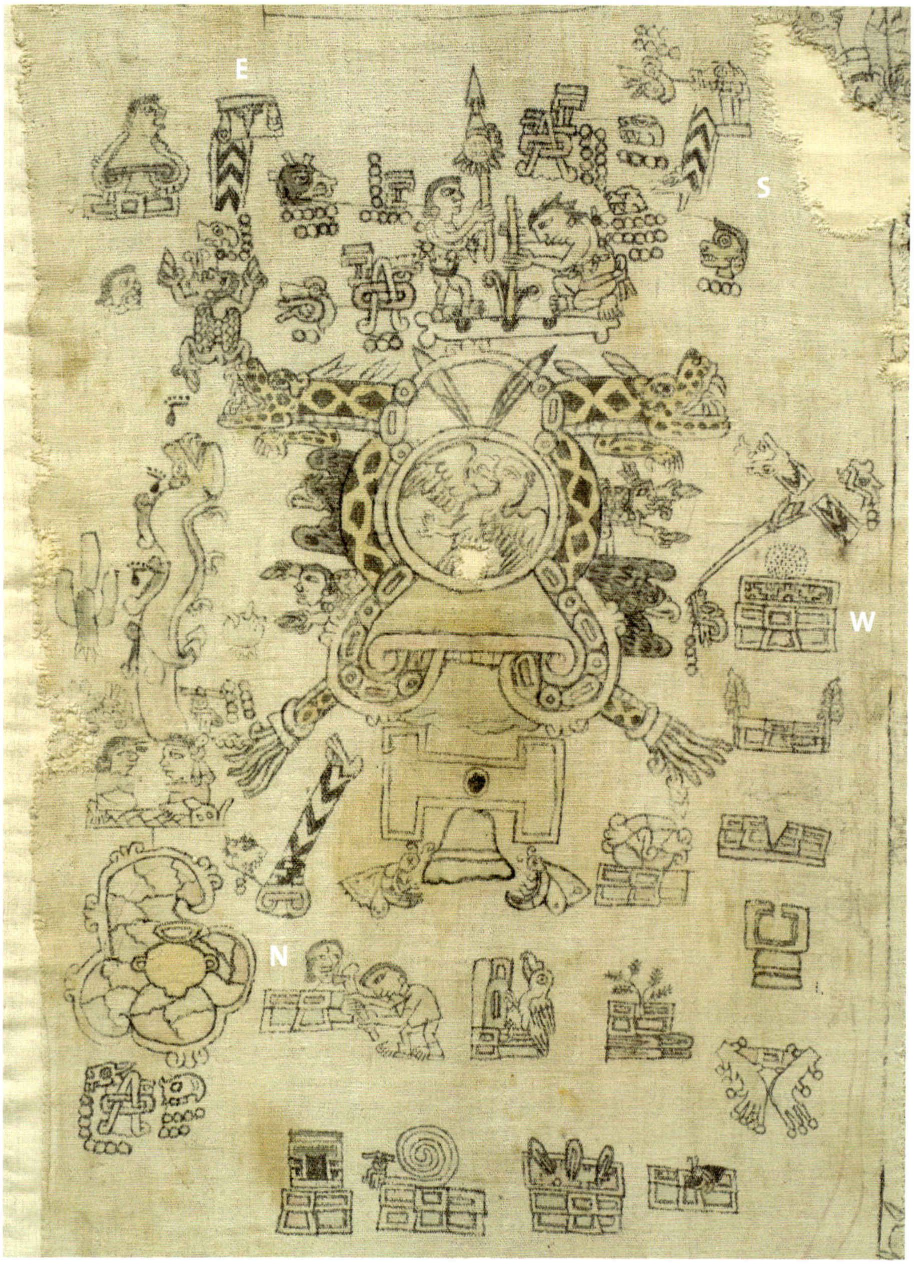

The large, serpent-entwined hill where the fire-making ritual takes place bristles with symbols of power and political inauguration (fig. 3.34). The two serpents, with jaguar paws, are knotted around the hill and jut out from its corners. Eagles and knife-wielding supernaturals known in Mixtec as *yahui* fly out on either side of the hill (Smith 1973b:60–64). Quetzal feathers ornamenting the hilltop and jade beads with red centers lining the bottom of the hill are of the same design as those of the quetzal and jade rivers. On top of the hill, a kneeling priest with shaggy hair produces fire by twirling a stick on a length of wood, or possibly bone, while a second priest holds aloft a ceremonial staff or spear. The performance of the fire-making ritual by the priests of 9 Wind signifies the founding of the rulership of Monte Verde, whose place sign and list of rulers follow directly above it.

Place signs grouped beneath the hill may be related to the circle of place signs that surrounds the same event on the Lienzo of Coixtlahuaca II, which appears to represent a confederation of ancient allies that existed or was formed at the time of the ritual and the founding of the Monte Verde lineage (see fig. 3.27).[27] On the Lienzo of Coixtlahuaca II, faded red lines radiate out from the central hill to thirteen of the sixteen surrounding place signs, but no lines lead to Monte Verde or to the places left and right of it at the top of the circle. To the left of Monte Verde is Miltepec, co-founder of Coixtlahuaca at a later date. To the right is an unidentified but probably local town that may also have contributed to this later formation. A list of rulers surmounts each of the three place signs. A fourteenth red line extends beyond the circle onto the much damaged lower right corner of the Lienzo of Coixtlahuaca II (see fig. 3.24). Although only fragments of this longer red line survive in this corner area and it is not clear where the line begins, it is possible that it originates from the ancestral couple whose son 7 Water becomes the founding ruler of Monte Verde. Perhaps this line refers to the movements of both 7 Water and the priests of 9 Wind from the home of the ancestors in regions north of Coixtlahuaca territory to Monte Verde and the enactment of the fire-making ritual within Coixtlahuaca territory.[28]

Going back to the Lienzo of Tlapiltepec, among its many details clustered around the hill of entwined serpents are four place signs that are found repeatedly in Mixtec and Coixtlahuaca Group manuscripts and that are known to stand for the cardinal directions (Jansen 1982a; 1982b, 1:223–77; 1998). Chevron bands signifying "enemy" or "war," attached to the directional signs, suggest that the founding of the rulership at Monte Verde by people from the north took place in hostile surroundings.

The sign for north is a small checkerboard hill to the lower left of the large hill (see fig. 3.34). Diagonally opposite is the sign for south, a temple in the form of a skull, above and to the right of the fire-making scene. The sign for east is a skyband of stars and a ray of the sun above and to the left. The sign for west, to the right of the hill, is a platform with a circle of ashes resting on it. The disposition of the directional signs is consistent with the cartography of the lienzo as a whole. The hill of entwined serpents and ritual activity taking place on its summit are themselves the center, the fifth cardinal direction, a vertical axis as opposed to the horizontal plane, in the Mesoamerican cosmographical scheme.

Above the fire-making ritual, the ancient ancestors, and the cave are the "Hill with Green Leaves" sign of Monte Verde and the seated figures of its first rulers, 7 Water "Eagle" and his wife 5 Vulture (see fig. 3.28). To the left of this scene, armed with a shield and obsidian-studded sword and accompanied by the chevron band that means enemy or war, is an individual named 4 Jaguar, thought to be identical with a powerful outside agent of this same name. Of possibly northern—that is, central Mexican—origin, he is prominent in the Mixtec screenfold histories. His warrior activities in this instance evidently helped establish 7 Water in the Coixtlahuaca area.[29]

Two other events from the early phase of Coixtlahuaca history on the Lienzo of Tlapiltepec involve relations with people and places located in the Mixteca south of the Coixtlahuaca Valley. In both cases, long black lines connect early members of the Monte Verde lineage, midway along the lienzo's left edge, with place signs and figures positioned along its upper edge.

In one instance a black line that originates from the hill marked with a black circle and swirl of liquid near the top center of the lienzo indicates that the wife of

7 Water's immediate successor at Monte Verde came from this town. The line parallels the branch of the ancestral system of red lines that leads to this place sign, and that shows 7 Water's sister migrating to this same, evidently important southern location (see figs. 3.14, 3.19).

A second black line with black footprints, ascending to the upper left corner of the lienzo, then traversing its upper edge, tells of an expedition into the south undertaken by the third ruler in the Monte Verde sequence, a man named 2 Flower. The ultimate destination of this line is the place sign sometimes known as "Town of Flint Knives"—now the archaeological site called Mogote del Cacique—a place of importance in the Mixtec screenfold histories and which may be the southernmost location portrayed on the Lienzo of Tlapiltepec. From the ruler of this place, 2 Flower received a jade nose ornament symbolic of great prestige (Doesburg and Buren 1997:116–17; Jansen 2007:272).

PATTERNS OF LINES

The network of connecting lines is a distinctive visual feature of the Lienzo of Tlapiltepec. Resembling an elaborate wiring diagram or circulatory system, a complex weave of lines stretches over the plain weave cotton cloth. The lines connect people and places, regions and periods of time, one section of the lienzo to another, one end to the distant other end. The lines explain these relationships as if speaking about them through a language: the language of lines.

The eye follows a line, catching on the human footprints beside it, and moves with the line as it curves and threads its way up, down, or across the lienzo. One sees that the line is red or black and parallel to or crossing other lines. Often the individual line is part of a configuration of two or more lines, and this system dovetails or overlaps with other systems. The lines originate from central or peripheral, northern or southern positions on the lienzo and lead from one area to another.

There are red lines with red footprints (and one or two without them); black lines with black footprints; black lines without footprints; in one area, black double lines, or roads, but lacking footprints; and undulating black lines for rivers. All together, a variety of types and configurations of lines communicate the details of genealogical and geographical relationships and make them comprehensively visible: a pattern of lines.

The building blocks from which this pattern is largely constructed, the leitmotif of the drawing, are the systems of branching lines: two or more lines that originate from one place sign, human figure, or married couple and from one location in the lienzo geography and one position on the large sheet of cloth and fan out to other place signs and figures elsewhere on the lienzo.

Branching lines signify derivation from common origins, division, multiplication, expansion, and kinship or other affiliation. On the Lienzo of Tlapiltepec, the ancient ancestors, followed by the founding of Coixtlahuaca and then its later re-founding, are each the source of a configuration of this type. The conquest of multiple towns by rulers of Tlapiltepec is also represented on the lienzo in this manner, and the converging lines of Coixtlahuaca Valley rivers are this form in reverse.

From the ancestors on the lower left edge of the lienzo, red lines fan out to a son, founder of the Monte Verde lineage, and three daughters (see figs. 3.28, 3.30). This particular system bifurcates: two lines lead south to the son at Monte Verde and a daughter at an unknown site farther south in the Mixteca; and two lead north to other daughters at Cholula and Tenochtitlan in Puebla and the Valley of Mexico.

Encompassing the north-south geographical span of the lienzo, the red lines that originate from the ancient ancestors are goalposts placed at the ends of a long, narrow playing field at the beginning of a game. The gaze is drawn upward by them toward the top of the lienzo, toward the roof of the building and the sky when the lienzo is hung vertically on the side of a building, and downward to where it rests on the ground. The ancestral lines involve the viewer at the outset in the scale of the lienzo.

A second system of long, red lines spreads out over the lower or northern half, from the founding rulers of Coixtlahuaca, armed with bows and arrows and meeting with other warriors at an unidentified Coixtlahuaca Valley site referred to here as Two Rivers. Starting at the right midsection of the lienzo, these lines expand downward, if the lienzo is displayed vertically, into the immediate field of vision of the viewer standing in front of it (see figs. 3.13, 3.21). These lines lead to towns in northern Oaxaca and south and central Puebla, and refer to an incursion into these regions, as well as signifying relationships: rulers of the northern towns descend from rulers of Coixtlahuaca.

A third fan of red lines, contained entirely within the northern section of the lienzo, merging with a branch of the Two Rivers system, tells of the family of a woman named 13 Rabbit who marries one of the men who migrated north from Coixtlahuaca: her parents, three uncles, maternal grandparents at Butterfly Water, and the group of towns they ruled (see fig. 3.21).

Lines associated with the re-founding of Coixtlahuaca, some two centuries after its original founding and after the meeting of warriors at Two Rivers, stem from the husband and wife who were Coixtlahuaca's first rulers in the new location. These lines, two black and one red, lead south rather than north, to their daughters at towns on the upper edge of the lienzo (see fig. 3.19).

Also held together by branching systems of connecting lines are people and places at the core of the map surrounding Coixtlahuaca, the area from which these other north- and south-directed systems of lines depart. Two major systems overlap on this upper right area of the lienzo, one of them genealogical and the other the undulating lines of Coixtlahuaca Valley rivers.

In the genealogical system in the core area, a loop of black lines and footprints leading from Coixtlahuaca to Tequixtepec and Tejupan and back indicates that two couples of the eight generations or so separating the founders of Coixtlahuaca from its later re-founders became rulers at these other towns (see fig. 3.20). Other lines branching off this loop show offshoots of the Coixtlahuaca lineage establishing themselves at Tlapiltepec and another, unidentified site.

Rivers are represented on the lienzo by a single system of wavy black lines, with the trunk of the system of converging lines located northeast of Coixtlahuaca and the branches spreading west and southwest to their sources. Place signs attached to the ends of the branches identify the towns and other sites where each of the various tributary streams originates (figs. 3.35, 3.36; letters in following section refer to these place signs).[30]

To the southwest, the prominent source of the rivers on the lienzo, as in the actual geography, is Monte Verde (**A**) and the other two mountains clustered with it. The visually strongest—blackest, least faded—of all of the river lines on the lienzo is one that leads diagonally from the large "Hill with Green Leaves" sign of Monte Verde across the lienzo to the entwined serpents and "Heart Rock" sign that stands for Coixtlahuaca, and more specifically, for the sector of the town founded by rulers from Monte Verde. Tlapiltepec (**B**) and a nearby hill are the source of a western branch of the river system, and other tributaries of the system originate from Two Rivers (**C**), whose precise location in the actual landscape is uncertain, and from Tulancingo (**D**).

Not all important rivers of the Coixtlahuaca Valley are included in the system of wavy lines on the Lienzo of Tlapiltepec. Conspicuously absent is any line that might represent the Río Grande, the main northern channel of the valley drainage system, which flows northeast past Ihuitlán (**E**) and Tepelmeme (**F**). Those two towns, however, are on the lienzo.

The river lines differ from all other lines on the lienzo in that they introduce a sense of the actual landscape, the physical valley, into the otherwise abstract geography of the lienzo. This physical aspect is heightened by the corner trio of landmark mountains from which some of the wavy lines flow. As Boone observed, the river lines signal that this is real territory.[31] Moreover, they speak of a certain territory that is not the Coixtlahuaca Valley as a whole, but more specifically, the southwestern part of it.

Taken as a whole, the pattern of lines built up from the individual branching systems on the right side of the lienzo is outward-radiating. In the core area, river lines overlapping other lines of human activities and relationships weave together a loose knot of lines, and from this knot, combed-out fringes of red and black lines radiate north and south.

Parallel configurations of lines on the lienzo occur across time as well as across space. The branching lines of the ancient ancestors on the left side of the lienzo prefigure branching lines depicting later historical developments on the map on the right side. The ancestral system concerns the genesis of the Monte Verde lineage and includes branches that lead to the north and south ends of the lienzo; later systems extending north and south from Coixtlahuaca signify events of regeneration in the history of this lineage. The drawing suggests that the later historical developments were understood as repetitions or fulfillments of the ancient original semi-mythical one.

Also on the left side of the lienzo, echoing the map on the right side in embryonic form, is the setting of the fire-making ritual related to the founding of the Monte Verde lineage. The hill with its knot of serpents and scene of priests drilling fire on its summit stand in the center of the configuration, and surrounding them are the cardinal direction signs marked by bands of chevrons signifying enemy or war (see fig. 3.34). It is difficult not to see this five-point image as foreshadowing the map that is elaborated on the right side of the lienzo: the core with its foreign margins.

Color is also part of the pattern, for red lines evidently have special significance. Red lines emanating from the ancient ancestors begin the genealogical history on the Lienzo of Tlapiltepec. The story culminates with red lines leading from Coixtlahuaca to towns and rulers in areas of Oaxaca and Puebla north of Coixtlahuaca. Specifically, the genealogy begins with red lines that trace the family tree of the founder of the Monte Verde lineage of Coixtlahuaca back to the birth of the earliest ancestors from a river of quetzal feathers and a river of jade beads. Red lines follow the dispersal of the

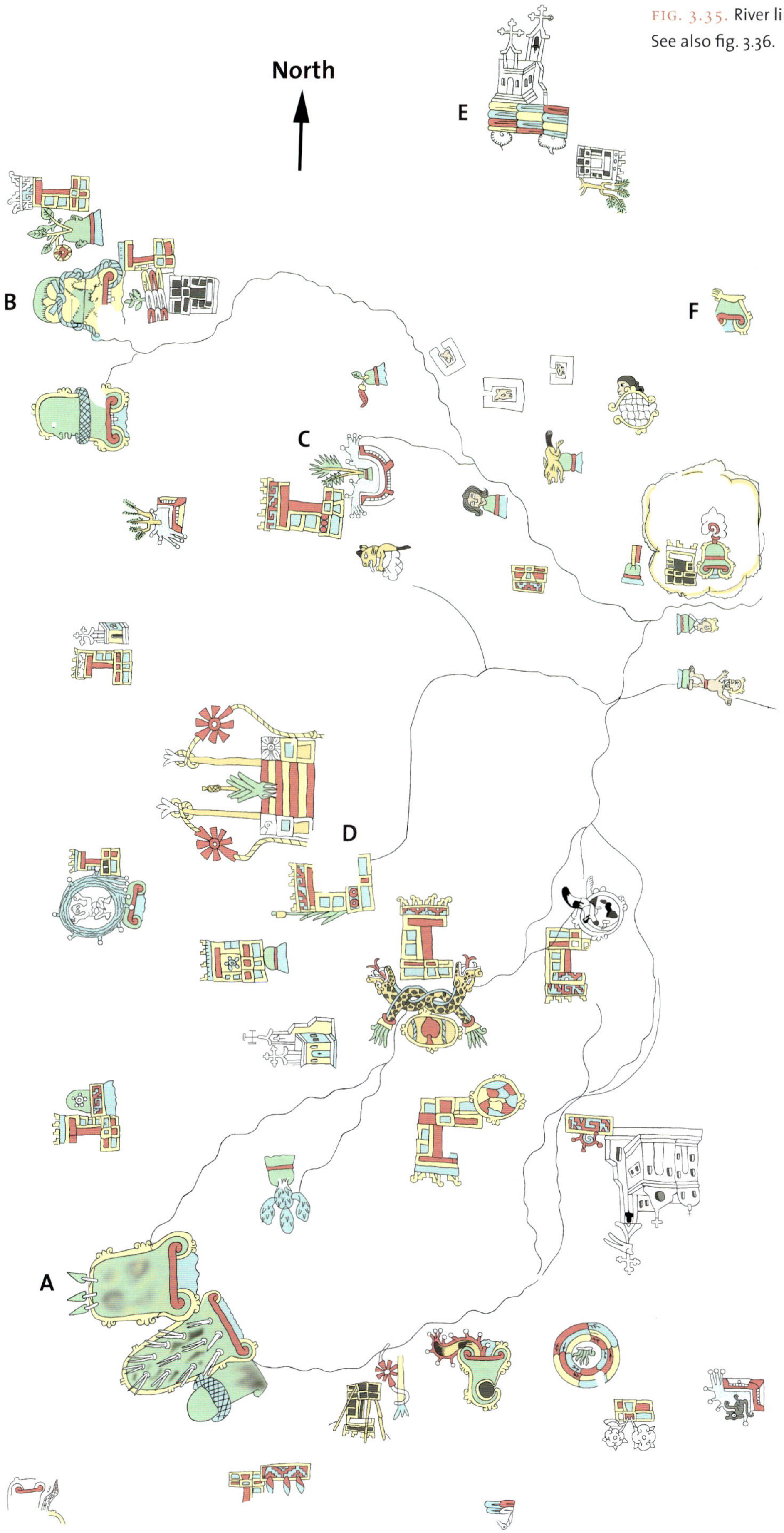

FIG. 3.35. River lines on Lienzo of Tlapiltepec. See also fig. 3.36.

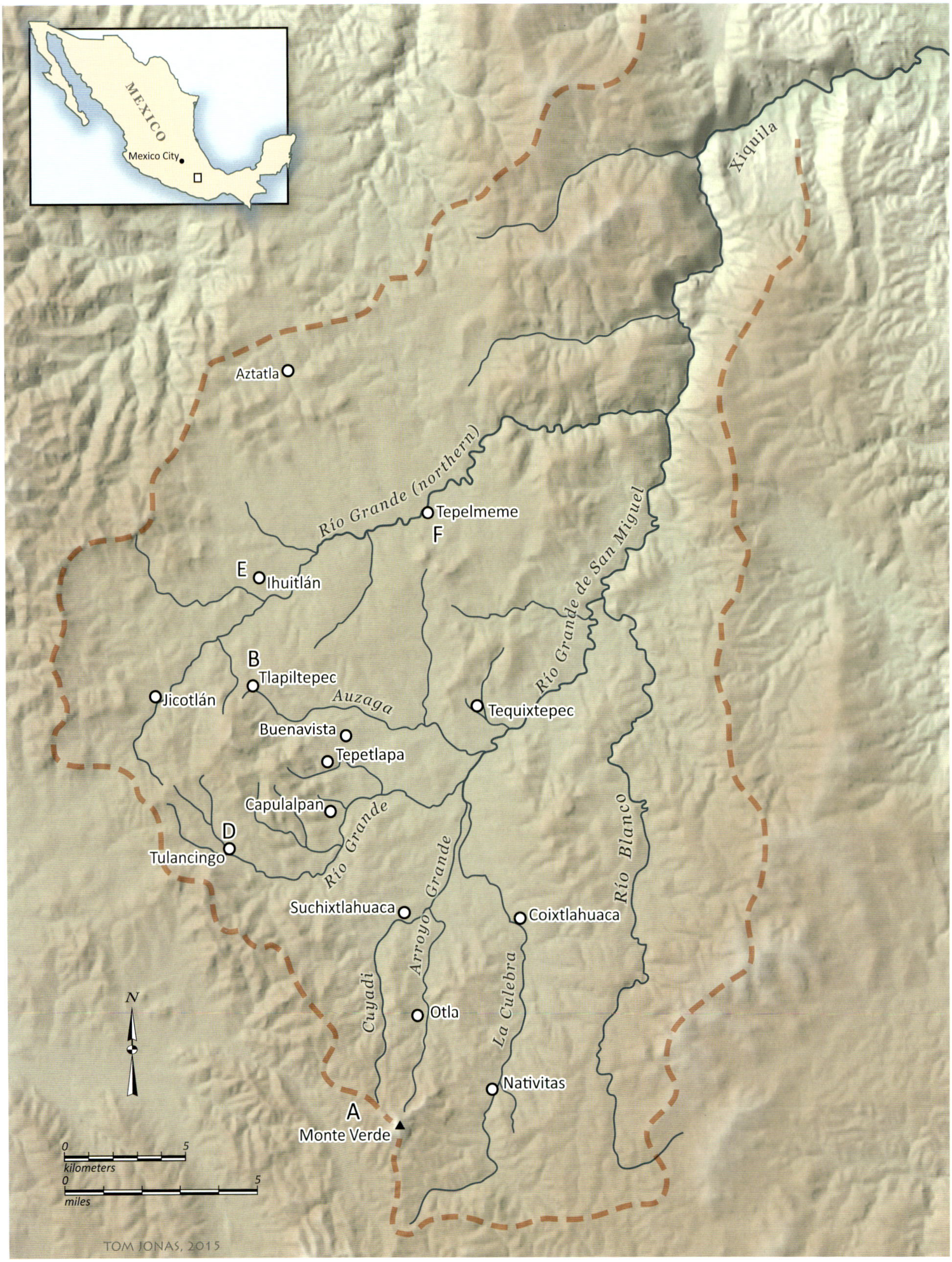

FIG. 3.36. Rivers of the Coixtlahuaca Valley. See also fig. 3.35. © 2015, University of Oklahoma Press.

founder's siblings to other important towns in Puebla and the Valley of Mexico in the north and the Mixteca in the south.

No ancestry is given for the lienzo's second lineage of Coixtlahuaca rulers. The ancestral system of red lines pertains exclusively to the origins of the Monte Verde lineage, which suggests that the red lines that lead to towns and rulers on the northern section of the map might signify continuity with these origins, and descent of the northern rulers from the Monte Verde lineage.[32]

Not all lines or footprints linking members or offshoots of the Monte Verde lineage are red, however. In fact, all genealogical lines in the core area of the map are black rather than red. Two of three lines originating from the re-founders of the lineage within the core (fig. 3.19, A) but then extending beyond the core to daughters on the southern edge of the lienzo, also are black. The line to the third daughter for some reason is red. What distinguished this particular daughter, the town she moved to, or the family she married into, from her sisters or their towns?

Nor do all red lines on the lienzo originate exclusively with members of the Monte Verde lineage. Red lines indicate the parents, uncles, and Butterfly Water grandparents of the woman 13 Rabbit, mentioned above, who marries a ruler of Tepexi, himself derived from Coixtlahuaca via a red line, on the northern section of the map. Perhaps this means that the wife's family was genealogically related to the Monte Verde lineage after all, even though it is not otherwise explicitly stated.

It may also be that red lines on the Lienzo of Tlapiltepec imply some ethnic or cultural quality that the Monte Verde lineage of Coixtlahuaca rulers considered themselves to share with rulers of other towns located mainly north of Coixtlahuaca. On the Lienzo of Coixtlahuaca II, red lines attached like the spokes of a wheel to the circle of towns and rulers surround the fire-making ritual. There the red lines appear to signify some ancient original bond that united Monte Verde with the rest of the towns that complete the circle.[33]

VISUAL STORYTELLING IN THE LIENZO AND MIXTEC SCREENFOLDS

A priority for the designer of the Lienzo of Tlapiltepec was that one thing should lead to another and that the lienzo tell a story. In this quality of visual narrative, the Lienzo of Tlapiltepec recalls the pre-Hispanic Mixtec historical screenfold manuscripts. The lienzo and screenfolds differ in their physical architecture, but in their graphic and structural linearity they have much in common. If history is represented in the screenfold manuscripts as an intricately patterned line, it is represented on the lienzo as a pattern of lines.

The screenfold manuscripts utilize the back-and-forth line of a continuous corridor of space outlined by red guidelines, the line built up of figures that fill the channel, and lines formed by elements such as trails of footprints, roads, and umbilical cords connecting the figures (see figs. 3.2, 3.5). The Lienzo of Tlapiltepec utilizes branching, dovetailing, and crisscrossed connecting lines as well as various major and minor dividing lines.

With its long, narrow shape and division into two columns of space, like two strips (tiras) or perhaps two flattened-out screenfolds, placed side-by-side, the lienzo also has something of the form of these manuscripts. The column on the left is like a vertically oriented manuscript of the tira or screenfold type that reads from bottom to top, and the column on the right is like a screenfold that reads most prominently from top to bottom. The lienzo merges the strip-shaped tira or screenfold format with a map that is also strip-shaped, long from north to south but narrow from east to west. It synchronizes the predominantly upward- and downward-directed paths of the reader who is following the story with the north-to-south and south-to-north movements of the protagonists featured in the story.

Unlike many of the cartographic manuscripts known from the colonial period, the Lienzo of Tlapiltepec is not a map of land boundaries. It is fully an account of historical events and genealogical-political relationships. This quality also relates it to the screenfold manuscripts. Indeed, the Lienzo of Tlapiltepec and its fellow Coixtlahuaca Group manuscript, the Lienzo of Coixtlahuaca II, are the most detailed examples painted in single-sheet, cartographic form, rather than screenfold form, of the type of genealogical history that was customarily produced in the Mixteca. The Lienzo of Coixtlahuaca II, however, *is* a boundary map. Its territorial expanse spreads out more or less equally in all directions from a center point, rather than having a beginning and an end and a distance to be traversed between them.

There exist in total five Mixtec historical screenfold manuscripts of the pre-Hispanic type in which the pages are divided into vertical or horizontal interconnected bands or registers. They are Codex Bodley, Codex Selden, Codex Vindobonensis or Vienna, Codex Colombino-Becker I, and Codex Nuttall or Zouche-Nuttall. Codices Bodley and Selden contain the genealogical histories of town rulers. Codex Vindobonensis tells in great detail of the activities of the gods and ancestors at the beginning of Mixtec history; a genealogy was added later to its reverse side. Codex Colombino-Becker I is devoted entirely to the biography of the legendary eleventh-to-twelfth century Mixtec ruler named 8 Deer "Jaguar Claw," and Codex Nuttall has a version of 8 Deer's life on one side and genealogies and origin stories on its second side.[34]

No screenfold manuscripts survive from the Coixtlahuaca Valley. They were undoubtedly produced there as elsewhere in the Mixteca; the layout of the Lienzo of Tlapiltepec is a testament to this. The multiple-register screenfold in the Mixteca was the chosen form of manuscript for comprehensively recording history and fully elaborating pictorial narratives. Screenfolds were likely often the source from which history was excerpted, summarized, mapped, and then writ large on lienzos.

In the chronologically organized screenfold manuscripts, the figures follow one another in regimented rows or columns. They are read incrementally, register by register and page by page. In the lienzos the arrangement is often cartographic, and an important part of the meaning comes from the view of the arrangement as a whole, but these are not simple alternatives. In the screenfolds, the single-file sequence of motifs contains the central thread of the story, but other aspects of the composition across the spread of pages may also be significant and require that the screenfold, like the lienzo, be viewed more comprehensively.[35]

For example, columns of figures in the screenfold manuscripts are occasionally combined with landscape, as in the case of a large mountain or mountain range that fills a pair of facing pages in the Mixtec Codex Vindobonensis (fig. 3.37).[36] In the upper right corner of this scene, protagonists drill fire and gesture with a handful of plants toward a row of twelve named mountain peaks. Many other place signs follow, listed in columns within the mountain and stacked in vertical registers, separated by red guidelines, over the next several pages of the codex.

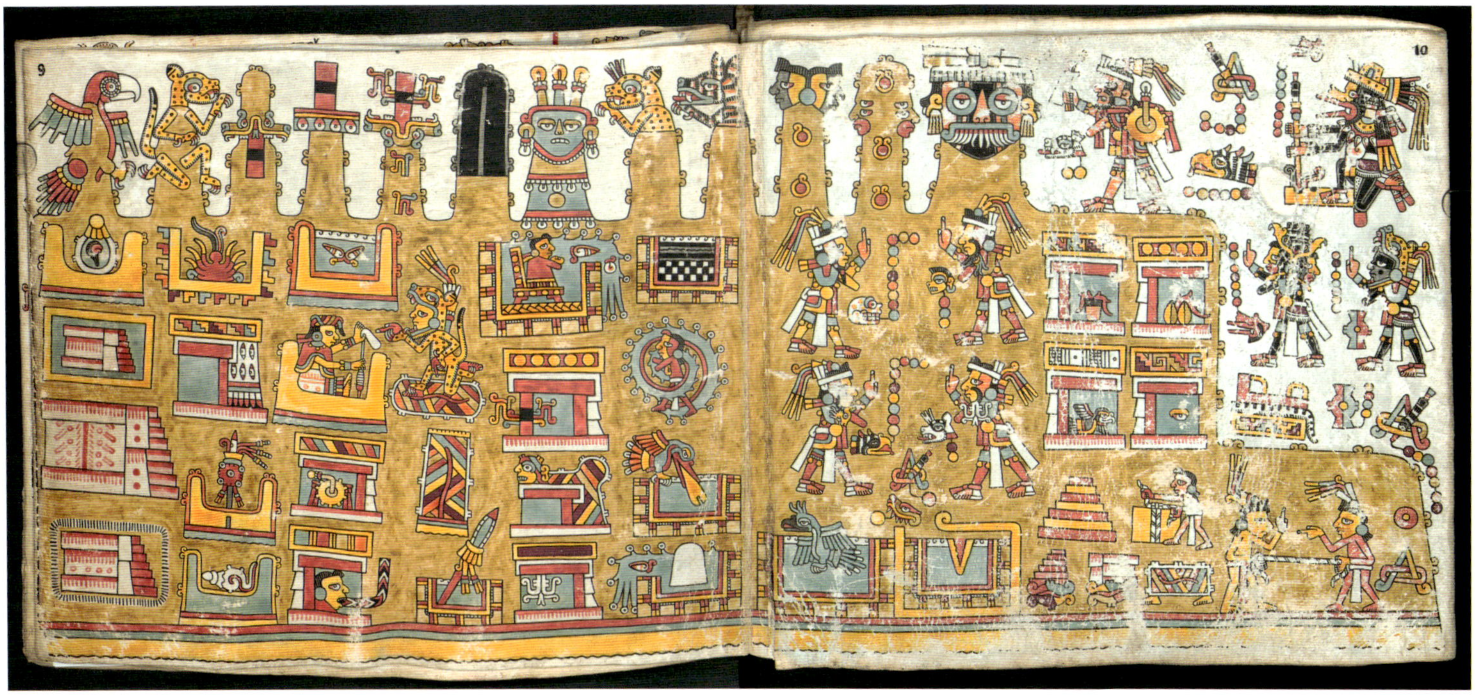

FIG. 3.37. Mountain landscape from Codex Vindobonensis, pp. 9–10. Courtesy of the Österreichische Nationalbibliothek Bildarchiv und Grafiksammlung, Vienna, Codex Mexicanus I, fol. 9v and 10r.

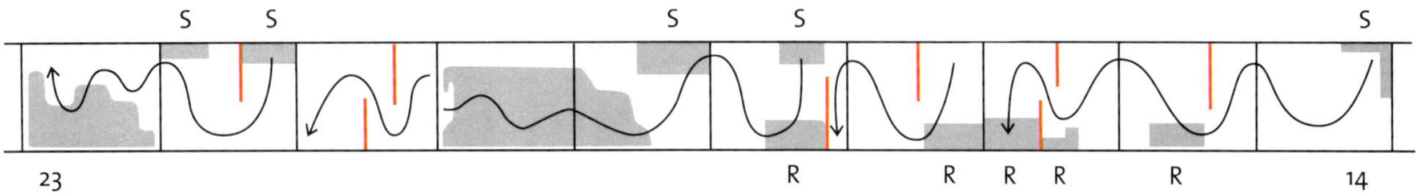

FIG. 3.38. Diagram showing locations of skybands (S), rivers (R), and large mountains on Codex Zouche-Nuttall, pp. 14–23. Arrows indicate reading path through the vertical registers of these pages.

Another example of merging a regimented chain of elements with the depiction of a spatial environment in the Mixtec screenfold format is found in a section of Codex Nuttall that concerns the origins and activities of a semi-mythical ancestral couple named 3 Flint and 12 Wind.[37] The woman, 3 Flint, is associated throughout the ten-page section with rivers, or more generally the earth, while the man, 12 Wind, comes from the sky. Their eventual marriage suggests a fertile alliance of the two regions.

In this instance the correspondence between the space of the manuscript and real space is sustained across the pages not by substituting the system of registers and guidelines with a mountain or other encompassing landscape feature, but by arranging the sequence of images in the vertical registers such that the star bands that represent the sky always fall at the tops of the registers and the rivers always fall at the bottom of the registers (fig. 3.38). The result is a spatial framework of sky above and earth below that is integrated with the regular progression of figures and scenes in alternately upward- and downward-reading registers separated by red guidelines. The story of 3 Flint and 12 Wind may be followed register-by-register and page-by-page, turning over the leaves of the screenfold like those of a book. But this ten-page section must at times have been opened out and viewed as a whole, as a frieze-like representation of the vertical world, with the regular pulse and flow of the storyline threaded through it.

The effect is not radically different from the combination of history and map found on the Lienzo of Tlapiltepec. In Codex Nuttall, the spatial environment in which the

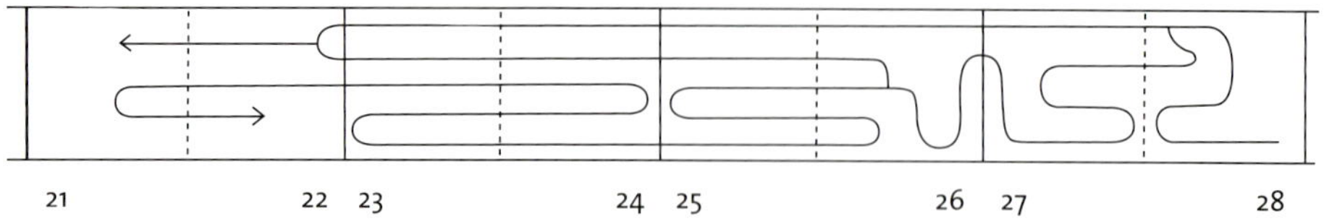

FIG. 3.39. Diagram showing multiple parallel reading paths through Codex Bodley, pp. 28–21; guidelines omitted.

story takes place—especially the vertical dimension—is represented through the sky signs distributed along its upper edge and river signs along its base. On the right side of the lienzo, an arrangement of place signs around Coixtlahuaca according to the cardinal directions makes the sheet of cloth a map of the horizontal geographical plane.

In Codex Nuttall, guidelines divide the pages into a single continuous channel of space containing a single sequence of figures and scenes; a single line, versus the network of lines of the Lienzo of Tlapiltepec. In parts of Codex Bodley, the guidelines divide the pages into two and even three parallel channels of space containing parallel and interrelated genealogical-historical narratives. In one eight-page section of the codex, a lower system of registers branches off an upper register and later generates a third, middle branch, which rejoins the upper one at the end: in other words, a pattern of lines, as on the Lienzo of Tlapiltepec (fig. 3.39).[38]

Thus, as these examples illustrate, the pre-Hispanic Mixtec screenfold manuscript is not a mere sequence of signs and symbols. The story may be shaped and meaning derived from many other variables in the way the elements are arranged in the space of the screenfold, in addition to their one-by-one succession as organized by the systems of registers and guidelines.

Consider the biography of 8 Deer "Jaguar Claw" in Codex Colombino-Becker I.[39] What makes this manuscript a dramatic visual story is not merely the plot of the "rise to power" (Troike 1974:422) of this important eleventh–twelfth century figure of Mixtec history, or the lively painted scenes of travel, conquest, procession, and pursuit that fill the manuscript's pages. It is the way in which these have been combined with a three-register variant of the Mixtec multiple-register screenfold format that makes the Colombino-Becker I so effective.

An example of this fusion is the manuscript's account of 8 Deer's journey to Tututepec. In this episode, centered on facing pages 5–6 of the Colombino portion of the manuscript, but beginning on the preceding pages 3–4 and continuing through pages 7–8, 8 Deer is seen traveling to the Pacific coastal town of Tututepec, where he becomes its ruler and confers with his older half-brother, 12 Movement, then sets out to conquer many other towns in the area (fig. 3.40).

In following this sequence of events, the reader of the manuscript moves with 8 Deer and his entourage from left to right, place sign to place sign, across the lower register on pages 3–4. Turning over the next leaf of the screenfold, the reader continues with the travelers across the same register on pages 5–6 (fig. 3.41). At the lower right corner of page 6, 8 Deer makes an offering of burning incense in a ballcourt. From there, representing the final stage of the journey, unnamed members of 8 Deer's traveling entourage make their way back along the middle register to Tututepec on page 5, represented by a large place sign that includes a hill, an eagle, and a tall temple, located at the end of this register.

On the upper register of page 5 of Colombino-Becker, now as ruler of the town, 8 Deer confers with his half-brother, 12 Movement, and continuing on this register, the armed figure of 8 Deer as an attacker begins a series of conquests of other towns,

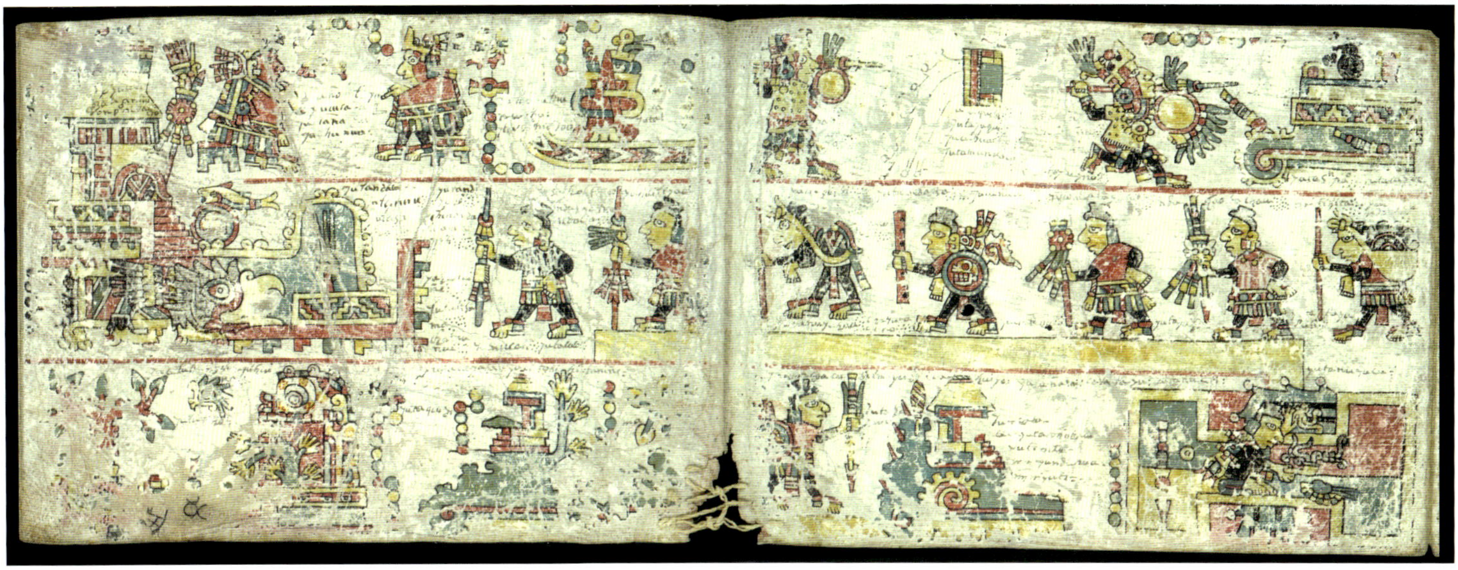

FIG. 3.40. Eight Deer travels to Tututepec, on Codex Colombino, pp. 5–6. The journey reads from left to right across the bottom register, then from right to left as the entourage approaches Tututepec on the middle register. Reproduction authorized by the National Institute of Anthropology and History, Mexico.

FIG. 3.41. Journey to Tututepec, Codex Colombino, pp. 3–6. Drawing by Nicholas Johnson.

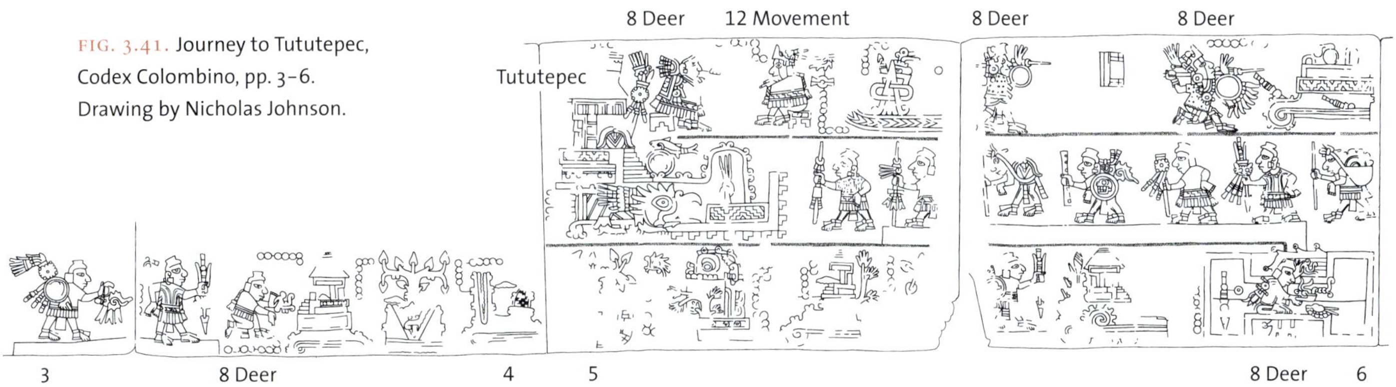

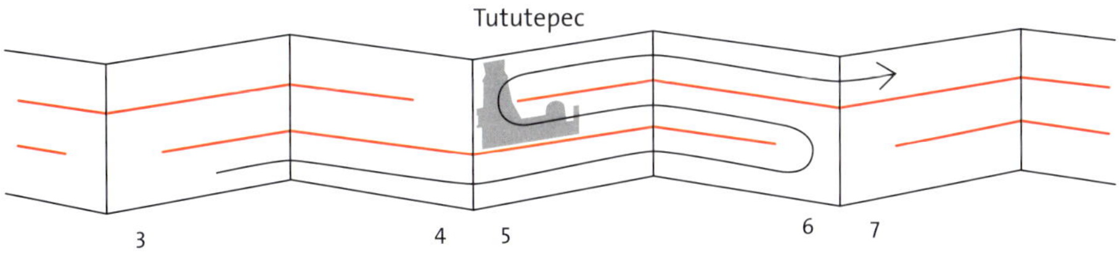

FIG. 3.42. Diagram of journey to Tututepec, Codex Colombino, showing the shape of the journey in the screenfold manuscript.

the litany of which continues all through the manuscript's following pages 7–8. The long, forward-moving upper and lower registers; switchbacks onto and off of the shorter, backward-moving middle register, and the closing of one two-page spread and opening of the next combine with the painted scenes to shape this episode and animate it. They give the episode a sense of tension leading to Tututepec as its climax, and to the further consequence of the conquest other towns of the area. The anchor of the design, the visual fulcrum, as it were, around which these transitions and the tensions of the episode revolve, is the oversized place sign of Tututepec. Positioned at the end of the backward-moving middle register, Tututepec anchors the design at the turning point where the momentum changes and becomes movement forward again (fig. 3.42).[40] Movement toward the center is followed by movement radiating outward.

This is also the configuration on the Lienzo of Tlapiltepec. The story begins on the edge of the large sheet of cloth with the cave and rivers of origin of the ancestors. The story progresses to the interior of the sheet as descendants of the ancestors establish themselves at Coixtlahuaca, then radiates outward as Coixtlahuaca develops ties and expands its influence beyond its home territory into regions to the north and south. The lienzo, like the screenfold, is dynamically polarized around a core area.[41]

CONCLUSIONS

I began this chapter with an overview of the Lienzo of Tlapiltepec as seen in its original size and as it might have appeared to a viewer if hung vertically on the side of a building. Missing from reproductions of the manuscript in books or on computer screens are the effects on the viewer of the size and proportions of the lienzo. In person, one is conscious of an optical narrowing and crowding toward the top of the lienzo and opening out toward the bottom, as well as the earth-to-sky setting that accompanies the lienzo when it is displayed in this manner. These too are part of what the lienzo is, and of how in visual terms it tells a story.

Emphasized throughout this chapter are the spatial layout, visual dynamics, and overall narrative coherence of the manuscript. Significant in this regard are the division of the manuscript into two columns of space, the cartographic framework of the presentation, and its signature graphic feature, the network of red and black connecting lines. Broadly defined, connecting lines play a variety of structural roles in Mixtec-style manuscripts, and in screenfold and lienzo contexts they take a variety of pictorial forms.

As a map, the Lienzo of Tlapiltepec covers an area extending from the Valley of Mexico in the north, at the bottom of the lienzo, to the central Mixteca of Oaxaca in the south, at the top. Coixtlahuaca and other significant sites nearby form the core of the map at the upper right, and other towns are arranged around them. Towns located north of Coixtlahuaca, at the lower right, compose nearly half the map, and those south of Coixtlahuaca, at the upper right, form another significant cluster.

Three focal points in time, some two centuries apart—three historical plateaus—divide the span of time covered by the lienzo. The original founding of the lienzo's two lineages at Monte Verde and Miltepec are the first of these focal points of the cartographic-historical narrative. These events are represented non-cartographically at the middle left of the lienzo. The founding of Coixtlahuaca by members of the two lineages some two centuries later, in the core of the map at the upper right, is followed by the re-founding of the town at a second pair of southern Coixtlahuaca Valley locations approximately two centuries later.

The most significant consequence of the regime established by the two lineages at Coixtlahuaca as portrayed on the Lienzo of Tlapiltepec is an expansion of influence into areas of Oaxaca and Puebla lying north and northwest of the Coixtlahuaca Valley. This expansion begins with an expedition into these areas instigated by the founders of the regime, and results over time in the rise to power of descendants of the regime in Cuauhtinchan and Tecamachalco, Puebla, and other towns that make up the northern section of the lienzo map.

Northern geography is prominent in the history of Coixtlahuaca portrayed on the Lienzo of Coixtlahuaca II as well, but in its case the north is a peripheral zone on the right-hand edge of the lienzo beyond Coixtlahuaca's territorial boundaries. Furthermore, while north is an important direction of incursions and political expansion arising from events surrounding the founding of Coixtlahuaca on the Lienzo of Coixtlahuaca II, it is not the sole direction of these activities as it virtually is on the Lienzo of Tlapiltepec.

North is also significant in Coixtlahuaca history, according to both lienzos, as the point of origin of the founder of the Monte Verde lineage, 7 Water "Eagle," or Atonal (I), as he was known in the Valley of Mexico. On the Lienzo of Tlapiltepec, the southern migration of 7 Water from a northern location, and travels of priests southward from a place of seven caves to the hilltop site where they perform foundation rituals, are juxtaposed at the lower left of the manuscript, with the northward developments of a later era that occupy one quarter of the manuscript at the lower right. On the Lienzo of Tlapiltepec the story begins in the north at the lower left and later returns to the north at the lower right.

On the Lienzo of Coixtlahuaca II, as on many other cartographic-historical lienzos of the colonial period, an image of the home territory, consisting of a central space framed by a rectangular perimeter of boundary signs, is the dominant motif. On the Lienzo of Tlapiltepec wavy lines representing rivers define a geographically significant core area, but this is limited to the southwest portion of the Coixtlahuaca Valley. The much larger area encompassed by Coixtlahuaca's boundaries is not indicated on the manuscript.

The Lienzo of Tlapiltepec is not a boundary map. Rather, it is an account of events and relationships leading up to and arising from the formation of Coixtlahuaca as a widely influential political entity, an account such as might be found inscribed in greater detail in a screenfold manuscript of many pages. It is a large, single-sheet, cartographic summary of Coixtlahuaca's establishment and its consequences. In these features, as in its map of interregional scope, the Lienzo of Tlapiltepec is unique among cartographic-historical manuscripts from the Mixteca.

Connecting lines on the Lienzo of Tlapiltepec direct the reader and engage the viewer. In abstract and diagrammatic terms, forming patterns, the lines signify developments occurring across geographical space as well as through historical time. Lines and trails of human footprints extending lengthwise along the vertical edges of the lienzo and centrally from the Coixtlahuaca core toward both ends represent interactions taking place along a north-south axis, one of the manuscript's most prominent themes. Branching red lines on the left side of the lienzo tell of the origins of the initiator of the Monte Verde lineage and his three siblings and describe their dispersal to the north and south. Even more red lines fanning out from the later founders of Coixtlahuaca at the upper right of the lienzo lead to destinations in Oaxaca and south and central Puebla, north of Coixtlahuaca, at the lower right. Lines from subsequent re-founders of Coixtlahuaca lead to other towns on the upper edge of the lienzo.

On the right side of the lienzo, the pattern as a whole is one of lines radiating from a tangled core where lines and footprints representing human activities and relationships are interwoven with undulating lines that stand for rivers of the southern Coixtlahuaca Valley. This outward radiating pattern on the right side of the lienzo is foreshadowed on the left side by the branching lines of the ancestors and their northern and southern offspring, and by the configuration of the hill of entwined serpents where ritual fire is kindled, with the serpents' heads and tails radiating out from the corners of this knotted core and the signs of the cardinal directions arranged cartographically around it.

The Lienzo of Tlapiltepec is in some respects closer to the pre-Hispanic Mixtec screenfold manuscripts than it is to other cartographic lienzos of the early colonial period. Similarities between the lienzo and the screenfolds—the best surviving evidence of pictorial narrative traditions of the Mixteca—include aspects of form and an overall sense of narrative purpose. The Lienzo of Tlapiltepec is a document whose shape is simultaneously that of a map of an area that is long in one direction—north to south—but narrow in the other, and of a manuscript of similar proportions, such as a tira or screenfold, that is designed to tell a story.

Divided lengthwise into two narrow columns of space, the Lienzo of Tlapiltepec suggests an arrangement of two manuscripts in strip form placed side-by-side. In the left-hand column, the Coixtlahuaca genealogy is presented chronologically from ancient origins at the base of the column to the most recent historical rulers at the top, as it might be in a history painted on a tira or screenfold. While the organization of the material in the wider right-hand column is more complex, it is also dominated by a chronological progression that leads from the founding of Coixtlahuaca in the upper half of the column to relations with towns located in areas north of Coixtlahuaca in the lower half.

Seen in this way, connecting lines on the lienzo are the equivalent of lines that structure the narrative in the pre-Hispanic Mixtec screenfold manuscripts. This includes the apparatus of registers and guidelines that structure continuity in the screenfolds, as well as the vocabulary of forms of elongated shape such as roads and umbilical cords that often colorfully tie together and group the figures in these screenfolds. Comparison of the lienzo with the pre-Hispanic screenfolds in this regard helps to suggest something of the substance or weight of meaning contained in a simple connecting line on the early colonial lienzo.

The Lienzo of Tlapiltepec is an elaborately integrated combination of map and history: a spatial environment comprehensively viewed and the threads of a story sequentially followed. Related constructions from the Mixtec screenfold manuscripts include the incorporation of a mountain landscape into the pages of Codex Vindobonensis and a framework of earth and sky defining vertical space in a section of Codex Nuttall. Multiple strands of the genealogical-historical narrative in sections of Codex Bodley are comparable to the network of connecting lines on the Lienzo of Tlapiltepec.

Parallels between the early colonial Lienzo of Tlapiltepec and the pre-Hispanic Codex Colombino-Becker I screenfold lie in the importance of central and peripheral zones in the space of the two manuscripts, in action that leads from the periphery to the center and out toward the periphery again in both, and in the progression of the narrative from a beginning to a middle and an end.

In the journey of 8 Deer to Tututepec in Codex Colombino-Becker I, a buildup and release of tension derives from the movement from outer register to inner one and to outer one again, as well as from the actions of turning over the leaves of the screenfold to close one pair of pages and advance to the next. On the lienzo, on the other hand, drama arises not from transitions from register to register or page to page, but rather from confrontation with the whole of Coixtlahuaca geography and history condensed onto the single large sheet of cloth—more than twice the height of the human viewer and as wide as the viewer is tall—and from following these developments upward and downward over its surface.

NOTES

1. Gruzinski (1993:41–45) discusses characteristics of native sketch maps of the colonial period.
2. This chapter's summary of the map and history inscribed on the Lienzo of Tlapiltepec highlights prominent developments but does not specifically mention every event represented on the lienzo. The internal history of the Coixtlahuaca Valley community of towns, in particular, as reflected on the Lienzo of Tlapiltepec, is only slightly touched on. This history is explored in detail in the works of Bas van Doesburg, including chapter 2 of this book. See Doesburg 2000, 2001, 2004, 2010a. My summary relies on sources listed in chapter 1, notes 4 and 11, with Doesburg and Buren's synthesis, "The Prehispanic History of the Valley of Coixtlahuaca, Oaxaca" (1997), being especially helpful.
3. On iconographic and stylistic characteristics of a selection of native maps from the Mixteca in the colonial period, see Smith (1973a:162–71). Mundy (1996) examines native mapping traditions as they were affected by European cartography and Spanish colonization. Boone (e.g., 2000b:77–85; 1998) discusses structures and purposes of native maps and cartographic histories.
4. The Toltec origins of the Monte Verde lineage of Coixtlahuaca rulers are discussed by Bas van Doesburg in chapter 2 of this book. See also Annals of Cuauhtitlán (Bierhorst 1992:42, 107–108, 136), Caso (1977:134), Jansen (1982b:419), Pohl (1994a:150–52), Doesburg and Buren (1997:107–13), Jansen and Pérez Jiménez (2011:380–81, 452–53).

   Two Coixtlahuaca rulers called Atonal are mentioned in the Annals of Cuauhtitlán, and both appear on the Lienzo of Tlapiltepec as well as other Coixtlahuaca Group lienzos: Lienzo of Coixtlahuaca II (Seler II) and Lienzo of Ihuitlán; with the earlier Atonal alone appearing on the Lienzo of Tequixtepec I. The earlier Atonal of the eleventh or twelfth century is founder of the Monte Verde lineage and is named 7 Water "Eagle" on the Coixtlahuaca lienzos. We refer to him here as Atonal I. The later Atonal, his fifteenth-century descendant, is named 6 Water on the Coixtlahuaca lienzos. He was killed during the Aztec conquest of Coixtlahuaca of 1458–62. On the Lienzo of Tlapiltepec, 6 Water is the nineteenth, and final, ruler in the column of rulers that appears near the upper left edge of the sheet. Concerning Coixtlahuaca's war with the Aztecs as reflected in the Coixtlahuaca manuscripts, see Doesburg, this volume, chapter 2.

   There has been uncertainty concerning the significance of the eagle depicted adjacent to 7 Water on the Lienzo of Tlapiltepec. The eagle likely represents 7 Water's personal name, as it does on the Lienzo of Tequixtepec I (Parmenter 1982:66); 7 Water and his three sisters all have personal names on the Lienzo of Tlapiltepec. At the same time, since it is attached to the house next to 7 Water on the Lienzo of Tlapiltepec, the eagle may have an additional meaning. Doesburg and Buren (1997:110) consider the eagle-house combination to be a place sign for the specific Monte Verde site where the rulership of 7 Water "Eagle" was established. Confirming a double connotation, the Lienzo of Coixtlahuaca II shows 7 Water wearing an eagle helmet—representing his personal name—while, distinct from this, his place sign includes the combination of a house and an eagle. It has also been suggested that the eagle-house sign refers to the town of Cuauhtinchan, Puebla, which is represented by a similar place sign near the lower right corner of the Lienzo of Tlapiltepec, and with which Coixtlahuaca is known to have had important ties at a later stage of its history (Topsey 1985:31; Pohl 1994a:151).
5. On the Lienzo of Coixtlahuaca II, a side-by-side pair of rivers or currents of water emerge like springs from the base of a hill. Between the rivers at their source is what appears to be a small human face or mask. Attached to one side of the hill is a house or palace and to the other side a tree, and on top of the hill there is a second, smaller house (see fig. 3.23). On the Lienzo of Tulancingo, the sign consists of the hill with the pair of rivers flowing from its base and a tree (Doesburg 2000:180 and figs. 8, 12). As in the manuscript of the Coixtlahuaca Group known as Codex Baranda, the place sign on the Lienzo of Tulancingo is accompanied by the date of the meeting of warriors but not the scene of this event. In Codex Baranda the place sign is a hill with a cactus and another plant but only a single river.

   Previously, Doesburg and Buren (1997:122) suggested that the meeting of warriors took place at a site called Omeapan that no longer exists but is mentioned in an early colonial document (Archivo General de la Nación [hereinafter AGN], Civil, vol. 726, exp. 7, f. 4). The name "Omeapan" (from the Nahuatl *ome*, "two," plus *a(tl)*, "water," plus locative suffix *-pan*, "on") accords with the two rivers in the place signs on the Coixtlahuaca II, Tulancingo, and Tlapiltepec lienzos. While the above-mentioned document did not indicate clearly where Omeapan was located, another document, recently discovered by Doesburg, refers to Omeapan with more geographical precision (AGN, Tierras, 2787, 1751, f. 92, Jicotlán contra Tlapiltepec). According to this second document, the valley of Omeapan was located between Ihuitlán and Jicotlán, immediately north of Tlapiltepec. On the Lienzo of Tlapiltepec, the place sign I refer to as Two Rivers is positioned east rather than north of Tlapiltepec. Nevertheless, it could still be Omeapan. Its position on the lienzo, close to Tulancingo and Coixtlahuaca in the right-side core of the map and at the center of the composition, may reflect pictorial narrative priorities.
6. A possible clue to the identity of the warriors who meet with the Coixtlahuaca founders at Two Rivers in this scene is found in the manuscript known as the *Historia tolteca-chichimeca*, from Cuauhtinchan, Puebla. Cuauhtinchan is one of the towns to which the red lines that extend north from Two Rivers on the Lienzo of Tlapiltepec lead. According to the *Historia tolteca-chichimeca* (Kirchhoff, Odena Güemes, and Reyes García 1976:205, para. 322), the migration of "los mixtecas los popolocas" from Coixtlahuaca into the Cuauhtinchan area was somehow prompted by a visit from a Cuauhtinchan group called the Colomochca. Perhaps the warriors who meet with 1 Wind and 4 Jaguar on the Lienzo of Tlapiltepec are the Colomochca from Cuauhtinchan. On the relationship of the Coixtlahuaca Mixteca-Popolocas to the Cuauhtinchan Colomochca as documented in the *Historia tolteca-chichimeca* and other sources, see Reyes García (1977:56–62).
7. See Doesburg and Buren (1997:121–22).
8. Regarding the documented name of the site represented by the Coixtlahuaca "Round Stone" sign and the uncertainty of its exact location, see Doesburg (2001:58 n. 27).
9. See note 4, above.
10. It is possible that a woman named 10 Wind, who appears at the top right corner of the Lienzo of Tlapiltepec, was a fourth daughter of 10 Serpent, even though no line connects them (Johnson 1992; Doesburg, personal communication, July 2011); like the three other daughters of 10 Serpent, 10 Wind is accompanied by a place sign but no husband is shown. The place sign with 10 Wind has been identified by Jansen (2011:300–301) and independently by

Hermann Lejarazu (2011) as representing Teposcolula, southwest of the Coixtlahuaca Valley. The town associated with daughter 11 Death, in the upper left corner of the lienzo, remains unidentified. The town of daughter 9 Grass is identified by Doesburg as Yanhuitlán (fig. 2.1, this volume). The town of daughter ? Vulture (name sign partly destroyed), represented by a platform with four-petaled flowers, is Suchixtlán, 10–15 km south of the Coixtlahuaca Valley (Jansen 1982b:276; see also Smith 1973a:79).

11. Research for the Royal Ontario Museum's color illustration of the Lienzo of Tlapiltepec reproduced in this book indicates that the spiral of liquid in this Coixtlahuaca place sign was originally red. This same site on the Lienzo of Coixtlahuaca II is represented by a hill and flowing blood, rather than the frieze and spiral. Doesburg (2001:44–46) demonstrates that the site referred to by both place signs was probably Yestepeque, "Blood Hill," known to Mixtec speakers as *Tineñe,* "Little Place of Blood," mentioned in colonial documents as a sector of the town of Coixtlahuaca that was inhabited by Mixtecs.
12. Only fragments of the once-red connecting lines—now pale pinkish-gray—are clearly visible in photographs of the lienzo. In 1988, I made a tracing from the original lienzo of all its connecting lines and trails of footprints, black as well as red. It is possible that some connecting lines, and certain that parts of lines, have disappeared entirely. I then transferred the traced lines onto a smaller, complete tracing of an enlarged photograph of the lienzo (Johnson 1994).
13. Ross Parmenter, having discovered that the upper half of the right side of the Lienzo of Tlapiltepec contained a map of the Coixtlahuaca Valley, realized that the lower half was a continuation of the map into areas north of the valley (Parmenter 1982:37). In conversations Parmenter referred to this lower right section of the manuscript as "the northern map." Cuauhtinchan and several other towns in central Puebla were first identified on the lienzo and described as destinations for an expedition originating from the Coixtlahuaca Valley by Jansen (in Jansen and Gaxiola 1978:14–15), and Jansen continued to develop this theme, often in papers devoted primarily to other manuscripts and topics (1982b:416–18; 1989:73–74; 1992:27–30; also Jansen 1983, and Jansen and Pérez Jiménez 2000:153–58; 2011:140, 350–52, 431). For discussion of this "northern map" section of the Lienzo of Tlapiltepec and related material on the Lienzo of Coixtlahuaca II and in manuscripts from Cuauhtinchan and Tecamachalco, Puebla, and the Valley of Mexico, see Doesburg and Buren (1997:128–40), Johnson (1994:125–42), and Doesburg, this volume, chapter 2.
14. It may be noted that this system of red lines originates specifically from the woman 11 Deer at "Butterfly Water" rather than from between 11 Deer and her husband 3 Flint.

    Smith (in Smith and Parmenter 1991:31–33) tentatively proposed that the town of one of the sons of this couple, represented on the lienzo by a man with closed eyes seated in an L-shaped container of splashing water, was Chila, Puebla, northwest of the Coixtlahuaca Valley in the Mixteca Baja; a related sign in the tira known as Codex Tulane, representing one of the two towns featured in that manuscript, was identified by Smith as Chila. Smith's argument hinged to some extent on the possibility that the Mixtec name for Chila as recorded in the sixteenth-century Mixtec grammar of Antonio de los Reyes (Reyes 1976 [1593]:90), "*toavui*," was a misprint for *touvui*. Doesburg, during fieldwork in the Chila area in 2009, determined that the Mixtec name for the town is still *Toavui*, as Reyes stated, not *Touvui*, and that it is therefore unlikely that the sign on the Lienzo of Tlapiltepec or the similar sign in Codex Tulane represent Chila as Smith contended (Bas van Doesburg, personal communication, July 2011). But see also Jansen and Pérez Jiménez (2011:338–39), whose interpretation of the name *Toavui* leads them to agree with Smith that the place signs in Codex Tulane and on the Lienzo of Tlapiltepec both do represent Chila.

    Doesburg has suggested identifications for place signs associated with two other offspring of the "Butterfly Water" couple. A hill with blood flowing over it may represent the former village of Yestepec (San Francisco Yestepec; not to be confused with the site of the same name at Coixtlahuaca, mentioned above in note 11) referred to in colonial documents as having been located not far north of Texcalhueyac (now Las Palmas), northwest of the Coixtlahuaca Valley in the Mixteca Baja. Yestepec means "Blood Hill" (from the Nahuatl *extli*, "blood," and *tepetl*, "hill"). A second "Blood Hill" sign on the Lienzo of Tlapiltepec, shown as conquered by rulers of Tlapiltepec, may represent this same place. Another possible identity for one or both of these "Blood Hill" place signs, as was suggested to me by Mary Elizabeth Smith, is the town of Tonalá, also in the Mixteca Baja (see Jansen and Pérez Jiménez 2000:139–40; 2011:332).

    Another place sign associated with the "Butterfly Water" offspring consists of an L-shaped container of flowing water; within it, a green semicircular object with a cord knotted to it. The semicircular object, Doesburg observes, resembles marcasite mirrors that had leather cords tied at the back, found in archaeological contexts and depicted in other manuscripts. Doesburg suggests this place sign represents the village of Atexcal (from the Nahuatl *atl*, "water," and *tezcatl*, "mirror") located southeast of Tepexi in central southern Puebla. On the lienzo a daughter of the "Butterfly Water" couple marries the ruler of this village. Subsequently a daughter of this couple, named 13 Rabbit, marries 9 Monkey, a ruler of Tepexi, who originated from Coixtlahuaca, either directly or as a descendant, as indicated by a red line. Other evidence that the water-mirror place sign on the Lienzo of Tlapiltepec is Atexcal is discussed by Swanton and Doesburg in this volume, chapter 2, appendix B.
15. See *Historia tolteca-chichimeca* (Kirchhoff, Odena Güemes, and Reyes García 1976, pp. 205–206, para. 322–27, and pp. 219–20, para. 362–64; also Leibsohn 1993:353, 358–59). For discussion of the Mixteca-Popolocas from Coixtlahuaca as they appear in the *Historia tolteca-chichimeca* and Cuauhtinchan Maps nos. 2 and 3, all from Cuauhtinchan, Puebla, and on the Map of Tecamachalco (Lienzo Vischer I), from Tecamachalco, Puebla, see Reyes García (1977:56–62; 1998), Yoneda (1981, 1996, 2005), Johnson (1994:125–42), Doesburg and Buren (1997:128–40). The Mixteca-Popolocas of the Puebla and Coixtlahuaca manuscripts are mentioned frequently in Carrasco and Sessions (2007); see contributions of Asselbergs, Aveni, Yoneda, and Wake, among others, to that volume, devoted to Cuauhtinchan Map no. 2. My own understanding of the links between the Lienzo of Tlapiltepec and the Puebla manuscripts began with a meeting with Keiko Yoneda and Luis Reyes García arranged by Carlos Paredes Martínez (1988), for which I remain ever grateful.
16. As explained to me by Luis Reyes García (1988), the Mixtec name for Tecamachalco, represented on the Lienzo of Tlapiltepec by a platform with thatched house and plant, was the same as, and was derived from, the name of the village where the important Mixteca-Popoloca ruler of Tecamachalco, called 12 Lizard on the

Tlapiltepec and Coixtlahuahca II lienzos and Quetzpaltzin in Puebla sources, originated. The Mixtec name of 12 Lizard's village was *Yucutnuyaca* and the Nahuatl name Huitzcolotla or Huixcolotla (present-day San Salvador Huixcolotla, located northwest of Tecamachalco). Huixcolotla/*Yucutnuyaca* was a Mixteca-Popoloca village. Quetzpaltzin/12 Lizard was born there (see Celestino Solís and Reyes García 1992:19). The Mixtec and Nahuatl names of the village have the same meaning: *huixcolotl* and *tnuyaca* both refer to a type of spiny tree whose thorns were used for ritual self-mutilation.

In the Mixtec grammar of Antonio de los Reyes of 1593, the Mixtec name for Tecamachalco is given as "*yucutduyaca*," which Smith (1973a:78) suggests is a misprint for *yucutnuyaca*; and in a gloss on the right-hand margin of the Lienzo of Coixtlahuaca II it is *chiyotnuyaca*. The unrelated Nahuatl place name, Tecamachalco, means "Place of the Stone Jawbone" (Smith 1973a:78).

17. The Lienzo of Coixtlahuaca II is the largest and most comprehensive of the Coixtlahuaca Group of lienzos and the one most closely related to the Lienzo of Tlapiltepec. The American Museum of Natural History's (hereinafter AMNH) copy of the Lienzo of Coixtlahuaca II stands in here for the original (Ethnologisches Museum Berlin), which was not accessible for photography (fig. 3.24). Except for parts of the painting that are so faded and damaged as to be barely legible on the lienzo itself, the AMNH copy is a generally exact, full-size reproduction of the original. Material missing altogether from the copy, largely from the right side of the document, includes, among other details, several human figures, a series of rectangles bordering a river—perhaps signifying plots of land—and some of the lienzo's connecting lines and footprints. The AMNH copy was painted on lightweight cotton cloth that was originally cream colored but has since darkened to an ochre brown, against which the paint colors no longer stand out (Johnson, 1994b).

The AMNH copy is signed, "W. v. d. Steinen, Berlin 1899, Copie n.d. Original." Wilhelm von den Steinen was an artist and illustrator of ethnographic and archaeological material who provided drawings for many of Eduard Seler's publications. The copy of the Coixtlahuaca II lienzo was discovered in a storage area of the AMNH in 1991 rolled up together with a copy of the Lienzo of Zacatepec 1, also signed by Von den Steinen. While the AMNH has no record of the acquisition of the two lienzo copies, Eckehard Dolinski found both mentioned in a letter from Seler to the museum dated May 8, 1899, Berlin (AMNH, Archives of Department of Anthropology). In this letter Seler states that he has mailed a copy of the Lienzo of Zacatepec to the museum and that he is also having a copy made for them of the Lienzo of Coixtlahuaca that he hopes to send within a few months (Eckehard Dolinski, personal communication, 2000). The Von den Steinen reproduction is one of two known copies of the Lienzo of Coixtlahuaca II, the other being a full-size black line tracing, with no color, made by Seler himself (Ibero-American Institute, Berlin). König (1984:234) notes that the latter was not carefully made. I thank Eckehard Dolinski for bringing Seler's tracing to my attention and for providing me with a photocopy.

18. One of the more legible of this group of northern place signs on the Lienzo of Coixtlahuaca II is a hill with a maguey on its peak. A perhaps related "Hill with Maguey" appears on the lower left corner of the Lienzo of Tlapiltepec, above and to the right of the seven-chambered cave, Chicomoztoc. Doesburg (personal communication, 2011) suggests the sign on the Lienzo of Coixtlahuaca II represents Metzontla (Los Reyes Metzontla, from the Nahuatl *metl*, "maguey," and *tzontli*, "place where there is an abundance of something") southwest of Tehuacán.

19. The Map of Tecamachalco / Lienzo Vischer I is reproduced in black and white as a large foldout in Burland (1960). The document is discussed in more detail in Reyes García (1998).

20. Another family depicted on the northern section of the Lienzo of Tlapiltepec that has representatives on the Map of Tecamachalco is the self-contained group that consists of the rulers of "Butterfly Water" (3 Flint and 11 Deer), their three sons and a daughter, and a granddaughter who marries a ruler of Tepexi (see fig. 3.21). This family's origins are not explained on the Lienzo of Tlapiltepec. Reyes García (1993) contends that this family, as represented on the Map of Tecamachalco, also originated from Aztatla, but it is not clear that this is the case. Reyes García reads the sequence of rulers that includes the "Butterfly Water" couple on the Tecamachalco manuscript downward from top to bottom, whereas the Lienzo of Tlapiltepec shows that the genealogy on the Tecamachalco manuscript probably should read upward from bottom to top. On the Lienzo of Tlapiltepec, the "Butterfly Water" couple, 3 Flint and wife 11 Deer, are followed by their daughter 8 Death and her husband 12 Movement, followed next by this couple's daughter 13 Rabbit and her husband 9 Monkey. On the Map of Tecamachalco, 1 Death and her husband 6 Movement, followed by 13 Rabbit and husband ? Monkey—who, in spite of the discrepancies are likely these same people—are the third and fourth couples, respectively, above the "Butterfly Water" couple, 3 Flint and 11 Deer (Johnson 1994:136, 138 n. 19).

21. The small, partly black house that accompanies the ancestors' place sign is one of seven or eight black houses on the Lienzo of Tlapiltepec. Perhaps these buildings represent pre-Hispanic temples.

A hill surmounted by a diamond-shaped net on the right-hand edge of Cuauhtinchan Map no. 2 is identified by Yoneda as Matlatlan, present-day Maltrata, in western Veracruz, south of the volcano Pico de Orizaba, which itself, in the form of a large snow-capped mountain, also appears near Matlatlan on Cuauhtinchan Map no. 2 (Yoneda 1981:141, plate 31; Yoneda in Carrasco and Sessions 2007:184 and illustration sections G and H). Matlatlan is also found on Cuauhtinchan Map no. 1 (Yoneda 1981:140, plate 30); in the section of Codex Mendoza that records Aztec conquests (folio 10v; Berdan and Anawalt 1992, 2:18–19); and possibly in Codex Dehesa, p. 18.

22. The genealogy of 7 Water "Eagle" and his three sisters is included in three other manuscripts of the Coixtlahuaca Group: Lienzo of Coixtlahuaca II, Lienzo of Tequixtepec I, and the Gómez de Orozco Fragment (see Parmenter 1982:70–71). On the Lienzo of Coixtlahuaca II, all that remains of the faded figure of 1 Wind "Flower Serpent" is part of the person's face and head, part of the outline of the serpent with flowers attached to its back, and a line that could be the back of a throne upon which 1 Wind is seated. Almost nothing survives of the place sign associated with 1 Wind on Coixtlahuaca II. Where there may have been a black disc, as in the sign on the Lienzo of Tlapiltepec, on Coixtlahuaca II there is now a perfectly circular hole in the cloth. However, above these remains of the figure and place sign on Coixtlahuaca II, a written gloss, weak but still faintly legible in photographs of the lienzo, appears to give the Mixtec place name *ayuu*. This suggests that the Mixtec name of 1 Wind's town, represented by the destroyed place sign on Coixtlahuaca II and by the hill with black circle and flowing liquid on the Lienzo of Tlapiltepec, was *Ayuu*.

The Mixtec manuscript known as Codex Muro contains a similar place sign that is also glossed *ayuu*. The sign, Codex Muro, p. 3, is a hill with a black circle enclosed within its summit and a human jaw placed within the lower part of the hill. It is possible that this sign in Codex Muro and the place signs associated with 1 Wind "Flower Serpent" on the Lienzo of Coixtlahuaca II and Lienzo of Tlapiltepec, apparently identified as *Ayuu* on the former and containing a black disc on the latter, all refer to the same place. Finding no town named *Ayuu* in the Mixteca Alta where Codex Muro is from, Hermann Lejarazu (2003:145–46) tentatively identified the town mentioned on p. 3 of Codex Muro as a town of similar name, existing still as the village of Santa María Ayú, located near the Oaxaca-Puebla border in the Mixteca Baja.

On the Lienzo of Tlapiltepec, 1 Wind "Flower Serpent" and the associated place sign are located near the southern edge of the map, at the center of a group of towns of the Mixteca Alta *south* of the Coixtlahuaca Valley. The position of this place sign at the south end of the lienzo is surely cartographically meaningful. In the scheme of north-south interactions emphasized on the Lienzo of Tlapiltepec, the town of 1 Wind "Flower Serpent" is an important southern focal point. Therefore, it is difficult to imagine that this place sign on the Lienzo of Tlapiltepec represents the *Ayuu* (Santa María Ayú) that is located *northwest* of the Coixtlahuaca Valley in the Mixteca Baja. If it does in fact stand for a town called *Ayuu*, as the gloss on Coixtlahuaca II suggests, it must have been a different *Ayuu*.

The name *Ayuu*, analyzed by Hermann Lejarazu (2003:144), means "Place of the Stone." The name contains the Mixtec word for "stone," *yuu*, represented in the sign in Codex Muro by the black disc, plus the locative prefix *a-*, "in" or "place," represented in Codex Muro by a human jaw. The black disc is not the normal sign for *yuu* or "stone" (see Smith 1973a:46–50). As noted by Hermann Lejarazu (2003:145), the disc motif frequently refers to the mirrors of polished obsidian made by the ancient Mexicans, called in Mixtec *yuu tata* (*yuu*, "stone," and *tata*, "dark or dark brown"), a term also applied to the dark glassy stone from which the mirrors were made. In the place sign associated with 1 Wind "Flower Serpent" on the Lienzo of Tlapiltepec, and likely the destroyed sign accompanying 1 Wind on the Lienzo of Coixtlahuaca II, if indeed these signs stand for a town called *Ayuu*, the black circle would represent *yuu*—dark stone, or mirror made from it. Another identification proposed for the town of 1 Wind "Flower Serpent" is the Mixteca Alta town of Tiltepec, called *Yucu tnoo* in Mixtec, the Nahuatl and Mixtec names both meaning "Black Hill." Doesburg (personal communication, 2011) and Jansen and Pérez Jiménez (2011:286 n. 7) have both made this suggestion.

23. Origin caves containing seven openings are not exclusively central Mexican. See Boone (2003:209–11) and Jansen and Pérez Jiménez (2007:105–107, 115, 333 n. 51) for some examples from southern Mexico.
24. The introduction of the cult of 9 Wind "Quetzalcoatl" into the Coixtlahuaca Valley is discussed by Doesburg, this volume, chapter 2. On 9 Wind "Quetzalcoatl" in pictorial manuscripts from the Mixteca as a whole, see Nicholson (1978, 2001) and Jansen and Pérez Jiménez (2007). Detailed commentaries on Codex Vindobonensis are those of Furst (1978); Jansen (1982); and Anders, Jansen, and Pérez Jiménez (1992b; with facsimile reproduction of the codex).
25. See Boone (2000b:154). On the Lienzo of Tlapiltepec, the lienzo's earliest female ancestor, 4 Movement, is positioned in front of "Deer River." Perhaps we are to understand that she was from there.
26. Caso (1961:255) suggests this second black line could mean that the male of the third ancestral couple, named 12 Flint, originated directly from Chicomoztoc, and that it was his wife, also named 12 Flint, who was the descendant of the river-born lineage.
27. It is not certain that any of the place signs arranged in a circle around the fire-making ritual on the Lienzo of Coixtlahuaca II are equivalent to any of the signs grouped beneath the ritual on the Lienzo of Tlapiltepec, but there are possible correlations, such as a split hill on the Lienzo of Coixtlahuaca II and split temple platform on the Lienzo of Tlapiltepec. Another is a partly destroyed glyph that includes a hill with a mask, at the top of the circle of towns on Coixtlahuaca II, and a glyph that includes a temple platform and a man who appears to be carving a mask in the group on the Lienzo of Tlapiltepec. The position of the group beneath the large hill of entwined serpents on the Lienzo of Tlapiltepec suggests these places might be located somewhere north of it.
28. I am grateful to Eckehard Dolinski for his photographs of the original Lienzo of Coixtlahuaca II, confirming the red color of these fourteen lines.
29. Concerning 4 Jaguar on the Lienzo of Tlapiltepec and in the Mixtec screenfold manuscripts, see Jansen (1982b:419–20); Jansen (1996, in which Jansen proposes that this 4 Jaguar is identical with the Toltec ruler Topiltzin Quetzalcoatl); Jansen and Pérez Jiménez (2007:215, 268); Ruíz Ortíz and Jansen (2009:29–33); Jansen and Pérez Jiménez (2011:379–82, 508–509); Byland and Pohl (1994:139–52); Doesburg and Buren (1997:114–16); and Nicholson (2005, who questions Jansen's identification of 4 Jaguar as Topiltzin Quetzalcoatl).
30. Figure 3.36 includes only those streams which on a 1984 topographical map of scale 1:50,000 are shown as having water in them year-round. The names of the rivers in figure 3.36 are those found on this map. *Carta topográfica*, 1:50,000; Secretaría de Programación y Presupuesto, Instituto Nacional de Estadística, Geografía e Informática, Mexico, 1984; sheets E14D15, E14D16, E14D25, E14D26.
31. Elizabeth Hill Boone (May 1998), commenting on an earlier outline of what eventually became my contribution to this book.
32. Two other manuscripts of the Coixtlahuaca Group, the Lienzo of Coixtlahuaca II and Lienzo of Tequixtepec I, employ red connecting lines in genealogical-historical contexts. On both, red lines are reserved for movements and relationships pertaining to the primordial era of Coixtlahuaca history, and exclusively to the Monte Verde lineage of Coixtlahuaca rulers. The same applies to the ancestral system of red lines on the Lienzo of Tlapiltepec.

On the Lienzo of Coixtlahuaca II, red lines tie the fire-making ritual that signifies the founding of the Monte Verde rulership to place signs and rulers arranged in a circle around it (see fig. 3.24).

On the Lienzo of Tequixtepec I, a short road, consisting of a trail of red human footprints sandwiched between parallel red lines, connects the parents of 7 Water, founder of the Monte Verde lineage, and their place sign, to a sign consisting of a crenellated enclosure and blood plus a hill and an eagle. Red connecting lines are uncommon in manuscripts from the Mixtec region. In Codex Colombino-Becker I (pp. 8–9), fine red lines link a sequence of signs, but this is the only instance of their use in the surviving pre-Hispanic-style Mixtec screenfold manuscripts. To my knowledge, red connecting lines are not found on lienzos or other panel-form manuscripts from the Mixteca except for the Tlapiltepec, Coixtlahuaca II, Tequixtepec I, and Otla lienzos from the Coixtlahuaca Valley.

Two manuscripts not from the Coixtlahuaca Valley that include red connecting lines are the Mixtec screenfold Codex Egerton (Burland 1965; König 1979; Jansen 1994, with color facsimile), and the Map of Tecamachalco / Lienzo Vischer I, painted on a large sheet of animal hide (no published color illustrations; Burland 1960; Reyes García 1998), both of them postconquest. In both the Egerton and Map of Tecamachalco, as on the Lienzo of Tlapiltepec, red lines connect subsidiary figures to the main ruling line. The Map of Tecamachalco and possibly also Codex Egerton are, like the Lienzo of Tlapiltepec, from transitional areas between the Mixteca and the Valley of Mexico (Map of Tecamachalco is from Tecamachalco, Puebla; Egerton may be from the northern Mixteca Baja as Smith suggested [1973a:17–19, 82; Smith in Smith and Parmenter 1991:90; Jansen and Pérez Jiménez 2007:219]). Also from this transitional zone, on the map that accompanies the 1579 *relación geográfica* from Huehuetlan, Puebla, roads are represented variously by red lines (Acuña 1981–88, vol. 5, 2nd map after p. 214).

Codex Egerton and the Map of Tecamachalco, like the Lienzo of Tlapiltepec and other manuscripts from the Coixtlahuaca Valley, show the influence of central Mexican manuscript painting in a variety of ways (see, for example, Smith 1973a:18) and it is possible that their red lines reflect this influence. Among the central Mexican manuscripts that feature red connecting lines are the "Genealogía de una familia de Tepeticpac" from Tlaxcala (Glass 1964:70–71, plates 28–29; Reyes García 1993:210), and the genealogy of Aztec rulers in Codex Mexicanus (Mengin 1952, plates VI–VII). Some other Valley of Mexico manuscripts that contain red connecting lines are Codex Boturini (Corona Núñez 1964–67, 2:7–29) the Tira de Tepechpan (Noguez 1978; Diel 2008), Códice de Santa María Asunción (Williams and Harvey 1997) and Codex Kingsborough (Paso y Troncoso 1912). An orange-red line links the series of scenes that constitute the Lienzo of Jucutacato (Glass 1964:43, plate 7; Roskamp 1998) from western Mexico.

33. In addition to systems of red connecting lines accompanied by red footprints, the Lienzo of Tlapiltepec contains an isolated red line that lacks footprints. This line is attached at one end to the hill-with-knotted-rope sign of Tlapiltepec on the right edge of the lienzo. The line runs parallel to the edge of the lienzo under a row of three Tlapiltepec ruling couples and the assemblages of weapons that appear before them, and above another, earlier group of rulers of this town (see fig. 3.13). The lienzo contains various black dividing lines—the upper and lower groups of Tlapiltepec rulers, for example, are both separated from other material by short black lines—but no other red dividing lines. This sole red dividing line recalls one in the early colonial Mixtec screenfold Codex Becker II (Nowotny 1961), where it separates an upper register from a lower. A potential additional meaning is that the line on the Lienzo of Tlapiltepec is intended to include the Tlapiltepec rulers who appear above it, who contributed militarily to Coixtlahuaca's northern expansion, in the network of relationships that is indicated by red connecting lines on the lienzo. This red dividing line is one of a number of features on the lienzo that graphically emphasize Tlapiltepec. The town is shown as a hub of incoming and outgoing connecting lines of variously genealogical, expeditionary, military, and river significance.

34. On the format, content, and style of the Mixtec genealogical-historical screenfold manuscripts, including these five multiple-register manuscripts and two screenfolds of simpler design that are often grouped with them, see Smith (1973a:9–19); Boone (2000b:87–124); Dennis (1994); Johnson (2005a); and Jansen and Pérez Jiménez (2011). Codex Selden, although divided into registers like the pre-Hispanic members of the group, was actually painted forty years after the Spanish conquest of Mexico (Smith 1994).

The title "Codex Colombino" is derived from Christopher Columbus, and Becker I from the nineteenth-century German collector Philip J. Becker; the other manuscripts are named after the libraries, collectors, and scholars that have been associated with them. Jansen and Pérez Jiménez (e.g., 2004; 2005:14; 2011:42–95) have proposed a series of Mixtec names for the manuscripts, related to their origins and contents, and meaningful to modern Mixtecs. Because Codex Colombino-Becker I is a biography of the Mixtec ruler 8 Deer "Jaguar Claw," it would be known as Codex Iya Nacuaa (Mixtec *iya* = lord, *nacuaa* = 8 Deer).

35. Some of the ways in which meaning is derived from aspects of the painted composition as a whole in the Mixtec screenfold manuscripts are explored by Hamman (2004) and Johnson (2005a).

36. See Boone (2000b:89–96) for a summary of the contents of Codex Vindobonensis. Furst (1978) and Jansen (1982b) are book-length commentaries. For color screenfold facsimile reproductions of the codex, see Adelhofer (1963, 1974) and Anders, Jansen, and Pérez Jiménez (1992b, which includes a page-by-page reading of the manuscript).

37. Anders, Jansen, and Pérez Jiménez (1992a), with screenfold facsimile reproduction, is a detailed account of Codex Nuttall. Troike and Anders (1987) include a screenfold facsimile of the codex. The visual composition as a whole of the story of 3 Flint and 12 Wind in Codex Nuttall is weighed by Hamann (2004:101–107; see also Hamann 2002) and Johnson (2005a:178–88). Other discussions of this story include Jansen (1982b:332–44), Furst (1986), Byland and Pohl (1987), Dennis (1994:427–66), Pohl (1994b:32–35), and Jansen and Pérez Jiménez (2011:280–83).

38. The two sections of Codex Bodley that contain multiple parallel channels of space are the opening seven pages (40–34) and final eight pages (28–21) on the reverse side of the screenfold. Detailed readings of the codex are found in Caso (1960, with screenfold facsimile), and Jansen and Pérez Jiménez (2005, with color reproductions of all of its pages).

39. Caso and Smith (1966) include commentary by Caso on both the Codex Colombino and Codex Becker I portions of this manuscript, plus a screenfold facsimile reproduction of the Colombino section (both republished in Caso 1996). Nowotny (1961) includes a color reproduction of the Codex Becker I section. Troike (1974) includes a reconstruction of the fragmented Codex Colombino-Becker I and a thorough discussion of its badly damaged painted narrative.

40. On the Tututepec pages of Codex Colombino-Becker I and elsewhere in the codex, we repeatedly see sequences of events leading to important destinations or goals represented by oversize place signs or scenes. The sequences begin on the upper or lower registers and progress to their conclusions on the middle register, followed by consequences and new developments again on the upper or lower registers.

41. The Lienzo of Tlapiltepec is not the only single-sheet, cartographic-historical manuscript from the Mixteca in which the narrative moves from the edge of the sheet into the center, then expands outward toward the edges again. Another notable example of this design is the Lienzo of Zacatepec 1 (Johnson 2005a:323–28, 333–37).

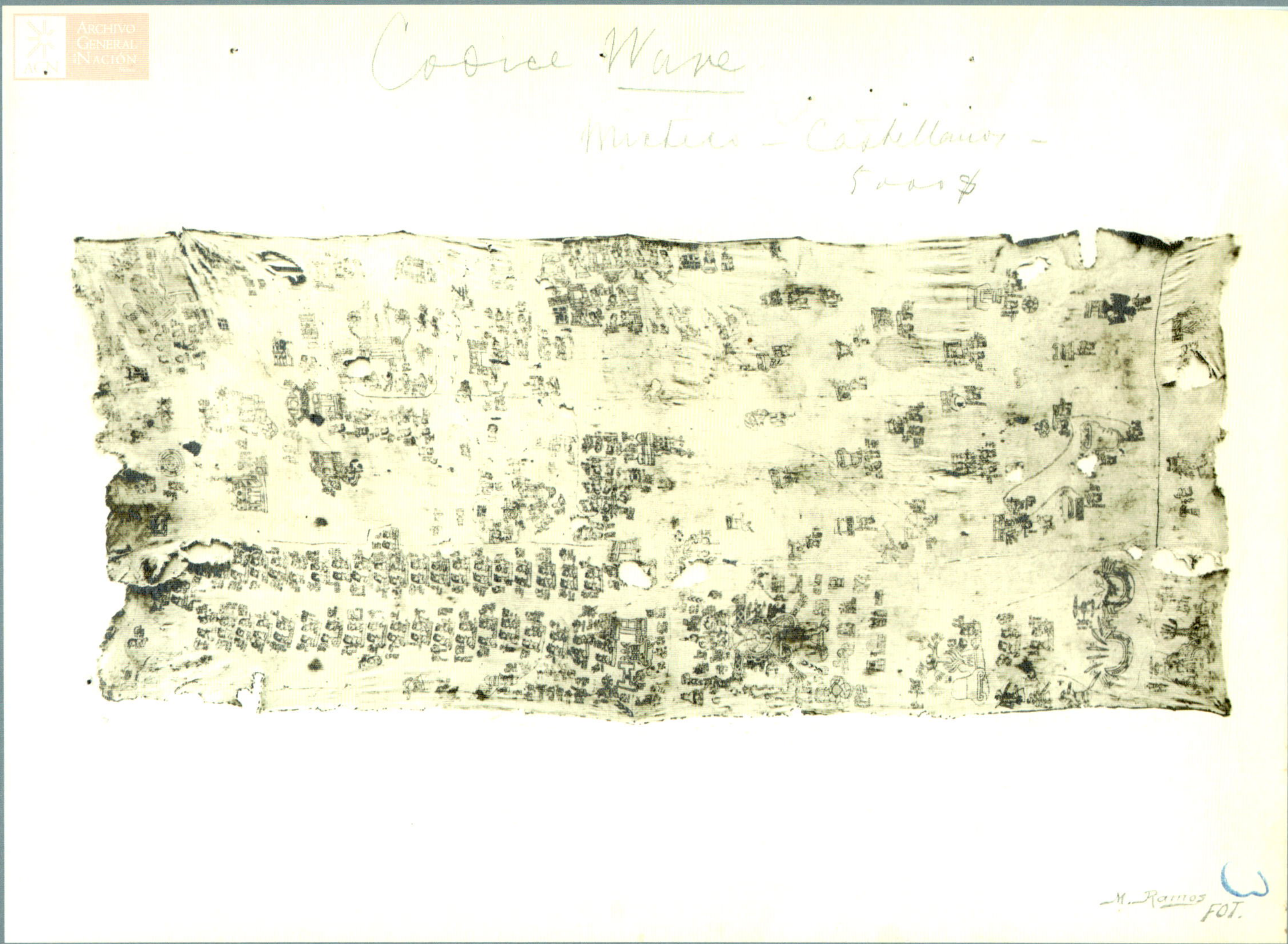

FIG. 4.1. Earliest known photograph of the lienzo, taken around 1908. Inscribed: "Códice *Wave* [Huave]. Mixteco—Castellanos—5000$" and signed, "M.[anuel] Ramos. FOT." Preserved in the Archivo General de la Nación, Mexico.

CHAPTER 4

Illustrating the Lienzo

ARNI BROWNSTONE AND ECKEHARD DOLINSKI

A freshly painted lienzo must have been a wonder to view. Its myriads of boldly outlined and brilliantly colored small figures, organized over an immense, pale field, narrated a complex array of events with economy and clarity. The secret of its legibility lay in how precisely the figures stood out against their neutral cotton background. Looking at the same lienzo today, its figure-to-ground relationship has shifted drastically, its black outlines much subdued and its colors and background merging toward gray. This aging process poses a significant impediment to our scholarly understanding of lienzos, and we look to visual aids to facilitate our study. Photographs are useful for analyzing details of lienzos but seldom do photos adequately capture overall views (fig. 4.1).

As a solution to the problem of how to provide visual access to these documents, scholars have traditionally turned to schematic illustrations, usually based on tracings of the original. This is particularly true in the present study. The story behind our illustration of the Lienzo of Tlapiltepec is told here so the reader can better gauge its reliability and formal qualities as a visual aid.

Over the past one-and-a-quarter centuries, a number of partial and complete illustrations of the Lienzo of Tlapiltepec have been made. The first was probably the colored detail made freehand by the Tlapiltepec schoolteacher Fidel López Sandoval at the request of historian Manuel Martínez Gracida between 1888 and 1892 (fig. 4.2).

Illustrations have long been produced by tracing the figures of an original manuscript onto a transparent or semi-transparent film. In 1912 Rickards (1913:47) noted at the International Congress of Americanists in London that Eduard Seler, the leading figure in Mesoamerican archaeology from about 1880 to 1920, and Paul Henning, an archaeologist who worked in Mexico at the Museo Nacional de Arqueología from 1909 to 1911, had both made illustrations of the complete lienzo (Rickards 1912:47). At the general meeting of the same congress on May 29, 1912, Alfred Maudslay, president of the Royal Anthropological Institute, "called attention to the large copy of the post-Columbian painting, called Codex Rickards, and the album

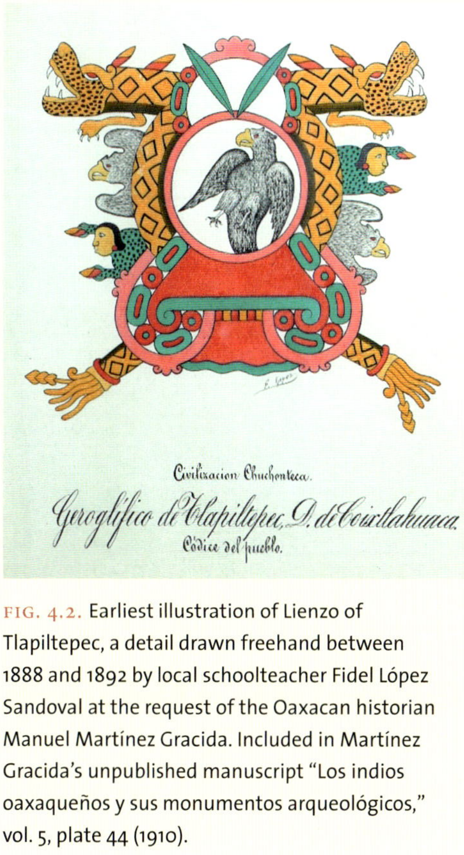

FIG. 4.2. Earliest illustration of Lienzo of Tlapiltepec, a detail drawn freehand between 1888 and 1892 by local schoolteacher Fidel López Sandoval at the request of the Oaxacan historian Manuel Martínez Gracida. Included in Martínez Gracida's unpublished manuscript "Los indios oaxaqueños y sus monumentos arqueológicos," vol. 5, plate 44 (1910).

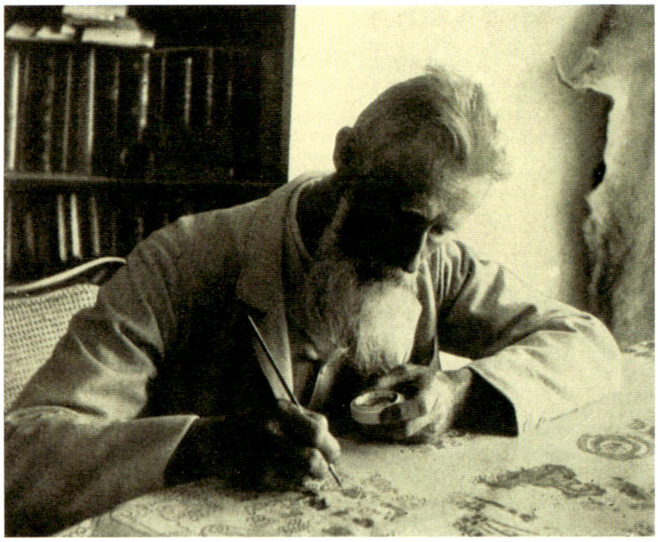

FIG. 4.3. Eduard Seler colors his tracing of the Lienzo de Tlapiltepec in Oaxaca, September 1910, probably at the home of Constantine Rickards. Photograph by Caecilie Seler-Sachs. Reproduced from Seler-Sachs, Lehmann, and Krickeberg (1927). The original photograph is lost.

of photographs of Zapotecan antiquities presented to the Congress by Mr. Constantino Rickards, of Oaxaca" (International Congress of Americanists 1913:xlii). Soon after the conference, Adela Breton, secretary of the congress, donated a full-size negative blueprint, presumably based on a partially colored-in tracing of the lienzo, to the British Museum Library (Manuscript Catalogue 1911–15). The figures are delineated in white on blue paper backed with white cloth. The blueprint is in two pieces measuring 161.4 by 33.5 inches and 155.7 by 33.5 inches. Breton noted that the copy contained errors, and later, Cottie Burland of the British Museum speculated that these were due to the tracing process. He suggested that because of the soft surface of the lienzo, sketching its figures with a pencil on tracing paper would have made a tracing too faint to produce a readable blueprint. Thus it was later gone over with ink (Parmenter 1982:19). A note written on the blueprint's storage box states: "Codex Rickards, photostatic copy, post-conquest genealogy. Constantine G. Rickards, 10 October 1926. Additional Mss 38,845." This suggests that Breton gave the copy to the library on Rickards's behalf. The copy does not appear to have been based on Seler's tracing, nor does it match the line drawings in Rickards's 1913 publication. It thus seems most likely that the blueprint is of the tracing made by Henning, but this has not been confirmed, as efforts to locate Henning's original have failed.

Fortunately, the location of Eduard Seler's tracing is known. Seler made his sixth and final research trip to Mexico in 1910. In September of that year he presided over the Seventeenth International Congress of Americanists, in Mexico City. It may have been then, when Abraham Castellanos gave the first public lecture on the Lienzo of Tlapiltepec, that Seler learned that the document resided in Rickards's home in Oaxaca. Seler had already collected two lienzos for the Ethnological Museum Berlin—Lienzo Seler I and Lienzo Seler II—and he hoped that the Lienzo of Tlapiltepec would become Lienzo Seler III. Rickards's price was too steep, however, and Seler settled for making his own life-size traced illustration (fig. 4.3). Seler wrote to Konrad Theodor Preuss, his assistant at the Ethnological Museum Berlin, "I came here [to Oaxaca] because I had the opportunity to get a lienzo, which is in private ownership (the owner bought it for 2000 pesos + 4000 marks). It is 4.4 m long and 1.4 m wide, is made in the good traditional style and has hieroglyphics in the character of Codex Borgia. However, the symbols that were drawn beside the hieroglyphs look very strange. I have copied them completely and colored them (six days' hard work)."[1]

At this time the lienzo must have been faded, much as it is today, with color no longer discernible in some passages. About a year later, Rickards (1913:48) noted, "At one time [the lienzo] must have been gorgeous with rich deep colors which have almost disappeared; but in parts, especially where animals are drawn, one can see vestiges of dark red, yellow, black and blue." Early twentieth century photographs show that virtually all the fading must have occurred before the date of collection, a fact

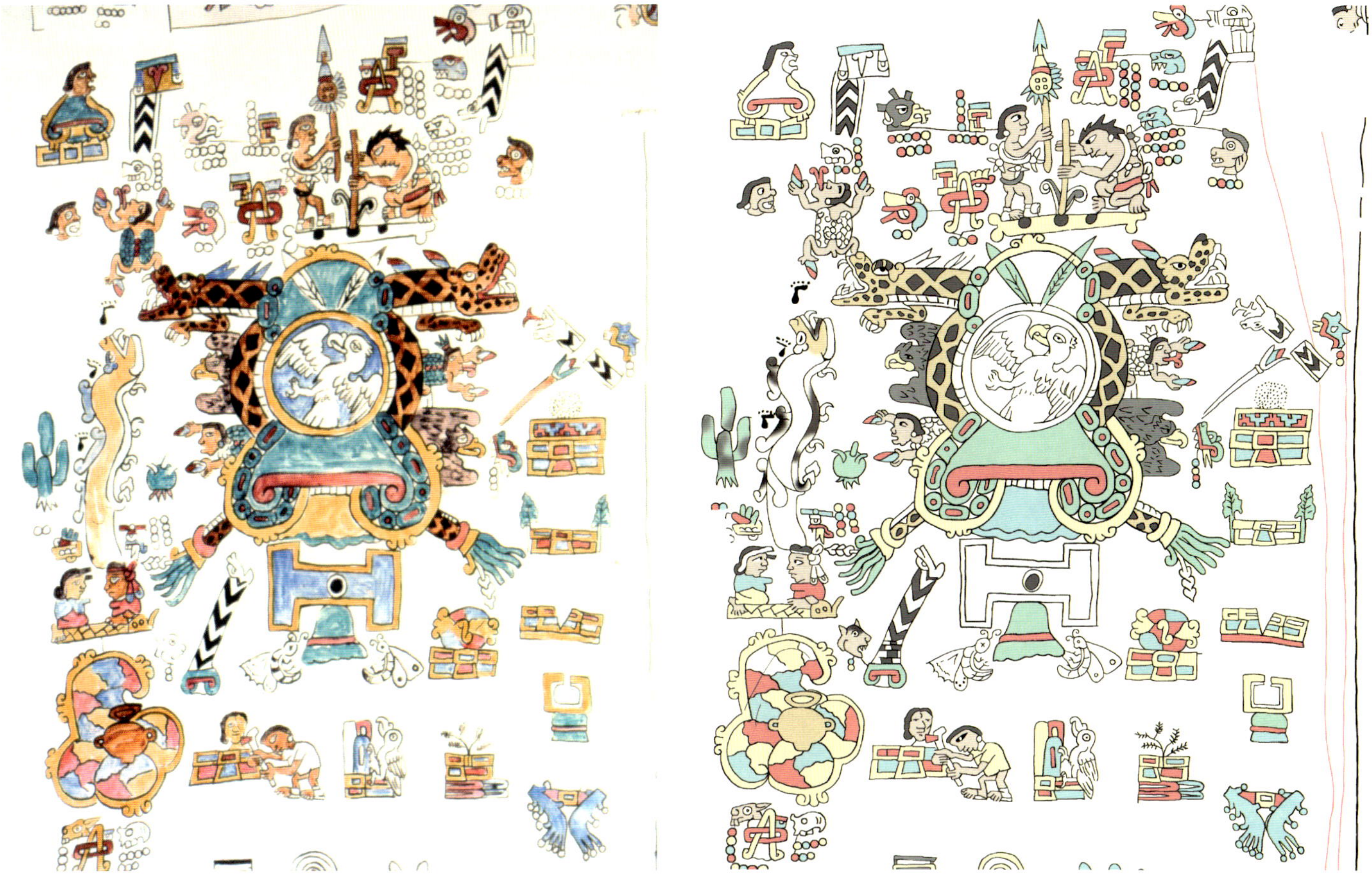

FIG. 4.4. Detail from Seler's illustration, *left*, compared with the illustration made for this book, *right*. Photo by Eckehard Dolinski.

supported by the likelihood that the lienzo has not been on display for more than a week during its hundred years at the Royal Ontario Museum.[2] Because Seler set out to create a schematic illustration rather than a reconstruction, he increased the intensity of his colors significantly beyond their original strength, much as he had on the thousands of brightly colored glyph cards that he produced for purposes of analysis over the course of his long career. Although color was indiscernible in many passages, Seler knew from experience that most of these passages had almost certainly once been filled in. He also knew that the distribution of colors was for the most part formulaic. Accordingly, Seler completely filled in almost all the figures on his illustration with bright colors that still stand out crisply against the overlapping, meter-wide sheets of white "Imperial Tracing Cloth" glued onto a sheet of canvas. While his illustration is in many respects excellent, Seler did miss a number of details, including several connecting lines and footprints. Most notably, he did not distinguish between red and black pathway lines. He also neglected to add color to the small circles that represent numbers in date and name signs. In creating the Royal Ontario Museum illustration, we refrained from consulting Seler's illustration and took our cues exclusively from the original. However, it is interesting to compare the two illustrations (fig. 4.4)

Seler deposited his illustration in the Ethnological Museum Berlin. Around 1937 it was moved from that museum to the Ibero-American Institute, Berlin, no doubt by Walter Lehmann, Seler's former student and successor.[3] More recently, between No-

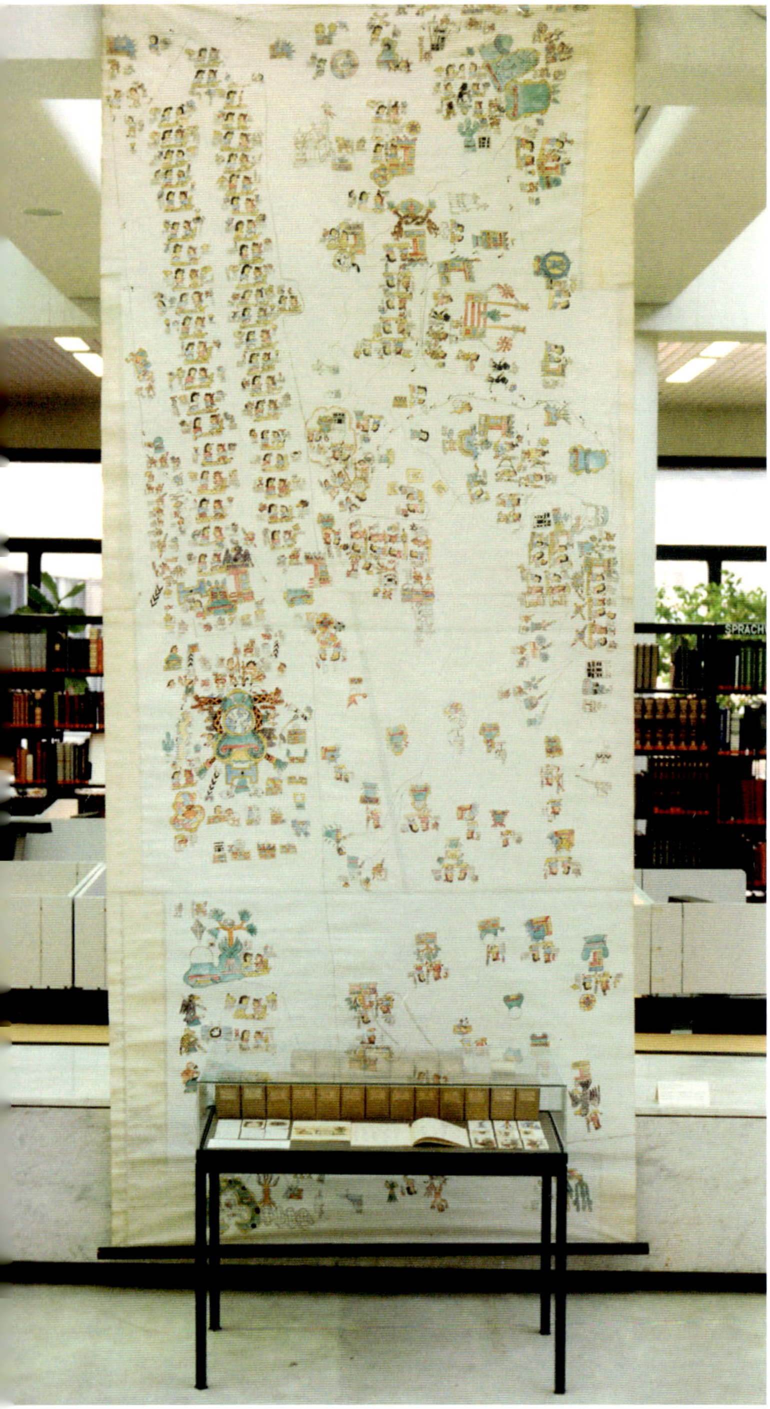

FIG. 4.5. Eduard Seler's illustration of the Lienzo of Tlapiltepec on display at the Ibero-American Institute, Berlin, November 11–December 31, 1991, in the exhibition "Eduard Seler: Pionier der Altamerikaforschung." Photo by Eckehard Dolinski.

vember 1991 and January 1992, Seler's tracing was put on public display at the Ibero-American Institute as part of an exhibition celebrating its creator (fig. 4.5). It was later displayed in the exhibition that accompanied an international colloquium on Seler, held at the Museo Nacional de Antropología e Historia in Mexico City in March 1999. Apparently, neither Seler's nor Henning's (now lost) versions have been published.

Howard Cline, editor of the *Guide to Ethnohistorical Sources* of the *Handbook of Middle American Indians*, noted additional early twentieth century illustrations of the lienzo: "Partial copies by Saldaña made about 1912 (*Boletin del Museo Nacional* ser. 3, 1:205, 262, Mexico, 1912) may correspond in part to copies itemized in an unpublished inventory of copies in the MNA [Museo Nacional de Antropología] in 1934 and now unknown." Around 1960 Cline set out to make his own illustration based on tracings from photographs. To that end, he requested a set of 8 × 10 prints from the Royal Ontario Museum in order to make a schematic diagram of the place glyphs on the Lienzo of Tlapiltepec. He noted, "As you can imagine, [it is] sometimes difficult to identify, let alone trace, some of the glyphs of such a large item as yours in the 8 × 10 size" (Cline to Kidd, May 5, 1961). We do not know whether Cline completed his illustration.

In 1988 Nicholas Johnson, a contributor to this book, made a new tracing of the lienzo. His primary focus was on the role of connecting lines. Many of the lines, especially the red ones, were too faded to be visible in photographs, so Johnson traced all the connecting lines from the original onto Mylar film. Then on a second piece of Mylar he traced a sixty-inch photograph of the lienzo to produce a line drawing of all the visible elements. To this he added the connecting lines freehand, based on his first tracing. His final illustration was in black and white, using dashes to represent the red lines (fig. 4.6). Johnson's tracing has been reproduced in a number of publications, including Johnson (1994, 1997), Brownstone (1996), Boone (2000b), and Doesburg (2000, 2010).

Around 1990 Helmuth Fuchs, then curator in the ethnology department of the Royal Ontario Museum, set out to make a full-size color illustration based on a tracing of the original, but stopped less than a quarter of the way through. More recently, the Club Rotary La Villa in Mexico City sponsored the production of another life-size illustration of the lienzo on September 21, 2011, and presented it to the community of San Mateo Tlapiltepec during its annual patron saint celebrations. It reproduces the black outlines of the figures, painted on a white cloth with no fill-in color. In her article published in a Oaxacan online journal, *Ciudadanía Express*, Beatriz García

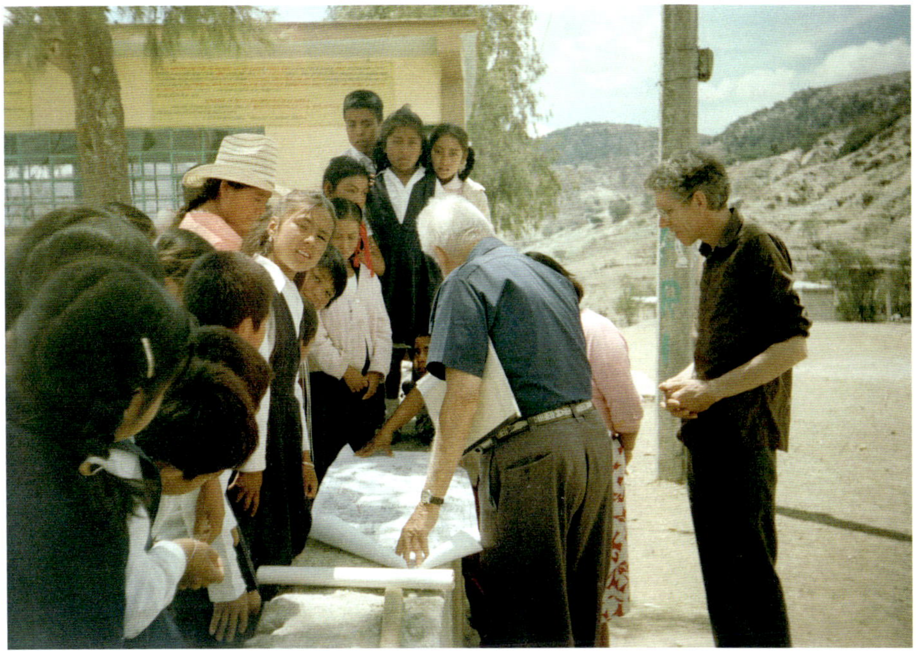

FIG. 4.6. Students and teachers (Socorro Quiroz Cruz and Eloisa Cruz Mejía) listen to Ross Parmenter interpret the images on an intermediate rendering of Nicholas Johnson's illustration of the lienzo. Johnson is at right. San Mateo Tlapiltepec, Oaxaca, April 15, 1988.

quotes a Tlapiltepec council member who believed that the new reproduction was based on a copy of the lienzo left by several historians who visited the community in 1986.[4] Although we have only seen this reproduction through several low-resolution images on the Internet, it appears to be drawn freehand, probably from a black-and-white photograph or drawing. The lower right corner, the only part visible in detail, shows a number of errors and omissions. Regardless of its quality, the very existence of the reproduction indicates the community of Tlapiltepec's continued interest in the lienzo and further confirms the need for an accurate and fully colored illustration, as brought forward in this volume.

Our illustration is the result of a collaborative effort. Arni Brownstone, coauthor of this chapter, has extensive experience producing electronic illustrations based on tracing Plains Indian pictographic paintings. He largely coordinated between the three other contributors. Georgia Guenther, the Royal Ontario Museum artist, rendered the illustration electronically using a stylus and tablet in Photoshop. It was the task of Eckehard Dolinski, the other coauthor of this chapter, to detect colors on the original through digital imaging. Nicholas Johnson's deep knowledge of the visual vocabulary of Mesoamerican manuscript painting guided us through areas of uncertainty.

The first version, completed in 2008, was intended to serve both for this book and the Latin American section of the Royal Ontario Museum's galleries as a life-size stand-in printed on vinyl, for the original could not be exhibited due to its sensitivity to light. The outlines were traced from eight overlapping high-resolution digital photographs of the lienzo, each taken from the same distance and camera angle. After all the figures were electronically traced, the underlying photographs were deleted, leaving eight black-and-white line drawings. These were then "stitched together" into a single outline drawing of the entire lienzo. Drawing electronically allows for considerable control, and we strove to lay down the line work as faithfully to the original as possible, avoiding the idealization of details in areas where the original artist lacked technical control; for example, in the delineation of toes on feet. In some instances the original painter purposely drew feet with the toes squared off.

The task of coloring was far more complex than tracing the outlines. From the beginning, we conceived of the illustration not so much as a copy of the lienzo in its current state, but as an interpretive rendering that maximized the readability of the visual information as it was conveyed in the original, freshly painted document. Between one iteration and another we progressively shifted away from replication and toward greater idealization. We began by adding color as if painting with a brush and filled in only those passages in which the color was readily discernible. For guidance on color strength and hue we looked to less-faded lienzos from the same region, relying most heavily on the Lienzo of Tequixtepec I. As we became practiced at detecting color in more faded areas, we grew more confident that almost all the figures on the lienzo had originally been completely filled in. We began to have a clearer understanding of how the lienzo was originally intended to appear, and our illustration evolved accordingly. We intensified our search for passages where color could be discerned, in part motivated by our understanding that the more figures we filled in, the more legible our illustration would be. To identify extremely faded colors on the lienzo, we employed color enhancement software called DStretch, developed by Jon Harman to make rock paintings more discernible.[5] DStretch is built on research by the U.S. National Aeronautics and Space Administration (NASA). It employs "decorrelation stretch" to manipulate digital images and is based on the "removal of the inter-channel correlation found in the input pixels" (see Ronald E. Alley, 1996, NASA website).

Hundreds of digital images of details of the lienzo were viewed through the "color spaces," or filters, that DStretch uses to distort and detect colors, as well as through filters available in Photoshop. Validation of a color was achieved in DStretch when it persisted after being viewed through successive "color spaces." Perhaps the greatest advantage to this exercise was that it stimulated us to repeatedly review details of the original afresh, and it somehow aided the naked eye to see with greater acuity. In the process we discovered and verified the presence of faint color in more and more passages.

The colors of certain details, such as strings of circles representing numbers and items of clothing, may vary considerably from painted manuscript to painted manuscript in the Mixtec and Chocho traditions. Still, overall, the manuscript painters predictably followed a great number of conventions or tendencies in their use of color. They used naturalistic color, painting vegetation and hills green, water and water-name signs blue, skin brown, and so forth. To make elements more distinguishable, they used contrasting colors for adjacent elements within any one figure. From manuscript to manuscript, painters also colored name and date signs with some consistency. In this context, we became better able to anticipate the identity of faded colors. We applied these predictable tendencies with caution, however, knowing that there were exceptions to the rule.

Despite our efforts to identify faded colors, areas of uncertainty held us back from completing the illustration. For example, we believed the palm or reed woven mats below ruling couples to be a pale yellow, while stronger yellow ochre was reserved for other elements, particularly those that were naturally more strongly colored, such as jaguars. Yet pale yellow could be detected in only a minority of mats. As another example, human skin was conventionally tinted brown, with women occasionally a lighter tone than men. Manuscripts that distinguish between men and women through contrasting flesh tones include the Tira de Tepechpan (Diel 2008:31) and Codex Magliabechiano from central Mexico, and Codex Egerton from the Mixteca. Influenced by such knowledge, Eduard Seler also differentiated between genders by shifting the tone on his illustration of the Lienzo of Tlapiltepec. As on the original today, Seler would have been able to discern that only a few faces were darker than the surrounding unpainted background, with no distinguishable difference in tone between men and women. Furthermore, in many cases we were not able to distinguish blue areas from green, notably in the case of hill place-signs.

To help us better understand the coloration of the lienzo, a team of specialists from the Canadian Conservation Institute (CCI) generously agreed to examine the document in early 2013.[6] They first attempted to enhance the lienzo's readability by imaging extremely faded areas under infrared and ultraviolet fluorescence photography; however, this exercise did not yield useful results. Color measurements were also taken using a spectrophotometer. In very faded areas, such as faces and reed mats, the reflectance spectra were indistinguishable from the unpainted support. Similar measurements taken in more strongly colored areas indicated that the lienzo painter employed a limited palette. Areas the naked eye faintly perceived as blue-green reflected spectra that were indistinguishable from areas thought to be blue. Color measurement also indicated that the painter used only one red and one yellow pigment.

In addition, the team conducted a detailed analysis of small samples of color to reliably identify the nature of pigments, fillers, and binding media. Paint samples taken from nineteen locations on the lienzo were analyzed using a combination of techniques, including color-scanning electron microscopy–energy dispersive spectrometry (SEM-EDS), Raman spectroscopy, Fourier transform infrared spectroscopy (FTIR), polarized light microscopy (PLM), and gas chromatography–mass spectrometry (GS-MS). The analysis of unpainted fabric areas consistently indicated the presence of low concentrations of a number of compounds: animal fat, beeswax, collagen-type protein, gallic acid, caffeine, *Pinaceae* resin, and DDE (a breakdown product of the insecticide DDT). According to the CCI report:

> The DDE is clearly from a modern treatment of the textile. The animal fat, beeswax, protein and *Pinaceae* resin could be original constituents that were applied during the preparation of the textile for weaving and/or painting. However, these materials could have been applied later. For instance, pine resin was commonly added to soap in the 19th century and, therefore, the use of resin soap to clean the lienzo might account for the trace amounts of *Pinaceae* resin in all the samples (Jean 1873). The caffeine and gallic acid are from a plant source but the reason for their presence is unknown.

Analysis of the thickly painted areas yielded organic compounds, likely corresponding to the paint medium. The major constituents identified in these were gum, collagen-type protein (glue), animal fat, and beeswax. While the lienzo did not appear to have an overall surface coating, it is possible that the constituents of the paint medium were also applied superficially to the unpainted areas.

The composition of the various pigments on the lienzo was also analyzed and identified. Samples of both dark and pale yellow were taken. Under a microscope, dark yellow appeared as a heavy accumulation of pigment, whereas light yellow appeared as pale staining of the textile fibers. The dark yellow proved to be composed of yellow ochre (consisting of goethite and silicates) and calcium carbonate. Tests of the pale yellow fibers did not indicate the presence of either yellow ochre or an organic yellow colorant, likely because the color was too faded or abraded. Red paint samples were found to contain cochineal with a trace of charcoal black and calcium carbonate. Cochineal derives from the scale of the dried female insect of the species *Dactylopius coccus*. Under the microscope, both the village hill signs, thought to be blue-green, and blue wavy lines in bodies of water appeared as similar accumulations of turquoise paint on the fibers. In both cases, it was found that the pigment was composed of Maya blue (a complex of palygorskite clay and indigo), calcium carbonate, and a small amount of iron oxide (hematite)—seemingly with no difference in composition between areas considered blue and those considered green. (Traces of yellow iron oxide were detected in one village hill sign.) However, Maya blue is believed to vary from blue to greenish depending on the ratio of indigo to clay (Helwig et al. 2013). Thick black paint used in outlines was shown to be composed of charcoal black, made from burned wood, and calcium carbonate, while gray paint contained a small amount of charcoal black. In sum, the analysis of the chemistry of colors revealed that the lienzo employed a total of four paint sources: cochineal red, Maya blue, yellow ochre, and charcoal black. The materials detected by the CCI are consistent with the main paints known to have been employed during the late pre-Hispanic and early colonial periods (see, for example, Olphen 1966; Altamirano Rocha 1982; Pareyón Moreno 2002). Not investigated were the few areas of white paint, as on a snow-capped mountain and between blue wavy lines in bodies of water.

While the CCI examination and analysis revealed significant information on the physical properties of paint on the lienzo, it did not resolve, and in some cases, added to our uncertainties about the coloring of the illustration. But it did bring us to a point where final decisions needed to be made. We decided to fill in some areas with color even though laboratory tests did not detect pigment there: brown on human skin, yellow on seating mats, and green on hill place-signs. We did so because we were sufficiently convinced by hints of those colors to the naked eye and confident in our knowledge of the visual language of the Coixtlahuaca lienzos and other related and comparable documents. In the end, relatively few passages on the lienzo were so elusive as to be left the color of the support textile, signifying that we were unable to reach a confident decision on the likely color of those areas. Furthermore, on the basis of better-preserved lienzos and other manuscripts substantially in the pre-Hispanic style, we realized that their painters strove to apply color as flat, stain-like fill-ins. Consequently, we once again began with a clean electronic line drawing and completely re-colored the illustration, this time filling in color passages uniformly instead of varying the tonality as in the previous version. The only exceptions were the few areas where we believed the original artist intended to modulate color tonality, and in several place signs where yellow appears to have been added as a means of identifying a desert or arid locality, such as the "Hill of the Knot" (Tlapiltepec) place sign in the middle right side of the lienzo.

Whenever possible we have relied on hard evidence as our guide in coloring the illustration; however, in many instances we were forced to apply calculated probabilities and educated generalizations. We took these decisions in an effort to represent the lienzo's original, newly painted state, culminating in an idealized rendering that we believe shares the same objectives of accuracy and legibility as the sixteenth-century lienzo painters.

NOTES

1. Seler to Preuss, October 30, 1910, p. 3. Ethnology Museum Berlin, Travels of Prof. Dr. Seler to America in the years 1906/07 and 1910/11. Seler's measurements are inaccurate, as the actual size of the Lienzo of Tlapiltepec is 3.97 × 1.67 m. His reference to strange symbols beside hieroglyphs is unclear.
2. The photographs, collected by Walter Lehmann in Mexico before 1919, are virtually contemporaneous with Seler's 1910 tracing and show the Lienzo of Tlapiltepec in much the same state at it is today (Lehmann Papers, Ibero-American Institute, Berlin). Parmenter (1961:10) noted that the lienzo had never been displayed in the Royal Ontario Museum (hereinafter ROM) but did not support his claim. There appears to be no record of the lienzo having been on display in the ROM. The only memory of it on display is in the 1990s when the ROM held a week-long celebration of Mexican culture.
3. Lehmann lost his position at the Ethnological Museum Berlin in 1934, apparently as a result of a plot by his colleague Walter Krickeberg (1885–1962), who sympathized with the National Socialists, then gaining power. He likely deposited the illustration, along with his papers, at the Ibero-American Institute when he began working there in 1937, shortly before his death in 1939.
4. http://ciudadania-express.com, October 17, 2011.
5. More about this enhancement technology is available at www.dstretch.com.
6. The team comprised Kate Helwig, Jennifer Poulin, Dominique Duguay, Season Tse, and Carl Bigras. Their results are found in the Canadian Conservation Institute report no. CSD 5032, CCI 125143, dated April 12, 2013.

REFERENCES

Acuña, René, ed.

1981–88 *Relaciones geográficas del siglo XVI.* 10 vols. Mexico City: Universidad Nacional Autónoma de México, Instituto de Investigaciones Antropológicas.

Adelhofer, Otto

1963 *Codex Vindobonensis Mexicanus I.* Introduction, color photographic screenfold facsimile. Reprinted 1974 with new facsimile reproduction. Graz, Austria: Akademische Druck- und Verlagsanstalt.

Aguilera, Carmen

1984 *Códice de Huamantla. Manuscrito de los siglos XVI y XVII, que se conserva en la Sala de Testimonios Pictográficos de la Biblioteca Nacional de Antropología e Historia y en la Biblioteca Estatal de Berlin. Estudio iconográfico, cartográfico e histórico.* Serie Códices y Manuscritos Tlaxcala 2. Tlaxcala, Mexico: Instituto Tlaxcalteca de la Cultura.

1986 *Lienzos y códices de Tepeticpac: Estudio iconográfico.* Serie Códices y Manuscritos Tlaxcala 4. Tlaxcala, Mexico: Instituto Tlaxcalteca de la Cultura.

Aguirre Beltrán, Hilda Judith

1997 "El Lienzo de Cuauhquechollac, algunos ejemplos de lectura." In *Códices y documentos sobre México: Segundo Simposio,* 2 vols., edited by Salvador Rueda Smithers, Constanza Vega Sosa, and Rodrigo Martínez Baracs, 1:377–91. Mexico City: Instituto Nacional de Antropología e Historia; Consejo Nacional para la Cultura y las Artes.

Altamirano Rocha, Sara Eugenia

1982 *Tecnología y conservación de los lienzos de Tuxpan, Ver.* Thesis, Escuela Nacional de Conservación, Restauración y Museografía Manuel del Castillo Negrete, Mexico City.

Altamirano Rocha, Sara Eugenia, and Alma Rosa Rubí

1989 *El lienzo de Carapan: Estudio histórico, iconográfico y de restauración.* Cuaderno de Trabajo 2. Mexico City: Dirección de Restauración del Patrimonio Cultural; Instituto Nacional de Antropología e Historia; Secretaría de Educación Pública.

Anawalt, Patricia Rieff

1981 *Indian Clothing before Cortés: Mesoamerican Costumes from the Codices.* Norman: University of Oklahoma Press.

Anders, Ferdinand, Maarten Jansen, and Gabina Aurora Pérez Jiménez

1992a *Crónica mixteca: El rey 8 Venado, Garra de Jaguar, y la dinastía de Teozacoalco-Zaachila. Libro explicativo del llamado Códice Zouche Nuttall.* With color photographic screenfold facsimile. Madrid: Sociedad Estatal Quinto Centenario; Graz, Austria: Akademische Druck- und Verlagsanstalt; Mexico City: Fondo de Cultura Económica.

1992b *Origen e historia de los reyes mixtecos. Libro explicativo del llamado Códice Vindobonensis.* With color photographic screenfold facsimile. Madrid: Sociedad Estatal Quinto Centenario; Graz, Austria: Akademische Druck- und Verlagsanstalt; Mexico City: Fondo de Cultura Económica.

Asselbergs, Florine G. L.

2004 *Conquered Conquistadors: The Lienzo de Quauhquechollan, a Nahua Vision of the Conquest of Guatemala.* Leiden, Netherlands: Research School of Asian, African, and Amerindian Studies (CNWS), Leiden University.

Austin Krumholz, Jeanne, Marjorie Kalstrom Dolson, and Miguel Hernández Ayuso

1995 *Diccionario popoloca de San Juan Atzingo, Puebla.* Tucson, Ariz.: Summer Institute of Linguistics.

Batalla Rosado, Juan José

2008 "Un glifo de la tradición escrituraria mixteca: El signo 'cerro' con doble voluta." In *Mixtec Writing and Society: Escritura de Ñuu Dzaui*, edited by Maarten E. R. G. N. Jansen and Laura N. K. Broekhoven, 305–25. Proceedings of the Colloquium, Amsterdam, September 2005. Amsterdam: Koninklijke Nederlandse Akademie van Wetenschappen Press.

Belmar, Francisco

1901 *Breve reseña histórica y geográfica del estado de Oaxaca.* Oaxaca, Mexico: Imprenta del Comercio.

Berdan, Frances F., and Patricia Rieff Anawalt

1992 *The Codex Mendoza.* 4 vols. Berkeley: University of California Press.

Bernal, Ignacio

1948 "Exploraciones en Coixtlahuaca." *Revista Mexicana de Estudios Antropológicos* 10:5–76.

Bierhorst, John

1992 *History and Mythology of the Aztecs: The Codex Chimalpopoca.* Tucson: University of Arizona Press.

Boone, Elizabeth Hill

1998 "Maps of Territory, History, and Community in Aztec Mexico." In *Cartographic Encounters: Perspectives on Native American Mapmaking and Map Use*, edited by G. Malcolm Lewis, 111–34. Chicago: University of Chicago Press.

2000a "Bringing Polity to Place: Aztec and Mixtec Foundation Rituals." In *Códices y documentos sobre México: Tercer Simposio Internacional*, edited by Constanza Vega Sosa, 547–73. Mexico City: Instituto Nacional de Antropología e Historia.

2000b *Stories in Red and Black: Pictorial Histories of the Aztecs and Mixtecs.* Austin: University of Texas Press.

2003 "A Web of Understanding: Pictorial Codices and the Shared Intellectual Culture of Late Postclassic Mesoamerica." In *The Postclassic Mesoamerican World*, edited by Michael E. Smith and Frances F. Berdan, 207–21. Salt Lake City: University of Utah Press.

2007 *Cycles of Time and Meaning in the Mexican Books of Fate.* Austin: University of Texas Press.

Boone, Elizabeth Hill, and Walter D. Mignolo, eds.

1994 *Writing without Words: Alternative Literacies in Mesoamerica and the Andes.* Durham: Duke University Press.

Borah, Woodrow

1943 *Silk Raising in Colonial Mexico.* Ibero-Americana 20. Berkeley and Los Angeles: University of California Press.

Borah, Woodrow, and Sherbourne F. Cook

1958 *Price Trends of Some Basic Commodities in Central Mexico, 1531–1570.* Ibero-Americana 40. Berkeley and Los Angeles: University of California Press.

Brownstone, Arni

1996 "Lienzo of Tlapiltepec: A Weaving of Ancient Mexican History." *Que Pasa* (Toronto) 1, no. 4 (Winter 1996): 15–18.

Burgoa, Francisco de

1934 *Palestria Historia.* Publicaciones del Archivo General de la Nación, vol. XXIV. Mexico City: Archivo General de la Nación.

Burland, Cottie A.

1955 *The Selden Roll: An Ancient Mexican Picture Manuscript in the Bodleian Library at Oxford.* Monumenta Americana 2. Berlin: Verlag Gebr. Mann.

1960 "The Map as a Vehicle of Mexican History." *Imago Mundi* 15:11–18.

1965 *Codex Egerton 2895, British Museum, London.* Introduction, color photographic screenfold facsimile. Graz, Austria: Akademische Druck- und Verlagsanstalt.

Byland, Bruce E., and John M. D. Pohl

1987 "The Marriage of 12 Wind and 3 Flint at White Hill." *Thesis* 2: 10–17.

1994 *In the Realm of 8 Deer: The Archaeology of the Mixtec Codices.* Norman: University of Oklahoma Press.

Campbell, Lyle

1997 *American Indian Languages: The Historical Linguistics of Native America.* Oxford Studies in Anthropological Linguistics 4. New York: Oxford University Press.

Carrasco, Davíd, and Scott Sessions, eds.

2007 *Cave, City, and Eagle's Nest: An Interpretive Journey through the Mapa de Cuauhtinchan no. 2.* Albuquerque: University of New Mexico Press.

Caso, Alfonso

1949 "El Mapa de Teozacoalco." *Cuadernos Americanos* 8 (5): 145–81.

1954 *Interpretación del Códice Gómez de Orozco*. Mexico City: Talleres de Impresión de Estampillas y Valores.

1958 "Comentario al Códice Baranda." In *Miscelánea Paul Rivet, octogenario dicata,* 1:373–89. Mexico City: Universidad Nacional Autónoma de México. Reprinted in Caso 1989, 63–73.

1960 *Interpretation of the Codex Bodley 2858*. Commentary, color photographic facsimile screenfold. Translated by Ruth Morales and revised by John Paddock. Mexico City: Sociedad Mexicana de Antropología.

1961 "Los lienzos mixtecos de Ihuitlán y Antonio de León." In *Homenaje a Pablo Martínez del Río en el vigésimoquinto aniversario de la primera edición de* Los origenes americanos, 237–74. Mexico City: Instituto Nacional de Antropología e Historia. Reprinted in Caso 1989, 75–103.

1965 "Mixtec Writing and Calendar." In *Handbook of Middle American Indians*, vol. 3, *Archaeology of Southern Mesoamerica*, edited by Gordon R. Willey, 948–61. Austin: University of Texas Press.

1977 *Reyes y reinos de la Mixteca*. Vol. 1. Mexico City: Fondo de Cultura Económica.

1979 *Reyes y reinos de la Mixteca*, Vol. 2, *Diccionario biográfico de los señores mixtecos*. Mexico City: Fondo de Cultura Económica.

1989 *Alfonso Caso: De la arqueología a la antropología*. Preface by Rafael Pérez Taylor. Mexico City: Universidad Nacional Autónoma de México.

1996 *Códice Alfonso Caso: La vida de 8-Venado, Garra de Tigre*. Introduction by Miguel León-Portilla; color photographic facsimile of the combined codices Colombino and Becker I with Caso's 1966 commentary. Mexico City: Patronato Indígena.

Caso, Alfonso, and Mary Elizabeth Smith

1966 *Interpretación del Códice Colombino / Interpretation of the Codex Colombino* [by Caso]. *Las glosas del Códice Colombino / The Glosses of the Codex Colombino* [by Smith]. With color photographic screenfold facsimile of Codex Colombino. Mexico City: Sociedad Mexicana de Antropología.

Castañeda de la Paz, María, and Sebastián (Bas) van Doesburg

2008 "Coatepec en las fuentes del centro de México y su presencia en el valle de Coixtlahuaca." In *Pictografía y escritura alfabética en Oaxaca*, edited by Sebastián (Bas) van Doesburg, 161–96. Oaxaca, Mexico: Instituto Estatal de Educación Pública.

Castellanos, Abraham

1912a "La cronología indiana." *Anales del Museo Nacional,* 3rd ser., 3:435–85.

1912b "El rayo de la luz y la cronología indiana." In *Reseña de la segunda sesión del XVII Congreso Internacional de Americanistas efectuado en la ciudad de México durante el mes de septiembre de 1910*, 120–33. Mexico City: Imprenta del Museo Nacional.

1917 *Conferencias histórico-pedagógicas*, 1–21, 41–44. Mérida, Yucatan.

Celestino Solís, Eustaquio, and Luis Reyes García

1992 *Anales de Tecamachalco, 1398–1590.* Mexico City: Centro de Investigaciones y Estudios Superiores en Antropología Social (CIESAS); Gobierno del Estado de Puebla; Fondo de Cultura Económica.

Chimalpain Cuauhtlehuanitzin, Domingo Francisco de San Antón Muñón

2003 *Séptima relación de las différentes histoires originales.* Paleography and translation by Josefina García Quintana. Mexico City: Universidad Nacional Autónoma de México.

Coe, Michael, and Justin Kerr

1997 *The Art of the Maya Scribe.* London and New York: Thames and Hudson.

Cordero Avedaño de Durand, Carmen

2001 *Lienzo del pueblo del señor San Pedro Nexicho.* Oaxaca, Mexico: Instituto Estatal Electoral de Oaxaca.

2004 *Interpretación y estudio del lienzo de San Juan Chicomezúchitl: El mapa o pintura de los cogues o señores.* Oaxaca, Mexico: Instituto Oaxaqueño de las Culturas; Gobierno del Estado de Oaxaca.

Corona Núñez, José

1964–67 *Antigüedades de México basadas en la recopilación de Lord Kingsborough.* 4 vols. Vol. 2, Codex Boturini, 7–29. Mexico City: Secretaría de Hacienda y Crédito Público.

Cortés, Hernán

1986 *Hernán Cortés: Letters from Mexico.* Translated and edited by Anthony Pagden with Introduction by J. H. Elliott. New Haven and London: Yale University Press.

Covarrubias, Miguel

1957 *Indian Art of Mexico and Central America.* New York: Alfred A. Knopf.

Dennis, Bryan Jerome

1994 "Hypertext and the Mixtec Screenfolds: Explorations in Writing, History, and Power." Ph.D. diss., University of California at Los Angeles.

Díaz del Castillo, Bernal

1956 *The Discovery and Conquest of Mexico, 1517–1521.* Translated by Irving A. Leonard, edited by Genaro García. New York: Farrar, Straus and Cudahy.

Dibble, Charles E.

1996 *Códice Xolotl.* 2 vols. Mexico City: Universidad Nacional Autónoma de México; Instituto Mexiquense de Cultura.

Diel, Lori Boornazian

2008 *The Tira de Tepechpan: Negotiating Place under Aztec and Spanish Rule.* With color reproduction of the manuscript. Austin: University of Texas Press.

Doesburg, Sebastián (Bas) van

1998a "Los lienzos pictográficos de don Francisco Belmar." *Mexicon* 20 (3): 52–54.

1998b “Commercializing Coixtlahuaca History: The Twentieth-Century Adventures of the Lienzo of Tlapiltepec.” *Mexican Codices and Archaeology.* Special issue, *Indiana Journal of Hispanic Literatures* 13 (Fall): 59–66.

2000 “Origin of the Lienzo de Tulancingo: New Facts about a Pictographic Document from the Coixtlahuaca Region.” *Ancient Mesoamerica* 11:169–83.

2001 “De linderos y lugares: Territorio y asentamiento en el Lienzo de Santa María Nativitas.” *Iconografía y Gobierno Indígena*. Special issue, *Relaciones: Estudios de Historia y Sociedad* 22, no. 86 (Spring): 17–82.

2002 *Documentos antiguos de San Miguel Tequixtepec, Oaxaca: Los primeros cien años de la colonia (1533–1617).* Leiden, Netherlands: Research School of Asian, African, and Amerindian Studies (CNWS), Leiden University.

2004 “El siglo XVI en los lienzos de Coixtlahuaca.” *Journal de la Société des Américanistes* 89 (2): 67–96.

2010a “Asentamiento y transición en el Lienzo de San Jerónimo Otla, Coixtlahuaca.” *Legitimación de la tierra entre los indígenas del México colonial*. Special issue, *Relaciones: Estudios de Historia y Sociedad* 31, no. 122 (Spring): 55–105.

2010b “Una colección olvidada: Los 5 lienzos de don Francisco Belmar.” In *El filólogo de Tlaxiaco: Un homenaje académico a Francisco Belmar*, edited by Francisco Barriga Puente, 129–38. Mexico City: Instituto Nacional de Antropología e Historia.

2012 “Collective Memory in Oaxaca: Reshaping Indigenous History.” In *Mesoamerican Memory: Enduring Systems of Remembrance*, edited by Amos Megged and Stephanie Wood, 129–46. Norman: University of Oklahoma Press.

Doesburg, Sebastián (Bas) van, and Olivier van Buren

1997 “The Prehispanic History of the Valley of Coixtlahuaca, Oaxaca.” In *Códices, Caciques y Comunidades*, edited by Maarten Jansen and Luis Reyes García, 103–60. Cuadernos de Historia Latinoamericana, no. 5. Ridderkerk, Netherlands: Asociación de Historiadores Latinoamericanistas Europeos.

Doesburg, Sebastián (Bas) van, and Michael W. Swanton

2008 “La traducción de la ‘Doctrina cristiana en lengua mixteca’ de fray Benito Hernández al chocholteca (ngiwa).” In *Memorias del Coloquio Francisco Belmar: Conferencias sobre Lenguas Otomangues y Oaxaqueñas*, vol. 2, edited by Ausencia López Cruz and Michael Swanton, 81–118. Oaxaca, Mexico: Biblioteca Francisco de Burgoa, Universidad Autónoma Benito Júarez de Oaxaca; Colegio Superior para la Educación Integral Intercultural de Oaxaca (CSEIIO); Fundación Alfredo Harp Helú Oaxaca; Instituto Nacional de Lenguas Indígenas (INLI).

2011 “Mesoamerican Philology as an Interdisciplinary Study: The Chochon (Xru Ngiwa) ‘Barrios’ of Tamazulapan (Oaxaca, Mexico).” *Ethnohistory* 58 (4): 613–52.

Durán, Fray Diego de

1984 *Historia de las Indias de Nueva España e Islas de la Tierra Firme*. 2 vols. Mexico City: Editorial Porrúa.

Fernández de Miranda, María Teresa

1961 Toponimia popoloca. In *A William Cameron Townsend en el vigésimoquinto aniversario del Instituto Lingüístico de Verano*, 431–47. Mexico, n.p.

Fernández Gatica, Andrés, José Alberto Figueroa Silvestre, Gerardo Morales, and Ignacio González Cejudo

2002 *Proposición de lectura del Lienzo de Zacatepec: Método galarziano. Los dos lienzos de Zacatepec, Oaxaca, siglo XVI.* Puebla, Mexico: Asociación Anahuacayotl de Tlaxcalancingo.

Forsyth, L[ouis] N.

1912 "Notes on the Mixteca." *Records of the Past* 11:266–69.

Freed, Stanley A.

2012 *Anthropology Unmasked: Museums, Science, and Politics in New York City.* 2 vols. Wilmington, Ohio: Orange Frazer Press.

Fuentes, Patricia, ed.

1963 *The Conquistadors: First-Person Accounts of the Conquest of Mexico.* New York: Orion.

Furst, Jill Leslie

1978 *Codex Vindobonensis Mexicanus I: A Commentary.* Institute of Mesoamerican Studies, publ. no. 4. Albany: State University of New York.

1986 "The Lords of 'Place of the Ascending Serpent': Dynastic Succession on the Nuttall Obverse." In *Symbol and Meaning beyond the Closed Community: Essays in Mesoamerican Ideas*, edited by Gary H. Gossen, 57–68. Albany: State University of New York, Institute of Mesoamerican Studies.

Galarza, Joaquín

1972 *Lienzos de Chiepetlan: Manuscrits pictographiques et manuscrits en caractères latins de San Miguel Chiepetlan, Guerrero, Mexique.* Mexico City: Mission Archéologique Française au Mexique.

García Icazbalceta, Joaquín

1891 *Colección de documentos para la historia de México.* Vol. 3. Mexico City: Imprenta de Francisco de León.

García Valencia, Enrique Hugo

2008 "El morral huasteco." In *El arte de los pueblos indígenas de México: Memoria del II Coloquio Nacional de Arte Popular*, edited by Arturo Gómez Martínez, 29–34. Xalapa,Veracruz, Mexico: Gobierno del Estado de Veracruz; Consejo Veracruzano de Arte Popular.

2010 "Urdimbres y tramas complejas." Paper presented at Instituto de Antropología, Universidad Veracruzana, Xalapa, Veracruz, August 25, 2010, and annual meeting of Society for American Archaeology, Sacramento, Calif., March 30–April 3, 2011.

n.d.a "Memoria histórica: Tecnología y estética." Unpublished draft paper.

n.d.b "La colonización del cuerpo: Género y política en el uso del calzón y el quechquemitl." Unpublished draft paper.

Garibay, Angel María

1979 *Teogonía e historia de los mexicanos: Tres opúsculos del siglo XVI.* Mexico City: Editorial Porrúa.

Gerhard, Peter

1986 *Geografía histórica de la Nueva España, 1519–1821.* Mexico City: Universidad Nacional Autónoma de México.

1992 *Síntesis e índice de los mandamientos virreinales, 1548–1553.* Mexico City: Universidad Nacional Autónoma de México.

1993 *A Guide to the Historical Geography of New Spain.* Rev. ed. Norman: University of Oklahoma Press. First published 1972 by Cambridge University Press.

Glass, John B.

1964 *Catálogo de la colección de códices.* Mexico City: Museo Nacional de Antropología; Instituto Nacional de Antropología e Historia.

1974 *Lienzo Totomixtlahuaca 1570 (Códice Condumex).* Mexico City: Centro de Estudios de Historia de México Condumex.

1975 "A Survey of Native Middle American Pictorial Manuscripts." In *Handbook of Middle American Indians*, vol. 14, *Guide to Ethnohistorical Sources*, pt. 3, edited by Howard F. Cline, 3–80. Austin: University of Texas Press.

Glass, John B., and Donald Robertson

1975 "A Census of Native Middle American Pictorial Manuscripts." In *Handbook of Middle American Indians*, vol. 14, *Guide to Ethnohistorical Sources*, pt. 3, edited by Howard F. Cline, 81–252. Austin: University of Texas Press.

Graulich, Michel

2002 "Los Reyes de Tollan." *Revista Española de Antropología Americana* 32:87–114.

Gruzinski, Serge

1993 *The Conquest of Mexico: The Incorporation of Indian Societies in the Western World, 16th–18th Centuries.* Translated by Eileen Corrigan. Cambridge, England: Polity Press.

Gudschinsky, Sarah

1959 *Proto-Popotecan: A Comparative Study of Popolocan and Mixtecan.* Indiana Research Center in Anthropology, Folklore and Linguistics 15. Supplement to *International Journal of American Linguistics* 25 (2). Baltimore: Waverly Press.

Guevara Hernández, Jorge

1991 *El lienzo de Tlapiltepec: Extinción de un señorío zapoteco.* Mexico City: Instituto Nacional de Antropología e Historia.

Hagen, Victor Wolfgang von

1999 *The Aztec and Maya Papermakers.* Mineola, N.Y.: Dover Publications. First published 1944 by J. J. Augustin.

Hamann, Byron

2002 "The Social Life of Pre-Sunrise Things: Indigenous American Archaeology." *Current Anthropology* 43, no. 3 (June): 351–82.

2004 "Seeing and the Mixtec Screenfolds." *Visible Language* 38 (1): 66–124.

Helwig, Kate, et al.

2013 "Examination and Analysis of Samples from the Lienzo of Tlapiltepec for Royal Ontario Museum." Conservation Science Division, Canadian Conservation Institute, Government of Canada, Ottawa. Report no. CSD 5032, CCI 125143.

Hermann Lejarazu, Manuel

2003 *Códice Muro: Un documento mixteco colonial. Estudio, interpretación, paleografía y traducción.* Oaxaca, Mexico: Gobierno del Estado de Oaxaca, Secretaría de Asuntos Indígenas.

2010 "El Lienzo de Tlapiltepec." *Arqueología Mexicana* 18 (106): 16–17.

2011 "Los glifos de Teposcolula y Yanhuitlán: La identificación de dos topónimos elusivos." *Cuadernos del Sur* (Oaxaca) 30.

Hopkins, Nicholas A.

1984 "Otomanguean Linguistic Prehistory." In *Essays in Otomanguean Culture History*, edited by J. Kathryn Josserand, Marcus C. Winter, and Nicholas A. Hopkins, 25–64. Vanderbilt University Publications in Anthropology, no. 31. Nashville, Tenn.: Vanderbilt University.

Huerta, Alejandro, and Eugenia Berthier, eds.

2002 *El Lienzo de Cuetzpala, Puebla: Un estudio integral.* Mexico City: Instituto Nacional de Antropología e Historia.

International Congress of Americanists

1913 *Proceedings of the XVIII Session, London, 1912.* London: Harrison and Sons.

Jäcklein, Klaus

1978 *Los Popolocas de Tepexi, Puebla: Un estudio etnohistórico.* Wiesbaden, Germany: Franz Steiner Verlag.

1979 "Apuntes sobre la historia prehispánica de los popolocas de Puebla." In *Mesoamerica, homenaje al doctor Paul Kirchhoff*, edited by Barbro Dahlgren, 194–211. Mexico City: Instituto Nacional de Antropología e Historia.

Jansen, Maarten E. R. G. N.

1982a "The Four Quarters of the Mixtec World." In *Space and Time in the Cosmovision of Mesoamerica*, edited by Franz Tichy, 85–95. Lateinamerika Studien 10. Munich: Wilhelm Fink.

1982b *Huisi tacu: Estudio interpretativo de un libro mixteco antiguo: Codex Vindobonensis Mexicanus I.* 2 vols. Amsterdam: Centrum voor Studie en Documentatie van Latijns Amerika.

1983 "La expedición hacia Cuauhtinchan: Contactos entre mixtecos, chocho-popolocas y nahuas en la época postclásica." Paper presented at the annual meeting of the Grupo de Trabajo Latinoamericano, Leiden University, October 12, 1983.

1988 "The Art of Writing in Ancient Mexico: An Ethno-Iconological Perspective." In *Visible Religion: Annual for Religious Iconography*, vol. 6, *The Image in Writing*, 86–113. Leiden, Netherlands: E. J. Brill.

1989 "Nombres históricos e identidad étnica en los códices mixtecos." *Revista Europea de Estudios Latinoamericanos y del Caribe* 47:65–87.

1992 “Mixtec Pictography: Conventions and Contents.” In *Supplement to the Handbook of Middle American Indians*, vol. 5, *Epigraphy*, edited by Victoria Reifler Bricker and Patricia A. Andrews, 20–33. Austin: University of Texas Press.

1994 *La gran familia de los reyes mixtecos: Libro explicativo de los códices llamados Egerton y Becker II*. With color photographic screenfold facsimiles of Codex Egerton and the Vienna fragment of Codex Becker II. Graz, Austria: Akademische Druck- und Verlagsanstalt; Mexico City: Fondo de Cultura Económica.

1996 “Lord 8 Deer and Nacxitl Topiltzin.” *Mexicon* 18 (2): 25–29.

1998 “La Fuerza de los Cuatro Vientos. Los manuscritos 20 y 21 del fonds mexicain.” *Journal de la Société des Américanistes*, 84-2: 125–61.

Jansen, Maarten E. R. G. N., and Margarita Gaxiola

1978 *Primera Mesa Redonda de Estudios Mixtecos: Síntesis de las ponencias*. Estudios de Antropología e Historia, no. 15. Oaxaca, Mexico: Centro Regional de Oaxaca, Instituto Nacional de Antropología e Historia.

Jansen, Maarten E. R. G. N., and Gabina Aurora Pérez Jiménez

2000 *La dinastía de Añute: Historia, literatura e ideología de un reino mixteco*. Commentary on Codex Selden, with line drawing of the manuscript. Leiden, Netherlands: Research School of Asian, African, and Amerindian Studies (CNWS), Leiden University.

2004 “Renaming the Mexican Codices.” *Ancient Mesoamerica* 15:267–71.

2005 *Codex Bodley: A Painted Chronicle from the Mixtec Highlands, Mexico*. Treasures from the Bodleian Library 1. Oxford: Bodleian Library, University of Oxford.

2007 *Encounter with the Plumed Serpent: Drama and Power in the Heart of Mesoamerica*. Boulder: University Press of Colorado.

2011 *The Mixtec Pictorial Manuscripts: Time, Agency and Memory in Ancient Mexico*. Leiden, Netherlands: Brill.

Jean, F.

1872 “Note on the Analysis of Soap.” *American Chemist* 3, nos. 1–12 (July 1872–June 1873): 164–65.

Jiménez, Blanca M., and Samuel L. Villela

1998 *Historia y cultura tras el glifo: Los códices de Guerrero*. Mexico City: Instituto Nacional de Antropología e Historia.

Jiménez Moreno, Wigberto, and Salvador Mateos Higuera, eds.

1940 *Códice de Yanhuitlán*. Mexico City: Secretaría de Educación Pública; Instituto Nacional de Antropología e Historia; Museo Nacional.

Johnson, Nicholas

1992 “The Genealogical Map on the Lienzo of Tlapiltepec.” Master’s thesis, University of New Mexico.

1994a “Las líneas rojas desvanecidas en el Lienzo de Tlapiltepec.” In *Códices y documentos sobre México: Primer Simposio*, edited by Constanza Vega Sosa, 117–44. Mexico City: Instituto Nacional de Antropología e Historia.

1994b Report on the Copy of Lienzo Seler II (Lienzo of Coixtlahuaca 2) at the American Museum of Natural History, New York. Unpublished report on file at the AMNH, 1994.

1997 "The Route from the Mixteca Alta into Southern Puebla on the Lienzo of Tlapiltepec." In *Códices y documentos sobre México: Segundo Simposio*, 2 vols., edited by Salvador Rueda Smithers, Constanza Vega Sosa, and Rodrigo Martínez Baracs, 1:233–68. Mexico City: Instituto Nacional de Antropología e Historia; Consejo Nacional para la Cultura y las Artes.

2000 "Lienzos Made from Cloth Originally Woven for Other Uses." In *Códices y documentos sobre México: Tercer Simposio Internacional*, edited by Constanza Vega Sosa, 574–94. Mexico City: Instituto Nacional de Antropología e Historia.

2005a "The Format of the Prehispanic Mixtec Historical Screenfold Manuscripts." Ph.D. diss., Tulane University.

2005b "Roads as Connectors in Mixtec Pictorial Histories." In *Painted Books and Indigenous Knowledge in Mesoamerica: Manuscript Studies in Honor of Mary Elizabeth Smith*, edited by Elizabeth Hill Boone, 129–42. Middle American Research Institute publ. 69. New Orleans: Tulane University.

Joyce, Arthur A., Andrew G. Workinger, Byron Hamann, Peter Kroefges, Maxine Oland, and Stacie M. King

2004 "Lord 8 Deer 'Jaguar Claw' and the Land of the Sky: The Archaeology and History of Tututepec." *Latin American Antiquity* 15 (3): 273–97.

Kirchhoff, Paul, Lina Odena Güemes, and Luis Reyes García

1976 *Historia tolteca-chichimeca*. Facsimile and Spanish translation. Mexico City: Instituto Nacional de Antropología e Historia.

König, Viola

1979 *Inhaltliche Analyse und Interpretation von Codex Egerton*. Beiträge zur mittelamerikanischen Völkerkunde XV. Hamburg, Germany: Hamburgisches Museum für Völkerkunde.

1984 "Der Lienzo Seler II und seine Stellung innerhalb der Coixtlahuaca Gruppe." *Baessler Archiv*, Neue Folge, 32:229–320.

1993 *Die Schlacht bei Sieben Blume: Konquistadoren, Kaziken und Konflikte auf alten Landkarten der Indianer Südmexikos*. Bremen, Germany: Edition Temmen.

1999 "Lienzo Seler II and the Coixtlahuaca Group of Lienzos." *Latin American Indian Literatures Journal* 15, no. 2 (Fall): 147–210.

2011 *La batalla de Siete Flor: Conquistadores, caciques y conflictos en mapas antiguos de los zapotecos, chinantecos y mixes*. Spanish version of König 1993. Oaxaca, Mexico: Secretaría de las Culturas y Artes de Oaxaca; Dirección General de Culturas Populares del CONACULTA; Fundación Alfredo Harp Helú Oaxaca.

Kranz, Travis Barton

2007 "Sixteenth-Century Tlaxcalan Pictorial Documents on the Conquest of Mexico." Article published online at whp.uoregon.edu/Lockhart/Kranz.pdf. Based on "The Tlaxcalan Conquest Pictorials: The Role of Images in Influencing Colonial Policy in Sixteenth-Century Mexico." Ph.D. diss., University of California at Los Angeles, 2001.

Lara Tenorio, Blanca, Eustaquio Celestino Solís, and Elisa Pérez Alemán

2009 *Anales de Tepeteopan: De Xochitecuhtli a don Juan de San Juan Olhuatecatl, 1370(?)–1675*. Mexico City: Instituto Nacional de Antropología e Historia.

Leibsohn, Dana

1993 "The 'Historia Tolteca-Chichimeca': Recollecting Identity in a Nahua Manuscript. Ph.D. diss., University of California at Los Angeles. Includes author's English translation of Historia Tolteca-Chichimeca, 311–93.

Lenz, Hans

1973 *El papel indígena mexicano*. Mexico City: Secretaría de Educación Pública (Sep-Setentas).

León, Nicolás

1905 "Data about a New Kind of Hieroglyphical Writing in Mexico." In *Proceedings of the International Congress of Americanists, Thirteenth Session, New York*, 175–88. New York: Eschenbach Printing Company.

1982 *Códice Sierra: Traducción al español y explicación de sus pinturas jeroglíficas*. Mexico City: Editorial Innovación. 1st publ. 1933, Mexico City: Museo Nacional.

MacNutt, Francis Augustus

1912 *De Orbe Novo: The Eight Decades of Peter Martyr D'Angheira*. 2 vols. New York: G. P. Putnam's Sons.

Maldonado Alvarado, Benjamin, and Mauricio Maldonado Alvarado

1995 "La historia en la piel: Otra lectura posible del Códice Colombino (mixteco prehispánico)." *Cuadernos del Sur* (Oaxaca) 3, nos. 8–9 (September 1994–April 1995): 29–41.

Maldonado Alvarado, Mauricio, and Benjamin Maldonado Alvarado

2004 *La sabiduría de las pieles: De las técnicas de curtición de los códices a la curtiduría tradicional actual en Oaxaca*. Oaxaca, Mexico: Instituto de Investigaciones en Humanidades de la Universidad Autónoma Benito Júarez de Oaxaca; Secretaría de Asuntos Indígenas del Gobierno del Estado de Oaxaca; Instituto Nacional de Antropología e Historia, Oaxaca.

Martínez Gracida, Manuel

1910 "Los indios oaxaqueños y sus monumentos arqueológicos." 4 vols. of text and originally 4 vols. of plates, 1 vol. now missing. Unpublished manuscript in the Genaro Vásquez Collection, Biblioteca Pública Central del Estado de Oaxaca, Oaxaca, Mexico.

Mastache de Escobar, Alba Guadalupe

1971 *Técnicas prehispánicas del tejido*. Mexico City: Instituto Nacional de Antropología e Historia.

Matos Moctezuma, Eduardo, Johanna Broda, and Davíd Carrasco

1987 *The Great Temple of Tenochtitlan: Center and Periphery in the Aztec World*. Berkeley: University of California Press.

Meade, Mercedes, and Rosaura Hernández

1984 *Lienzos de la fundación de Huamantla, Tlaxcala.* Tlaxcala, Mexico: Instituto de la Cultura Tlaxcalteca; Centro Social, Recreativo y Cultural de Huamantla.

Melgarejo Vivanco, José Luis, and Manuel Álvarez Bravo

1970 *Códices de tierras: Los lienzos de Tuxpan.* Commentary by Melgarejo Vivanco, photography by Álvarez Bravo. Mexico: Editorial La Estampa Mexicana.

Mendoza García, Edgar

1996 "Bienes de comunidad: Cohesión y autonomía de Santo Domingo Tepenene, Oaxaca, durante la segunda mitad del siglo XIX, 1856–1910." Thesis, Escuela Nacional de Antropología e Historia, Mexico City.

Mengin, Ernst

1952 "Commentaire du Codex Mexicanus nos. 23–24 de la Bibliothèque Nationale de Paris." *Journal de la Société des Américanistes*, n.s., 41 (2): 387–498.

Monaghan, John

1990 "Performance and the Structure of the Mixtec Codices." *Ancient Mesoamerica* 1, no. 1 (Spring): 133–40.

Monroy, Salazar

1946 *Museo Regional de Oaxaca.* [Oaxaca?]: n.p.

Mundy, Barbara E.

1996 *The Mapping of New Spain: Indigenous Cartography and the Maps of the Relaciones Geográficas.* Chicago: University of Chicago Press.

1998 "Mesoamerican Cartography." In *The History of Cartography*, vol. 2, bk. 3, *Cartography in the Traditional African, American, Arctic, Australian, and Pacific Societies*, edited by David Woodward and G. Malcolm Lewis, 183–256. Chicago: University of Chicago Press.

2005 "At Home in the World: Mixtec Elites and the Teozacoalco Map-Genealogy." In *Painted Books and Indigenous Knowledge in Mesoamerica: Manuscript Studies in Honor of Mary Elizabeth Smith*, edited by Elizabeth Hill Boone, 363–81. Middle American Research Institute publ. 69. New Orleans: Tulane University.

Nicholson, H. B.

1978 "The Deity 9 Wind 'Ehecatl-Quetzalcoatl' in the Mixtec Pictorials." *Journal of Latin American Lore* 4, no. 1 (Summer): 61–92.

2001 *Topiltzin Quetzalcoatl: The Once and Future Lord of the Toltecs.* Boulder: University Press of Colorado.

2005 "Ce Acatl Topiltzin Quetzalcoatl of Tollan = 4 Jaguar of 'Cattail Frieze' and Military Ally of 8 Deer 'Jaguar Claw'?" In *Painted Books and Indigenous Knowledge in Mesoamerica: Manuscript Studies in Honor of Mary Elizabeth Smith*, edited by Elizabeth Hill Boone. Middle American Research Institute publ. 69. New Orleans: Tulane University.

Noguez, Javier

1978 *Tira de Tepechpan: Códice colonial procedente del valle de México.* 2 vols., with color photographic reproduction. Mexico: Biblioteca Enciclopédica del Estado de México.

Nowotny, Karl Anton

1961 *Codices Becker I/II. Museum für Völkerkunde Wien Inv. Nr. 60306 und 60307.* Commentary, color photographic reproductions. Graz, Austria: Akademische Druck- und Verlagsanstalt.

Oettinger, Marion

1983 *Lienzos coloniales: Guía de la Exposición de Pinturas de Terrenos Comunales de México (siglos XVII–XIX).* Mexico City: Universidad Nacional Autónoma de México.

Oettinger, Marion, and Fernando Horcasitas

1982 *The Lienzo of Petlacala: A Pictorial Document from Guerrero, Mexico.* Transactions of the American Philosophical Society 72, pt. 7. Philadelphia: American Philosophical Society.

Olphen, H. van

1966 "Maya Blue, a Clay-Organic Pigment." *Science* 154 (3749): 645–46.

Oudijk, Michel

2000 *Historiography of the Bènizàa: The Postclassic and Early Colonial Periods (1000–1600 A.D.).* Leiden, Netherlands: Research School of Asian, African, and Amerindian Studies (CNWS), Leiden University.

Oudijk, Michel, and Sebastián (Bas) van Doesburg

2010 *Los lienzos pictográficos de Santa Cruz Papalutla, Oaxaca: Patrimonio en peligro.* Mexico City: Universidad Nacional Autónoma de México, Instituto de Investigaciones Filológicas; Oaxaca: Fundación Alfredo Harp Helú Oaxaca.

Parmenter, Ross

1961 "Twentieth Century Adventures of a Sixteenth Century Sheet: The Literature on the Mixtec Lienzo in the Royal Ontario Museum." *Boletín de Estudios Oaxaqueños* 20 (November 15). Mitla, Oaxaca: Museo Frissell.

1970 "The Identification of Lienzo A: A Tracing in the Latin American Library of Tulane University." Preprint of 1977 article in *Philological and Documentary Studies* 2 (5): 181–95. New Orleans: Middle American Research Institute, Tulane University.

1972 "The Testimony Showing that the Lienzo Called 'Antonio de León' Came from San Mateo Tlapiltepec in the District of Coixtlahuaca in the Mixteca Alta in the State of Oaxaca, Mexico." Unpublished manuscript in the Royal Ontario Museum, Toronto.

1982 *Four Lienzos of the Coixtlahuaca Valley.* Studies in Pre-Colombian Art and Archaeology, no. 26. Washington, D.C.: Dumbarton Oaks; Trustees for Harvard University.

1993 *The Lienzo of Tulancingo, Oaxaca: An Introductory Study of a Ninth Painted Sheet from the Coixtlahuaca Valley.* Transactions of the American Philosophical Society 83, pt. 7. Philadelphia: American Philosophical Society.

1994 "La identificación de Tulancingo en el Lienzo de Ihuitlán: Una valiosa aportación de un noveno lienzo del Valle de Coixtlahuaca." In *Códices y documentos sobre México: Primer Simposio*, edited by Constanza Vega Sosa, 101–15. Mexico City: Instituto Nacional de Antropología e Historia.

1997 "A Nativitas Ruler List on Lienzo A." In *Códices y documentos sobre México: Segundo Simposio,* 2 vols., edited by Salvador Rueda Smithers, Constanza Vega Sosa, and Rodrigo Martínez Baracs, 1:269–303. Mexico City: Instituto Nacional de Antropología e Historia; Consejo Nacional para la Cultura y las Artes.

Paso y Troncoso, Francisco del

1912 *Códice Kingsborough: Memoria de los indios de Tepetlaoztoc al monarca español contra los encomenderos del pueblo.* Madrid: Hauser y Menet.

Peñafiel, Antonio

1900 *Códice Mixteco. Lienzo de Zacatepec.* Mexico City: Secretaría de Fomento.

Pohl, John M. D.

1994a "Mexican Codices, Maps, and Lienzos as Social Contracts." In *Writing without Words: Alternate Literacies in Mesoamerica and the Andes*, edited by Elizabeth Hill Boone and Walter D. Mignolo, 137–60.

1994b *The Politics of Symbolism in the Mixtec Codices.* Vanderbilt University Publications in Anthropology 46. Nashville: Vanderbilt University.

2003 "Royal Marriage and Confederacy Building among the Eastern Nahuas, Mixtecs, and Zapotecs." In *The Postclassic Mesoamerican World*, edited by Michael E. Smith and Frances F. Berdan, 243–48. Salt Lake City: University of Utah Press.

Reyes, Antonio de los

1976 *Arte en lengua mixteca.* Vanderbilt University Publications in Anthropology, no. 14. Nashville, Tenn.: Vanderbilt University. First published 1593 by Pedro Balli, Mexico.

Reyes García, Luis

1977 *Cuauhtinchan del siglo XII al XVI: Formación y desarrollo histórico de un señorío prehispánico.* Wiesbaden: Franz Steiner Verlag.

1993 *La escritura pictográfica en Tlaxcala: Dos mil años de experiencia mesoamericana.* Tlaxcala, Mexico: Universidad Autónoma de Tlaxcala.

1998 "Documentos pictográficos del señorío popoloca de Tecamachalco." *Mexican Codices and Archaeology.* Special issue, *Indiana Journal of Hispanic Literatures*, no. 13 (Fall): 67–74.

Reyes Gómez, Félix A.

1998 *Historia de Tamazulápam* [sic]. Oaxaca, Mexico: Carteles Editores.

Rickards, Constantine George

1913 "Notes on the 'Codex Rickards.'" *Journal de la Société des Américanistes,* n.s., 10:47–57.

Rincón Mautner, Carlos

1994 "A Reconstruction of the History of San Miguel Tulancingo, Coixtlahuaca, Mexico, from Indigenous Painted Sources." *Texas Notes on Precolumbian Art, Writing, and Culture*, no. 64 (February).

1995 "The Ñuiñe Codex from the Colossal Natural Bridge on the Ndaxagua: An Early Pictographic Text from the Coixtlahuaca Basin." *Institute of Maya Studies Journal* 1 (2): 39–66.

1997 "Reading the History of Place-Becoming in the Codices from the Coixtlahuaca Basin." In *Latin American Indian Literatures: Messages and Meanings. Papers from the Twelfth Annual Symposium, Latin American Indian Literatures Association / Asociación de Literaturas Indígenas Latinoamericanas*, edited by Mary H. Preuss, 129–48. Lancaster, Calif.: Labyrinthos.

1999 "Man and the Environment in the Coixtlahuaca Basin of Northwestern Oaxaca, Mexico: Two Thousand Years of Historical Ecology." Ph.D. diss., University of Texas at Austin.

2000 "La reconstrucción cronológica del linaje principal de Coixtlahuaca." In *Códices y documentos sobre México: Tercer Simposio Internacional*, edited by Constanza Vega Sosa, 25–43. Mexico City: Instituto Nacional de Antropología e Historia.

2005 "The Pictographic Assemblage from the Colossal Natural Bridge on the Ndaxagua, Coixtlahuaca Basin, Northwestern Mixteca Alta of Oaxaca, Mexico." *Ketzalcalli* 2 (2): 2–69.

2007 "A Study of the 'Lienzo of San Jerónimo Otla' from the Coixtlahuaca Basin of Oaxaca, Mexico." *Latin American Indian Literatures Journal* 23, no. 1 (Spring): 74–95.

2012a "Cave, Mountain, and Ancestors: Weaving History and Cartography for the Preservation of Native Dominions in the Early Colonial Mixteca of Oaxaca." In *Mesoamerican Memory: Enduring Systems of Remembrance*, edited by Amos Megged and Stephanie Wood, 249–76. Norman: University of Oklahoma Press.

2012b "Linajes y casas señoriales de los Tolteca-Chichimeca de Coixtlahuaca en la Mixteca de Oaxaca." In *El Poder Compartido: Ensayos sobre la Arqueología de Organizaciones Políticas Segmentarias y Oligárquicas*, edited by Annick Daneels and Gerardo Gutiérrez, 115–72. Mexico City: Centro de Investigaciones y Estudios Superiores en Antopología Social; Zamora, Michoacan: Colegio de Michoacan.

Robertson, Donald

1994 *Mexican Manuscript Painting of the Early Colonial Period: The Metropolitan Schools*. Foreword by Elizabeth Hill Boone. Norman: University of Oklahoma Press. First published 1959.

Roskamp, Hans

1998 La historiografía indígena de Michoacán: El lienzo de Jucutácato y los títulos de Carapan. Leiden, Netherlands: Research School of Asian, African, and Amerindian Studies (CNWS), Leiden University.

Ruíz Ortíz, Victor Hugo, and Maarten E. R. G. N. Jansen

2009 *El Lienzo de Otla: Memoria de un paisaje sagrado. Edición e interpretación del manuscrito recién descubierto, acompañado por los cortometrajes "La epopeya de la princesa 6 Mono y del gran guerrero 8 Venado" y "Cantero."* Oaxaca, Mexico: Gobierno del Estado de Oaxaca; Yuu Núú.

Sacchi, Duccio

1986 "Imagen y percepción del territorio según los mapas mixtecos (1595–1617)." *Historias* 15 (October–December): 19–30.

Sampson, Geoffrey

1985 *Writing Systems: A Linguistic Introduction*. Stanford, Calif.: Stanford University Press.

Seler-Sachs, Caecilie, Walter Lehmann, and Walter Krickeberg, eds.

1927 *Einige Kapitel aus dem Geschichtswerk des Fray Bernardino de Sahagun, aus dem Aztekischen übersetzt von Eduard Seler*. Stuttgart, Germany: Strecker und Schröder.

Sellen, Adam

2004 The Face that Launched a Thousand Fakes? *Rotunda* (Member Magazine of the American Museum of Natural History) 36 (3): 32–39.

Sepúlveda y Herrera, María Teresa

2005 *Los lienzos de San Juan Cuauhtla, Puebla*. Mexico City: Consejo Nacional para la Cultura y las Artes; Instituto Nacional de Antropología e Historia; Editorial Miguel Ángel Porrúa.

Smith, Mary Elizabeth

1973a *Picture Writing from Ancient Southern Mexico: Mixtec Place Signs and Maps*. Norman: University of Oklahoma Press.

1973b "The Relationship between Mixtec Manuscript Painting and the Mixtec Language: A Study of Some Personal Names in Codices Muro and Sánchez Solís." In *Mesoamerican Writing Systems: A Conference at Dumbarton Oaks*, edited by Elizabeth P. Benson, 47–98. Washington, D.C.: Dumbarton Oaks.

1983 "The Mixtec Writing System." In *The Cloud People: Divergent Evolution of the Zapotec and Mixtec Civilizations*, edited by Kent V. Flannery and Joyce Marcus, 238–45. New York: Academic Press.

1994 "Why the Second Codex Selden was Painted." In *Caciques and Their People: A Volume in Honor of Ronald Spores*, edited by Joyce Marcus and Judith Francis Zeitlin, 111–41. Ann Arbor: University of Michigan.

Smith, Mary Elizabeth, and Ross Parmenter

1991 *The Codex Tulane*. Middle American Research Institute publ. 61. New Orleans: Tulane University.

Spinden, H. J.

1940 "Diffusion of Maya Astronomy." In *The Maya and Their Neighbors*, 162–78. New York: Appleton-Century.

Spores, Ronald

1974 "Marital Alliance in the Political Integration of Mixtec Kingdoms." *American Anthropologist* 76: 297–311.

Swanton, Michael

2008 "Multilingualism in the Tocuij Ñudzavui Region." In *Mixtec Writing and Society. Escritura Ñuu Dzaui*, edited by Maarten E. R. G. N. Jansen and Laura N. K. Broekhoven, 347–80. Amsterdam: Koninklijke Nederlandse Akademie van Wetenschappen Press.

Tedlock, Dennis

2010 *2000 years of Mayan Literature.* Berkeley and Los Angeles: University of California Press.

Tena, Rafael, paleographer and trans.

2004 *Anales de Tlatelolco.* Mexico City: Consejo Nacional para la Cultura y las Artes.

Terraciano, Kevin

2001 *The Mixtecs of Colonial Oaxaca: Ñudzahui History, Sixteenth through Eighteenth Centuries.* Stanford, Calif.: Stanford University Press.

Topsey, Harriot Wentward

1985 "The Coixtlahuaca Group of Mexican Manuscripts: An Examination." Master's thesis, University of Calgary.

Torquemada, Juan de

1986 *Monarquía indiana.* 3 vols. Mexico City: Editorial Porrúa.

Troike, Nancy P.

1974 The Codex Colombino-Becker. Ph.D. diss., University of London.

Troike, Nancy P., and Ferdinand Anders

1987 *Codex Zouche-Nuttall, British Museum London (Add. MS. 39671).* Color photographic screenfold facsimile with foreword by Ferdinand Anders and introduction by Nancy P. Troike. Graz, Austria: Akademische Druck- und Verlagsanstalt.

Velázquez, Primo Feliciano, trans.

1975 *Códice Chimalpopoca: Anales de Cuauhtitlán y Leyenda de los soles.* Mexico City: Universidad Nacional Autónoma de México.

Vences Vidal, Magdalena

2000 *Evangelización y arquitectura dominicana en Coixtlahuaca.* Salamanca: Editorial San Esteban.

Weitlaner Johnson, Irmgard

1966 "Análisis textil del lienzo de Ocotepec." In *Summa Anthropologica en homenaje a Roberto J. Weitlaner*, 139–44. Mexico City: Secretaría de Educación Pública; Instituto Nacional de Antropología e Historia.

1971 "Basketry and Textiles." In *Handbook of Middle American Indians*, vol. 10, *Archaeology of Northern Mesoamerica*, pt. 1, edited by Gordon F. Ekholm and Ignacio Bernal, 297–391. Austin: University of Texas Press.

1985 "Hilado y tejido." In *Esplendor del México antiguo*, 2 vols., edited by Carmen Cook de Leonard, 1:439–69. Mexico City: Centro de Investigaciones Antropológicas de México.

Williams, Ann, and Esther Pierson

1950 *Diccionario español-popoloca, popoloca-español.* Mexico: Instituto Lingüístico de Verano.

Williams, Barbara J., and H. R. Harvey

1997 *The* Códice de Santa María Asunción, *Facsimile and Commentary: Households and Lands in Sixteenth-Century Tepetlaoztoc.* Salt Lake City: University of Utah Press.

Winter, Marcus C., Margarita Gaxiola, and Gilberto Hernández

1984 "Archaeology of the Otomanguean Area." In *Essays in Otomanguean Culture History,* edited by J. Kathryn Josserand, Marcus C. Winter, and Nicholas A. Hopkins, 65–108. Vanderbilt University Publications in Anthropology, no. 31. Nashville, Tenn.: Vanderbilt University.

Yoneda, Keiko

1981 *Los mapas de Cuauhtinchan y la historia cartográfica prehispánica.* Mexico City: Archivo General de la Nación. 2nd ed. 1991 , Centro de Investigaciones y Estudios en Antropología Social; Fondo de Cultura Económica; Gobierno del Estado de Puebla.

1996 *Migraciones y conquistas: Descifre global del Mapa de Cuauhtinchan núm 3.* Mexico City: Instituto Nacional de Antropología e Historia.

2005 *Mapa de Cuauhtinchan núm. 2.* Mexico City: Miguel Angel Porrúa; Centro de Investigaciones y Estudios en Antropología Social.

Zeitlin, Robert N.

1990 "The Isthmus and the Valley of Oaxaca: Questions about Zapotec Imperialism in the Pacific Lowlands of Mesoamerica." *American Antiquity* 55 (2): 250–61.

INDEX

Page numbers in italic type indicate that the entry appears in an illustration or both in an illustration and in text on that page.

Art credits: Frontispiece, Detail of the Lienzo of Tlapiltepec showing a sixteenth-century Dominican monastery at Coixtlahuaca. Courtesy of the Royal Ontario Museum. Photo by Brian Boyle. P. 74, (*Top*) Seal used by the municipal authorities of Tlapiltepec ("mountain of the knot") during the mid-nineteenth century. Courtesy Municipal Archivo of Teposcolula. (*Bottom*) The glyph of Tlapiltepec from the Lienzo of Tequixtepec I. Photo by María de los Ángeles Romero Frizzi.

Copyedited by Katrin Flechsig
Indexed by Nicholas Johnson
Cartography by Tom Jonas
Design and composition by Julie Allred, BW&A Books, Inc.
Set in Adobe Minion and The Sans
Jacket design by Tony Roberts
Image prepress by University of Oklahoma Printing Services
Text printed and bound by Thomson-Shore, Inc.